MOLSON

The Birth of a Business Empire

MOLSON

The Birth of a Business Empire

DOUGLAS HUNTER

WITH ILLUSTRATIONS BY THE AUTHOR

PENGUIN

VIKING

VIKING
Published by the Penguin Group
Penguin Books Canada Ltd, 10 Alcorn Avenue, Toronto, Ontario, Canada
    M4V 3B2
Penguin Books Ltd, 80 Strand, London WC2R 0RL, England
Penguin Putnam Inc., 375 Hudson Street, New York, New York 10014, U.S.A.
Penguin Books Australia Ltd, Ringwood, Victoria, Australia
Penguin Books (NZ) Ltd, cnr Rosedale and Airborne Roads, Albany, Auckland
    1310, New Zealand

Penguin Books Ltd, Registered Offices: Harmondsworth, Middlesex, England

First published 2001

10 9 8 7 6 5 4 3 2 1

Copyright © Douglas Hunter, 2001
Illustrations © Douglas Hunter, 2001

Printed and bound in Canada on acid free paper ∞

NATIONAL LIBRARY OF CANADA CATALOGUING IN PUBLICATION DATA

Hunter, Douglas, 1959–
    Molson : the birth of a business empire

Includes bibliographical references and index.
ISBN 0-670-88855-9

1. Molson, John, 1763–1836. 2. Molson Companies—Biography.
3. Businesspeople—Canada—Biography. I. Title.

HC112.5.M64H85 2001   338'.04'092   C2001-901150-4

Visit Penguin Canada's website at **www.penguin.ca**

For Deb

The utility of History consists principally in the examples it gives of the virtues and vices of those who have gone before us; upon which we ought to make the proper observations.

—Lord Chesterfield, letter to his son, November 20, 1739

Introduction

WHEN I BEGAN THIS PROJECT in 1999, I knew only that I wanted
to write about the Molsons in some way. I spent nine months acquiring a basic understanding of the family and the associated corporate
history of the brewery and other ventures, a saga that stretches
back more than two centuries. I'm no James Michener, and I came
to an early conclusion that an all-inclusive, multi-generational
narrative was not for me. Part of the reason was writerly ego. That
book had already been written twice: the first time by Merrill
Denison with *The Barley and the Stream* in 1955, and then by Shirley
Woods with *The Molson Saga* in 1983. (As well, a monograph commissioned by the Molsons, *The Molson Family*, was written by
Bernard K. Sandwell in 1933.) I loathed the idea of having to shape
a narrative that had already been defined by previous authors. But
the main reason for not producing yet another wide-screen family
history was the sheer scale of the undertaking.

The Molson saga seduces the writer with its sweep, its panora-
mic view of politics, commerce and family history that also illuminates the birth and evolution of a nation. But its appeal is also a
siren's call: to tell this story, the writer must confront an overwhelming mass of primary research material. The main resource is
the Molson Archives at the National Archives of Canada. The
finding aid alone, which simply itemizes the holdings, is more than
four hundred pages long. My aversion to the task, I hasten to add,
wasn't laziness. Rather, I was convinced there was too much history—at least history in the way I approach it—to cram into one
volume. It would take me years to absorb all the primary materials
(for the Molson Archives, as voluminous as they might be, are only
the starting point for research), and in the end I would be forced to
distill it ruthlessly. In the process, a lot of good stuff would be left

unused. As well, I would have about fifty more years of history to accommodate than Denison, nearly twenty more than Woods, and the adventures of the Molson company over the past two decades alone deserve a book of their own.

There is certainly a need for books that tackle the grand sweep of history, and I am in particular indebted to Denison for making the effort, but my instincts as a writer have always been to strive to bring stories to life through detail and nuance, while incorporating historical context. I take my hat off to any writer brave enough to swallow the Molsons in one meal. I came to think of the Molson saga as the great white whale in *Moby Dick*: my quest was to carve off a substantial piece, not choke on the whole leviathan.

I decided, as a result, to address one particular era in order to bring more detail and new resources to the task of telling the story. I could see at least four different books hiding in the mountains of research materials. But I also wanted to write something with a beginning and an end that were determined by narrative—there had to be a substantial, cohesive story rather than a set of dates to bridge.

After my first months of preparatory research, I resolved to concentrate on the last fifty years of the saga, when the post-war Canadian brewing industry emerged. After digesting such material as the 1955 Restrictive Trade Practices Commission Report on the monopolistic behaviour of the Molson rival E.P. Taylor, I was ready to look at the Molson Archives themselves. I knew that to ground the narrative properly I had to pay at least some attention to the brewery's origins, and I wanted to see some of the pertinent primary materials for myself. And so, as fate had it, the first volumes of documents I requested from the Molson Archives contained the correspondence generated by the activities of the brewery's founder, John Molson, in the 1780s. It took perhaps an hour of reading these wonderful letters for me to change my mind completely about the story I would tell.

I realized that Denison, even in devoting about 175 pages to the life of the family patriarch in *The Barley and the Stream*, had left much of this material unused or at least unquoted at any length. Clearly there was a complex, fascinating story still waiting to be told. And so, rather than writing the end of the Molson story, I decided to write the beginning. My leading character became John Molson, the teenager who left Lincolnshire in 1782 to come to Montreal and make his own way onto what he memorably referred to in 1786 as "the Grand Stage of the World."

I don't know why I had to take such a circuitous route to the story I chose to tell. I'd long been interested in colonial history—I had written about controversies surrounding a proposal to raise the War of 1812 shipwrecks *Hamilton* and *Scourge* for *Canadian Geographic*, and had penned for the *Globe and Mail* a critique of the liberties taken with the historical record in the television movie *Divided Loyalties* (about the Mohawk leader Joseph Brant). In this, my eleventh book, I finally seized the opportunity to explore at length the eighteenth and early nineteenth centuries within the framework of a family and corporate history.

With my narrative choice made (and the Restrictive Trade Practices report of 1955 returned to the filing cabinet, retrieved only for the Epilogue), I began chasing down the minutiae necessary to tell the story. With a collection as thoroughly indexed as the Molson Archives, it is all too tempting to direct one's research according to what the finding aid tells you is there. But as researchers well know, vital clues appear in the least likely places. An offhand remark in the postscript of a letter can inform an incident that occurred more than a decade earlier. Business details turn up in personal letters, while information that sheds light on personal lives crops up in financial records. And for every day that I spent at the National Archives examining the Molson Archives, I probably spent another three looking for and examining supportive documentation in other collections. For as fundamental as the Molson Archives are to writing about the Molsons, considerable legwork is required to understand their content fully. In the end, in addition to published sources, I drew on materials in the National Library of Canada (helpfully housed in the same building as the National Archives of Canada), the Archives nationales du Québec, the Vermont State Archives, Britain's Public Record Office, the Boulton & Watt papers in the City of Birmingham Archives, and the municipal archives in Birkenhead.

All the while, I was looking back over my shoulder at Denison's *The Barley and the Stream: The Molson Story* (which carries the additional, curiously self-deprecating subtitle *A Footnote to Canadian History*). Denison's book is still a resource for writers and researchers, turning up regularly in footnotes and bibliographies. Commissioned by the Molson family and published by McClelland & Stewart in 1955, it was the product of several years of toil by Denison in concert with his research associate, Léon Trépanier. Because it was an official history, Denison's own drafts, correspondence and research notes became part of the Molson Archives when they were donated to the National Archives beginning in 1976. Very late in my own research, I had a look at the Denison files in an attempt to verify sources for certain assertions he had made, for which I had found no supportive evidence. These files include letters in which Denison complained about how the project was so much larger than he had anticipated. Having almost completed my own research, I could well understand Denison's frustration, and could even forgive him for some of the wild-goose chases on which he had led me.

The Barley and the Stream is an admirable effort, but it probably wasn't the book Denison hoped to write. He may have planned to produce a multi-volume work—his *A History of the Bank of Montreal,* another commissioned project, published by McClelland & Stewart in 1966, was issued in two large volumes. The bank history is also far more scholarly than his Molson book. Although Denison was diligent in sifting through the corporate archives, *The Barley and the Stream* is not remotely an academic work. Denison, an architect by training, had written theatrical pieces on Canadian history before taking on the Molsons and other subjects of Canadiana. He provided no bibliography or list of sources for documents from outside what were then private corporate papers, which meant that much of the book was fundamentally unsubstantiated. As Alfred Dubuc wrote of *The Barley and the Stream* in the entry for John Molson in the *Dictionary of Canadian Biography,* "Too many statements (including dates) are open to question and are not supported (and in some instances are contradicted) by primary sources."

Denison nonetheless is still relied upon as an important source on the Molsons, because in some instances, it appears, he was able to examine documents that, for whatever reason, did not become part of the Molson Archives at the National Archives. But the closer you read Denison, the more puzzles you find. I learned an early lesson in trusting Denison when I read that the convoy in which Molson travelled to Quebec in 1782 was under the escort of HMS *Preston*. Hoping to verify some of the incidents related by Molson in letters home after the voyage, I located the master's and captain's logs for the ship with the marvellous online search engine for Britain's Public Record Office, and ordered copies. Some $150 later, the logs arrived. They revealed that the *Preston* was escorting a convoy to St. Lucia at the time that Molson's convoy was bound for Quebec. Some basic sleuthing determined that Molson's convoy, in fact, was under the escort of HMS *Assistance* and *Surprize*. I have no clue why Denison asserted that the *Preston* was involved with Molson's convoy. While it may have been the sort of innocent mistake that all writers can make, it was an expensive lesson in the idiosyncrasies of Denison's book.

Unfortunately, some of the curiosities in Denison's book are due to deliberate obfuscation. As the author of an official history, Denison plainly was under pressure to bowdlerize or overlook certain details that the Molsons considered to be unfit for public airing in the 1950s. Denison was circumspect in his treatment of John Molson's obvious affection for his widow aunt, Ann Elsdale, although he had been more explicit in the surviving drafts of his manuscript. Most unfortunately, he wrote an entirely misleading account of Molson's relationship with Sarah Vaughan, the mother of his three sons. We know that they lived out of wedlock for fifteen years before marrying in 1801, but Denison implicitly had them marry in 1786, a year before the birth of their first son, by sending them off on a "honeymoon," and then made no mention of the 1801 wedding.

Because Denison is still regularly cited by writers, I decided to make direct references to him in important areas where I fundamentally disagreed with him—while at the same time giving him credit where it is due, which it often is. I have kept my Denison "corrections" to what I hope is a minimum, and I deliberately avoided reading Shirley Woods's 1983 book, not out of disrespect but because I didn't want to turn my own work into a running commentary on previous efforts.

In some aspects of the John Molson story, time has been on my side. In the last two decades, significant scholarship and research tools have emerged that greatly benefitted my understanding of his life and times. One of my aims with this project was to extend the resources used beyond the Molson Archives, the National Archives, and other traditional (though valuable) primary repositories such as the Archives nationales du Québec in Montreal. My instincts (which I believe have been proved correct) were that Vermont held many important clues to Molson's first years in North America. Denison had devoted only a few paragraphs to Molson's activities in that state, but I was able to learn far more through sources that were never available to him. In addition to valuable documents in the Vermont State Archives (some of which had already been cited by Denison), I profited enormously from the work of the late historian Allen L. Stratton, whose *History of Alburgh, Vermont*, Vol. I, was published posthumously in 1986; his incomplete manuscript for Vol. II, which addressed the genealogy of local families, was published by the Vermont Historical Society in 2000. Stratton's work, augmented for me by the local researcher and genealogist David M. Bell, was fundamental to my understanding of Molson's activities in and ties to northern Vermont.

I have also striven to expand our understanding of Molson's English roots, and to that end I was particularly well served by the Public Record Office in Surrey, which has transformed itself into one of the world's most service-oriented research facilities. The scope of this book would not have been possible for me only a few years ago, as I could not have afforded repeated trips to the PRO to search for and examine all the documents that I was, instead, able to retrieve by using the PRO's World Wide Web interface. I ordered copies of a wide variety of documents, from ships' logs to lawsuits, without ever leaving my office.

The Internet has changed the way history is (or can be) researched and written. For most writers and academics, who have unlimited curiosity but limited budgets, the trend towards placing catalogues for major collections online, and offering photocopies or other reproductions of documents by mail, has been a godsend. (Also invaluable are the sites posting transcripts and even original page facsimiles of historic works, such as the excellent Early Canadiana Online service.) When researching history, you hope to maximize the proportion of research expenses that actually produces worthwhile material. In the past, too much money has been swallowed by hotels and plane fare—better than ninety percent of a typical research budget is consumed by costs involved in actually getting to the research. Expenses have also precluded entirely the possibility of making some trips to archives that were longshot resources. I am a firm believer in examining, firsthand, original materials wherever possible, and there are many instances in this book when I could not have conveyed details without having held a particular letter in my own hands. At the same time, archival services contacted by telephone, the Web and e-mail allowed me to examine many more documents, usually as photocopies, than would have been possible otherwise. Money saved in transportation and accommodation was redirected to hiring researchers to assist in retrieving information.

Let me conclude, then, by thanking a long list of people who made it possible for me to cast a wide net in research. Hilbert Buist was an ever-reliable researcher as well as an invaluable sounding board. In addition to materials he supplied from his own files, he retrieved and copied documents on my behalf at the National Archives and at the Archives nationales du Québec and McGill University in Montreal. In Vermont, David M. Bell provided copies of family genealogies he had researched, and he chased down various clues in such arcane places as cemetery and tax-roll records. The brewery historian Ian Bowering did a superb job of providing me with a cogent analysis of the probable configuration of Molson's brewery in 1786 and the brewing process he likely followed, which became the basis for much of chapter 11.

At the National Archives of Canada, the staff were uniformly helpful and are too numerous to name. At the McCord Museum in Montreal, archivist Suzanne Morin deserves special attention for entering the archives with a flashlight in the midst of renovations to retrieve a letter written by John Molson to his son Thomas in 1824 that was unreadable on microfilm.

On the English front, I was selflessly well served by the descendants of John Molson's privateering uncle, Robinson Elsdale: Barbara (Henson) Elsdale, her son, Robert, and Robert's wife, Chris. They provided copies of a number of printed sources and a digital copy of a watercolour portrait of Robinson, and above all made for me a photocopy of Robinson's original manuscript in which he regaled his wife with his adventures at sea.

Still in England, Tim Proctor, project archivist with the Archives of Soho in the City of Birmingham Archives, did more than was called for in hunting down correspondence in the Boulton & Watt holdings containing references to the Molsons. There is no index for this material, and Mr. Proctor's interest in my work was solely responsible for the relevant letters turning up. Janice Taylor, archivist with the Wirral Archives Service in Birkenhead, unearthed documents in its Laird Bros. holdings that shed light on the design and construction of John Thomas Molson's *Nooya*.

Genealogy was a fundamental research area, one where I have been particularly well served by resources not available to earlier writers on the Molsons. I pitched my research base camp at the International Genealogy Index, maintained online by the Church of Jesus Christ of Latter-day Saints at www.familysearch.org. The reasons genealogy is so important to this church are better left to theologians; suffice to say that the church takes genealogy seriously enough to have compiled one of the world's great databases on births, deaths and marriages. While the portions of its online data that have been privately compiled must be approached cautiously, the church is well regarded for the effort it made in the 1960s to photograph official records worldwide and transfer them to microfiche, and their contents in turn have been transcribed to the online database. This primary material was a great help in sorting out names, dates and relationships in England in the eighteenth century and earlier. Another important online resource was the fee-based ancestry.com, which provided important supportive information in the form of historic professional city indices, military records, and U.S. and state censuses.

As noted, David Bell and the late Allen Stratton were critical to my understanding of the families of northern Vermont. I must also thank David Sinclair for providing information on his ancestors named Gibbins Pell, and Wendy Sawlor and Mike Vaughan for sharing what they know of the Vaughans and Sweets of Massachusetts and Rhode Island.

It seems that I can't write a book without leaning on an old publishing cohort, Robin Brass of Toronto, for some sort of assistance or advice. In this project, Robin steered me in the direction of the marine historian Robert Malcomson, who provided me with background on British naval activity on Lake Ontario during the American Revolution, and in turn put me on to Arthur Britton Smith's *Legend of the Lake: The 22-Gun Brig-Sloop Ontario, 1780.*

I have provided a full bibliography, but several works beyond those already noted do merit special mention. For understanding the history of Quebec during John Molson's life, two classic books were indispensable: Donald Creighton's *The Empire of the St. Lawrence* and A.L. Burt's *The Old Province of Quebec.* The history of early steamboat services in Canada is well served by Frank Mackey's *Steamboat Connections* and George H. Wilson's unpublished 1961 McGill University master's thesis, *The Application of Steam to St. Lawrence Valley Navigation, 1809–1840.* N.A.M. Rodger's *The Wooden World* particularly informed my perception of the Royal Navy during the eighteenth century. *The Dictionary of Canadian Biography* was absolutely indispensable, and I thank the many authors of the individual entries that I consulted in writing this book, in particular Alfred Dubuc and Robert Tremblay for their work on the Molsons. I also thank Ramsay Cook, its editor-in-chief, and Loretta James and the other DCB staff members at the University of Toronto for their assistance.

On the publishing front, I benefitted from an unusual comple-
ment of editors, which I assure the reader was not a symptom of a
book in desperate straits. Meg Masters, my long-standing editor at
Penguin Canada, was involved with this book at its inception,
along with publisher Cynthia Good. After Meg embarked on a freelance career, I was taken on by Barbara Berson, who had been my
editor on *Open Ice,* my first book published by Penguin, in 1994.
Circumstances beyond our control necessitated the additional
involvement of freelance editor Janice Weaver, who stepped into
the breach with aplomb, and the book was whipped into final shape
by copyeditor Dennis Mills, proofreader John Sweet and senior production editor Sandra Tooze.

Finally, I must thank Eric H. Molson and Stephen T. Molson for
permitting my access to the restricted materials in the Molson
Archives at the National Archives of Canada. I am also indebted to
John Paul Macdonald, Molson Inc.'s vice-president of corporate
affairs, for various favours small and large. *Molson* is not a work
authorized or commissioned by either the Molson family or Molson
Inc., but without the cooperation of Messrs Molson and Macdonald,
it would not have been possible.

My thanks to all.

A few words are merited on presentation. While I have taken the
research seriously, this is not an academic work, and I have not
attempted to provide an endnote on every source for every fact.
Where I have been particularly indebted to previous authors, I have
provided an endnote indicating my gratitude, and otherwise have
been fairly arbitrary in providing endnote sources for particular
facts. The bibliography provides a list of primary and secondary
sources, as well as online resources.

With quotations from historic documents, I have striven to be as
faithful to the handwritten originals as possible. To preserve their
flavour, all but the most confusing misspellings and grammatical
errors have been reproduced without notation. The letters are so
riven with errors in punctuation and spelling that I have chosen to
make minimal parenthetic corrections or [sic] citations. Addressing

every small error would have bogged the phrasing down to the point of unreadability and robbed passages of their charm. Long "em" dashes are often used as periods in these letters, and I have used my own unscientific judgment in selecting the appropriate punctuation. For typographic clarity, underlining has been replaced with italics. The only significant differences from the original documents come from my decision to avoid contractions confusing to modern readers. For example, "gfather" has simply been written as "grandfather," and "havg" as "having." Superscript has also been avoided. As well, "per" has been used wherever I encountered the corresponding symbol—it's unfamiliar to most people, and I can't even find it on my own keyboard.

Douglas Hunter
Port McNicoll, Ontario
June 2001

Genealogy Chart 1: William Mouldson (1540–1604) and descendants

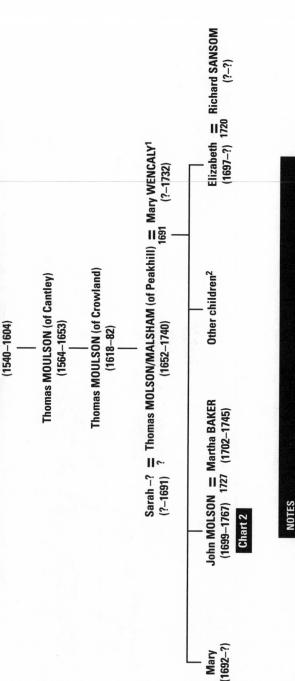

William MOULDSON (of Cantley)
(1540–1604)

Thomas MOULSON (of Cantley)
(1564–1653)

Thomas MOULSON (of Crowland)
(1618–82)

Sarah –? ═ **Thomas MOLSON/MALSHAM (of Peakhill)** ═ **Mary WENCALY[1]**
(?–1691) ? (1652–1740) 1691 (?–1732)

John MOLSON ═ **Martha BAKER**   Other children[2]   Elizabeth ═ **Richard SANSOM**
(1699–1767) 1727 (1702–1745)   (1697–?) 1720 (?–?)

Chart 2

Mary
(1692–?)

NOTES
1. Possibly Marie Winsley, born at Holbeach, 1668
2. Four children, including a son named Thomas, are thought to have died in infancy.

Genealogy sources: *The Molson Family* (Bernard K. Sandwell, 1933), Molson Archives,
Dictionary of Canadian Biography, Molson genealogy (Carruthers, 1995), author research

Genealogy Chart 2: John Molson (1699–1767) and descendants

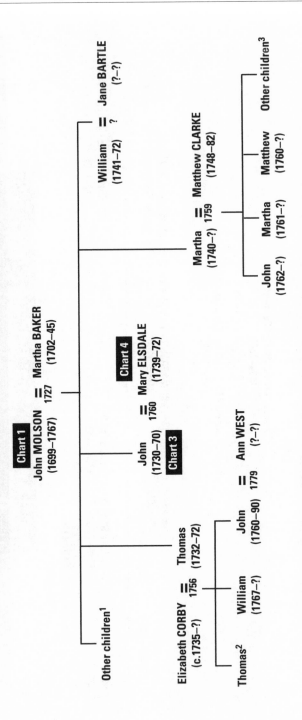

NOTES

1. At least five children of John Molson and Martha Baker died in infancy.
2. Two sons of Thomas Molson and Elizabeth Corby were christened, in 1760 and 1764.
3. A total of 14 children were christened at Moulton to parents named Martha and Matthew Clarke from 1760 to 1780.

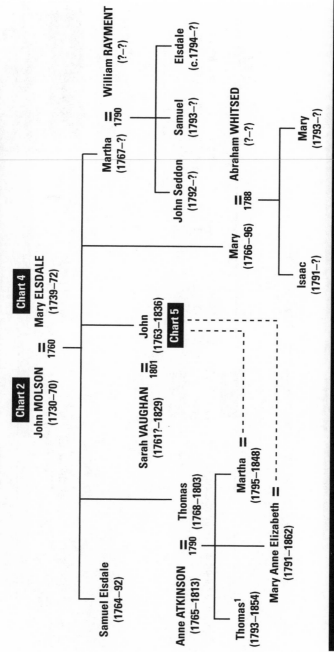

Genealogy Chart 3: John Molson (1730–70) and descendants

Chart 2

John MOLSON (1730–70) = 1760 **Mary ELSDALE** (1739–72)

Samuel Elsdale (1764–92)

Sarah VAUGHAN (1761?–1829) = 1801 **John** (1763–1836)

Chart 5

Anne ATKINSON (1765–1813) = 1790 Thomas (1768–1803)

Thomas[1] (1793–1854)

Martha (1795–1848) = -------

Mary Anne Elizabeth (1791–1862) = -------

Mary (1766–96) = 1788 Abraham WHITSED (?–?)

Isaac (1791–?)

Mary (1793–?)

Martha (1767–?) = 1790 **William RAYMENT** (?–?)

John Seddon (1792–?)

Samuel (1793–?)

Elsdale (c.1794–?)

NOTES

1. According to Bernard K. Sandwell (1933), Thomas Molson was married twice, to Elizabeth Ingolsby and Mary Anne Wyles. The Ingolsby marriage produced three children, Elizabeth, Edward and Harriet; the Wyles marriage produced a daughter, Mary Ann Elizabeth.

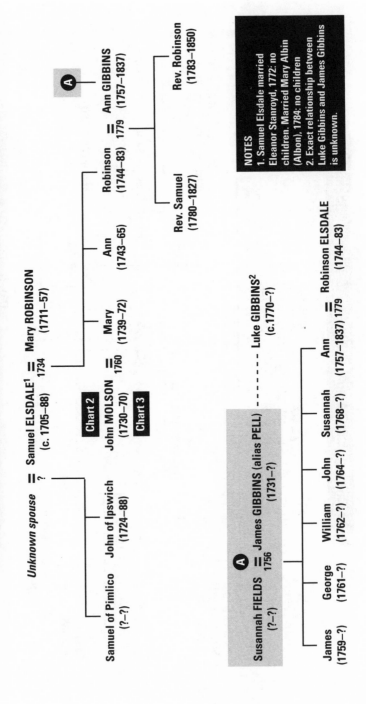

Genealogy Chart 4: Samuel Elsdale (c.1705–88) and descendants

Unknown spouse = Samuel ELSDALE[1] = Mary ROBINSON
= ?   (c. 1705–88)   1734   (1711–57)

A   Ann GIBBINS (1757–1837)

Samuel of Pimlico (?–?)

John of Ipswich (1724–88)

Chart 2

John MOLSON (1730–70) = 1760
Chart 3

Mary (1739–72)

Ann (1743–65)

Robinson (1744–83) = 1779 Ann GIBBINS (1757–1837)

Rev. Samuel (1780–1827)

Rev. Robinson (1783–1850)

A   Susannah FIELDS (?–?) = 1756 James GIBBINS (alias PELL) (1731–?) - - - - - - - Luke GIBBINS[2] (c.1770–?)

James (1759–?)

George (1761–?)

William (1762–?)

John (1764–?)

Susannah (1768–?)

Ann (1757–1837) = 1779 Robinson ELSDALE (1744–83)

NOTES
1. Samuel Elsdale married Eleanor Stanroyd, 1772: no children. Married Mary Albin (Albon), 1784: no children.
2. Exact relationship between Luke Gibbins and James Gibbins is unknown.

Genealogy Chart 5: John Molson (1763–1836) and descendants

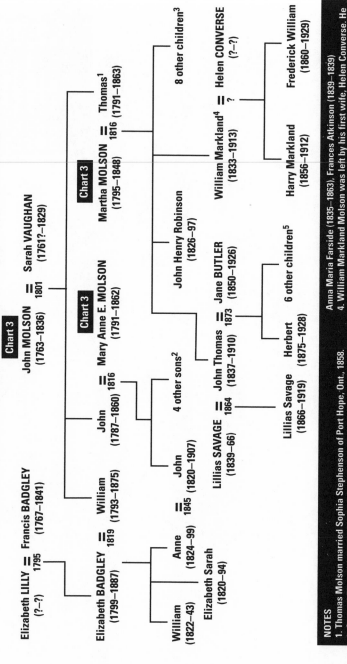

NOTES

1. Thomas Molson married Sophia Stephenson of Port Hope, Ont., 1858.
2. Samuel Elsdale (1822–1893), George Elsdale (1826–1866), Joseph Dinham (1829–1894), Alexander (1830–1897).
3. John (1817–18), Sarah Anne (1819–20), Thomas (1821–33), Martha Ann (1824–1900), Mary Anne Elizabeth (1828–1922), Harriet Bousfield (1830–1913), Anna Maria Farside (1835–1863), Frances Atkinson (1839–1839).
4. William Markland Molson was left by his first wife, Helen Converse. He subsequently married Pauline Nesmith. Helen Converse married Sir Edward Morris, premier of Newfoundland.
5. Naomi (c. 1876–?), Kenneth (1877–1932), Percival Talbot (1880–1917), Evelyn (1881–1969), Walter (1883–1952), Mabel (1888–1973).

Chapter 1

You are now so near the port which I have so long wished and laboured to bring you safe into, that my concern would be doubled, should you be shipwrecked within sight of it.
— Lord Chesterfield, letter to his son, September 12, 1749

BEFORE BEER BECAME AN industrial product—divorced from the agrarian calendar and fermented in factories around the clock by the tens of thousands of gallons—it was brewed in a traditional process that could begin no earlier than September. The harvested barley had been delivered, and when the weather was judged sufficiently cool for fermentation, the seeds would be "steeped" in the malthouse, soaked in water to coax them into germination. Starch became sugar; fermentation turned the sugar into alcohol; and the process of transforming cereal grain, yeast, hops and water into beer was underway.

Not yet twenty-three, John Molson began making his first batch of beer in his newly acquired brewery in the eastern suburb of Montreal known as St. Mary's Current on September 30, 1786, noting in his record book: "Steeped 30 bushels of Barley for the first time." Those bushels marked the beginning of an annual production cycle carried forward by successive generations of Molsons, each cycle demanding more barley, each generation enjoying greater revenues. Eighty years after that first steeping, this wheel of progress spun under the eye of the brewery founder's grandson, J.H.R. Molson. But in September 1866, J.H.R. was less concerned with the time-worn family routine of turning barley into liquid profit than he was with dying.

It had been an abysmal year for the "middle" branch of the Canadian Molson dynasty, the descendants of Thomas Molson, the second eldest of the patriarch John Molson's three sons. Thomas, J.H.R.'s father, had died in 1863, and the passing of that iconoclast had unleashed bitter disagreements and misadventures among his heirs, which had sullied the past three years—a sad repetition of the infighting that had blemished family relations after the death of the patriarch. The death in 1866 of the bride of J.H.R.'s youngest brother, John Thomas, in childbirth drew a deeply hued pall over the affairs of the brewing heir.

J.H.R.'s grandfather, on buying his first eight bushels of barley on July 28, 1786, had triumphantly announced in his record book: "Commencement on the Grand Stage of the World." Two generations later, the euphoric energy of the founder had dissipated into a dour consideration of death and its consequences by his grandson.

A family business invites a parallel business of family, with issues of inheritance, marriage, interdependence. The patriarch's arrival in Montreal in 1782 was an escape from the lives of countless English ancestors for whom opportunities and ambitions were strictly defined by bequeathal and the land's limited ability to support each new generation. Eighteen-year-old John Molson had broken free, physically and psychologically, on a new continent, with a new idea of how to make one's way onto that grand stage. But the old issues and habits had been impossible to shake. Some of his own children and grandchildren came to search for their own means of escape.

With a family business, the filial love of blood relations can become compromised or challenged by issues of commerce—who can be a worthy partner? who is fit to lead? who should be shunted aside or rebuked, even expelled? Home life and the life of enterprise become impossibly commingled, with no respite except through outright physical withdrawal. J.H.R.'s strong-willed father had disappeared from Montreal in a decade-long retreat, and J.H.R.'s brother William Markland would soon embark on his own self-imposed exile of more than two decades. The Molson family members, advantaged by the fruits of the patriarch's initial toil, had come to squabble within and across generations over how business—even *what* business—should be pursued. More often than not they had advanced their net worth, but sometimes they had reduced or even imperilled it. And in the autumn of 1866, they appeared in danger of actually losing it—of allowing the middle branch's core business of brewing to slip out of the family's hands.

On September 8, 1866, J.H.R. applied pencil to paper to write in an exceptionally precise hand a note on the practical consequences of his own death to his youngest brother, John Thomas. In the Regency period, there arose the notion that script in letters between friends, family and confidants should be rambunctiously casual, so as to distinguish the musings of the idle well-to-do from the workaday communications of the merchant classes. The precision of J.H.R.'s note to his youngest brother, rather than being anachronistic, was indicative of its true nature: a communication ultimately of commercial concern, despite the emotions that should have rocked the pencil. It was the least casual message that J.H.R. could have imagined writing.

He had been a sickly child, and his parents, Thomas and Martha, had been cursed by the death of two children in infancy before being blessed with a son, Thomas, in 1821. But Thomas died in his twelfth year, leaving J.H.R., born in 1826, the eldest male. As a testament to his parents' lack of faith in J.H.R.'s ultimate survival, when a final son arrived in 1837, they named him John Thomas, even though they had already given the pre-eminent male Molson name to eleven-year-old J.H.R.—John Henry Robinson.

The reason for the two brothers sharing a name lay in both the patriarch's will and their parents' marriage. Thomas had wed, unthinkingly, without a marriage contract, which left his bride, his cousin Martha, in a position to inherit half the brewery and even leave it to her family back in England. Thomas's misstep had forced his father to conceive of an inheritance scheme that would avoid the calamity of the brewery passing out of the direct chain of descent. In his deathbed will, dictated on January 11, 1836, he decided to skip over Thomas altogether and leave the brewery to Thomas's son, J.H.R. The brewery property was thus bequeathed to

"John Molson, son of my son Thomas Molson." In the event that Thomas's son John did not reach adulthood, or declined to take on the brewery, it would go to another grandson John, the son of the patriarch's eldest son, John Junior.

When his grandfather died, John Henry Robinson Molson was nine years old and apparently sufficiently wan to make his father fear that he would not live long enough to inherit the property when he came of age. If no "John Molson, son of my son Thomas Molson" reached the age of twenty-one, the middle branch would lose its grip on the brewing business. (Thomas's only other son, William Markland, born in 1833, was ineligible to inherit the brewery because he didn't have the requisite name.) For a man like Thomas, the predicament inspired a transparently obvious solution: if the survival of his existing son John was in doubt, he would simply have another son and name him John as well, and the terms of the will would be satisfied.

The oldest and youngest sons of Thomas Molson, forty and twenty-nine at the time of J.H.R.'s letter, were thus twins of a kind, joined by blood, by name, and by their strange roles of leading man and understudy on the grand stage that their long-dead grandfather had imagined. Though both had been named John, neither one embraced the name. While the family partnership that ran the brewery business in 1866 was known as John H.R. Molson and Brothers, the elder John was regularly known as J.H.R., and as a boy had named himself "Little Jackie." As for John Thomas, he was addressed by his pseudo-twin as Thomas. The name of John evidently carried too much weight in their lives for either man to be willing to bear it.

As it happened, their father's baptismal scheming to ensure a pair of potential brewing heirs proved unnecessary. J.H.R. lived to see twenty-one (and well beyond), and so had acquired the brewery assets in 1847. John Thomas, the spare heir, was provided for, in part, by being bequeathed his father's distillery at Montreal's Longue Pointe (which he then sold to J.H.R. in 1864). Yet the issue of inheritance, of the brewery business carrying forward through the middle branch, was far from settled, for J.H.R. had never married.

At forty, he had no heirs, and seemed to harbour no prospects of ever siring one. Casting a gaze of harsh judgment about his immediate family, he had decided that the only person worthy of receiving his earthly goods was the understudy who surely would have memorized the lines that J.H.R. had first been born to read.

"I have bequested everything I possess to you in a will which has been drawn up by Abbott and I have written it all with my own hand," J.H.R. explained to his favourite brother. He seemed to be preparing for his actual imminent death, as he elaborated, "My Uncle William Molson has it in his keeping and it will I suppose be read before or after my funeral as he may think best."

"I leave you everything," J.H.R. revealed, "as I think you are the best entitled to it[,] my brother Markland's ingratitude to me, when I have done so much for him—" He paused, reconsidering his condemnation of his other brother, and decided he could express his anger more precisely. He drew a careful line through "ingratitude" and the words that followed, and picked up the sentence again, so that it now read, ". . . Markland's untruthfulness & dishonesty making any bequest to him not to be thought of."

His dissatisfaction with the behaviour of his other siblings—his sisters Harriet, Mary Anne Elizabeth and Martha Ann—was only slightly less profound. "I leave my sisters nothing," he informed John Thomas, "as I consider they took advantage of the wording of my father's will to obtain a large sum of money which my father never intended them to have. You therefore have all. . . . I would wish the brewery property not to pass out of your hands if you can help it. I do not wish Markland ever to possess it."

But as much as he simply wished to see the family enterprise kept out of the despised hands of William Markland, J.H.R. ultimately aimed to deliver his fellow John Molson freedom from the confining obligations of a family enterprise that had trapped J.H.R. in unhappy partnerships, which had boxed him in as firmly as the coffin everyone appeared to have been waiting so long to craft. For as he expressed it to John Thomas in his note: "I hope what I leave you will[,] with what you now have[,] make you perfectly independent in every way."

John Thomas would not wait for his brother to die to experience independence in every way. Less than four years after receiving the note, with J.H.R. destined to live to the age of seventy, John Thomas withdrew from the brewery partnership and literally sailed away. The understudy who had become the chief beneficiary turned his back on his opportunities and (some surely said) his obligations. He had buried a bride of twenty-seven and resolved to steer clear of every hazard that had come to confound his elder brother. Yet another Molson had chosen self-imposed exile.

> *All material & workmanship to be of the best & generally equal to any steam yacht afloat—all doubtful or defective work or material upon discovery will be rejected. . . . Although of course there are many matters of detail omitted from this specification the builders must clearly understand that their price must include everything reasonably necessary to make her complete as a yacht should be & ready for her owners use—in fact equal in all respects both above and below to any first class yachts afloat, built by White, Harvey, Steele or any first class builder.*
> —from specifications drawn up by the designer St. Clare Byrne for an auxiliary screw steam and sailing yacht to be built by Laird Bros. of Birkenhead, England, for John Thomas Molson

In the middle of the day, with Liverpool well astern and the Isle of Man before him, John Thomas Molson duly noted that the temperature in the engine room of the Steam Vessel *Nooya* had reached 112 °F. The engine was less likely the source of the stifling heat than the coal fire and boiler nourishing it with steam pressure. The passage was about five hours old: at 7:55 on the morning of August 10, 1870, the S.V. *Nooya*, a luxurious, auxiliary-powered schooner measuring about 114 feet overall, had slipped away from the Sloyne, the principal anchorage in the River Mersey, which separated the industrial colossus of Liverpool from the Laird Bros. shipyard at Birkenhead. This, too, John Thomas had faithfully recorded. And he noted how his new vessel had moved downriver at half speed for about twenty minutes, when the order was given to the

The S.V. *Nooya* at anchor in Montreal, circa 1870. (The Molson Archives Collection/National Archives of Canada/PA-127503)

engineer to bring her up to full speed. After the Forinby Lightship was cleared at 10:07, John Thomas considered the voyage officially underway, and he began measuring miles against hours run.

John Thomas and his paid crew, led by the sailing master William Christall, were out on the Irish Sea, steering roughly northwest towards the Isle of Man. The sails remained unhoisted as the vessel split the glassy calm into chevrons of bow and stern waves; the temperature belowdecks rose as the 135-horsepower dual-cylinder engine strained to rotate the gunmetal screw, almost seven feet in diameter, a ponderous 120 revolutions per minute, the tips of its two blades lashing the ocean at thirty miles per hour. They were bound for Moville in northern Ireland, some two hundred miles from Liverpool, and from there, an entire ocean waited to be crossed before S.V. *Nooya* could end the cruise in Quebec City.

Back in Canada, a nation then three years young, the arrival of the thirty-three-year-old John Thomas and the weeks-old *Nooya* was anticipated by Arthur Radcliffe Boswell, honorary secretary of the Royal Canadian Yacht Club in Toronto. Boswell, latterly described in his own club's *Annals* as "silver haired and silver tongued," was a thirty-two-year-old lawyer who would serve as the R.C.Y.C.'s commodore fourteen times and be elected Toronto's mayor in 1883. He would acquire a prominent role in amassing the campaign war chests of Sir John A. Macdonald's Conservative party, and be rewarded with a King's Council appointment in 1887. But in 1870, Boswell was still a young member of Toronto's upper-class conservative strata, a man whose greatest achievement had been to drum up the funds necessary to build the newly completed R.C.Y.C. clubhouse on Front Street—in those days, Front Street actually fronted the harbour—opposite the provincial legislature. The club had been making do in a floating headquarters on the city's waterfront, but general rot, accelerated by an invasion of muskrats, had urged the membership back onto solid ground.

"I have the honour to inform you," Boswell had written John Thomas on March 8, "that at the Regular meeting of the R.C.Y.C. held last evening, you were unanimously selected a member." It would have been extraordinary for the membership to have decided otherwise. The Molsons of Montreal were prominent Conservatives and one of the nation's wealthiest and most established families, intermarried with other families of equal or greater standing. John Thomas's cousin Elizabeth was the wife of the Canadian railway czar Sir David Lewis McPherson, the business partner of Sir Casimir Gzowksi. Boswell, who had found the fundraising for the club's new headquarters a hard slog (the club's principal fleet, pre-*Nooya*, numbered only nineteen), could not have been more delighted when a Molson had abruptly presented himself as a candidate for membership during its construction.

Yet the *Nooya* would never progress above Montreal's Lachine Rapids. In mid-June 1871, the federal minister of marine and fisheries, Peter Mitchell, a New Brunswick shipbuilding magnate, would inform John Thomas of his "great pleasure in authorizing you . . . to explore and angle for salmon and trout in any of the vacant river[s] along the North coast of the River and Gulf of St. Lawrence, during the current season. Please, in return, to acquaint this Department with your proceedings, and convey any information of interest which you may obtain relating to the fishing etc."

No racing craft, the *Nooya* had been commissioned to serve as a floating estate in the Gulf from which John Thomas could indulge his passions for fly fishing and duck and caribou hunting with friends and family members.

S.V. *Nooya* was added to the fleet list of the R.C.Y.C. for the 1870 season, but the paucity of information—the list gave only her name (incorrectly, as *Neoya*) and her owner (as "Mr. Molson"), with no details of her size or type—betrayed the phantom status of John Thomas and his vessel. By 1870, beginning with his delivery of S.V. *Nooya* from Liverpool to Quebec City, John Thomas had also become a phantom in the affairs of the greater Molson family and the disparate, increasingly troubled businesses they pursued.

Painting: All the vessel to have equal to four coats of the best oil paint where required. Topsides black with gilt band & stern mouldings gilt—bottom copper or some other approved colour—bulwarks grained & varnished or done in immitation [sic] teak to match the deck fittings—spars all varnished (after being carefully scraped down) with best copal varnish (not lower masts)—Boats to be all bright varnished.

The *Nooya* was a magnificent craft, worthy in every way of being a gentleman's yacht, certainly ranking among the finest afloat anywhere in the world when she began her voyage to Quebec in August 1870. She was the culmination of more than a year of investigation by John Thomas into yachts and yachting. There had been other extravagances in the Molson family's recent past—palatial Montreal residences and summer homes—but the *Nooya* was exceptional, a physical manifestation of John Thomas's new freedom from the family enterprise, yachting's genteel version of running away to sea.

In finding himself a worthy vessel, John Thomas had sought the advice of a friend, Bryce Allan of the Montreal Allans. Bryce was the son of Hugh Allan, who would be knighted the following year for his services to the British Empire in transportation: his Allan Line of steamships delivered the royal mail between Liverpool and

Quebec City and Montreal. The Allans, like the Molsons, were a prominent Montreal family who maintained a summer home at Lake Memphremagog, east of Montreal. Acting on John Thomas's enquiries over matters of the proper yacht, Bryce Allan, who hung his hat at the Allan's Liverpool office, had made contact with St. Clare Byrne, a yacht designer and broker in Liverpool.

Initially, Byrne sought out a quality second-hand yacht for John Thomas. His client even came to England in the summer of 1869 to inspect one potential purchase, the *Hawk*, at Cowes, a yachting mecca on England's south coast, opposite the Portsmouth naval facilities. It was from these waters that John Thomas's grandfather had left England as a teenager, risking a wartime crossing to establish the enterprise that made it possible, almost a century later, for John Thomas to go shopping for the ultimate extravagance of Victorian leisure.

Back home in November 1869, John Thomas had concluded that a used vessel was not for him. He wrote Bryne: "I wonder what a composite auxiliary screw schooner would cost—say with four staterooms fitted with drawers etc. bath under floor—saloon with piano, library in it." By then, St. Clare Byrne had come to the same conclusion: that a man of John Thomas's means and standards would be served only by the creation of something entirely new. Knowing they would have to move quickly if a yacht were to be completed in time for the 1870 season (construction would likely take at least four months), Byrne had already submitted a set of unapproved specifications for quotation when he replied to Molson. Laird Bros. in Birkenhead had built David Livingstone's sidewheel steamer *Ma Robert* for the Dark Continent in 1858 and Francis McLintock's steam yacht *Fox*, which searched for the lost Franklin expedition in the Canadian Arctic in 1859. It was unquestionably the leading builder of luxury yachts with iron hulls. Although he knew other firms could create the yacht for twenty percent less than Laird Bros., Byrne stressed the importance of staying with "*very leading builders* for this class of work as it is quite a specialty."

John Thomas agreed to Byrne's proposal. The yacht's specifications were enclosed in a letter to Laird Bros. on January 21, 1870.

Three days later, Laird Bros. responded to Byrne, advising that "it seems to comprise all that is necessary to complete a first class yacht." The builder attached specifications for the engines and propulsion, and quoted a final price of £5,200, adding, "If we receive the order to proceed within three weeks from now[,] we calculate being able to complete her for delivery in June next, and will use our best endeavours to accomplish this." Three weeks would come in mid-February; on February 16, John Thomas wired St. Clare Byrne a simple message: COMMENCE YACHT.

> *Cabins etc: . . . It is proposed to have all the internal fittings of selected pitch pine french polished, or pine painted as owner may desire. . . . In two of the state rooms aft baths to be fitted in the floor to fill from sea & drain off into bilge as usual. . . .*

Byrne forwarded John Thomas's telegram to Laird Bros. the next day. "I have much pleasure in putting her in your hands," he said of the yacht commission. The construction schedule was tight. To reassure Laird Bros. that John Thomas was a client worth the effort, Byrne added that Bryce Allan "can tell you all about Mr. Molson."

For a shipbuilder moving ahead on a major commission with only a one-quarter payment, all that mattered was that Mr. Molson was a man of his word and was good for the money. To this, Bryce Allan could have casually testified, but how much more a man like him would have been able to convey if "all about" Mr. Molson was indeed of concern to Laird Bros.

John Thomas Molson? Thirty-three years old, wealthy most certainly. Single most unfortunately. Wife dead in childbirth, hasn't remarried. Surrounded by various friends of like sporting minds. Crack shot, a captain in the volunteer militia until he resigned in '64. Still very much of that sporting-officer mould, the uniformed English gentleman loose in the empire, bagging its game, only he isn't actually *English* English, having been born and raised in Montreal. One of those colonials who seems more English in his enthusiasms than the English themselves. Something of a stranger in his own land. Never happier than when he isn't actually in it, except of course when he's stalking caribou, shooting duck, or angling for salmon and sea trout in the Gulf of St. Lawrence—hence the yacht commission. Absolutely necessary if you're going to angle the north shore of the Gulf in style. Railways and steamboats will get you as far as the Saguenay, but after that you're on your own. Read George Thomas Good's guide to fishing the lower St. Lawrence, published at Quebec in 1862. In order to get to the prime streams along the north coast or at Anticosti, "you must charter a schooner for the voyage, unless lucky enough to find a chance conveyance by steam or sailer." Would a man like John Thomas rely on chartering or a chance conveyance when he could build something as fine as anything in the world for the very purpose? With bathtubs and a piano?

But we were talking about John Thomas, the stranger in his own land. Honeymooned in Italy. Fond of Europe, which is to say the Europe of finery and excellence, and beyond Europe of whatever spectacle of achievement the world has to offer. In another year he's going to travel the entire globe by ship and rail, do the grand tour, with a list of sight-seeing stops that would give a crown prince envy. San Francisco, Yokohama, Shanghai, Hong Kong, Canton, Saigon, Singapore, Batavia, Galle, Calcutta, Delhi, Bombay, Aden, Suez, Cairo, Alexandria, Malta, Gibraltar, Southampton, London, Liverpool, Quebec, Montreal. John Thomas will add it all up—27,602 miles in 203 days—and work it out to be 136 nautical miles per day, 5.66 nautical miles per hour. As if the vacation of a lifetime was the equivalent of a steamer-run to be plotted out to the mile and pound of coal and conducted with the utmost efficiency.

A brewer? Not at all. He doesn't have anything to do with running it, having bowed out of the operating partnership last year. He and his brothers bailed out of distilling—temperance guilt on his part at least, if you ask me—and have gotten into some other ventures: mining sands in the Gulf of St. Lawrence for iron; refining sugar, if you can imagine, right in the backyard of the Redpaths. Those ventures aren't going to work out, but John Thomas is managing the setbacks. He has that military craft of the family, going back to that great-grand-uncle of his—the privateer named Elsdale—and his grandfather and uncles, who served in the War of 1812, and his uncle John, who was wounded on Chambly Road during the rebellion of '37. The last decade has been nothing less than a carefully orchestrated retreat for John Thomas, fought to preserve strategic assets. His money is socked away in various stocks and bonds, with some of it in shipping because the family has had that affinity for the sea ever since Elsdale hacked and slashed his way around Hispaniola. Shame, though, about the family situation: the siblings who can't abide one another, the opportunities missed. The Molsons were in steamships decades before the Allans—they were global pioneers, absolutely—and railways, too. But look at them now. The Molson steamers are gone, given up, and the Allan Line rules the Atlantic. Father Hugh is going to be Sir Hugh, and he's going to build a railway to the Pacific. Ask me if there will be a Molson brewery in another ten years, and I won't be able to say for certain. But John Thomas's investments will still be delivering a return, and John Thomas will still be spending, sailing, spending, shooting, spending, fishing, spending, travelling. Go ahead and build, you Lairds.

> *Companions etc.: Companions, skylights, & all deck fittings of teak as light, small, & neat as possible consistent with strength & other requirements. . . . Steering wheel: To have a very neat brass mounted Teak Wheel with iron standards. . . . Boats: Three, say one gig 20 to 22 feet long fitted up complete in every way like a yacht gig. . . . Masts spars etc: . . . Sails will be all of finest narrow white yacht canvas & made by Lapthorne, Gordon or other approved maker. . . .*

What should this grand creation be called? John Thomas had determined that it would be a Canadian Native word, Indian or Eskimo, and he gathered from various experts the names of animals and bodies of water. He considered the "Esquimault" word for silver gull—*nooya*—and made his choice. His confirmation of the name, sent to Byrne on April 22, crossed in one Allan ship as an update on construction from Byrne, written April 21, made its way to Montreal aboard another one.

John Thomas upheld a long-standing tradition among custom-yacht clients by knowing just enough about vessels to both inform and exasperate his designer. There were the usual revisions to the interior, despite the very tight schedule, and John Thomas fretted about whether or not the yacht would be able to accommodate a piano as he insisted. Byrne set him at ease in his April 22 update: "By the way there *is* room for a piano in the dining room—I have tried it." After receiving word of John Thomas's decision on the name, Byrne wrote him: "I note your wish to name her 'Nooya'—I will arrange to have a pretty & well carved seagull for a figurehead—nothing could come in better."

Laird Bros. performed admirably. S.V. *Nooya's* keel touched the Mersey on June 4, but two more months would pass before the new vessel was sufficiently prepared to tackle the Atlantic. John Thomas invited Byrne along for the maiden voyage, from Birkenhead to Moville, but in his haste to be underway, the Molson heir left the *Nooya's* designer behind. Byrne was preparing to board the ferry at Liverpool for Birkenhead when he saw the *Nooya* heading down the Sloyne. It's doubtful he ever saw his luxurious creation again. Byrne subsequently made a point of inspecting the logs of incoming ships at Liverpool, and was relieved to see that they had been blessed with fine weather on their Atlantic crossings. He hoped the *Nooya* would enjoy the same.

John Thomas recorded no measure of elation or disappointment in the yacht's performance on the first day of the transatlantic cruise. At one point, the engine had to be shut down because of the over-heating of one machinery component, but the inconvenience paled beside his grandfather's experiences with his pioneering steamboat *Accommodation*, which thrashed and shuddered and regularly sur-rendered to the currents and tides of the St. Lawrence in 1809. The eighty-five-foot *Accommodation's* primitive power plant, operating on just two pounds of steam pressure, summoned up six mighty horsepower in turning a pair of paddlewheels. John Thomas's *Nooya* took advantage of the latest advances in engine and propulsion technology, including a propeller whose blades could be "feathered," or rotated, to reduce drag when under sail. Six decades of innovation had allowed John Thomas to employ steam technology in a leisure cruise of the Atlantic, where his grandfather had to build four steamboats before coming up with one that could defeat the river current that ran past the brewery.

The *Nooya* appears to have met John Thomas's expectations. His only concern during the first twenty-four hours was the way she rolled when a "considerable swell" met her beam-on as she rounded the top of Ireland on the final approach to Shore Head. Even so, he found her movements "perfectly easy." Favoured by the good weather St. Clare Byrne had both predicted and wished for, and making much of the voyage under sail power, she conquered the entire Atlantic passage, from the Liverpool bell buoy to Quebec City, in fifteen and three-quarter days.[1]

It is tempting to think of the swell that rose to meet John Thomas as a reverberation of his own deep past, an echo of the initial crossing his grandfather had made in the spring of 1782. Grandfather John's ship had none of the amenities of the *Nooya*— no piano, no staterooms equipped with private baths, no auxiliary steam engine—and many more uncertainties awaited him on the far shore. That passage was an eight-week battle through storms and potential boardings by American and French privateers in a leaky merchant ship commanded by a drunken captain.

John Molson, of course, had no idea of what his grandson John Thomas, born a year after his death, would be capable of accomplishing with his life and with the brewing fortune to be left to him. John Thomas, however, had every opportunity to appreciate the industriousness of his grandfather, if only through his considerable legacy. And if he had no personal inclination to carry on the energetic pursuit of wealth, then John Thomas at least had the opportunity to avail himself of the wealth bequeathed to him. Both men sailed for Quebec, but in truth they had very different destinations.

Chapter 2

---

*Never be proud of your rank or birth, but be as proud as you
please of your character. Nothing is so contrary to true dignity as
the former kind of pride. You are, it is true, of a noble family, but
whether of a very ancient one or not I neither know nor care, nor
need you, and I dare say there are twenty fools in the House of
Lords who could out-descend you in pedigree. That sort of stately
pride is the standing jest of all people who can make one; but dignity of character is universally respected. Acquire and preserve
that most carefully.*

    —Lord Chesterfield, letter to his godson and heir, to be
    delivered after his death (1773)

IT WAS AS IF, for one otherwise unremarkable hour, twenty-four-
year-old Horatio Nelson and eighteen-year-old John Molson had
confused their destinies. On the afternoon of Thursday, May 2,
1782, the future Montreal brewer was far closer than Nelson to the
apogee of Trafalgar, while the future lord admiral was far closer than
Molson to the allure of an adolescent North America.

Molson, a paying passenger aboard a merchant ship bound for
Canada, was waylaid at Portsmouth, England, in the intimate
company of the wooden machines of Nelson's future glory.
Nelson, meanwhile, who had taken command of HMS *Albemarle*
the previous August, was well on his way to the St. Lawrence. The
twenty-eight-gun frigate had emerged from several months of
repairs in the Portsmouth drydocks (after a collision with an East
Indiaman) to depart on April 20—the same day that Lord Howe,

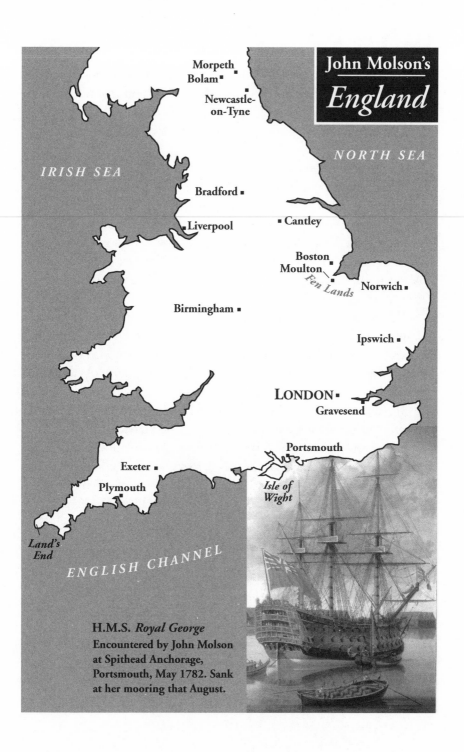

John Molson's
England

NORTH SEA

IRISH SEA

Morpeth
Bolam
Newcastle-
on-Tyne

Bradford

Liverpool

Cantley

Boston
Moulton

Fen Lands

Norwich

Birmingham

Ipswich

LONDON
Gravesend

Portsmouth

Exeter

Plymouth

Isle of
Wight

Land's
End

ENGLISH CHANNEL

H.M.S. *Royal George*
Encountered by John Molson
at Spithead Anchorage,
Portsmouth, May 1782. Sank
at her mooring that August.

newly appointed commander of the Channel fleet, hoisted his flag aboard Nelson's future flagship, HMS *Victory*. The day before Molson found himself off Portsmouth, Nelson and the *Albemarle* had arrived at Cork, Ireland, to help escort a convoy of some thirty to forty merchant ships through the hazards of the American Revolution to Quebec.

On the afternoon of May 2, Molson's ship, delayed by her captain's incompetence, had skulked back into Portsmouth harbour, her own convoy in danger of leaving her behind. She eased through the naval moorings off Spithead, gliding past three mammoth first-rate warships. "The tide of flood began to flow," Molson related in a letter home, "so we were obliged to put back amongst the Men of War (in the passing thro' them, we went along side the *Royal George*, the *Victory*, the *Sovereign*)."

The *Victory* was nearly a quarter-century away from Nelson's empire-saving martyrdom at Trafalgar, in 1805. The *Royal Sovereign*, still under construction, would be commissioned in 1786 and become the first ship at Trafalgar to draw French fire. As for the *Royal George*, she was mere months away from utter infamy.

In November 1759, a British fleet led by Admiral Edward Hawke aboard the *Royal George* had chased down the French Brest fleet at Brittany's Quiberon Bay. Fighting with almost brazen self-confidence, steering through a full gale towards a rocky lee shore, Hawke had become a national hero by seeing to the destruction of seven French battleships. Wolfe had bested Montcalm on the Plains of Abraham that September, and the Cape Breton fortress of Louisbourg had already capitulated in 1758. The triumph at Quiberon Bay helped seal Louis XV's loss of Canada by denying France the warships that might have made a success of the counteroffensive that followed Wolfe's victory. Instead, when Montreal fell on September 8, 1760, eastern North America had become wholly British. With his birth still four years away, John Molson had been secured a new land to explore by the *Royal George*'s gallantry.

The *Royal George*'s greatest moment was well behind her when John Molson saw her at Spithead. And less than four months later, on August 29, she would be carelessly heeled over at her mooring while stores were being loaded and repairs made. A gust of wind would press the open gunports below the waves, causing this storied relic to capsize and sink in sixty-five feet of water. She took with her about one thousand people, among them women and children who had moved aboard while she was idle in port. It is likely that many of them were watching from the rail as John Molson's humble merchant ship sought secure anchor in her company.

Delayed in his departure at Spithead, John Molson lay in the slack water between the tidal flows drawing the observer into past and future. The decisive violence of what had been and what would come was both recalled and promised by the tiers of the great ships' silent cannons. While the *Victory* was freshly prepared for new duties, the once glorious *Royal George* had been reduced to a floating facsimile of one of the market towns John Molson knew well.

"I was surprised at the number of people, men, women and children," remarked Olaudah Equiano, who as the young black slave of a Royal Navy officer came across the *Royal George* at Spithead about twenty years before Molson did.[1] "There were shops and stalls of every kind of goods, and people crying their different commodities about the ship as in a town." The ship's basic character would have been much the same when Molson encountered her. That all of it was about to end up on the bottom of the anchorage, with such harrowing loss of life, could not have been predicted by anyone.

"Kismet," Nelson would utter resignedly as he lay dying belowdecks on the *Victory* on October 21, 1805. Fate. On that May day in 1782, Nelson and Molson were in transit, the trajectories of their lives far from clear—although Nelson's would have been the more predictable. Nelson was brilliant and fearless, and his death from the musket ball of a French sniper during his greatest military accomplishment was almost preordained. His preparations for Trafalgar had been unfolding since he had joined the navy at the age of twelve, and before that battle he had been blinded in one eye and lost an arm. Already, he had narrowly avoided being killed by a polar bear in the Canadian arctic. Molson's past in a quiet corner of rural England had been far more prosaic, but his future as a middle-class Lincolnshire farmer would have seemed as preordained as

Nelson's martyrdom—which, perhaps, made Molson's actual destiny all the more improbable. As he set out from Portsmouth that spring, Molson, more than Nelson, was the young man whose present circumstances begged his own history for an explanation.

In medieval times, south Lincolnshire farmers would harden the feet of their geese with tar and drive great flocks nearly one hundred miles south to sell them in London. These fowl travelled farther than most people who saw them pass ever did. Unless compelled to bear arms and march off to war, the common crowd of rural England routinely lived and died within sight of a particular village for generation upon generation, never roaming more than the few miles to the nearest market town.

In this near-timeless age of immobility, a Molson ancestor in the seventeenth century took the noteworthy step of leaving Cantley, in the southern extreme of Yorkshire's West Riding, to begin anew in the grazing lands of south Lincolnshire, some seventy miles to the southeast. No one knows why, much less how. We cannot even say for certain if this was a singular pilgrimage, as opposed to a succession of relocations by different generations and family branches, for there would be far more Molsons in the south Lincolnshire countryside than John Molson's direct ancestry could account for.[2] But the meagre details are less important than the impression they leave: of a family suddenly unsettled and in motion, across geography and through the social strata.

The family lineage has been traced back into the fourteenth century, to a Thomas "Moldson" of Kylhome (the name of a particular manor farm) in the parish of Cantley, in the reign of Richard II (1378–99). The Moldsons/Molsons might even have been in that neighbourhood during the reigns of Richard I (1189–95) and his brother John I (1199–1216) and their struggles for control of the English throne—with Robin Hood running interference against John's reign. Those royal rivalries inspired Edinburgh's Sir Walter Scott to write his romantic epic *Ivanhoe*, published in 1791. Cantley was situated less than four miles from the town of Doncaster, which was, for a long time, the Don River's highest navigable point

The earliest preserved reference to John Molson's direct ancestors is in Britain's Public Record Office and dates to 1530 (C1/604). In a suit that survives in slightly damaged condition, a man named John Banaster argued before Sir Thomas More, Lord Chancellor of England, for ownerships of "messuages" (a dwelling house and outbuildings) and land that had belonged to a Thomas Molson in Brampton and "Kelholme" in Yorkshire's Cantley parish. The defendants were Richard (William) and John Molson, whose names are highlighted. It's worth noting that "Molson" had its modern spelling in a legal document of such an early date.

upstream from the Humber, and Scott opened his novel with the following paragraph:

> In that pleasant district of merry England which is watered by the river Don, there extended in ancient times a large forest, covering the greater part of the beautiful hills and valleys which lie between Sheffield and the pleasant town of Doncaster. . . . Here haunted of yore the fabulous Dragon of Wantley; here were fought many of the most desperate battles during the Civil Wars of the Roses; and here also flourished in ancient times those bands of gallant outlaws, whose deeds have been rendered so popular in English song.

Finding veritable forebears to John Molson in a past misted by the breath of dragons remains a challenge. As individuals—complete with characters, aspirations and life stories, however prosaic— these Molsons scarcely exist. Most of John Molson's known ancestors survive as little more than names on the family tree. Yet even where they survive only in a baptismal record, these ancestors still help illustrate the predominant facts of life in John Molson's time. The path from birth to death was corralled by issues of inheritance, bequest, succession and narrow opportunity. Along the way, one struggled to avoid falling into the depths of poverty, which was just a short step from middle-class life.

Previous writers have speculated that the Civil War of the 1640s, also known as the Puritan Revolution, may have impelled the Molson relocation from Yorkshire to south Lincolnshire. The conflict ravaged the communities along the Don.[3] The timing of the Molson migration, however, seems wrong for war to have been the motivation. John Molson's great-great-grandfather Thomas Moulson was the first direct ancestor to appear in south Lincolnshire, but he could not have moved until after his son Thomas was christened at Cantley in 1652, which was seven years after the fighting ended. If anything, Thomas Moulson was moving against the grain of contemporary politics. The role of church-warden (a parish lay position), which Thomas's descendants held in the Church of England, strongly associated the family with royalist factions. Yet Thomas had relocated to a republican stronghold: Lincolnshire was one of seven counties in the arch-republican Eastern Association.

The republican-minded "low" Protestants of Lincolnshire were distinguished by more than their broad sympathies for the Cromwellian cause. They were also synonymous with the English colonization of North America. The region of East Anglia, of which south Lincolnshire was a part, was closely associated with the Massachusetts Bay Colony, established in 1628. The Pilgrim fathers, who had left England from the south Lincolnshire town of Boston in 1609, and initially settled in the Netherlands, founded their colony at Plymouth, Massachusetts, in 1620. Eastern Massachusetts is strewn with place names inspired by East Anglia settlements, with Boston the most prominent. By the time our John Molson was born in 1763, south Lincolnshire had a transatlantic heritage generations old, giving it a world view of opportunity unlikely to have been found back in Yorkshire's West Riding.

The fact that the elder Thomas was remembered in the Molson family tree as "Thomas of Crowland" makes it clear he did abandon Cantley, for Crowland was a village in the southwestern extremes of south Lincolnshire. His relocation was probably provoked by a shortage of land, or at least the opportunity for new lands. Thomas of Crowland is identified as the youngest of three sons although, curiously, he, and not one of his older brothers, inherited his father's name.[4] Still, he would not have stood to inherit much, if any, property, which would have compelled him to look elsewhere. His eye evidently led him to south Lincolnshire.

While it is true that many individuals never wandered more than a few miles from their birthplace, commerce did span great distances, and Yorkshire and south Lincolnshire were linked by agricultural trade. Crops of rape were cultivated in the briny Lincolnshire lowlands and exported to both Yorkshire and Lancashire, to serve as livestock feed, while wool from Lincolnshire sheep travelled to Yorkshire for spinning. The novelist Daniel Defoe, who wandered extensively through Yorkshire (and made Robinson Crusoe the son of a Hull merchant who retired to York), noted in his book *Travels of a Gentleman through Great Britain* (1727) that Lincolnshire corn was making its way to Yorkshire. As yeomen—freehold farmers—the Moulsons of Yorkshire would have had some knowledge of south Lincolnshire, and personal contact with farmers who produced feed for them.[5]

Whatever his reasons for moving, Thomas Moulson relocated after western Europe had already warmed to far more ambitious migrations. While Sir Walter Raleigh's efforts to establish a colony in Virginia at Roanoke had failed in the late sixteenth century, Jamestown had been successfully staked out in 1607, one year before Champlain established Quebec. As noted, the Pilgrims of south Lincolnshire were in Massachusetts in 1620, and thousands of people, mainly from East Anglia, had migrated to Massachusetts Bay in the decade before the English Civil War. Some 120,000 "colonists," mainly Presbyterian Scots, were employed as shock troops of Protestant settlement in northern Ireland between 1620 and 1642. In this age of daring mobility, one or more ancestral

Molsons leaving south Yorkshire for a new life in south Lincolnshire is comparatively pedestrian. Nonetheless, these Molsons demonstrated a capacity for movement that remained latent in the family's genes for several generations. The new world colonies would eventually call out to one of them.

The general region of south Lincolnshire to which Thomas Moulson came was known as Holland. A rectangular coastal indentation called the Wash brought what was then known as the German Ocean (now the North Sea) into the marshy lowlands of the Fens. Crowland (or Croyland), where Thomas Moulson settled, had essentially been an island, some thirty miles from the Wash, when St. Guthlac arrived at the site of a future abbey in AD 699. Reclaiming these saltwater expanses for farming had been a local preoccupation since Roman times. A seawall was built at the Wash and stretched east along the salt marshes, and Holland was limned by dyke works and diversionary canals. Many of the improvements had been undertaken since about 1600, with the expertise of Dutch engineers and agriculturalists, and the region had acquired a distinct Dutch flavour in its geography, architecture, tulip production and population.

The improvements came at a price to the long-standing inhabitants of the Fen Lands, the people remembered as the Gyrvii, who had raised great flocks of market geese and resisted efforts to drain the marshes. Their displacement, however, was a mere footnote in the epic transformation of land ownership and usage, as tenant farmers lost their footing through the practice of enclosure, which turned common land into large private holdings. Enclosure had been prevalent in the sixteenth century under the Tudors, and it gained fresh momentum in the eighteenth. Improved agricultural efficiency led to a population boom, and the displacement of a growing populace (along with economic hardships) helped foster the desire for new land in Ireland and North America. Long before settlers began running natives off their land in the new world, Europeans had been busy uprooting and disenfranchising their own people in places like Ireland and south Lincolnshire.

South Lincolnshire provided dramatic contrast to the fabled woods and picturesque towns of south Yorkshire that Thomas Moulson had left behind. A visitor in the early nineteenth century described the Holland region as "an immense extent of low land, much of which was once marsh land, but is now become, by means of the exertions made during a period of almost two hundred years, one of the richest tracts in the kingdom: it is a region of fertility, without beauty, in a climate which is not salubrious to the human constitution."[6]

By 1799 an estimated 150,000 acres had been reclaimed for farming, and was mainly being used as pastureland for sheep (wool was the chief source of wealth for Lincolnshire), horses and cattle. The new land presented considerable challenges: the battle against seawater was constant. In many areas brackish water lay only a foot or two below the surface and would well up in a phenomenon known as the Soak.[7] And while there was a constant vigilance against seawater, soil during the growing season was often in danger of drought due to inefficient irrigation. Economic difficulties in the late eighteenth century would propel some Holland residents in the direction of the new world, following the example set by the local Pilgrims and East Anglian émigrés almost two centuries earlier.

No Molson would join the exodus until he enjoyed a critical mass of wealth, which would take several generations to accumulate and channel through successive male heirs. After Thomas Moulson established himself in Crowland, his descendants settled and farmed about ten miles north, within a specific corner of south Lincolnshire: the satellite villages to the south and east of the market town of Spalding. Moulson's eldest son became known as Thomas of Peakhill, in honour of a settlement in the parish of Cowbit. He identified himself as "Yeoman" in some surviving property leases that show him employing land in the agricultural communities of Holbeach, Cowbit and Moulton—leasing plots for his own use and renting some of his own holdings to a husbandman, or tenant farmer. He may have been the local churchwarden, but he was also illiterate, signing a number of surviving legal documents with a crude "T."

Thomas of Peakhill's third son, christened John in 1699, was the lone male offspring to survive to adulthood. This John, the first so-named to carry the lineage forward since a man known as John of Brampton died in 1549, was the grandfather of the John Molson who came to Canada.

In 1727 "Grandfather" John married Martha Baker, about whom we know nothing, except that she apparently came with a dowry of several hundred pounds. The previous year, Grandfather John had become the village of Moulton's churchwarden and justice of the peace, and in 1731 was made overseer of Moulton Grammar School.[8] Grandfather John, in short, was firmly planted in the leading ranks of the educated, rural middle class. In one generation, the Molsons had leapt from illiterate yeomen to erudite gentry.

With the marriage, Grandfather John received from his father a property at Moulton known by the disagreeable name of Snake Hall. The estate's appearance in the marriage settlement marks its debut in Molson family records. Thomas the great-grandfather likely acquired it through a marriage dowry—either from his first wife, remembered only as Sarah, or from Mary Wincely, whom he married just two months after Sarah's death in 1691.

The strategy of a man acquiring wealth by such means—by marrying it and thus possessing it outright—had become firmly established in English jurisprudence in the seventeenth century.[9] That era marked the blossoming of individual rights in English law, albeit rights under which women and their property became the property of their husbands. The eighteenth century, in turn, codified and exalted the rights of property. Ownership of land became a primary concern, a focal point of economic and physical survival. Land delivered power because it bestowed the right to vote in parliamentary elections; it also represented security, and ultimately it helped shape the dynamics of families and the destiny of individual members.

The importance of land was accentuated by the competing traditions of inheritance in England in the eighteenth century. The "gavelkind" principle saw the equal division of property among male heirs; more common among landowners was the practice of primogeniture—the first-born male received the bulk of the real property, leaving siblings either to marry well or to seek some profession as a means of survival. Primogeniture was reinforced by the common-law practice of assigning the fundamental inheritance right to the first-born male, with the right descending thereafter through the younger males. That operative principle of lineage led directly to our John Molson.

Property ownership and opportunities for those offspring other than first-born males, which may have driven Thomas Moulson from Cantley to Crowland in the seventeenth century, became prominent and sometimes contentious family issues throughout the eighteenth and nineteenth centuries. Long after the Molsons of south Lincolnshire became the Molsons of Montreal, ancient issues of bequest welled up in their lives like the Soak in the Fen Lands. It was as if, standing in their thriving brewery on the shore of the St. Lawrence River, thousands of miles and decades removed from Snake Hall and its pastures, they would sense this insistent, brackish water cooling the soles of their shoes. Try as John Molson might to build one, no dyke could hold back the crises it provoked.

Snake Hall as it appeared in 1988. It's doubtful if even the original portion of this much-renovated estate dates to John Molson's time. (Courtesy the Elsdale family)

As the eighteenth century progressed, the Molson fortune gathered momentum, with marriage and inheritance creating an ever-larger bequest for the eldest male heir of each successive generation. At the heart of that bequest was Snake Hall ("Snakes Hall" in the will of our John Molson's father), which by the late 1760s consisted of a home and various outbuildings associated with thirty-eight acres (in five parcels) in the heart of the drained marshland. A house known as Snake Hall still stands on the property, much modified, although at its core is a two-storey brick structure in a severe Georgian style.[10] Thomas of Peakhill's great-grandson John Molson would never have been able to establish himself in business in Canada without it.

Grandfather John's first effort to produce a male heir with Martha Baker resulted, in 1728, in a boy named John, who died in infancy. A second boy was born in 1730, and this next John—Father John—introduced an exciting dynamic to the lineage through his marriage.

The bride at the wedding on September 11, 1760, in Surfleet, a northern satellite town of Spalding, was Mary Elsdale, eldest daughter of Surfleet's Samuel Elsdale and his wife Mary Robinson. Mary Elsdale's wedding to thirty-year-old Father John came two months after her twenty-first birthday. It is doubtful that her fifteen-year-old brother Robinson attended the ceremony, for he had gone to sea in 1756 at the age of twelve, entering the Royal Navy at the beginning of the Seven Years War.[11]

Mary Elsdale is as anonymous as so many of the Molson ancestors, but her brother Robinson shines spectacularly from an otherwise dim past. On the evidence of Robinson's life, the Elsdale bloodline delivered the Molsons the vitality and daring not often found in a lineage of yeomen. The Molsons had demonstrated a capacity for movement; the Elsdales infused movement with action. In Robinson, the dynamism of the first Canadian Molsons had a firm precedent. For generations after the union between John Molson and Mary Elsdale, the Molsons of Canada paid tribute to Mary's family by naming their children Robinson, Mary, Samuel and Elsdale. These descendants were Molsons in name, but substantially Elsdales in heart and spirit. More than any other person, Robinson Elsdale provides a glimpse of the mettle from which our John Molson was made. Character, as Lord Chesterfield had impressed upon his son, was so much more important than simple lineage, but in Robinson Elsdale both qualities were indivisibly fused. We cannot say if John Molson was his father's son, but certainly he was his uncle's nephew.

Chapter 3

[T]he world can doubtless never be well known by theory; practice
is absolutely necessary; but surely, it is of great use to a young
man, before he sets out for that country, full of mazes, windings,
and turnings, to have at least a general map of it, made by some
experienced traveller.
—Lord Chesterfield, letter to his son, August 10, 1749

THE MOLSONS OF SOUTH LINCOLNSHIRE were doubly enriched
by the union between John Molson (Father John) and Mary Elsdale
in 1760. About two weeks before the wedding, Father John
received Snake Hall from Grandfather John, and Mary brought to
the union a parcel of land at Pinchbeck valued at £600. This was a
substantial sum. Converting currency values across centuries is difficult, but we can say Mary Elsdale enriched Father John, and ultimately his heirs, by the modern equivalent of about £64,600.[1]

More important, the Molson lineage was enriched in character
by Mary's brother Robinson, who had enjoyed the auspicious christening date of Christmas Day, 1744. Robinson Elsdale's dashing life
at sea, which lasted until his retirement in 1779, injected the staid
Molsons with a spectacular dose of glamour and adventure. Elsdale
provided an enigmatic role model to the Molson family as well as
the general population around Spalding.

Residents of the Holland region had long struggled against the
encroaching sea to wrest a respectable living from drained land.
Robinson Elsdale effectively leapt over the seawall, and rode the
ocean to personal glory. He was a local celebrity who would be

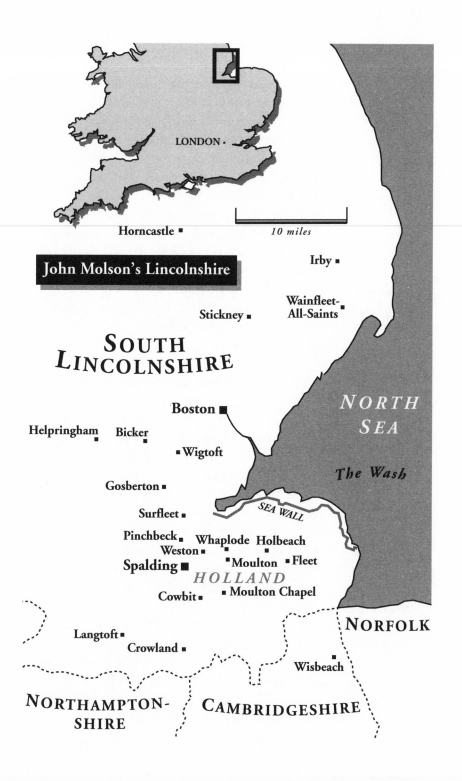

LONDON ·

Horncastle ■

10 miles

John Molson's Lincolnshire

Irby ■

Wainfleet-
All-Saints ■

Stickney ■

SOUTH
LINCOLNSHIRE

Boston ■

Helpringham ■   Bicker ■

■ Wigtoft

Gosberton ■

Surfleet ■

Pinchbeck ■   Whaplode Holbeach
Weston ■   ■
Spalding ■   ■ Moulton ■ Fleet

HOLLAND

Cowbit ■   ■ Moulton Chapel

*NORTH
SEA*

The Wash

SEA WALL

NORFOLK

Langtoft ■
Crowland ■

Wisbeach ■

NORTHAMPTON-
SHIRE

CAMBRIDGESHIRE

included in Britain's *Dictionary of National Biography* (DNB), and his circle of family and friends would play fundamental roles in John Molson's critical first years in Canada.

English boys dreamed of adventure in the glorious age of fighting sail the way they do today of conquering football pitches. Positions on warships for boys as young as six were formally arranged with ship captains and other senior commissioned officers through patronage and personal favour. These boys were known as servants, but the term did not have its modern connotations. They were aboard as future officer material, and were trained accordingly. Naval ships were constantly in need of crew, and officers took it upon themselves to recruit from within their home districts; thus Robinson Elsdale probably went to sea at age twelve under the patronage of a south Lincolnshire officer. The thriving seaport of Boston was only about ten miles from Surfleet, and may have provided a springboard for Robinson Elsdale's career.

Samuel Elsdale appears to have had either the wherewithal or the connections to arrange the beginning of a naval officer's career for his son. Such a career was considered desirable and respectable in the eighteenth century, not to mention potentially profitable during wartime, as all men aboard a warship shared whatever prize money became available. (No such booty was available in the army.) And while Hollywood has helped create an image of a cruel and depraved eighteenth-century British Navy (mainly through grossly distorted versions of the *Bounty* mutiny), it was actually one of the more progressive public institutions of the time, and placed a high priority on the welfare of its carefully trained men.[2]

While British life was riven with patronage and nepotism, boys like Robinson, after getting their feet aboard a warship, advanced largely on merit. Unlike in the army, commissions in the navy could not be purchased, although in the higher ranks politicking was an inevitable feature of advancement and command.[3] We can scarcely imagine what little room Robinson Elsdale's world left otherwise for "merit," which essentially implied entitlement, and entitlement was invariably a result of the circumstances of birth, not of an individual's intelligence and character.

The opportunities for advancement on the basis of ability and personal industry were dauntingly narrow. By modern standards, life was suffocatingly preordained by birth, with the most esteemed public institutions held through inheritance or outright purchase. Parsonages in the Church of England were the property of individuals or families; the House of Lords was the purview of inherited privilege; and about one-third of the seats in the House of Commons belonged to "rotten boroughs"—rural seats that had perhaps fifteen eligible voters or fewer, while entire cities coming into industrial greatness (such as Manchester) had no representation at all. Holland was one of those corners of England without any representation in the House of Commons, despite its growing population and economic importance.[4] Because the rotten boroughs had so few voters, a majority could—and inevitably did—band together and sell their seat to whoever was willing to pay for a political career in the House of Commons. The problems in Parliament were widely recognized in the late eighteenth century, but the excesses of the French Revolution helped set back the reform movement in England by half a century, and had a direct impact, in turn, on the political stability of the Canadian colony to which John Molson was bound in 1782.

Commerce and industry were opening new avenues to aspiring Englishmen, but for Robinson Elsdale (and his nephew John) advancement was equated with escape, if not from distinctions and prejudices of class, then from the limiting boundaries represented by the walls of seawater surrounding the kingdom. The sea itself, however, was a trackless void with its own opportunities, and across the North Atlantic was an entire continent incomplete in description and unresolved in propriety. The sea was both an end in itself and a means to an end, and in the Fen Lands it was an alluring alternative—an expanse of navigable water beyond the seawall and an encroaching welling underfoot in the pastures, tens of miles from breaking surf.

Elsdale joined the Royal Navy during a period of rapid wartime mobilization that saw a pre-war navy of 10,000 men absorb about 70,000 new recruits between 1756 and 1759. We don't know what ship or ships Elsdale sailed on, but as a servant he would have spent his mornings in shipboard schooling (larger warships carried a schoolmaster) learning navigation, astronomy and trigonometry, and the rest of his time mastering shipboard skills and routines such as handling sails and maintaining a watch. Once he became a mid-shipman, his goal would have been to achieve a lieutenant's rank, by passing a verbal exam for which his own captain recommended him and which was administered by three other captains.

Despite the fundamental appeal of a naval officer's career, Samuel Elsdale's apparent decision to arrange the first step towards one for his son Robinson is initially puzzling, for such a career was traditionally desirable only to children who did not stand to inherit substantial property, and Robinson has long been remembered as Samuel's only son. It was a good option for a second-born, but a first-born's obligations and opportunities rested with the family estate. The Royal Navy represented for most candidates the best of a handful of limited career choices. As the historian N.A.M. Rodger has noted, for all its relative appeal as a middle-class pursuit, it still was "an arduous, dangerous and [outside of wartime] ill-paid profession." Further, a stint as a servant on a Royal Navy vessel, particularly during wartime, would have been extremely foolhardy for a boy expected to live long enough to inherit the bulk of the family's wealth.

Robinson Elsdale in fact had two brothers (or half-brothers) who have been left off the family tree. They emerge in the Molson Archives amidst the wrangling over the estate of Robinson's father. John, a tanner at Ipswich, died at age sixty-four in 1788, which means Samuel Elsdale was only nineteen when John was born. He must have been a child of a marriage by Samuel that preceded the one to Mary Robinson in 1734, when Samuel was twenty-nine. The other son, Samuel, who lived in the London suburb of Pimlico, may also have been a product of this now-forgotten first marriage.[5]

As prosperous as Samuel Elsdale of Surfleet apparently was, he must have been compelled to spread his bequeathed wealth thinner than he would have liked. According to his obituary in *The Gentleman's Magazine*, he had a considerable number of dependants.

"His disposition was benevolent, humane, and charitable in the extreme. He provided most liberally for a large family in his life-time; distributed his assistance most generously to a long list of relations, and effectually provided for more than 60 helpless orphans." In addition to providing a generous dowry for Mary and probably setting up his sons from his first marriage in business, Samuel also had to make special provisions for his other daughter, Ann. Her health was obviously poor, as she died young at Bath, a traditional convalescent retreat, and her father had to establish a trust to care for her. Ultimately, the Elsdale family's complex inheritances would trigger one of the most fractious episodes in our John Molson's life, damaging reputations in his family almost beyond repair.

Having realized that Robinson would have to find his own way to independent wealth, Samuel Elsdale took the risk of securing him a naval apprenticeship during the world's first global war. It so happened that Robinson thereafter chose to carve a path to wealth with a cutlass.

To become eligible for the lieutenancy exam in the Royal Navy, Robinson Elsdale had to complete six years of service (or "rated time") at sea, at least two of them in the navy as a midshipman, and reach the age of twenty (although the age requirement was some-times waived when shortages of officers, particularly in wartime, called for accelerated promotion). To advance past a lieutenant's rank and secure a captaincy, however, required either further patronage or an especially noteworthy performance, and not simply a demonstration of general competence.

Had Elsdale stayed for his full six years of rated service, he would have completed his minimal spell as a midshipman at eighteen, in late 1762. French Canada had fallen in 1760, and the Treaty of Paris that formally ended the Seven Years War against France and Spain was signed early in 1763. His DNB entry attributes his depar-ture from the navy to "the slowness of promotion." We don't know if his captain refused to recommend him for the lieutenant's exam at an early age—understandable, given the new age of peace—only that Elsdale left the navy even before he turned eighteen, to begin a new career as a privateer.

Elsdale had never actually "joined" the navy—at the time, men signed on for hitches with individual king's ships, not an arm of the military, and experienced sailors were wont to move between the navy, merchant shipping, fishing and privateering as opportunity arose. (The notorious impressment system, however, permitted the always short-staffed navy to collect sailors at land or sea.) Whatever the circumstances of his departure, Elsdale at least would have been exceptionally well trained in naval combat under the new divisional system.[6]

A privateer was essentially a pirate licensed by the Crown to inflict punishment on enemy property through acts of reprisal. The Crown got a share of the spoils, and the privateer and his crew—and the ship's owner—divvied up the rest. While the officers and crews of warships were entitled to prize money in addition to pay (which no one on a privateer received), privateering was sometimes far more lucrative than naval duty. Certainly during the new era of peace following the Treaty of Paris, privateering provided infinitely more opportunities for prize money than a navy no longer seeing combat duty.[7]

Privateering, however, was a far from logical career option for a lieutenant-in-training like Elsdale in the closing years of the Seven Years War. When peace descended on the Royal Navy and deposited even experienced officers ashore on half-pay, midshipmen working towards a lieutenancy generally moved into merchant shipping, along with officers who were given leave, so that they could continue developing their sea legs. (Nelson would spend ten years in the merchant service waiting for renewed hostilities with the French to open the door for career advancement in the navy.) Yet if the merchant service was considered a second-rate pursuit, privateering was the career equivalent of plunging off the edge of the respectable world. Robinson Elsdale went from being a naval officer-in-training to a licensed buccaneer.

Privateers had ended the Seven Years War desperately short of men, as the service was so wanting in comparison with what the man-hungry Royal Navy offered. After the war, privateering was a career option for those who desired a fortune that could no longer be provided through wartime naval prize money. It did, however, present high risks, not the least of which were one's fellow crew-members, who were often little more than murderous criminals. As he came of age, Robinson Elsdale was clearly motivated by financial considerations, not professional ones. His desire for lucre could well have been echoed by his nephew John when he wrote to his attorney in January 1787: "My continual theme is *Money & Money* I must have."

John Molson's uncle, the celebrated privateer Robinson Elsdale. (Courtesy the Elsdale family)

When our John Molson was born at Snake Hall, on December 28, 1763, his uncle Robinson, who had just turned nineteen, was already a battered veteran of the privateering business. According to the account of his sea-going exploits he wrote for his wife,[8] in the course of a single 1762 cruise off Hispaniola (when he was only seventeen) Elsdale captured a rich French merchantman in a bloody and traumatic attack; participated in a near-disastrous land raid, in which he was ordered by his captain to protect several young ladies of the attacked household against the advances of his fellow crew-members—one of whom he had to shoot with a pistol; was captured in a joint assault by French and Spanish privateers, in the process seeing his captain slain and having his arm broken and all his possessions stripped; and, fortuitously, was then liberated by another English ship when his own vessel and fellow prisoners were being taken away by a prize crew.

Elsdale supposedly spent the better part of seventeen years plundering French ships around the Atlantic and Caribbean. He did not devote all of his time in those years to privateering, however: the anecdotes he wrote for his wife, based on the first years of his career out of the navy, include non-privateering voyages to west Africa in which he participated in the slave trade, a passage from Lisbon to Virginia in a ship named the *Sally & Kitty,* and a spell in the Greenland whale fishery.

Privateering was a brutal business, and we are fortunate that a retired Elsdale was sufficiently educated and motivated to write an entertaining account of his years at sea. It so impressed the celebrated novelist Frederick Marryat—when he was shown a copy of it[9] —that he pilfered the unpublished work for much of the first seven chapters of his 1846 novel *The Privateersman: Adventures by Sea and Land, in Civil and Savage Life, One Hundred Years Ago.* While most of the novel is forgettable, the first chapters are riveting, and are sometimes almost a verbatim rendering of Elsdale's narrative. Apart from changing Elsdale's name to Elrington, Marryat essentially published an edited transcription.

Elsdale wrote the manuscript to entertain and enlighten his wife, and some of it plainly is harmless fiction. In one adventure, as the captive servant of a fetching African princess, he hunts tigers, which makes for a dramatic narrative, but the animals are on the wrong continent.[10] Nonetheless, for an amateur writer his prose was carefully crafted and justified his eventual inclusion in the DNB—not as a privateer, but as an autobiographer.

Elsdale's manuscript, which ranks among the best eyewitness descriptions of life at sea at the apex of the age of fighting sail, reveals an intelligent, thoughtful and educated man—certainly the most unusual participant in the blood-soaked history of privateering. He wrote his wife in the introduction:

> I have painted, without reserve, exactly the feelings of my Heart, in the different situations describ'd; Instead of the fearless insensibility of the Seaman, viewing with indifference surrounding dangers, she will find me trembling & astonish'd at impending fate; but, let her remember, she sees a Man describing the feelings of his own breast, not his behaviour, in those black moments when the Soul shrinks back upon herself & startles at destruction.

Elsdale went on to father two exceptional sons, Samuel and Robinson (a daughter, Sarah, died in infancy). Both sons graduated from Oxford and became Anglican priests; Samuel also became an acclaimed poet.[11]

The anecdotes he recorded for his wife came from his first years at sea, at the close of the Seven Years War, before he gained command of his own vessel. He opened his collection—as Marryat wisely chose to imitate in his novel—in the thick of action, as a sailor (likely a midshipman) serving on the fourteen-gun schooner *Revenge* under a Captain Wetherall.

Elsdale recounted how the *Revenge* intercepted a substantial merchant ship off Hispaniola. It was carrying home a Frenchman, his wife and their seventeen-year-old son, along with the fortune he had made in the West Indies. The privateers boarded the armed six-hundred-ton vessel and cornered the crew on the quarterdeck:

> The French cou'd retreat no further, our first men were forc'd forwards, impell'd by those behind crowding forwards to share

in the Action. Crowded thus together & all further retreat cut off, they contested this decisive struggle with all the mutual animosity & rage excited by so obstinate a combat. Here was the tug of Battle, cool Valour, deliberate resolution guided by conduct, yielded to the blind Wish for Vengeance & eager thirst for blood, fir'd with equal fury all was savage rage & fiend like ferocity. Wedg'd in one Mass, for want of room to wield their weapons, the combatants grappled together & sought each others hearts with shortened weapons: or, struggling fell together upon the deck, where they rowld mixt with the dead and dying: & trod underfoot by the survivors; who yet maintain'd the contest, with unabated fury.[12]

The attack on the merchant ship ended horribly. The courageous Frenchman, determined to protect his wife after the battle had been lost, lunged at one of the *Revenge*'s officers with his sword. "Rous'd at the Lieutenants danger," Elsdale related, "I fir'd a pistol at his Breast & the Ball entering his Heart the bravest & most Gallant Gentleman I ever saw fell dead at our feet, oer power'd by Numbers & unequal weapons." The dead man's son was wounded with an axe, but survived[13]; his widow was given protection by Captain Wetherall and restrained from injuring herself in her grief. Elsdale was devastated and sickened by the outcome:

But who can paint the condition of the unhappy Lady, who stood by a witness to this scene, her Eyes blasted with the sight of her beloved Husband slain before her face, her only Son sore wounded weltring groaning in his blood, whilst she herself stript of the fair fortune she but that morning arose mistress of, a wretched captive, to the Ruffians whose Hands yet reek'd with the blood of all the World dearest to her... When I return'd to the deck, soften'd with the unutterable anguish I had been witness to; I cou'd not contemplate the prospect before me with[out] consternation & horror; the whole space was cover'd with the dead & dying or swimming in blood, the Victors & Vanquished indiscriminately mix'd, & all this carnage only the Consequence of trying, wether the Property on

Board shou'd remain to the first owner or be torn from him. The Quarrels of Princes, at that moment appear'd a poor justification: reason, Religion & humanity, clouded the Pride of Triumph; the Rage of fight had subsided & I remain'd anxious, unquiet'd & dissatisfied, & droop'd with heighten'd remorse, as I knew the whole of what was gain'd by this waste of blood, wou'd be devoted to the wild waste of riot & the senseless Extravagance of dissolute debauchery.

Elsdale survived to command his own ship by the age of twenty-four, gaining the rapid advancement the navy could not provide. How long he used this command for legal piracy is open to question. Marryat, a former Royal Navy captain, shared his own past profession's general low regard for the privateersmen in his novel. His protagonist, Elrington, makes an early exit from the nasty business on moral grounds. As Elsdale demonstrated his own capacity for remorse and regret, one must wonder if he, like his fictional alter ego, also eventually turned his back on an enterprise he recognized as treacherous and often senseless.

In a communal letter that survives in the Molson Archives, dated April 23, 1769, several south Lincolnshire friends, writing to Elsdale through a merchant in Helsingor, Denmark, praise a recent privateering triumph. But the single surviving legal document of his days at sea, a charter contract from February 10, 1770, indicates that Elsdale and his ship, the *Duke of Ancaster*, based at Boston, were hired (at least on this occasion) to transport coal and other goods for Paul Jackson of Newcastle, from the Tyne to Lisbon. Rather than being a full-time privateer, Robinson Elsdale was probably, at the most, an armed merchantman. As the master of his own vessel, he would have taken what commercial work came along and engaged in privateering when the opportunity presented itself.

However men like Elsdale were held in the esteem of men like Marryat, Robinson was a hero in his old neighbourhood. "I believe we shall get very Drunk tonight," assured George Chapman, one of the signatories of the 1769 letter, "for we are Toasting you and your ship's crew about famously, and you may Depend upon us if we shall not be limited to one Bowl only in Remembrances to you, but shall drink an unlimited number. . . ." It was evidently a wild night, as it took until the next morning for the correspondence to be completed.

The revelry was unfolding under the auspices of the newly formed Ancaster's Club—probably a facetious reference to Elsdale's ship, the *Duke of Ancaster*. It was left to James Gibbins to wrap up the raucous letter:

> Now Capt, it falls to my share to finish this Noble warlike musical Drunken piece for your to understand. Business whent on so fast in Drinking, singing, with Horn & flutes that I had not time to Compleat this till 10 this morn; we was verry happy in thinking that you and crew was as joyous as our selves, I never saw an Engagement carryd on with Better Courage till about 4 oclock I fell but my wound was not mortal, but not haveing strength enough to go through the Battle, so I made my [way] to bed, but Resolute George Warlike George gave chase and fired a 4 pounder at my chamber door and continued for severall rounds but my fortification being Bomb Proof could not take it by storm, but that Brave Commander, took it by stratagem, in this maner—he wrenchd the door open at top and threw a candle in the room upon the Bottom of a Chair, which took fire then ran down stairs and alarmed the House, with that I had left my Candle Burning and had fell down and sett fire to the Chair so the Key was deliverd imeadiately, and he master of the fort, and I, a prisoner, I was then Brought before my Uncle to receive sentence he being chairman, my crime was deemd Capital, I was admited to plead my own case and got clear for drinking [a] Bumper [a cup or glass filled to the brim]—and promising never to do the like more in particular a Club night our Worthy Members departed about 8 this morning verry Drunk and so we spent the last 12 Hours. . . .
>   PS
> Ah [Rough] Enough the Weomen are Kinde
> There's the thing, Capt, Capt, there's the Thing
> My Honest and Worthy friend. . . .

This James Gibbins was almost certainly Robinson Elsdale's future father-in-law, who was thirty-six when the letter was written and George Chapman smoked him out of his room with a tossed candle. Gibbins had married Susannah Fields in 1756, and they had six children, the eldest of whom was Ann. On March 31, 1779, three months after Ann would have reached the age of majority, the thirty-four-year-old Robinson Elsdale took as his bride at Pinchbeck a woman recorded in the parish registry as Ann Gibbins. There is no doubt James Gibbins's daughter and Robinson Elsdale's bride were one and the same person. The DNB's entry on Robinson Elsdale would describe his young wife as "a lady of great beauty and intelligence." She was only six years older than her nephew, John Molson, and she would provide a major romantic complication in his life. John Molson had always loved his uncle Robinson, and he would discover that he loved Ann as much, if not more.

By the time Robinson Elsdale retired from the sea in 1779 to wed the alluring Ann, the British Empire he had helped build and enrich was on its heels. The American colonies were in full revolt, although the tide would not turn against the mother country for another two years. In south Lincolnshire, families were chafing under the limited opportunities the land presented them. Britain was a small island nation, and there was no more fen to be drained or salt marsh to be reclaimed around Spalding. In the years that followed Wolfe's victory over Montcalm on the Plains of Abraham, North America had been flooded with immigrants—an estimated 30,000 from England, 55,000 from Ireland and 40,000 from Scotland between 1760 and 1775.[14]

Father John possessed a modest real-estate portfolio in the late 1760s. In addition to the thirty-eight acres attached to the Snake Hall estate, there were about seventy-six acres of pasture land around Moulton, about thirty acres in Pinchbeck from his wife's dowry, twenty acres in Whaplode and Holbeach, two acres in Cowbit and three acres in Weston. Except for Snake Hall and the Moulton pastures, these lands were largely occupied by tenant farmers, and in the case of the Whaplode and Holbeach acreages they included an unspecified amount of "copyhold" land—acreage that was not owned outright by the Molsons. It was a respectable port-folio for a middle-class Englishman, but was eclipsed by the hundreds of acres being offered to individual newcomers by speculators in the American colonies.

Father John's last will and testament (January 5, 1769) promised to parcel out these lands among his wife and five surviving children: John (born in 1763), Samuel Elsdale (1764), Mary (1766), Martha (1767) and Thomas (1768). (Several other children, as was depress-ingly routine, had died in infancy.) Citing their marriage settlement, Father John agreed to surrender title to Snake Hall to his wife, Mary, upon his death; the estate and its thirty-eight acres would then become the property of their eldest son, John, upon her death.

To provide for his daughters' dowries, Father John bequeathed Martha the Pinchbeck lands from her mother's dowry, and Mary the twenty acres in Whaplode and Holbeach that had been passed on to him by his own father. As for his second-eldest son, Samuel Elsdale, Father John left him only £100, as "my Father in Law Mr. Samuel Elsdale hath faithfully promised me to take care of and provide for [him]."

Father John's youngest son, Thomas, was given the seventy-six-odd acres at Moulton plus the small parcels at Weston and Cowbit, but the large Moulton holding would be his only until the age of twenty-one, when he was required to surrender it to his brother John. When the will was written, Father John's children were all under the age of six; Thomas, the youngest, was only two months old. Were Father John to die in the near future, Thomas would benefit from the revenues the above lands could generate on his behalf for about two decades. When he came of age at twenty-one, Thomas would be awarded these revenues by his guardian and trustee, while the majority of the lands that generated them, the Moulton pas-tures, would pass into the hands of his brother John.

As it happened, Father John did die the year after the will was written; he was only forty when he succumbed on June 4, 1770. Grandfather John had died and bequeathed him the bulk of his property three years earlier. Grandfather and Father John's deaths were a prelude to a catastrophic series of losses in 1772. William, one of three brothers of Father John, was the first to be lost, probably that spring (his will was proved April 17), age thirty-three. Thomas, brother of Father John and William, then died on May 20, age forty-one. Finally, the widow Mary, thirty-three, died on September 21. In the space of five years, two Molson generations in south Lincolnshire were virtually eradicated.[15] Perhaps, as the early nineteenth-century visitor to south Lincolnshire wrote, the Fen Lands truly featured "a climate which is not salubrious to the human constitution."

Our John was six when his father died, eight when he lost his mother and became an orphan. To oversee the finances and upbringing of his children, Father John had named four guardians and trustees: his father-in-law, Samuel Elsdale; his brother, Thomas; and two Lincolnshire friends, Boaz Baxter of Helpringham and John Richards of Spalding. After Father John's death, John's financial affairs were overseen by his uncle Thomas, but in September 1771 Thomas turned over the duties of trustee and guardian to John's maternal grandfather, Samuel Elsdale, perhaps because his health was failing—he would be dead the following spring.

John Molson and his siblings spent virtually no time at Snake Hall after their mother's passing. Her household possessions were auctioned off in October 1772, raising little more than £90, and Samuel Elsdale moved to lease out the estate and various lands left to the children. His first expenditure on John's behalf was recorded on April 7, 1771: "To Ben. Seamour for Turnips for Sheep feed 4/14/6."*

So began more than a decade of careful itemizing by Samuel Elsdale of "disbursements"—expenses incurred in raising the orphan John Molson and maintaining the properties he would inherit when he turned twenty-one on December 28, 1784. The charges against Molson's inheritance included pocket money, stockings, shirts, watch mending and cleaning, land taxes, the

---

* 4/14/6: Denotes 4 pounds, 14 shillings, 6 pence. Style in this book is to present the same pounds, shilling and pence as £4 14s 6d. A shilling was worth 12 pence; a pound was worth 20 shillings.

purchase of a mare and repairs to Snake Hall. The detail of the account maintained by Elsdale leaves the distinct impression of a stingy overseer. In his defence, he was only meeting his obligation as the trustee to account for all revenues and expenses until John was old enough to claim his inheritance. When John came of age, Elsdale would have to provide a final accounting, and turn over to John the difference between the value of the estate (including revenues generated since Father John's death, with interest due thereon) and the monies spent on John's behalf. However, the boy may have carried into adulthood bitter memories of his grandfather's penchant for charging the smallest expenses against his inheritance, down to the buckle on his belt. Molson's initial draft of his 1810 will, in which his property was left to his eldest son, John Junior, directed that he give his two younger brothers "board, lodging & washing during the time of their Minority."

Removing the Molson children from Snake Hall after their mother's death at least allowed Elsdale to rent out all the properties to the benefit of their inheritances. We don't know where each sibling ended up; however, based on Elsdale's accounting of estate expenses, John was sent to live with William Robinson (a family member of Samuel Elsdale's late wife). In 1776, when John was twelve, he was consigned to the care of a Mr. Whitehead, who was paid for John's board and education until 1780, when he was sixteen.

The long list of disbursements on John Molson's behalf tell us precious little about his youth. It has been said he was a sickly boy, but this seems to have been based solely on his grandfather's notation of a six-week expense for board and nursing in February 1773, when Molson was nine, and a suggestion in a letter home after he reached Quebec that his health had recovered. John's education was relatively brief—just four years—for someone who would soon show such entrepreneurial spirit. At the very least, he learned to read and write, and to keep—and understand—elementary financial records. It was only two years after the end of his formal education, while still a teenager, that John Molson made an ambitious bid for independence in the new world. Mr. Whitehead, whoever he was, had taught him well in what little time he had.

John Molson's formal education was nearing its end when his uncle Robinson retired from the sea to marry Ann Gibbins. When Captain Elsdale put behind him his swashbuckling days, John Molson assuredly was an impressionable teen who doted on his uncle's tales of derring-do and consumed every ounce of counselling he provided, and we can imagine that once Mr. Whitehead was through with him, uncle Robinson provided the finishing school. Robinson Elsdale's life may have begun—and would end—in south Lincolnshire, but he had lived to the utmost on the global stage. Elsdale's influence was accentuated by the early deaths of both John's parents and so many other elder Molsons. Once home from the sea, he plainly was a major presence in the lives of all the orphaned Molson children. Robinson Elsdale was, as John's sister Martha would describe him, "the best and truest Friend we ever had."

As John Molson waited to claim his inheritance, south Lincolnshire witnessed an exodus of families determined to begin anew in America. Their situations must have been dire for them to choose to quit England for a colony in the midst of a bloody revolution. There may well have been more émigrés (evidence of others who preceded them surfaces in letters preserved in the Molson Archives), but it is certain that three men known personally to Robinson Elsdale planned to leave for the rebel colonies in the spring of 1781. They carried with them a letter of introduction to a New York storekeeper written by a man named William May on May 30.

The Mays were a long-established Lincolnshire family, and the letter writer was likely a Captain May known to Robinson Elsdale. May was also probably in the Royal Navy, as the letter of introduction was written at Portsmouth, the base of the British Channel fleet. Its contents indicate that, five months earlier, May had written a similar letter, purposes (and present whereabouts) unknown, for Robinson Elsdale.

"I now do myself the like in recommending three other Friends—*equally* Interesting to me as [Robinson Elsdale]," wrote May for the three Lincolnshire men. "They are inclined to become adventurers in your yet unbounded Continent." May explained they were interested in agriculture and hoped "to settle in the Jersey's—Pennsylvania or Long Island—What think You of going towards Albany?" All of these places offered Loyalist strongholds. The men could not have foreseen that the surrender of Cornwallis at Yorktown, the foundation of the rebel victory, was only months away.

The fact that this William May had already written a letter of introduction for Robinson Elsdale suggests that Elsdale travelled to America ahead of, or with, the three Lincolnshire men. It is possible Elsdale visited America after his marriage, to scout opportunities in commerce, land speculation or resettlement. We know from the anecdotes written for his wife that he had been to Virginia aboard the *Sally & Kitty*, and he must have visited America more than once during his nautical career. While he apparently decided against relocating, he must have impressed upon the Lincolnshire trio the advantages of America, revolution be damned.

The three Lincolnshire men were William Haw, Thomas Loid and James Pell. Haw figures no further in John Molson's life. Loid and Pell, on the other hand, would play leading roles. Loid is a cipher; as he sails through the young Molson's life, it is as if we can see the wake but not the ship, the course and destination but not the point of departure. Beyond the fact that he was married (to an unknown woman), nothing is known about Loid's life in Lincolnshire before he reached North America—his age, his origins, his trade. His anonymity could be due to the fact that, like James Pell, Thomas Loid was travelling incognito. For James Pell in truth was James Gibbins, Robinson Elsdale's father-in-law.

The extraordinary fact that James Pell was the newly adopted name of James Gibbins was plainly stated in a letter to John Molson, in Montreal, from his friend Jack Baxter in September 1786: "James Gibbins alias Pell with 2 [actually three] Sons are fixed at Montreal and of course you must think I have a desire to hear of their Wellfare but you say not a Word, give my Comp[lemen]ts to them & if you write me again pray let me hear of them, or be assured I will send by first ship to Montreal a few Hand Bills which shall make their Names Public."

There can be no doubt that Jack Baxter was writing the truth. The known offspring of James Pell match precisely those of James Gibbins. Like James Gibbins, "Pell" had sons named James Junior, George and William, all of whom made appearances in North America. That James Pell was actually James Gibbins places the subsequent events in John Molson's life in a much clearer—and deeper— context. But why would James Gibbins rename himself and his sons "Pell"? Presumably, as might have been the case with John Molson's great-grandfather Thomas of Peakhill, who transformed himself into a "Malsham" for a few years, there was something unsavoury to hide. However, a survey of civil and criminal court cases in Britain's Public Record Office turns up no formal incident of wrongdoing involving a Gibbins from the years leading up to the emigration to North America.

Some shameful event need not have been behind the name change. The transformation of the Gibbins clan was related exclusively to their passage to, and residence in, North America. The change was strictly observed in letters between England and Canada (except for one from Martha Molson to her brother John in Montreal in November 1783, in which she broke form by asking him to "pray Remember me to Gorgey Gibbins"—a reference to James Senior's son George). When in England, these Pells were always referred to by their real names. Since the "Pells" made several transatlantic passages during the Revolutionary War, the name change may have been designed to avoid the British impressment for naval service.

Legally, the "press" was permitted to collect sailors only in the merchant or fishing fleets in limited circumstances, not simply any able-bodied soul who could be overwhelmed on a dark street by a press gang. (In times of desperation, however, the British Navy would resort to an illegal "hot press," in which it grabbed anybody it could.) Signed warrants would be carried by the impressment service to slap on eligible males between the ages of eighteen and fifty-five. James Senior was forty-nine when William May wrote the letter of introduction, and his three eldest sons, James Junior, William (Bill) and George, ranged in age from nineteen to twenty-two. All of them came to North America, and the boys in particular may have had some experience in the merchant service, perhaps in association with Robinson Elsdale, which would have made them vulnerable to the press. At the beginning of the revolution, the Royal Navy stripped New York of thousands of young men. Perhaps the Gibbins men determined the best way to avoid being conscripted into service, on land as well as at sea, was to travel under false identities.

As to why they chose the name Pell, there is no clear reason.[16] James Gibbins was a clever if exasperating man. It would not have been beyond him to turn his name into an elaborate pun—James Gibbins becoming James Pell because Jimmy Pell was a winking nod to *je m'appelle*—"I am named" in French. Perhaps, more prosaically, he was inspired by Thomas Loid's middle name, Pelgrave— if indeed Thomas P. Loid was even travelling under his proper name (the letter of introduction written by William May actually identified him as Thomas Lawd). There were a number of Pells around Lincolnshire and, to avoid impressment, one or more of the Gibbins could have adopted the identity of a known Lincolnshire Pell to make use of an exemption certificate held by whomever they were impersonating.[17]

The peregrinations of the Lincolnshire men and their families are obscure, but circumstantial evidence indicates that once in North America they must have made fresh plans after the shocking Yorktown surrender in October 1781, which ruined any prospects of settling under the King's rule in the Thirteen Colonies. James Gibbins and the Loids would have joined the Loyalist evacuation to Quebec.

Their participation in the exodus would not have been easy. While the port of New York was in British hands, and Albany, near the headwaters of the Hudson River, was a Loyalist stronghold, George Washington's arm of the Continental Army was wintering over about fifty miles up the Hudson River from New York at Newburgh. The fact that hostilities had largely ceased for the winter may have made the journey less perilous than we imagine. In any event, Thomas Loid was not an actual continental Loyalist in flight, and his subsequent actions would make it clear that he was far from slavishly devoted to the Crown. The Lincolnshire party would have eased its way up the Hudson River valley, through Albany and into Vermont, which, as an independent republic, was not one of the rebel colonies and was providing a safe passage for the Loyalists streaming into Quebec.[18]

Here the Loids and Gibbins evidently created a plan for establishing themselves on the island of Montreal. Gibbins would set up a butchering operation, while Loid would build a brewery. Gibbins returned to England, probably from Quebec City, with the fall 1781 convoy, to collect his eldest son, James Junior, and came back to Montreal in the spring of 1782. All the equipment and provisions both men needed for their new ventures would have been travelling with Gibbins in the spring of 1782—or were consigned to another merchant vessel. Because no mention is made of Gibbins's wife, Susannah Fields, in relevant correspondence, and because he was considering marrying in Montreal in 1785, Gibbins was likely a widower at the time of his emigration. How or when the other sons, George and Bill, reached Quebec is unknown, but they were settled there by the autumn of 1785.

On May 2, 1782, James Gibbins Senior and Junior left Portsmouth aboard a merchant ship bound for Quebec City in the company of eighteen-year-old John Molson. Molson never named in letters home the ship that he boarded with two men travelling under false identities. It was the beginning of a pattern of omission, evasion and deceit in John Molson's life.

Why did John Molson go? And why did his guardian, Samuel Elsdale, let him? Even without an unresolved rebellion, an Atlantic crossing was hazardous in the late eighteenth century. And the fact that peace negotiations were about to begin in Paris didn't eliminate all hostilities. Both American and French privateers were active against British shipping and property on both sides of the Atlantic. The British government had been striving to minimize losses by organizing shipping to and from Quebec into spring and fall convoys. (It took about eight weeks to cross the Atlantic, against the prevailing winds, from England to North America, four weeks from North America to England.) The convoy system did tend to limit American privateering in the Gulf of St. Lawrence to the early and late weeks of the season, when the Royal Navy escorts were absent, but the Atlantic crossing was still a passage tainted with menace.

Merrill Denison proposed, reasonably, in the official Molson family biography, *The Barley and the Stream*, that Robinson Elsdale "probably helped to break down Samuel Elsdale's opposition" to John Molson's visiting Canada. Denison, however, did not realize that the "Pells" were actually Robinson Elsdale's father-in-law and brother-in-law. The fact that John Molson would be crossing the Atlantic with the Gibbins clan could have as easily unsettled Samuel Elsdale as assuaged him, for we have no idea what he thought of his daughter-in-law's alias-equipped menfolk. The parting of Samuel and his grandson was brittle, and John would devote much energy to winning back his grandfather's approval.

Robinson Elsdale, for his part, surely would have approved of his nephew making the trip to assess his affinity for the sea—at John's age, he was already one frenetic year into his privateering career. John was probably so saturated with uncle Robinson's tales of high-seas adventure that he could not resist experiencing life before the mast firsthand, even if it had to be in a dowdy, lightly armed merchant ship. It seems, based on John's subsequent letters, that simply making the ocean crossing and assessing the potential of a sea career was as much a motivation for joining the Gibbins men as was a relocation to America.

That said, the need to begin anew in a land with almost unlimited elbow room and opportunity must have occurred to Molson. For while he was poised to inherit the Snake Hall estate and the Moulton acreages that were to benefit his youngest brother, Thomas, until Thomas turned twenty-one, John must have concluded that it would be difficult to maintain a middle-class lifestyle without all of the property his father had held. Even with the lands that were to serve as dowries for Mary and Martha and the five meagre acres in Cowbit and Weston that were left exclusively to Thomas, John Molson's father apparently had been land rich but cash poor. The only monies specified in his 1769 will were the £100 left to Samuel Elsdale Molson and another £100 for his widow, Mary; Father John expected the rents from various lands to support her. Granted, Father John had inherited the properties from his own father only three years before his death, leaving little time to amass the sort of cash holdings that his father was able to dispense in his will. But a 1794 parliamentary initiative to improve the drainage systems in the Holland area suggests that the land was becoming difficult to work. That Holland was in an economic slump is reinforced by a letter John Molson received from his cousin John (the son of his late uncle Thomas) in February 1784, in which he noted, "Times are much better than they were when you left us."

The thin prospects for himself and his siblings likely haunted the teenaged John Molson. He must have known that the inherited properties would not provide any of them with real prosperity. His sisters, hopefully, would marry well enough to be provided for; Samuel (Sammy) and Thomas would largely have to fend for themselves. Samuel, whose health was poor, was overly dependent on the generosity of his namesake grandfather, as his late father had entrusted his future well-being to the seventy-seven-year-old man who was known to the surviving children as the Old Gent. Thomas would benefit from the income of the Moulton pastures until he was compelled to turn them over to his older brother when he came of age; the five acres he would be left with were barely a starting point for a yeoman's career.

They were all coming of age in an England being transformed by commerce, colonial misfortune and industrialization. America might be all but lost as a colony, but the terms of peace would be generous enough to the rebels—initial talks almost went as far as relinquishing to the Americans all of British North America—to ensure a solid trading partner for the former mother country. The merchant class presented fresh opportunities beyond working the land, and industrial innovations were promising their own revolution. In 1769, six years after John Molson's birth, James Watt determined how to apply steam pressure to both sides of an engine cylinder through a slide valve and so produce thrust with both strokes of the piston. He built the first model with his partner, Matthew Boulton, in 1776; Boulton & Watt gave the world the reciprocating engine, which would power the Industrial Revolution.

While John Molson was about to cross the Atlantic under the power of sail, experiments were already underway to place steam engines in ships' hulls and do away with the vagaries of the wind. It would take John Molson another twenty-seven years to catch up with it, but he would become a global pioneer in steamship construction and operation, employing Boulton & Watt engines to find his way to sea in a manner neither he nor his uncle Robinson could have foreseen.

But first, John Molson had to reach Montreal. And so he set sail with the Gibbins men in the spring of 1782. And they very nearly didn't make it.

Chapter 4

Caesar, when embarking in a storm, said it was not necessary he should live, but that it was absolutely necessary he should get to the place to which he was going.
—Lord Chesterfield, letter to his son, November 24, 1749

A PECULIARITY OF SHIPBOARD LIFE was that when Captain James Worth received his sailing orders at ten in the evening, he had one foot in the present and the other in the future. In the town of Portsmouth, it was May 1, 1782, but in the adjacent naval mooring at Spithead, where Captain Worth's *Assistance* lay, it was already May 2. On a naval vessel, the date turned at noon, not midnight. With the sun at its apex, the noon sighting was taken with a sextant to determine position, the distance travelled in the past twenty-four hours was noted in the ship's log and a new watch-cycle of seven shifts began (five each of four hours, and two "dog" watches of two hours each). On land, sailors obeyed the standard calendar, but once a ship had its orders and was preparing to get underway, the captain and crew began living twelve hours ahead of landsmen. And so, two hours before John Molson's new day dawned, Worth was already ten hours into the next calendar page, bearing orders to begin escorting the convoy of thirty-two merchant ships that would transport Molson to Quebec. The frigate *Surprize* was also placed under Worth's ultimate command as commodore of the convoy.*

---

* Hereafter, events are reported according to traditional calendar days, not the days of the ship's log.

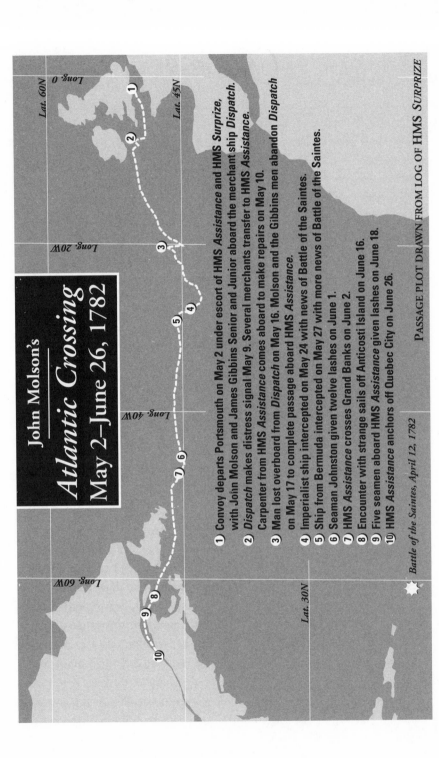

John Molson's
Atlantic Crossing
May 2–June 26, 1782

① Convoy departs Portsmouth on May 2 under escort of HMS *Assistance* and HMS *Surprize*, with John Molson and James Gibbins Senior and Junior aboard the merchant ship *Dispatch*.

② *Dispatch* makes distress signal May 9. Several merchants transfer to HMS *Assistance*. Carpenter from HMS *Assistance* comes aboard to make repairs on May 10.

③ Man lost overboard from *Dispatch* on May 16. Molson and the Gibbins men abandon *Dispatch* on May 17 to complete passage aboard HMS *Assistance*.

④ Imperialist ship intercepted on May 24 with news of Battle of the Saintes.

⑤ Ship from Bermuda intercepted on May 27 with more news of Battle of the Saintes.

⑥ Seaman Johnston given twelve lashes on June 1.

⑦ HMS *Assistance* crosses Grand Banks on June 2.

⑧ Encounter with strange sails off Anticosti Island on June 16.

⑨ Five seamen aboard HMS *Assistance* given lashes on June 18.

⑩ HMS *Assistance* anchors off Quebec City on June 26.

Battle of the Saintes, April 12, 1782

PASSAGE PLOT DRAWN FROM LOG OF HMS *SURPRIZE*

Lat. 60N   Long. 0

Lat. 45N

Long. 20W

Long. 40W

Long. 60W

Lat. 30N

Launched the previous year in Liverpool, the fifty-gun *Assistance* was a belated response by the cash-strapped Admiralty to the deteriorating state of the once invincible Royal Navy. Underfunded during the decades of peace that followed the Seven Years War, the navy had been reduced to a flotilla of warships with sprung seams, decks that leaked water into the bunks of crewmen, rotting woodwork, shattered spars and torn sails. French seapower had determined the political map of North America seven months before John Molson found himself in the Spithead anchorage, gazing upon almost ten thousand tons of warships that had not been available for the colonial struggle.

The fact that the *Victory*, the *Royal Sovereign* and the *Royal George* were idle at Spithead testified to the navy's hard-pressed resources. None of these great ships had been available when an outnumbered British fleet was turned away by the French blockade of the Chesapeake that had forced Cornwallis's surrender at Yorktown the previous October. The blockade sealed the rebel victory in the American Revolution, and the British Parliament resolved to negotiate peace in the spring of 1782. Lord North's government, whose penny-pinching treatment of the navy in peacetime had caused its deterioration, gave way to a new ministry formed by the Marquis of Rockingham after the House of Commons passed a resolution on March 4 holding that anyone advising or attempting the continued prosecution of war in America would be declared an enemy of the state. On April 12, over the objections of George III, Rockingham's government had sent the London-based Scottish merchant Robert Oswald to Paris to begin negotiating a peace accord with Benjamin Franklin.

But hostilities were far from ended: French and American privateers threatened British shipping in the Atlantic, and Britain was still at war with not only the French but Spain and Holland as well— every major naval power of Europe was allied against her. Less than three years had passed since the waters off Portsmouth had bristled with the masts of an invasion fleet comprising sixty-six French and Spanish warships, the sight of which had caused widespread panic in coastal England. Poor planning by the would-be invaders had saved the country from an actual landing. But the French had moved on to other targets. Since their success at the Chesapeake, they had been stalking Britain's possessions in the Caribbean, determined to wrest control of its vast plantation economy.

Led by the Comte de Grasse aboard the magnificent *Ville de Paris* (at 110 guns, the largest warship in any navy), the French had collected St. Eustatius, St. Kitts and the settlements of Demerara and Essequibo in what is now Guyana. Although bad weather had prevented de Grasse from taking Barbados, he was preparing for a joint attack with Spain on Britain's prize Caribbean possession, Jamaica.[1] After recovering at Bath from bladder surgery, Admiral George Rodney had taken thirteen ships of the line back to the Caribbean in mid-January 1782, arriving at Barbados in March as the British Empire teetered on the brink of disaster. Rodney, working just short of cross purposes with Admiral Samuel Hood, was being depended upon to thwart the accelerating Franco-Spanish campaign, which could cripple the British economy.

Whatever had become of Rodney and Hood's joint fleet was unknown to Captain Worth, or to anyone else back in Britain. Navy and merchant ships were the empire's lines of communication, and the Atlantic was like a great moat of silence. Information moved at the speed of sail power and was beholden to the weather and the seaworthiness of the vessels. Captain Worth was like a modern astronomer staring into the far reaches of the universe: the deeper he looked, the farther back in time he saw. Already a half-day ahead of the terrestrial world in his shipboard routine, it would take him almost a month to reach the point where he could then look back nearly two months, to learn what had already transpired, and what was to be, while the most powerful politicians and military leaders he left ashore in Britain remained mired in ignorance.

A few days earlier, a spring convoy of fifty-nine merchant ships had left Britain for the Caribbean under the stewardship of HMS *Preston*,[2] with no idea of whether the islands to which they were bound—Barbados, St. Lucia, Jamaica—were French or English. Captain Worth's convoy had more reasonable expectations of a friendly welcome—no one seriously expected the French tricolour to be waving once again above the Quebec citadel as they drew near. Hostile privateers were the main concern and, in addition to the goods in the merchant fleet, there were a number of noteworthy passengers who demanded safe delivery.

Foremost was Henry Hamilton, the former lieutenant-governor of Fort Detroit. Colonel Hamilton had captured the abandoned rebel post on the Wabash at Vincennes in "Indian country" on December 17, 1778. Two months later, he was forced to surrender with his garrison to General Rogers Clark, and had been sent to Virginia as a prisoner. There, Governor Thomas Jefferson reluctantly permitted him to be included in a prisoner exchange, after keeping him in irons for several months. An investigation strongly indicated that Hamilton had been paying native allies bonuses for rebel scalps, but not for live captives. Jefferson had feared the influence Hamilton might have in promoting frontier atrocities if he ever returned to North America, and now "the Hair Buyer" was on his way to Quebec to serve as the province's new lieutenant-governor.

Also in the convoy were Hugh Finlay, the colony's deputy postmaster-general and a member of Governor Haldimand's advisory executive council; Brigadier General Allan McLean, who had commanded the Quebec garrison when the Americans tried and failed to capture the colonial capital in 1775–76; and Lieutenant-Colonel Henry Hope, a future lieutenant-governor.

These high-ranking bureaucrats and officers were being delivered to a colony facing administrative crisis. There had been no chief justice active in the colony since 1776.[3] And while Britain's finances were a scandalous mess, Quebec's books were especially in disarray, owing in part to a failure to collect the mutation fines—the *quints* owed by seigneurs and the *lods et vents* from town lots in what had been the royal domains of Quebec City and Trois-Rivières. The fact that such tithes existed, paid or not, underlined the ungainly structure of post-conquest Quebec. Molson and the Gibbins men were on their way to a reunion with Thomas Loid in the most unusual corner of the British Empire, a colony unmatched in its political, social and legal complexity.

Quebec's conquerors of 1760, if only out of practicality, declined to expel, subjugate or assimilate the province's French subjects. Instead, the British generously accommodated the new colony's French fact. Catholic rights were recognized, and the old land system of seigneuries—the quasi-feudal holdings that denied freehold ownership—was permitted to continue. The colony was placed under the control of a series of governors who, as military officers, had participated in the conquest of French Canada. From the beginning, they showed more sympathy for the rights and needs of the francophone Canadians (albeit mainly the elite) than they did for the British merchant class, whose members arrived on the heels of conquest and were still clamouring for expanded powers and rights of their own as Molson departed Portsmouth.

The merchants had been waiting since 1760 for the legal accommodations to which they felt entitled as British subjects. Those who expected relief from Westminster were enraged by the Quebec Act of 1774, which at last gave the colony a legal framework. In addition to enshrining Catholic rights a half-century before they were granted in Britain (where Catholics were banned from practising law, sitting on juries, voting in elections or holding office), the act continued to uphold the seigneurial system and the old French civil law, with no jury trials in civil cases, leaving mercantile disputes to be settled by politically compromised judges. British criminal law was imposed, but without the benefit of rights under the Habeas Corpus Act, which protected against illegal detention and imprisonment. (There were a few accommodations. Among them, the old civil code could not restrict traditional British freedom of bequest or prevent the execution of wills according to British law.) And while the Quebec Act suggested that the colony would eventually have an elected assembly—Nova Scotia had been governed by one since 1758—under the act, the colony continued to be administered with the input of a council appointed by the governor, who tended to rule with the limited involvement of an extra-legal "privy" council, rather than the council as a whole. An elected assembly (in the lower house only) would not come until 1791, when Quebec was divided into Upper and Lower Canada.

Much blame for the merchants' unhappy situation rested with the merchants themselves, who had promoted such blatantly selfish causes as a Protestant-only elected assembly. But the colonial assemblies in America were all as restrictive on Catholic rights as Britain, and there was also a significant social schism in play in the merchants' lack of lobbying success. The governors, with their military backgrounds, were by nature inclined to look down upon the commercial ranks. General James Murray, the first governor, from 1760 to 1768, pronounced the merchants "ignorant, licentious, factious men." The disdain in which military officers held merchants was substantially due to snobbery. But the divide between the old order of landed gentry (allied with commissioned soldiers) and the new wealth generated by trade and industry would prove increasingly anachronistic in a world being transformed by individual initiative, protracted electoral reform and technological advances.

In some ways the colonial administration in the Quebec citadel (forthrightly military under Governor Frederick Haldimand, since his simultaneous appointment in 1778 as commander-in-chief of the British forces in North America) was literally holding the fort against the new social order. Haldimand, a professional French-Swiss soldier "who had much of the charm and the inappropriateness of a medieval ruin," in the memorable words of the historian Donald Creighton, "was appalled at the possible social consequences of the jury system in Canada [for civil cases]. There were foreign troops serving His Majesty in America; and he shook his head solemnly over the dreadful prospect of a German baron being tried by a jury of Canadian shopkeepers."[4]

But Haldimand was determined to protect the rights of ninety-seven percent of the colony's population against the narrow interests of the hated British merchant class, whose members had a habit of abusing positions of appointed authority to enrich themselves. Despite his class prejudices, Murray had not been entirely wrong about the lot of them, and military dislike for the merchant ranks was reinforced by the poor quality of food and general supplies the fighting ranks sometimes received from profit-bloated provisioners, and by the corruption of those who held the provisioning contracts.

Haldimand's intransigence, however, extended to pointedly ignoring some of the instructions sent to him by the home government. London had directed him in March 1779 to move on several reforms he found odious: the introduction of British commercial law, jury trials for torts and mercantile disputes, and the application of habeas corpus. On April 12, 1781, the colonial secretary, Lord Germain, formally reprimanded Haldimand, writing, "Your withholding from the council the instructions which you were originally commanded by the king to communicate to them, and that command repeated by an additional and special instruction from His Majesty, is considered by His Majesty, as well as the lords of trade and myself, as such an instance of disobedience to the royal authority as ought not to be passed over, if longer persisted in."[5]

But the continuing hostilities—not on council but with the Americans and their allies—frustrated efforts to have any of the reforms adopted. And financial misadventure by the colonial administration, going far beyond its failure to collect mutation fines, was steering the colony towards an economic calamity. John Molson gave no inkling of understanding what truly awaited him on the far side of the Atlantic.

At seven o'clock on the morning of May 2, a cannon boomed from the deck of the *Assistance*, signalling the masters of the ships in the Quebec convoy to come aboard and receive their instructions for the passage. At nine, the *Assistance* was actively preparing to leave Spithead, and by noon she was five miles off Dunnose, on the southeast coast of the Isle of Wight.

Harbourbound were John Molson and James Gibbins Senior and Junior, travelling as the Pells. Molson never bothered to name either the ship they were aboard or her captain, and left no clues as to the ship's size or the number of crew and paying passengers.[6] However, from Worth's log and a shipping notice in the *Quebec Gazette* of June 27, 1782, we know that Molson and the Gibbins men were aboard a London merchant ship called the *Dispatch*, commanded by John Smith.

Their captain had turned their departure into a desultory, maddening disarray. He was not even on board when the rest of the convoy departed, "so we were obliged to keep tacking about to wait for him," Molson recounted in a letter to his uncle Robinson. At noon, the captain came aboard with his wife and children, but the *Dispatch* could not leave until the family was returned to shore. When the tide turned against them, they sought refuge in the Spithead anchorage in the company of the three great ships of the line. By two o'clock, the wife and children were back on shore, but the ship was forced to wait another hour for the tide to reach ebb before finally getting underway. The sun was setting when Molson and company cleared the Isle of Wight and at last gained the English Channel, alone, with no sign of their protective convoy.

Two merchants on board were unnerved by their isolation, knowing that their cargo (unspecified by Molson in subsequent letters) would appeal to French privateers. By piling on all available sail and running before the light easterlies, John Molson's ship was able to close with the convoy by nine the next morning.

Molson reported that on the morning of May 3, "The Commodore lay too for us & we joined in about an Hour. The Commodore signal[led] for our Capt. to go on Board him & he gave him sevear Cheek for delaying him." This may well have happened, but Molson could also have been mistakenly recalling a general meeting of all shipmasters in the convoy held by Worth on the morning of the fourth.[7] Land's End had been cleared, and Worth was likely taking the opportunity to review basic convoy discipline and the procedures that would help ensure an orderly crossing.

It was a long passage that could easily take eight weeks, with the convoy working against the Gulf Stream, the prevailing winds and the North Atlantic storm tracks. In modern times we have all but lost the profound sense of life suspended in transit, even held in the balance, that was experienced by eighteenth-century travellers—of months being occupied in motion from one existence to another, of travel being so much more than distance logged. John Molson removed himself from south Lincolnshire and embarked for another world on a voyage that was itself another world. For Molson, this world was not so much the trackless ocean as it was the culture of its roving mariners. He was moving inside the life of his beloved uncle Robinson, and the voyage would steer him through the narrative of his uncle's career at sea as surely as if he were turning pages of his memoirs.

The spring convoy of 1782 from Portsmouth to Quebec was a direct ancestor, in spirit and practice, of the Allied fleets that played cat-and-mouse with German U-boats in the First and Second World Wars. The warships seconded to this duty had to be swift, manoeuvrable, capable of spending the vast majority (upwards of eighty percent) of their days at sea, and sufficiently armed to ward off single attackers. The twenty-eight-gun frigate *Surprize* was perfectly suited to this work; the *Assistance* was probably given the role because she wasn't good for much else. At fifty guns, she was too small to take her place in the line of battle without being shot to flinders, and too large to be called a true frigate, which generally carried no more than forty guns.

Since the Cruisers and Convoys Act of 1708, escorting merchant ships had been a principal duty of the Royal Navy, but the legislative imperative did not make the task any more welcome to its officers. They loathed the work—which was, by and large, dull, and complicated unnecessarily by the incompetence of some merchant captains and the unseaworthiness of their vessels. It could well have occupied much of Robinson Elsdale's time in the service during the Seven Years War, and would have convinced him that privateering, in addition to being far more lucrative, would be infinitely more interesting. Molson's ship, the *Dispatch*, was a textbook example of the albatrosses that men like Captain Worth had to bear. Molson, for his part, despised his captain—"as Big a fool, & Drunkerd; as he would frequently get drunk & sleep a whole night together," he related. And he would soon come to despise the ship just as much.

How Molson wound up on what proved to be such an unseaworthy vessel under the care of such an incompetent master is as mysterious as it is surprising. In the future, Molson would show great care in selecting specific captains and ships for transatlantic assignments, whether carrying people or property, and he made these choices based on either personal experience or gathered intelligence. His first crossing, easily his worst, could not have been arranged by a man presumably as discerning and well connected as his uncle Robinson. His uncle's father-in-law, James Gibbins, had almost certainly booked their passage, if only because he was the senior member of the party, and his subsequent disappointing performances when entrusted with Molson's property suggest an inherent slipshod approach to details. However Molson came to be tossed around on the Atlantic in this hulk, his life was soon in serious danger.

Several months after the passage Molson committed his account to paper. He correctly recalled that the convoy cleared Land's End on Sunday the fifth, then vowed that for almost two weeks "nothing Material happened," until a gale greeted them, at noon on Friday the seventeenth.

The gale in fact came much sooner. "Fresh gales" had been noted by Worth on the fourth, and on the afternoon of the seventh, as the fleet passed the treacherous Scilly Isles, light northerlies began to give way to gale-force south-westerlies. By the eighth, Worth was noting: "strong gales & cloudy with rain." In deteriorating weather, Worth had only the most rudimentary tools for not losing control of his convoy. The sophisticated flag signalling system that Nelson would use to such critical effect at Trafalgar in coordinating the attack of his fleet would not appear in book form until 1803. Flags based on ideograms (rather than coded phrases, as at Trafalgar) were used by admirals to communicate with their fleets at the time of Molson's crossing, but the system could function only if the receiving ships' crews knew how to read them. This would have been completely beyond the skills of the merchant sailors in the convoy. The only alternative was a basic system of commands based on cannon fire. Worth's crew was kept busy touching off signal guns, filling the air with powder-concussions in an effort to keep the convoy's ships within sight of each other, so that no stragglers could be picked off by privateers.

Molson recalled how, by three o'clock in the afternoon on the day the gale struck, they were taking on water through a leak in the upper works, which flooded the hull to a depth of four feet in only an hour. Wooden ships tended to leak the worst when they were most vulnerable: in a heavy sea, when the flexing of the hull in large waves opened up seams. Molson's ship was beginning to work herself apart.

With the hold flooding at an alarming speed, they decided to fire a distress signal with one of their cannons, but no one responded; as the ship began to wallow, the rest of the convoy drew away from her in the storm. Left to their own salvation, they threw cannons overboard. It was almost the end of them, for as they ditched the cannons, "she shipped a sea forward that almost filled her, she being a deep waisted vessel she rose verry barely, & had we shipped another sea we should all have gone together to the Bottom." Every available hand was assigned to spelling each other off on the pumps.

By midnight the gale began to ease; the constant pumping continued, and by nine o'clock the next morning, the wind had abated to the point where more sail could be set and the lost convoy pursued. By eleven that night, they at last came within sight of it— presumably the stern lamps in the dark. The convoy shortened sail and allowed them to close. They made contact with what must have been the *Surprize* (although no mention is made of the encounter in the *Surprize*'s log) and told her of their plight: "that we keep one pump continually going & with difficulty keep her free," according to Molson. The *Surprize* instructed them to signal the *Assistance* with a gun (they must not have ejected all of their cannon) to speak directly with the commodore. Having already been rebuked by Worth for holding up the convoy at departure, Molson's captain must not have relished having to turn to him for aid now.

The commodore, Molson wrote:

> shortened sail for us, and we came under his lee Quarter, we told him our having sprung a Leak, & being obliged to heave our guns over board, he asked us whether we had a carpenter on board, we told him no. He said he would send his on board to exammin us which he did. The [carpenter] told us that the upper works were verry mean & must be caulked or else the Vessle could not live if any more bad weather came, which we could hardly expect having all fine in so long a passage.

Molson's recollection may have combined more than one event into a single episode, but Captain Worth's log does record that at 4:30 on the morning of the ninth, "the *Dispatch* Mercht Ship of London made the Signal of Distress: hoisted out the Cutter* & sent her on board with the Carpenter & Crew to give her every Assistance."

Worth recorded that "the boat return'd & brought on board two passengers." Molson wrote how "the Merchants which I never mentioned before thought it was most prudent to go on board the Man of War as they knowing the Lieutenant which came on board with the Carpenter to see our Condition, which he saw was very bad." The merchants had chosen to leave behind whatever goods they had consigned to the *Dispatch* in the commendable cause of saving their lives. The fact that Molson and the Gibbins men did not follow them, when they knew the *Dispatch* to be in such dire shape, makes it more likely that the Gibbins men were disguised as Pells to avoid impressment by the navy. They would commit themselves to the safety of a British warship only as an absolute last resort, and Molson appeared to be stuck with them. But if all the necessary goods to establish both the Gibbins men and Thomas Loid in business in Montreal were aboard the *Dispatch*, they would have been very reluctant to abandon it all.

The *Dispatch* was informed that the carpenter would come back to make repairs "the first fine day," according to Molson. With the gale having subsided, the following day proved suitable. A team of carpenters returned to make extensive repairs: "they caulked the Larboard side & some of the starboard & went on board again in the Evening," wrote Molson.

The good weather did not last. From Sunday the twelfth to Monday the twentieth, Worth recorded either fresh breezes or gales, and the *Assistance* actually lost ground from the sixteenth to the seventeenth. Except for losing contact with the convoy again, Molson avowed that "nothing material happe[ne]d only our Wretched Situation in regard to our being so leakey, & loosing

---

* *Cutter:* A ship's boat, usually about twenty feet long.

our Convoy, however we joined them the next day the Weather tolerable fine, but could not pursuade our Capt. to speak the Commodore to get his Carpenters to [caulk] the remainder [of the leaks]."

Molson wrote how "we were in hopes we should have no more gales to encounter in such a wretched ship as we were in." But there was a new problem: they had all but run out of coal and wood to fuel the galley. Captain Smith—"an idle diletary man"—had squandered his opportunities to ship enough aboard before the voyage, and was then dissuaded from doing so on the confused day of departure by the merchant passengers, who feared any further delay would cause the loss of the convoy escort and leave their cargo at the mercy of French privateers. Now two of the merchant passengers had abandoned ship for the security of the *Assistance*, and everyone left behind was on cold rations of biscuits, cheese and butter.

And then the weather deteriorated again, beginning to blow "verry fresh" around six P.M., on what was probably the sixteenth (Molson said the twenty-third) and was increasing. Molson recalled how it "blowed a Heavier Gale than it had done yet," and how he and his fellow passengers consulted with the mate, Mr. Bell. Together they argued for the captain to fire another distress signal while the convoy was still within hearing distance, as they were again falling behind. Smith, however, "was an obstinate fellow a Scotchman who would harken to nobody's advice at all," and they struggled on alone.

John Molson was now sharing with his uncle Robinson the storm-tossed mariner's terror of the immediate and dread of the eventual. Elsdale had presaged Molson's crossing with his own account of a hellish passage from Senegal home to England. Where Molson's captain was (by Molson's estimation) a bull-headed fool, his uncle's captain had been contemptibly useless:

[W]e applied to the Captain, who hung by the weather mizen shrouds in an agony of terror, for orders: but finding him astonish'd & terrified, I demanded, with an earnest oath, whether we shou'd wear her or lye there to perish; do as you please, sigh'd out the daunted mortal, & going below into the cabbin appear'd no more upon deck, during the terrors of that black night.

Having faced concerted lobbying to fire a distress signal, John Smith at last relented, but by then the convoy, as feared, had moved beyond the range of hearing, "we being all reddy lain too & so consequently falling to leeward." And when the mate, Mr. Bell, went down the lazarette to fetch a powder cartridge for the shot, he "found that the Vessel had sprung a fresh leak by her stern posts, the water making an amaseing noise."

Bell "supposed it would sink us." This was a terribly final pronouncement from a man whom Molson considered "a verry clever fellow." Bell had been sobered by the fatal mechanics of such a leak. A ship's pumps normally were located midships; as water flooded in at the stern, the rear of the ship settled deeper than the bow, making for an uphill course to the pump intake. But with Bell's guidance, they were able to get the *Dispatch* sufficiently level for the pumps to draw.

At some point in this gloomy night, they lost "one of the best Sailors aboard" in the most humiliating way: dangling from the mizzen-mast rigging while relieving himself, he suddenly disappeared over the side. An astonishing number of men were lost this way; for the common sailor, the only available toilet was the open ocean.

Molson had just brushed against one of the most celebrated episodes in his uncle's nautical career: his daring rescue of a man overboard while travelling from Lisbon to Virginia aboard the *Sally & Kitty*. While at the helm in rough weather, Elsdale was surprised to hear his name called out from the sea: "I ran to the side & saw Richard Vallant a Youth in the water going astern." The boy was the son of prosperous friends of the captain in Ipswich. Elsdale volunteered to swim to Vallant with one end of the deep-sea lead line, normally used to take soundings. When the line came loose from the ship, "All the Horrors of my situation rush'd on me at once, I thought death innevitable but still struggled hard for life." Elsdale very nearly drowned along with the boy, but both were narrowly rescued.

The poor sailor lost overboard from the *Dispatch* encouraged no such heroic rescue. The weather was judged too rough to go after him, and perhaps his family did not own enough property in Ipswich. Molson testified, "we could do nothing to save [him] but throw a few things overboard which however would only have prolonged his Misery as the sea was mountains high being impossible for any open boat to live. This however rather put a damp [on] us all losing one of our best Men and [the] Gale increasing. . . ."

Fortunately, the water did not gain on the pumps, and on the morning of May 17 they were still afloat. The convoy was now 270 leagues—about 810 miles—west of the Scillies, tracking roughly along the forty-fifth latitude, which would guide it below Newfoundland's Cape Race and into the Gulf of St. Lawrence. In fresh gales, the *Assistance* had been pressed hard to maintain order in the convoy: "fired a Shot at some of the Convoy for not Obeying the signals to bear down," Captain Worth recorded. At two o'clock that afternoon, Worth signalled for the *Surprize* to draw nearer; an hour later came the signal for the convoy to come under the *Assistance*'s stern. At four in the afternoon, a distress shot from the *Dispatch* was heard.

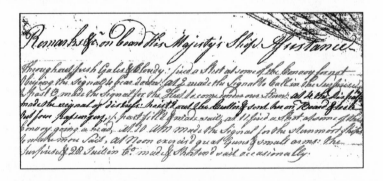

The log of Captain James Worth aboard HMS *Assistance* records the abandonment of the *Dispatch* by John Molson and the Gibbins men on the afternoon of May 17, 1782: "at 4 the Dispatch made the signal of distress[,] hoisted out the Cutter & sent her on Board & took out four passengers." (Public Record Office, ADM 51/72)

After hearing the distress signal, Worth ordered his cutter over to the *Dispatch*, and the vessel "took out four passengers," according to Worth's log. Three of them were Molson and the Gibbins men, who by now could not have wished to risk another four weeks on the *Dispatch* instead of taking their chances with impressment on the *Assistance*.

Molson recounted how Captain Worth

> told us that if [Captain Smith] chused he would take him (on Board) (& his Crew) & scutel the ship & sink her which however the Capt. refused; tho' I'll assure you I did not, for I acquainted the Commodore that I was a Passenger, & would be verry much obliged to him if he would take me, he told me by all means & I got on Board him directly, & left the Capt & Crue in their Wretched Condition (the Crue would have been glad to had come with me, but the Commodore would not take [them] without the Capt.)

And so John Molson, the two Gibbins men and an unnamed fourth party escaped the leaky *Dispatch* "only with what was on our backs," leaving the clever Mr. Bell and the rest of the unfortunate crew to continue risking their lives on the crossing with the obstinate John Smith, who was not yet prepared to allow the navy to sink his ship for him. And all the goods Loid and the Gibbins men were depending on were probably in her leaky hold.

At once, Molson was at the heart of Britain's fighting navy, and back within his uncle's life story. Worth placed him with the midshipmen for the balance of the voyage, and so introduced Molson to the dawn of Robinson Elsdale's nautical career. Life aboard a British warship had not changed appreciably since Elsdale was a teenaged midshipman during the Seven Years War, and the eighteen-year-old Molson would have been surrounded by youths in age from twelve to twenty, working towards a lieutenancy, as Elsdale once had. A young man considering a career at sea could not have asked for a more tolerable introduction to naval life. He was among the midshipmen for more than a month, but beyond the fact that regular meals and shipboard order pleased him, he said little more of his company than "I was treated verry civilly, as I was by every Body On Board."

The day after Molson and the Gibbins men came aboard, the *Assistance* broke away from the convoy to chase down a strange sail. It turned out to be a Danish merchant ship bound from St. Thomas in the Virgin Islands to Copenhagen, and the *Assistance* steered back into the convoy. The fleet had completed less than one-third of the passage and was coming into the shipping tracks of vessels passing above the Azores on their way between the Caribbean and northern Europe.

The weather continued to hammer at the convoy, and the *Assistance* was in a constant state of repair. On May 22, five tons of water had to be pumped aboard to help balance her. On the twenty-third, the convoy began making solid progress as the worst weather passed, and at four in the afternoon of Friday the twenty-fourth, another strange sail was sighted to the west.

Worth ordered the *Surprize* to intercept it. The frigate fired two shots at the unknown vessel and reined her in. "She prov'd to be an Imperialist from Curasso bound to Ostend who told us that the Day instant [before her departure] a French 74 Gun Ship arriv'd there dismasted & much damag'd," noted the *Surprize*'s Captain Ferguson in his log. The *Surprize* rejoined the convoy to share the incredible news borne by the intercepted merchant ship from the enemy alliance.

James Worth broke with form, entering into a log normally filled with perfunctory jottings of onboard events the opinion that the intercepted ship carried "arguably important intelligence." Indeed, this ship, outbound from Curaçao in the Netherlands Antilles, carried news of an action between Rodney and the French fleet. She had reported that three French ships of the line had put in at Curaçao the day before she had sailed, "dismasted & otherwise much Damaged, that the french Fleet had suffer'd considerably but that the [number] taken sunk & burnt was kept a secret: they say a three Decker however of ours was blown up."

On the afternoon of the twenty-seventh, another strange sail was sighted, and the *Surprize* was again ordered to give chase. The

Assistance had just conducted a burial at sea of a marine, John Deady, and was contending with more gale conditions and damage. At ten o'clock on the night of the twenty-eighth, the *Surprize* was at last able to share the fresh intelligence.

The second intercepted ship was a brig that had left Bermuda for Bristol on May 15. Before leaving, noted Worth, she had heard accounts of "an Action between Sir George Rodney & the French Fleet in which we had taken five, sunk two & Burnt one of the Line." The brig said the *Ville de Paris* was among them.

Worth had been overtaken by the leading edge of a shockwave generated by something seismic in geopolitics, a truly transforming event that would reaffirm the scope and strength of empire. He could share the news with the colonial VIPs on board, savouring the rare privilege of knowing the nation's fate before the nation did. The *Assistance* had gathered some of the first news beyond the Caribbean of a momentous engagement that had taken place on April 12—ironically, the same day that the Marquis of Rockingham's government dispatched Oswald to begin negotiating a peace with Franklin in Paris. This naval engagement would be remembered as the Battle of the Saintes, and it represented the most significant British victory at sea since Hawke's triumph at Quiberon Bay in 1759. "The Saintes" endures as a watershed in naval strategy;[8] indeed its tactical significance tends to overshadow the fact that it saved Britain's possessions in the Caribbean and averted the ruination of the colonial mercantile empire just as the American colonies were being lost.

The confrontation had come at the Dominica Passage, the dividing line between the Windward and Leeward Islands of the eastern Caribbean. In the waters between Basse-Terre, in the French island group of Guadeloupe, and the nearby islets of Isle des Saintes, which overlook the Dominica Passage, thirty French warships under de Grasse had encountered a British fleet thirty-six strong—the first time since France had sided with the rebel Americans in 1778 that Britain had enjoyed numerical superiority in both ships and total guns during a fleet engagement. Aboard the French fleet were 5,500 soldiers ready for the land assault on Jamaica.

The intelligence reports the *Surprize* had gathered were of vary-ing accuracy. Rodney had, in fact, triumphed over de Grasse as reported, and the *Ville de Paris* had been taken. Mercilessly pound-ed, the *Bismarck* of her day was captured by Admiral Hood's *Barfleur* as she tried to escape. Almost 300 men had died aboard the *Ville de Paris*, and when British sailors came aboard her, blood washed over their boots as it pooled around the deck scuppers.

All told, the French lost six ships (including the bulk of the siege battery being transported for the now abandoned invasion of Jamaica) and an estimated two thousand men. Britain lost about one thousand men. The report from the Imperialist ship—that a British warship had exploded—and from the Bristol-bound brig—that a French ship had burned—were both half right. The British prize crew that went aboard one of the captured "Seventy Fours" broke into the alcohol and, in their drunken revelry, knocked over a candle that set the ship alight. When the powder magazine exploded, all sixty members of the prize crew and four hundred Frenchmen died. Those who were not killed outright by the fire and explosion were torn apart in the water by sharks, which had already been worked into a feeding frenzy when the French ships dumped their dead overboard during the battle. Nor did the carnage end there. In transporting home their prize ships, including the *Ville de Paris*, the British encountered a hurricane that sank the ships and with them about 3,500 men.

The Saintes was an almost operatic orgy of bloodshed and calamity, but the British public cheered it heartily, in part for the essential naval victory, in part for its decisive defence of Britain's treasured Caribbean holdings. Molson never breathed a word of it in his letters home. It is possible that James Worth shared the gath-ered intelligence only with his senior officers and the colonial VIPs on board. However, once in Quebec no effort was made to withhold the news—the information, as gathered by the *Surprize*, was pub-lished in the *Gazette* the day after the convoy's arrival at Quebec. Molson may not have understood the magnitude of the event, or he may have thought it old news by the time he wrote his first letter home in August.

The effort to strip Britain of her precious Caribbean possessions had failed. The victory gave the empire hope—and the means to deal with the rebel Americans and their European allies at the negotiating table with reasonable strength, by providing intact bargaining chips if they were needed. But perhaps Molson never mentioned the Saintes in letters home because the outcome of this clash of empires did not matter to him. He was in pursuit of fresh opportunities, and the ancient game of geographic pawns and negotiated borders drawn without regard to the logic of terrain probably seemed irrelevant. But he would soon learn how disruptive simple lines on maps, drawn thousands of miles from the soil they etched, could be.

Molson was more affected by the flogging of a crew-member that took place aboard the *Assistance* on June 1. On a day made miserable by fresh gales, fog and rain, Molson was one of the ship's company compelled to assemble at two in the afternoon as a man was tied to a grating in the open air of the main deck and lacerated with a cat-o'-nine-tails—a whip with nine strands of line, with knots tied in them, that ripped into the flesh of the back. Worth noted how he "punished Mr. Johnston seaman with 12 Lashes for Drunkenness & neglect of duty." The dozen lashes were no small punishment, as they could reduce a man's back to bloodied strips, and routine punishments sometimes proved fatal. Molson complained in a letter home how the punishment was meted out "for little or nothing but just to satisfy the arbitrary will of the Capt." Whatever positive impression he had formed of the captain when he was taken aboard from the *Dispatch* was irreparably damaged: he confessed, "my mind altered for I always hated to see arbitrary sway carried on."

Discipline aboard British warships was largely discretionary, and as such was entirely subject to the good judgment or ill temper of the commanding officer. The British Navy's rules of crime and punishment, the Articles of War, were seldom employed as written, and even when followed literally, the death penalty was rarely invoked.[9] Most punishments under the Articles required a court martial, a difficult thing to arrange as prescribed in port, with officers from different ships sitting in judgment. Overwhelmingly, commanders strove to maintain discipline within the bounds of their own discretionary powers.

The Articles of War were read aloud to the assembled crew of the *Assistance* on June 5, and several times to the crew of the *Surprize* during the crossing. It was a common shipboard practice that reminded sailors of the worst-case scenario of discipline. Nowhere in the Articles is the use of the lash mentioned, however. Seaman Johnston's transgression of "drunkenness and neglect of duty" also had no literal place in the Articles of War. ("Drunkenness" was cited only in an article pertaining to the conduct of officers.) Given the stupendous daily ration of beer that sailors enjoyed, it would have been impossible for them not to be inebriated. Even so, "drunkenness and neglect of duty" was a common reason given for punishment and implied further transgressions (according to N.A.M. Rodger) such as fighting and shirking duty. The navy's *Regulations and Instructions relating to His Majesty's Service at Sea,* which spelled out the duties of an officer, allowed that he could have a man punished with up to twelve lashes at his discretion. For anything more, a court martial was required. However, commanders routinely exceeded the maximum the *Regulations* allowed, and faithfully recorded doing so in the logs. Seaman Johnston got the maximum flogging of a dozen strikes, a typical punishment for his crime.

The day before Johnston's flogging, Worth had begun to sound for the edge of the Grand Banks, but after hoving to and lowering 130 fathoms (780 feet) of lead line on both May 31 and June 1, no bottom was found. The fog was so thick on June 1 that the *Assistance* fired guns on the hour as a signal to the convoy. Finally, at one in the morning on June 2, the *Assistance* found bottom at thirty-four fathoms. Tallow on the lead line's weight brought back fine sand with black specks. For the next week the *Assistance* felt her way westward towards the Gulf of St. Lawrence through persistent fog, sampling the bottom (gravel, sand, broken shells) for further clues to her progress. At one in the afternoon on June 9, a day lashed by strong gales, the *Assistance* signalled the convoy that land had been sighted. They were passing south of Newfoundland's Cape Race, about to reach, at last, the Gulf of St. Lawrence. If ever they were to encounter American privateers, it would come in these waters, and on the eleventh the *Assistance*'s gunners were put to work filling shot bags with powder.

Another death: midshipman John Leach was buried at sea on the eleventh, a day that brought more rain and gale-force winds. On the twelfth, the *Assistance* lost contact with the *Surprize*. By the sixteenth, the *Surprize* had still not reappeared, and thick fog settled around the *Assistance*. The convoy had arrived in Canadian waters intact, only to have its collective security collapse in the prime cruising grounds of the privateers.

John Inglis had one eye on duty and another on advancement. The captain of His Majesty's twenty-four-gun *Pandora* was not shy to parade his initiative before his superiors, and so he rained down on General Haldimand at Quebec one breathless letter after another, dispatched from his compact 114-foot command as he cruised the Atlantic seaboard. After escorting a convoy from St. Lucia to Charleston that spring, the *Pandora* had delivered another fleet of merchant ships from Charleston to Halifax, chasing off privateers along the way. Captains like Inglis of small warships enjoyed large rations of independence as they patrolled alone on cruises they often assigned themselves.

After the Charleston convoy was safely tucked into Halifax, Inglis had steered the *Pandora* into the Gulf of St. Lawrence. "I have been cruizing a long time in the Gulph," Inglis wrote Haldimand on May 21. "I believe it is too early for the Privateers. I shall take great care to prevent the Trade from being taken."

On June 11, Inglis sent Haldimand an update: "Having intelligence at Halifax by the Annual Ships that the Quebec Convoy was to Sail Early this Year, I stood to Northward of Eastward to pick up those of the Convoy that might be separated by thick weather." On the tenth he had collected a ship called the *Woodlands Transport*, and the next day the *Pandora* came across the *London*. Both had been cut away from Worth's escort on the ninth in a "hard Gale of Wind. I shall see those or any others that I may fall in with out of Danger," Inglis vowed to Haldimand.

As the *Pandora* continued her search for convoy stragglers, Captain Worth felt his way into the fog-bound Gulf. The *Surprize* was still nowhere to be seen: the *Assistance* was alone in defending herself and the convoy members that had not wandered off.

At eleven on the morning of June 16, off Anticosti Island, according to her log, the *Assistance* "saw four strange ships in the WSW: hove to and Cleared Ship for action." Molson explained in a letter home that the fleet had become separated in the fog in the Gulf for several days, "after which we saw four sails of ships to Windward, which when we saw rather supposed to be Paul Jones"— the euphemism for an American privateer, in honour of John Paul Jones.[10] "All hands were Beat to Quarters, and every thing got ready to receive them[,] all the fleet being lain too." In preparing for action, John Molson and James Gibbins Junior were sent to help with the fore topsail braces, the controlling lines for the upper squaresail on the forward mast. It placed them on deck in what would be "the warmest part of the ship," as Molson noted. Through cold practicality or happy coincidence, the butcher James Senior was assigned to assist the doctors in the cockpit.

Two of the four strange ships approached first, "which we could plain see to be Frigates," Molson related. "We fired our Gun at them to bring them too which they did not." As the strange ships closed with the *Assistance*, a sharp-eyed officer identified one of them as the *Surprize*, fortunately before the first defensive shot could be fired. The other ships proved to be the *Woodlands Transport* and the *London*, travelling with the *Pandora*. Molson lamented that "immediately the Capt. ordered the guns to be taken in lashed as usual, the which I was sorry for as [I] should have liked to [have] seen something of the kind."

A battle at sea had been the final experience Molson required to complete the tour of his uncle Robinson's essential nautical adventures. He clearly invited it, even though single combat against two small frigates—just as Elsdale's *Revenge* had been ambushed by two rival privateers—would have pressed the *Assistance* to the brink of survival. If attacked simultaneously from both sides, the crossfire would have been horrendous. For all his boyish enthusiasm, Molson could not have had any illusions about the carnage of a full-pitch battle. Even without knowing the gory details of the recent fleet action at the Saintes, he would have heard enough of his uncle's youthful exploits to know the destructive power of cannon fire and the murderous grappling that followed a boarding. And perhaps he even understood by now (helpfully pointed out by the midshipmen with whom he messed) that walls on the gundecks of a British warship were painted bright red to disguise the distracting splatters when enemy fire tore apart the gun crews.

Yet the incident illuminates Molson's character better than any other one from his youth. As with the rest of the crossing's trials, he related the near-disastrous encounter with the *Surprize* and the *Pandora* in his letter home without melodrama or self-aggrandizement. The crossing had come with obvious risks, and when those risks became real hazards, he met them with genuine fortitude. Having faced so capably the possibility of death at sea more than once in a single crossing, Molson could not possibly be overwhelmed by anything he faced in the future.

On the eighteenth, the *Assistance*'s deck, no longer primed for battle, was readied for punishment. In what must have been a shocking episode, which Molson nonetheless never mentioned in his letters, the assembled crew were first read the Articles of War at ten in the morning. Then three seamen—Michael McLaughlin, Thomas Wood and Robert Mitchele—were given a dozen lashes each for "drunkenness & Theft." Two more seamen, Edward Fitzpatrick and Robert Elliott, were subjected to two dozen lashes each—twice the number James Worth was permitted to inflict without a formal court martial—for the same offence. Like other captains who exceeded their authority, Worth understood he could get away with it. The only recourse for the flogged sailor was to demand proper justice, which, under the Articles of War, was a court martial on the charge of theft—and that carried a maximum penalty of death. Not surprisingly, wronged sailors accepted their lashes rather than pursuing a judicial hearing that could cost them their lives, or at the least further lashes, if found guilty.

After this brutal outburst, nothing beyond the routine occurred. On Monday, June 24, as the *Assistance* approached Île d'Orléans above Quebec City, General Haldimand had a warm welcome delivered to Captain Worth: "I received with great Pleasure the News of the safe Arrival of your Convoy, attributed to your great Care and Attention, on which I beg leave to congratulate you. I hope I have the pleasure of seeing you at Quebec." All thirty-two ships in the convoy, even the battered *Dispatch*, had reached Quebec City.

At seven in the evening on Wednesday, June 26, the passage came to an end as the *Assistance* moored in twelve fathoms off Pointe Lévis. Benedict Arnold had established a battery for shelling Quebec City here in April 1776, after the failure of the American rebel assault on December 31, 1775. British shelling in the siege of 1759 had destroyed about one-third of the city's homes, and the crowded and unprotected lower town was still littered with rubble when Molson's convoy arrived. This area was now the haunt of the British merchant class, whose homes, offices and warehouses were crowded along the flats above the tideline.

The *Quebec Gazette*—the weekly broadsheet whose content was printed in both French and English—announced the arrival of the convoy's individual vessels, and listed their more noteworthy passengers. In addition to the senior colonial officials, the *Gazette* noted the debarking of a number of military officers, merchants and private citizens. John Molson and the Gibbins men were not worth mentioning. They set foot in the colony with their anonymity—and pseudonymity—intact, arranging for passage on a schooner upriver to Montreal.

To travel upriver on a ship, rather than overland by stage on the old *chemin royal*, they must have been carrying a significant amount of goods. Whether recovered from the *Dispatch* or the hold of another ship in the convoy, the equipment Thomas Loid required to establish a brewery probably travelled upriver under the eye of

John Molson. Although it's unlikely he had any real involvement with the brewery venture at this point, Molson had already done Loid a great service in ensuring that the vital components (which would have included a copper brewing kettle) reached Montreal. If it was all aboard the *Dispatch*, Molson had risked his life to ensure that Loid's equipment survived the passage. As he worked the pumps in the foundering *Dispatch*, he could not have foreseen that he was preserving the means to his own fortune.

When John Molson wrote his uncle Robinson that autumn, he remarked how the eight-week voyage "was reckoned a very quick one, tho' the first part was rather disagreeable. The Sea suits my Constitution exceedingly well, & if the Continent does not, I believe I shall go [to] sea all my Life." To his grandfather he wrote: "The Sea has fully answered my expectations for I am in as good health as every [sic] I was in my Life." And while the end of the crossing proved to be the end of John Molson's brief career as a sailor, he would not so readily shake his enthusiasm for ships in general. The lower town where he had come ashore in Quebec City would one day feature his own wharves and warehouses, to accommodate the passengers and goods carried aboard his own ships.

At the beginning of July, the *Assistance* was moved to a dockside berth for repairs before sailing to New York. The ever-dutiful Captain Inglis, back on patrol in the Gulf of St. Lawrence with the *Pandora*, ran down the fourteen-gun privateer *Despatch* of Salem, Massachusetts, off Prince Edward Island's North Cape, and captured the 150-ton vessel and her crew of forty. On the eighteenth, James Worth assembled a court martial at New York to try twenty-five men from HMS *Narcissus* on the charge of mutiny.

Mutiny varied widely in character, from a violent uprising to a peaceful strike over working conditions and pay. In most cases, the navy tended to show tolerance, and the death sentence specified under the Articles of War was rarely invoked. With the *Narcissus* uprising, the court was assembled for an entire week before coming to a decision on July 25. Seventeen men were acquitted. One man was to receive 200 lashes, another man 500. Six were condemned to die.

No man could endure so many lashes at once. Instead, the convicted were condemned to "go through the fleet"—rowed from one ship to another to receive twenty to thirty lashes aboard each, as an example to sailors on other vessels. According to an eyewitness of one such parade, "The torture is, therefore, protracted till, to use a sailor's phrase, 'their very soul is cut out.' After this dreadful sentence they almost always die."

The men condemned to hang were strung from the yards of their own ship on the twenty-seventh, as Worth and the *Assistance* prepared to go to sea again. Such was the lot of a workhorse warship and her discipline-minded captain. Neither James Worth nor the *Assistance* ever figured in any major battle. *Assistance's* most noteworthy accomplishment would come in 1800, when she transported Prince Edward, Duke of Kent, from Halifax to Plymouth.

None of the British warships involved in the 1782 convoy from Portsmouth to Quebec ended their service with distinction. The *Surprize* was sold by the navy in April 1783, as peacetime returned. The light-footed *Pandora* was lost on Australia's Great Barrier Reef in August 1791. And in March 1802, the *Assistance* was wrecked off Dunkirk, under the command of a different captain. She deserves to be remembered better as the ship in His Majesty's Navy that ensured the safe arrival in Quebec of a seemingly inconsequential teenage émigré whose ambition and personal industry would help transform the colony.

Chapter 5

The knowledge of the world is only to be acquired in the world, and not in a closet.

　　　　　—Lord Chesterfield, letter to his son, October 4, 1746

THE ST. LAWRENCE ABOVE TROIS-RIVIÈRES widens into Lac-St-Pierre, but becomes constricted with islands where the Richelieu drains into it, at Sorel. This was the highest point on the river that sea-going ships could reliably reach. Navigation further upriver, in contrary currents and winds, became less predictable for sailing vessels, which could spend weeks striving to cover a few miles against the outflow of the Great Lakes basin and the Ottawa River. There were, perhaps apocryphal, stories of sailors downbound from Montreal encountering ships at anchor, awaiting conditions favourable to pressing further upriver, and finding them still waiting for the conditions to improve when they returned to the town. It would become John Molson's habit to travel entirely by land between Quebec City and Montreal, a four-day trip along the old French royal road, until his own steam-powered innovations revolutionized transportation in the province.

If the lives of the Canadians, the presence of natives, the novel Catholicism of the communities, the agitation of the British merchants, the emerging importance of the fur trade to Montreal or the atmosphere of a rebellion not yet concluded made any impression upon this young man as he moved upriver by schooner, he did not record it. After travelling down the river from Montreal to Quebec City in 1749, the Swedish naturalist Pehr Kalm marvelled at how the shore appeared as one uninterrupted village. This picturesque panorama, which evoked images of Normandy for other travellers, glided by John Molson without encouraging a single written remark.

Judging a man's character solely by his correspondence is hazardous: the fact that Molson's letters were almost exclusively pragmatic in content does not mean that Molson himself was almost exclusively pragmatic in nature. It was an early sign of his belief— however socially impoverishing—that letters were largely instruments of business. He was far from a cold man, but his calculations were clearly apparent in letters, where he declined to bed them in descriptive colour. With time, his failure to communicate the most fundamental facts about his new life in letters home would produce incredible oversights. By then, his conviction that letters were professional instruments could no longer excuse his deliberately bottled silence.

His failure to reflect at length on the life and times of the colony should not mark him as naive or disinterested, although his singular enthusiasm for Quebec at such a turbulent time is nearly comical. He was taken, almost from his arrival, with the possibilities of the province in particular and the continent in general. The panorama that so delighted Kalm must have impressed Molson, or at least set off no alarms. He may well have travelled to the new world already convinced that, whatever its character, it would present opportunities superior to anything in south Lincolnshire. Considering that he had willingly come here during an unresolved revolution, it would likely have taken air filled with flying hatchets and musket balls to cool his enthusiasm. If his transatlantic voyage with the Gibbins men was meant only as a test of his sea legs, it quickly became apparent that he was determined to plant them on this novel, dry ground.

Molson and James Gibbins Senior and Junior almost certainly disembarked from the schooner at the island of Montreal's east end,[1] at the parish village of Pointe-aux-Trembles, so named for its trembling aspens. The Paris-based Order of Saint-Sulpice, seigneurs of the entire island of Montreal, had erected a fortified mill here about 1670, and the spire of the village's church, built in 1709, would have guided the approach of Molson's vessel from several miles downriver. Nestled against the broad stretch of river above Île Ste-Thérèse, which constricted the St. Lawrence at the island of Montreal's east end, the village was a convenient port of call, although as a port it offered nothing more elaborate than a riverbank.

John Molson's New World: Eastern North America *circa* 1782

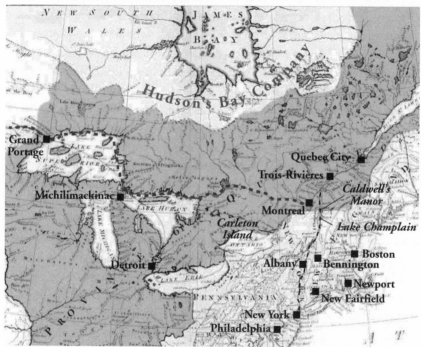

Background map: "The United States of America, with the British & Spanish Territories," 1784

Quebec territory (Quebec Act, 1774)
- - - - Lake Champlain–Hudson River corridor
■ ■ ■ ■ North West Company fur trade route

For John Molson and the Gibbins men, Pointe-aux-Trembles was the final landfall in a long and difficult journey. It was as if after the passage up the St. Lawrence they stepped ashore at the first opportunity and set to work building new lives. The town of Montreal still lay nine miles upriver, beyond the seigneurial farms and nascent suburbs, long since built over and paved under.

One can imagine Thomas Loid awaiting them on the shore by the village, ready to help them set down roots and enlist them in his own endeavours. Over the winter of 1781–82, he would have scouted more carefully the local opportunities for both himself and the Gibbins men, and would have been surprised and doubtless pleased to see John Molson in their company. This imperceptible man, as thinly drawn for us as his signature on a 1787 petition— one of the few tangible relics of his life—loomed over Molson's future in a way we can now appreciate but never understand. The paper trail has left behind many references to Loid, but no real explanation for him. Molson was in search of opportunity, and Loid would prove to be the instigator, catalyst and obstacle; he was also a mirror that would reflect Molson's confidence, trust and disillusionment.

They had all pulled up short at a place that was strategically and psychologically significant. Their focus was still on the descending river. Rather than moving to the precipice of civilization, a place from which they could stare into the unexploited interior of the continent, they had found a vantage point that afforded a view of an established, yet developing, world, not an untamed one. The idea of pressing forward, into what he vaguely called the "Upper Country," would cross John Molson's mind, but only idly. Pointe-aux-Trembles was not some remote address, the bottom of a colonial well. It was navigational high ground, and in looking back downriver, Molson would have had a comforting sense of being atop a panorama of opportunity, not beneath it.

At the height of summer in 1782, Montreal's church of Nôtre-Dame might have been visible beyond Pointe-aux-Trembles's poplars, but little else was.[2] Come autumn, the fires from four hundred concentrated households and a variety of institutions would smudge the horizon. Montreal was reached most easily from Pointe-aux-Trembles overland, along a simple dirt road that entered the town through a gate at its narrow eastern end, becoming rue Nôtre-Dame. Just inside the fortified wall was the citadel housing the British Army headquarters, the administrative heart of a profound defeat. It was a loss not yet officially negotiated, but the latest news of Britain's efforts to secure a peace, buoyed by the fresh intelligence of some wonderful, half-understood success by Admiral Rodney in the Caribbean, would have pressed westward against the great river's outflow along with Molson and raced him to the eastern gate. Peace would not necessarily bring prosperity.

Historians have long struggled to create a precise picture of Montreal as John Molson found it in 1782. Molson has not helped matters by having nothing at all to say about it. Systematic studies of architecture and property ownership conducted in the last decade have improved our impression of the old town, but much remains speculative.

The town was defined by its fortifications until their dismantling began in 1804. A wooden palisade had been torn down to make way for stonework and gates in 1717, and these more robust defences were in poor repair when Molson arrived. The walls, nonetheless, restricted the settlement to a compact rectangle about a mile long and little more than one thousand feet back from the river, opposite the islands of Ste-Hélène and Nôtre-Dame, although British merchants with the necessary funds had begun to establish country estates beyond the redoubts.

Here in 1642 some fifty devotees of the obscure Catholic organization known as the Société de Nôtre-Dame de Montréal had established Ville-Marie, the first permanent French settlement, a century after Jacques Cartier had placed the first European foot on the island. The religious outpost struggled through repeated attacks by the Iroquois, until, in 1663, the Société turned the island over to the Sulpicians, who operated it as a seigneury; the town and the island were still technically the property of the religious order when Molson arrived.

The Sulpicians built a church and a seminary and organized the town along a plan that survives today (as do many of the old stone buildings, including the seminary of 1684, in what is known as Vieux-Montréal).[3] Two main streets, St-Paul and Nôtre-Dame, followed their modern course, parallel to the river. The buildings were largely of wood, although stone was coming into greater use, as fire plagued the older structures—an inferno in 1765 had been particularly devastating. Piers and wharves were decades away. People and goods arriving by ship had to negotiate the muddy riverbank along makeshift boards to gain the town, just as they did at Pointe-aux-Trembles.

Despite its compact dimensions, late eighteenth-century Montreal was not compressed into narrow streets like the capital, Quebec City. Nor did it show any scars of battle, as it had never been battered by cannon fire. It had surrendered without resistance to both the British in 1760 and the main American assault in 1775. Many residences boasted sophisticated gardens in enclosed courtyards, which were both aesthetic and practical, providing a quiet respite while producing food for the household. It must have been an attractive provincial settlement—not exactly a sophisticated metropolis, but far from a typical lawless frontier boom town. On the other hand, there was no sewage system, and unless life had changed significantly from the first post-conquest years, pigs and other livestock would have been found within the town walls, even wandering at large in its streets.

The town had a pronounced religious component, as ecclesiastical concerns accounted for twenty percent of the property (including gardens and open ground) within the walls. In addition to the Sulpicians, the town was home to Récollet friars (whose property dominated the west end) and the Sisters of the Congregation of Nôtre-Dame. Montreal's heart was dominated by the Sulpician seminary, the Nôtre-Dame church and the convent of the associated sisters. Just outside the town's walls, the Grey Nuns operated the general hospital. The large religious population, in concert with the British military (particularly senior staff), would have given Montreal a fair dose of sobriety and stability. With about four hundred residences in the late eighteenth century, the

town was home to some three thousand people,[4] and the surrounding suburbs and rural parishes may have raised the island
population to five thousand.

Montreal had been a garrison town under French rule, and the
British military presence since the city's surrender in 1760 had
attracted the usual ranks of contractors who supplied provisions.
The British commercial community had begun to take root from
the moment of conquest. Exactly how large this merchant class was
when Molson arrived is impossible to say. A 1765 survey of the
Montreal district identified ninety-nine Protestants in the town
and another thirty-seven in the rest of the district, but only fifty
of the Montreal Protestants were identified as merchants.[5] The
term "merchant" can be applied to anyone from a humble cobbler
to a fur-trading giant. An optimistic guess would place the non-
francophone merchant ranks in Montreal at about one hundred
when Molson arrived. For those who depended on an active military campaign to fuel their business, the shift to a peacetime footing at this command post would mean recession, even ruin.

These merchants had come to Montreal from England, the
Channel Islands, Scotland and the American colonies, with some
of the minor ranks filled by discharged British soldiers. The most
famous were the Presbyterian Scots who developed the Montreal
fur trade and were at the heart of the North West Company, the
great rival to the Hudson's Bay Company (which was on the verge
of being formed by local traders when Molson stepped ashore at
Pointe-aux-Trembles).

Wrapped in its dilapidated stone walls, its territory less than one
hundred acres, Montreal was both a bastion against a vast continent of historic threats and a portal to the continent's equally vast
opportunities. The defensive posture was in rapid retreat with the
approaching peace: Montreal was becoming the hub of a new
nation, not a refuge from its dangers.

If land defined the limits of life in eighteenth-century Britain, it
was the basis of opportunity in North America. There seemed no end
to the "yet unbounded Continent" of William May's letter of introduction for the three Lincolnshire men of May 30, 1781, precisely

because it remained largely undescribed. Captain James Cook had sailed the survey ship HMS *Endeavor* up the coast of what would become British Columbia for the first time in 1778, only four years before John Molson left Lincolnshire, and Alexander Mackenzie of Montreal's North West Company would not begin his explorations (in search of more furs) until 1789 of what became the North West Territories.

Even that which was at least hazily understood was dauntingly vast. After the 1763 conquest, Quebec consisted of roughly a trapezoid of territory focused on the upper St. Lawrence. It took in the Gaspé and the modern Eastern Townships, and extended north of the St. Lawrence to a line drawn from Lake Nipissing (in what is now Ontario) over the top of Lac Saint-Jean and as far east as Rivière Saint-Jean on the north shore of the Gulf of St. Lawrence, at the west end of Anticosti Island. To the west, its border just crossed over the Ottawa River and ran from Lake Nipissing down to the St. Lawrence. The Quebec to which John Molson emigrated was much greater, thanks to the Quebec Act of 1774. That act annexed to the old colony the former French territories around the Great Lakes and the lands above the post-conquest province as far north as the watershed of Hudson Bay, beyond which was the private domain of the Hudson's Bay Company. The new dimension of Quebec included a great swath of land below the Great Lakes that reached to the banks of the Mississippi in the west and to the Ohio in the south and east. When the Quebec Act went into effect in 1775, this sprawling new Quebec helped ignite the American Revolution with the affront of the province's new dimensions. Because this land was set aside as native territory, it impeded further westward expansion by settlers and land speculators, and because the Quebec Act recognized Catholic rights long before they were granted in Britain or America, the new province surrounded the Thirteen Colonies in a loathed papal embrace.

Territories beyond the boundaries of 1763 Quebec were left (for the time being) to the fur trade, but the settled ribbon along the St. Lawrence circa 1782, inhabited by six generations of Canadians, was still fit for a king. The distance from Quebec City to Montreal

(160 miles) was on par with the trek from London all the way to Liverpool—or from London across the English Channel to Paris.

Montreal provided the introduction to a boreal wilderness that was, for the settlement's leading Anglo-Scot merchants, still essentially a vast resource of pelts. Until the American Revolution, moving upriver beyond Montreal was a task largely left to trading canoes, with rapids bypassed only by the most basic sluices. Proper canal construction around Montreal began only in 1779, and then as a military measure. One did not yet have to strike out for distant prairies to establish a homestead, for only a few miles from Montreal, arable land was uncleared, untilled, even unclaimed.

As noted, much of the land around the Great Lakes basin had been preserved from agriculture by the British, who promised their native allies, in treaties, to preserve native territories from exploitation. The American Revolution helped dismantle those barriers. American colonies could not control the westward pressure of their own citizens, and British negotiators at the 1782 peace talks callously abandoned the natives by surrendering so much former treaty territory (and what had been defined as Quebec below the Great Lakes) to the expansionist American republic. In Montreal, a town still largely built of wood, its defences neglected and crumbling since 1760, and its economy dependent on good relations with natives in the fur-trading networks, there was considerable fear. Erstwhile native allies surely were about to storm the town or commit atrocities in the surrounding countryside.

But the uprising never came. Critical allies, such as the Iroquois of New York under the Mohawk war chief Joseph Brant (Thayendanegea), relocated to reserves in what would become Upper Canada. The fur traders of the powerful North West Company, which coalesced from a number of independent operators in 1783, adjusted the basin of their empire to accommodate the new border, and prospered more. British North America, having withdrawn into a fraction of the vast colonial territory wrested from France only twenty years earlier, considered the influx of Loyalist immigrants and began to form its own plans for expansion within the untapped wilderness to which it limited itself in the peace of

1783. The clearing and settlement of what would become Upper Canada in 1791—the arable land around the lower Great Lakes, above the new border that cleaved them—was at hand. The surveying of the first five "Royal Townships" on the upper St. Lawrence, for settlement on lands purchased by the Crown from the Mississauga, would begin in 1783.

Initially, however, the former territory of post-conquest Quebec was the focus of much of the Loyalist resettlement. Refugees of the conflict moving north found property available on seigneuries, now often owned by British subjects—many of them senior army officers who had received them in payment for services rendered in the fall of Quebec or who had been able to purchase them cheaply from French nationals returning home after the conquest. Britain's decision to permit the continuation of the seigneurial system displeased Loyalists, who much preferred freehold land to tenancy, and their agitations helped spur the opening of Upper Canada to settlement. But many Loyalists seeking refuge during and after the American Revolution had to settle, at least initially, on the old seigneuries. They had come to live in the hybrid society of Quebec, where French civil and English criminal law coexisted uncomfortably in a mélange of post-conquest compromise.

In their midst were John Molson and his fellow émigrés from Lincolnshire, the Gibbins and Loids: opportunists moving among Loyalists and rebels, unallied, unmarked and unencumbered by the bitter colonial war that had set neighbour against neighbour. For John Molson, political allegiance was irrelevant; the continent was his to consider and, if it struck him, to explore.

Descended from generations of yeomen, John Molson was bred to view real estate as the foundation of personal prosperity and security. The new American sport of land speculation was not a voiced Molson ambition: working the land is how Molsons had always survived. None of his direct ancestors were traders, artisans, manufacturers or merchants, or middle-class professionals like clergymen, lawyers or physicians. True, John's uncle William had been set up in the tannery business by Grandfather John, but William had died when John was eight, minimizing what exposure, if any, he might have had to the trade. Beyond Robinson Elsdale's exploits at sea, the only way to make a living with which John Molson was familiar within his own family was the one practised since those distant days in Yorkshire. But with every passing month in Quebec, Molson's avowed interest in establishing himself in farming was contradicted by his own unreported actions in business.

In an undated letter to his uncle Robinson in the autumn of 1782, he made it clear that Lincolnshire no longer figured in his future. His impression of the climate was, for a modern Montrealer, endearingly optimistic: "The summer has not been particular Hot nor disagreeable, tho' I am told it has been the coolest for some years past, as for the Winters [I] do not dread at all as they have such Conveniences to keep a Person Warm."

As winter and its conveniences approached, Molson sketched the domestic and professional affairs of the Lincolnshire émigrés. While George Gibbins evidently had not yet arrived, William was now with his brother James and their father—either William had made a separate Atlantic crossing that year, or he had been with the Loids in North America all along. John Molson resolutely stuck to the Gibbins's alias of Pell in letters home, informing his uncle, "Mr. Pell has treated me exceedingly civelly during my absence from you, but I hope I shall have it in my Power to Make him amends here-after & you Sir I am greatly indebted for favors past, but I hope you will not find me ungrateful."

Molson had settled in with the Gibbins men, noting, "We have taken a House to our selves, which I am glad on. William and James have begun to Bucher which will answer verry well (they served ye shipping this years). Mr. Pell proposes taking a farm & him & me living in it but if I light of an opportunity of going to the Upper Country, I undoubtedly shall, & should be glad to see the Provinces before I come back, but that cannot be done unless there's a Peace. . . ."

Molson was impressed with the agricultural possibilities, but appalled by the primitive practices of the Canadians. "The Country is in general a verry Good mixt Soil, & in common is natural to clover, being between the three Rivers & Montreal the finest fields of Clover I ever saw in my Life." In south Lincolnshire, it was common practice to burn the fields to replenish the soil; in Quebec he saw only neglect. "The farmers manage their Land verry badly as they never fallow, but when it bring nothing, they let it lye Bastards two or three years & then plow it up again, & for all that there is verry few Weeds, besides Thistles. . . ." Molson offered a thorough shopping list of prices for wheat, barley, beef, butter, cheese and lamb, as well as servants' wages. Pleased with the values, as a consumer rather than a producer, he may not have realized that the rates had only recently plunged from the inflationary wartime years.

As for Thomas Loid, he had applied himself almost immediately to his brewing venture. "Mr. Lloyd is erecting a Malting [house] new from the Ground," Molson reported, "and there [is] no fear of it answering if he brought it to perfection, as he proposes to sell the Beer at L10 per hogshead.*" Molson promised to hold his opinion of the brewery until he had seen the results.

The operation was in a newly constructed building, built with four-inch squared logs, on a plot of land upriver from Pointe-aux-Trembles in the suburb of St. Mary's Current (or simply St. Mary), which was located just beyond Montreal's eastern wall. Loid had acquired the lot from a butcher and landowner named Pierre Monarque on September 3, with a £100 mortgage held by Monarque. The lot was a narrow ribbon, 40 feet wide and about 345 feet deep, which ran from St. Mary Street (as the local section of the shore road that became rue Nôtre-Dame within Montreal's walls was known) down to the bank of the St. Lawrence, where the foot of St. Mary's Current flowed past the island of Ste-Hélène. The Gibbinses, providing ships with butchered meat, were probably settled around Pointe-aux-Trembles to take advantage of the traffic, which called there rather than testing the strong St. Mary's Current to reach Montreal proper. Denison reasonably proposed that Molson was pitching in with the brewery from the very beginning, and doubtless helped Loid build it.

---

* *Hogshead:* A barrel of 52.5 Imperial gallons, or 55 wine gallons.

Having no idea of Thomas Loid's past, we cannot say if he was an experienced brewer exploiting his trade in the colony or a neophyte seizing the main chance. No evidence survives of how or where Loid obtained the brewing equipment—or even what much of that equipment was. The speed with which he established the brewery suggests that Loid approached the initiative with some forethought, and as noted he probably had the venture planned sufficiently in advance in the fall of 1781 for James Gibbins to return to England and arrange to have the necessary equipment shipped to Montreal for him in the spring of 1782. Brewing required a variety of specialized machinery and tools, particularly the brewing kettle. Loid would not have been able to purchase them in Quebec or import them easily from the American colonies in the midst of a revolution. He could have sourced them only in England.

The economic history of Montreal in the first decades under English rule is far from written, but it seems that Loid's rudimentary brewery was the only one operating in Montreal at the end of the American Revolution (although beer could have been made in small batches in household kitchens or hotels and taverns). Certainly the market was small: beer was unpopular with the Canadians, who much preferred wine and distilled spirits, and the town's British merchant community would have provided a small core clientele.

But Loid was poised to exploit a shift in local demographics. The influx of thousands of Loyalists promised a vast new market for the little brewery. And while operations were scaled back in peacetime, Montreal's importance as the British Army's military headquarters would continue, providing a brewer with a faithful clientele. There were other officers and men to supply at nearby posts, such as Fort Chambly and Fort St. Johns on the upper Richelieu, and the garrisons at the top of Lake Champlain, at Pointe-au-Fer and at Blockhouse Island (later North Hero Island).

The economy of the eighteenth century was rooted in basic commodities, and brewing, distilling and wine-making stood out in their ability to turn perishable agricultural produce into relatively imperishable, readily transportable goods. For generations, however, the drinking preferences of Canadians were a pox on the Quebec economy. Because they preferred wine, which required grapes that could not be cultivated domestically, everything consumed had to be imported, creating a serious drain on the money supply. New France's gifted superintendent, Jean Talon, saw beer as the solution to the trade imbalance. If a drink could be made from locally grown barley, the debilitating outflow of silver could be stemmed. Talon's royal brewery was completed in 1671, but lasted only a few years before public indifference to the product forced its closure.

Other brewery operations had come and gone during the history of New France, and by the time Thomas Loid established his brewery in 1782, the beer most widely produced was a spruce beer brewed in the summer. Technically, beer can be brewed from any cereal grain that can provide the starch for conversion into sugar and, through fermentation, into alcohol. While barley is the preferred grain for traditional ale and lager, other grains, such as oats and wheat, can be substituted. However, spruce beer (which John Molson would produce) relied on spruce boughs and branches essentially for flavouring, not fermenting, as well as for their antiscorbutic properties. (A native tea brewed from spruce bark saved many of Jacques Cartier's men from scurvy during the explorer's first catastrophic overwintering at Quebec in 1535–36.)

General Jeffrey Amherst, who accepted the capitulation of the French at Montreal in 1760, recorded in his journal that year a recipe for the local drink:

> Take 7 Pounds of good spruce & boil it well till the bark peels off, then take the spruce out & put three Gallons of Molasses to the Liquor & boil it again, scum it well as it boils, then take it out the kettle & put it into a cooler, boil the remained of the water sufficient for a Barrel of thirty Gallons, if the kettle is not large enough to boil it together, when milkwarm in the Cooler put a pint of Yeast into it and mix well. Then put it into a Barrel and let it work for two or three days, keep filling it up as it works out. When done working, bung it up with a Tent Peg

in the Barrel to give it vent every now and then. It may be used in up to two or three days after. If wanted to be bottled it should stand a fortnight in the Cask. It will keep a great while.

Brewing beer with molasses, a syrup produced in sugar refining, did nothing to free Quebec from its dependence on specie-draining overseas goods. But there was hardly a market to speak of for beer produced with traditional barley, until the Loyalists began supplementing the British military and merchant presence.

Because beer could be imported duty-free (unlike rum and molasses),[6] there was no outward financial incentive to establish a local operation. However, the experienced tastes of the military and Loyalists would have far preferred a good domestic brew to the idiosyncratic spruce beer—or something that had been sloshing in barrels in the bottom of a ship from England for two months. And if a brewery could be established, it would satisfy Jean Talon's frustrated vision of a value-added product created mainly from two local commodities—water and barley.

For a brewer, there was another advantage to the business: it operated on a welcomed cash basis. As Denison noted, the brewer's main purchases were on credit, while his sales brought coinage. Brewing generated pocketable revenues at a time when specie was in chronically short supply. If a brewery was run profitably, it could become self-financing and provide a literal cash flow that could be applied to other ventures.

But to generate that money required money to begin with, and the financial system under which John Molson found his way forward in the new world would have been utterly alien to a modern businessman luxuriating in instant electronic global transactions. There were no banks in Quebec, and hardly any British coinage (which was in short supply even at home) circulated in the colonies.

For the British Crown and Parliament, the North American colonies existed to supply the home country with valuable commodities, and to act as a market for the finished goods of British manufacturers. The mercantile system was dictated by the Acts of Navigation, which prescribed a long list of colonial commodities, such as tobacco and furs, that could be shipped only to Britain. The Acts of Navigation also limited large-scale manufacturing in the colonies, to protect British industry and artisans. And because the colonies existed for the benefit of Britain, the system was designed to funnel profits, and with them actual coinage, back to the mother country—hence no banks.

The solution to the resulting specie shortage normally would have been paper money, but inflationary problems moved the British government to bar the North American colonies from issuing it in 1764. Metal ruled, regardless of where it had been minted. Silver coinage in North America was a mélange of European currencies, mainly Spanish milled dollars, or "pieces of eight"—so-called for the way the coins were split into smaller pieces as a way of making change. Old French coins, such as the sou, were in circulation in Quebec, and there were also a few denominations of gold coin, mainly the Portuguese Johannes or "Joe" and the Spanish pistole. Even Mexican and Central American silver minted by the Spanish circulated. A summary of specie in Molson's possession drawn up on September 11, 1800, included doubloons, "half Joes," guineas, half-guineas, sous, "pistols," dollars (American or Spanish) and British crowns.

Each British colony in North America used the existing monetary units of the mother country, with one pound worth twenty shillings and a shilling worth twelve pence—albeit without being able to use the actual money to any significant degree. The colonial monetary system could function only by assigning conversion values to the hodgepodge of coinage in use. Every colony had its own exchange rate, and they were in active competition to prevent an outflow of coinage. At the first session of the Nova Scotia House of Assembly in 1758, the exchange rate devised in Massachusetts and adopted by the city of Halifax was made official for the entire colony. It rated a Spanish milled dollar, the dominant coin, at five shillings, rather than the four shillings and six pence it merited in sterling in London. In November 1760, Brigadier General James Murray, the new British governor of Quebec, adopted the rate there as well. This superior exchange rate, still in effect when John

Molson reached Montreal, was known as the Halifax currency in Quebec—hence the distinction made in many Molson communications between "pounds Halifax" and "pounds Sterling."[7]

It's important to realize that the Halifax pound was not an actual currency, but a rate of exchange for the circulating coinage. Because of the competitive exchange rate offered for silver and gold coins, a Halifax "pound" differed in value from a true pound sterling. But actual monetary values were further complicated by metal prices in London, the amount of silver or gold in a specific coin, and the real cost of shipping silver coins to London from the colonies, where they could be redeemed for the equivalent sterling.

The unusual system of exchange was exacerbated by the process by which money was actually used in America. In the American colonies it was avoided altogether by bartering goods, or by using a commodity with an agreed-upon value, like tobacco, as a substitute. But anyone living in North America who wanted to buy something in Britain had to pay for it there in sterling funds. And anyone who had sterling funds in Britain who wanted to employ that wealth in North America had to figure out how to put it to use.

Molson had money available to him back in England, though it was to be released at the discretion of his grandfather, Samuel Elsdale. Even after he came of age, Molson would still face considerable challenges in converting his equity in Britain into employable funds in Quebec. Shipping specie across the Atlantic was risky and costly. To turn British sterling in England into useful specie in Quebec, Molson had to use a transmogrifying device called a bill of exchange.

Such a bill, when drawn up by Molson, directed his banking house back in England to pay its bearer the sum noted—say, £100 sterling. Molson would first sell this bill of exchange to someone in Quebec—perhaps a merchant or fur trader who had available specie and needed the sterling represented by the bill of exchange to address a debt in Britain. Bills sold at a discount: Molson would receive the agreed-upon value in whatever circulating coinage was available—say £90 in Spanish-milled dollars for his £100 bill. The discount depended on a number of factors, including the number of bills of exchange and the amount of specie in circulation in Quebec. When specie was in especially short supply—and demand for it was high—the discount would naturally increase, and the opportunity arose for people with spare coinage to make tidy profits by purchasing bills at healthy discounts and redeeming them at full value. It was an opportunity for easy profit that would come to Molson with time, as the cash flow of the brewery allowed him to be an opportunistic buyer rather than a seller of bills.

The purchaser of one of Molson's bills would ship it to Britain to his creditor or banker, who, in turn, would present the bill of exchange to Molson's banker so that it could be redeemed from his sterling account. Bills of exchange could be issued "at sight," meaning the banking house would be required to redeem it as soon as it was presented. But they were regularly issued at thirty days' sight, which meant that the banking house was given thirty days in which to pay it after its acceptance—provided the banking house even accepted it. Bills could also be issued at sixty and ninety days' sight, the equivalent of an aggressively post-dated cheque.

Needless to say, this was an incredibly cumbersome way to do business, but provided he could find a ready buyer for his bill of exchange, Molson could at least convert the money (at some discount) in his sterling account into employable coins in Quebec with relative speed. But he faced additional complications.

First, there was the problem of finding a purchaser for the bill of exchange. One alternate method was for a representative of Molson back in England to transfer sterling funds to the London account of a merchant or banker who did business in Montreal, and who could then provide Molson with a letter of credit (to the equivalent) for use in Montreal. But the British merchant community in Montreal was small and had its own credit problems, which made it difficult for members to either purchase bills of exchange or provide goods or specie on a letter of credit. The foremost problem was the incredibly telescoped transaction process of Montreal's dominant enterprise, the fur trade. The business was based entirely on credit, and according to the North West Company's Alexander Mackenzie, it took almost four years for one season's trading to pass through the books and realize a profit.

The problem of finding merchants who would purchase a bill of exchange was exacerbated by the dramatic burst of a financial bubble just as Molson arrived in Quebec. In 1779, John Cochrane arrived in Quebec City as the Canadian agent for the London firm of Harley & Drummond, the new exchange contractors for the British Treasury. For motives that are not clear—he either was enriching himself or was put up to it by greedy Canadian merchants, or both—Cochrane convinced Haldimand that Canadian merchants should be allowed to purchase bills of exchange through Harley & Drummond using not just cash, but notes—in other words, on partial credit, using notes accepted on generous terms by the government. In 1781, Cochrane then persuaded the fiscally naive Haldimand to guarantee the notes of the merchants. As a result, merchants were taking advantage of the credit extended by Haldimand to lever more credit in the form of bills. Those who exploited this scheme were awash in inflated funds, and some of them took on considerable debt as they speculated in commodities. Grain was hoarded, and at one point the rum market was cornered. It took until the spring of 1783, and an order from the home government for Harley & Drummond to collect immediately on all outstanding debts, for the bubble to burst. As A.L. Burt put it, "The engines were suddenly reversed and, relatively speaking, Canada experienced the worst financial wreck in its history."[8] Virtually every merchant of consequence in Quebec was affected, as the debt crisis was piled atop the downturn brought about by the end of the wartime economy.

Even without the financial collapse of 1783, a significant problem Montrealers faced in using bills of exchange (and in managing funds and business in general in Britain) was the short shipping season on the St. Lawrence. John Molson became as wary as any other Quebec merchant of the tyranny of winter. Necessary goods had to be ordered in time for them to be consigned to "autumnal shipping" before pack ice closed the St. Lawrence until the following spring. During freeze-up, mail at least could be sent and received via the port of New York once the revolution was over, but service was spotty and would move Molson to provide elaborate instructions to his correspondents on how best to communicate with him—how postage had to be paid in advance, which private ship captains could be entrusted with correspondence in lieu of the mail packets (assembled at London for shipment to Quebec, Halifax and New York on the first Wednesday of the month), and which London coffee house should be used as a drop-off for outbound mail by private transport. Even when letters were not lost altogether, it could take six months for a message to get through via the circuitous winter shipping route. Meanwhile in London, a letter posted in the morning could be expected to arrive at another address in the city that afternoon; London and south Lincolnshire enjoyed next-day service. The protracted and unreliable communications system between Montreal and Britain would be the source of the young Molson's greatest frustrations in his first years in Canada. It was no system for a young man gripped by fiscal urgency.

Molson's financial world was further complicated by his own status as a minor. Until he reached the age of majority at the end of 1784, he had no direct control over his finances, and was utterly dependent on his grandfather Samuel's indulgence. Having parted with his grandfather on poor terms, Molson was concerned about the Old Gent's enthusiasm for his grandson's transatlantic adventure. "Should be glad if you would send me Word what my Grandfather [is] thinking of my getting to America," Molson wrote his uncle Robinson in the fall of 1782. Molson would assiduously cultivate allies in south Lincolnshire to plead his case before his grandfather as money became necessary.

Until he came of age, the only source of money Molson had back home was his grandfather, who would advance it to him against the value of the estate he stood to inherit. And being a minor, he had to use a sterling account that his Surfleet attorney Philip Ashley maintained with the Fleet Street banking firm Robert & Francis Gosling (Gosling & Son). Molson could write bills of exchange on Ashley's Gosling account; when they were eventually presented to Gosling & Son for redemption, the necessary funds had to be provided to the account by Ashley, using funds provided in turn by Samuel Elsdale. Ashley's involvement only exacerbated Molson's financial headaches. From the beginning, there were apparent problems with Molson's bills of exchange. On December 5, 1782, Robert Gosling sent Ashley a curt note: "We wrote to [you] the 30th respecting Mr. Molson's drafts [and] expected to have received an Answer before this. The parties who have the Bills are desirous of getting them accepted, we must therefore beg to have your determination about them by return of post."

In one important respect, Molson would move against the dominant commercial model of the colony. As a brewer, he became part of Quebec's second wave of economic development. He was not a fur trader harvesting the landscape and shipping the profits to England. Molson became a net benefit to the province, liquidating assets in England to turn them into equity in Quebec. The revenues of his commercial activities then remained almost entirely within the province, with investments fuelling further growth and diversification. Jean Talon probably would have been delighted to know him.

John Molson emerged from his first Canadian winter with his enthusiasm for the new world reinforced by the news of peace between Britain, the United States, France, Holland and Spain, signed at Paris in February 1783. By July, the nineteen-year-old's mind was made up: he would make his life on this side of the Atlantic. The financial catastrophe scandalizing the government and the merchants of the province appeared not to faze him. He may have had the good sense to realize that the influx of Loyalists was more important to his future than a burst speculative bubble among fur traders and army contractors.

He wrote a flurry of letters that month to an elite circle of south Lincolnshire recipients: Philip Ashley, his grandfather, his cousin John Molson, and the widow Alice Boulton, an old family friend. Beneath the occasional sing-song good cheer was a streak of deliberation. He was beginning to prepare the ground for his withdrawal from south Lincolnshire and the liquidation of the family estate he would not inherit for another eighteen months.

His most daunting task was informing his grandfather of his plans, and convincing him to go along with them so that he could move on opportunities before he came of age. "As the climate seems to agree well with my Constitution I am come to a full resolution to settle here and [am] going in to business Immediately," Molson wrote in a draft of the letter he sent Samuel Elsdale that month. "We have fine fertile land for nothing without either Town Dues or Taxes."

Having informed him he wasn't coming back, Molson now forth-rightly asked him for another £80, the equivalent of £6,400 today.[9] He had written Thomas Loid a bill of exchange for the sum, payable on a generous ninety days' sight, so that he would have time to remonstrate with his grandfather over the importance of it being paid. It was an obligation "which you must Honour if you mean I should keep any currency in this Country which I wish to have done as I mean to stay in the Country, I'll have not the least doubt but you'l be in the same way of thinking as myself, as well knowing that punctuality in Business is absolutely necessary . . . Believe me Dear Sir I cannot do without the Money I have drawn for, as I shall go directly into Business, being tired with an Idle Live." He added then crossed out in his draft "& spending of Money," reconsidering the wisdom of admitting to financial profligacy.

Molson also had to break the news that he had decided to undermine his grandfather's guardianship by granting power of attorney to Ashley "to settle all my affairs & to remit me all the money I have, as soon as may be after I arrive to the age of 21 years & hope you will assist him in expediting this Business. My reason for giving Mr. Ashley my Power of Attorney is thinking him a Proper Person for settling my Affairs with Mr. Molson [his cousin John] & giving me the drafts directly in his Bankers in London."

Molson was suggesting that a professional third party like Ashley was a better choice than his grandfather for dealing with another family member on financial matters. He would be entitled to sev-eral hundred pounds from his cousin John when he came of age. This was the income from Father John's estate that accumulated in the short period after his death, when Father John's brother Thomas served as the orphaned John's guardian and trustee. When Thomas died in 1772, the income from Father John's estate was folded into Thomas's estate and bequeathed to his eldest son, John (our John's cousin), to be accounted for when our John came of age.

John Molson clearly understood the parameters of his inheritance, and so another letter that July to his cousin John was to be expected, to prepare for a prompt settlement of the portion of his inheritance that had been swallowed by Thomas Molson's estate:

> I take this favourable Opportunity of informing you that I intend settling in this country, as there apears far greater Opertunities for a Person settling in Business here, than in all Probability will [be] in England for many years to come. I therefore wish you would be in readiness for to settle the Accounts that now stand between us & pay the Balance by Christmas with Mr. Ashley who I have impowered to receive it. I think it best to let you know my intentions a Twelve Month before Hand as it will be Impossible for me to do without the money & therefore hope you will not delay the payment longer than the time above mentioned as a month. I have spent a Twelve Month in this part of the World very agreeable, and since you have made a Peace for us, I purpose going into the United States, as soon as the Communication is open. Should take it as a favor receiving a few lines from you, hope your Family & all Friends are in good Health, Please to give my Love & Duty as due, & remember me to all inquiring Friends, particularly Miss Boulton. . . .

Yes, Alice Boulton, an old family friend who had been left a riding horse in the will of Father John's cousin John. The sixty-year-old widow could be depended on to put in a good word for his ambitions with the Old Gent. And so she too was dispatched a letter that July:

> I have the pleasure to inform you that my Constitusion has attained its usual Vigour, since my departure from Old England, and hoping these few lines will find you in the same agreeable state. Believe me, I cannot help wishing to hear after your state of Health since my Leaving you, which hath occured in my Thoughts since last I had the happiness of your

good company. I can assure you...I have spent my time verry egreable on this Side of Atlantic, knowing my Brothers & Sisters, hath you, my Grandfather, & Uncle Robinson Elsdale always to advise & direct them which I hope they will always with myself gratefully acknowledge. I have wrote to my Grandfather desiring a further supply of Money to the amount of four score Pounds, which hope you will be so kind as make intercession for me, as I could wish to appear a little Genteel, as I am thoroughly Convinsed it will be Money saved in the End, and not Injuring my Fortune at Present. Have wrote to my Friend Ashley, & Uncle Robinson to the same Purpose. . . .

Molson feared, with good reason, that his grandfather would not grant him advances against the value of Snake Hall so that he could start fresh on a new continent, particularly when it wasn't clear what he had in mind. His comments about "going into business" intimated a future that did not involve agriculture, but "business" was a catch-all term for professional activity that could apply to a political career or animal husbandry as readily as brewing. However, Molson's ongoing need for money would shortly become apparent. Thomas Loid's log brewhouse was beckoning.

Manoeuvring to remove his grandfather from the position of ultimate authority was potentially hazardous and likely impossible. Molson did not have the power to fire his grandfather as his guardian and trustee. Samuel Elsdale's essential duty was to give sober guidance to youthful wrong-headedness. While Molson harboured no enmity towards his grandfather, he did not have confidence in Samuel's ability either to judge the worth of opportunities an entire ocean away or to tend to the fundamental matters of his inheritance. As he explained in a letter to his uncle Robinson on September 30, "I earnestly desire you to Assist Mr. Ashley (who I have equally informed of my Intentions) with my Grandfather & also in Executing the Business as I am well assured my Grandfather is a perfect stranger therein."

Molson was determined to engineer the settlement of his inheritance without having to return to Lincolnshire to do it in person.

As he revealed to his uncle in his undated autumn letter: "One Reason for my not returng to England is My Grandfather always complains [so much] of Scarcity of Money that I do not consider myself a proper person to settle with him, therefore have give Mr. Ashley & you, my power of Attorney to do that Business for me . . . if any thing goes contrary to your wishes you may have it in your power to interceed in my behalf; which I make no doubt but you will, as you always have done—hope you'l not find me ungrateful." But Molson would not be able to avoid Samuel's disapproval by contriving to eliminate him from the decision-making process. Samuel's authority was vested in him by Father John's will; he was to oversee the bequests to all the Molson children, until they were old enough to assume title to them.

Molson's letters were more than a little rash and contradictory, as well as premature. His friendly warning to his cousin John to prepare to relinquish the proportion of his inheritance buried in the estate of Thomas Molson came almost eighteen—and not, as he stated, twelve—months in advance of the settlement date. His instruction to remit the balance to Ashley "by Christmas" was surely misstated, for he wasn't entitled to the money until December 28, 1784, not Christmas 1783. In his defence, Molson may have been factoring in time for the transit of the letter when he wrote of giving twelve months' warning, and he may have had good reason for stating so early his intention to collect the money. A sum of £300 was the equivalent of £24,000 today, and liquidity could have been an issue with his cousin in land-rich, cash-poor Lincolnshire.

On the matter of power of attorney, he was unquestionably in a rush and a muddle. He stated he had given his uncle Robinson and Philip Ashley his power of attorney when in fact he had not and could not. By the time he wrote Ashley on August 21, it had begun to occur to him that replacing his grandfather with Ashley and Uncle Robinson might not be so straightforward. It might have to wait until he turned twenty-one and was no longer a minor:

I shall send you my Power of Attorney next Summer, to settle the whole of my affairs, & to remit me the Money, as soon as possible, after I am at Age, as I do not intend to return to England to Lose any time.

If there's any difficulty about the Power of Attorney, on account of my being under Age, I will send you another directly after I am which will be the 28th of December 84; or if the Power of Attorney be not to your mind, give your advice by Letter, which way you would have me proceed.

If you had any Correspondence in any of the United States, would thank you for a Letter of Introducement, as perhaps I may travel through some of them.

Should be glad to hear from you as soon as possible. . . .

John Molson was a young man in a hurry in a world that scarcely seemed familiar with movement.

Chapter 6

People are, in general, what they are made, by education and company, from fifteen to five and twenty; consider well, therefore, the importance of your next eight or nine years; your whole depends upon them.
—Lord Chesterfield, letter to his son, April 1, 1748

AFTER RECEIVING A LETTER from his uncle Robinson written August 10, 1783 (which has been lost), John Molson promised to write him with cost-of-living details for the colony. These he provided on September 30, reeling off an exhaustive list of market prices for barley, wheat, chicken, duck, partridge, hare, beef, veal, turkey, mutton, butter, cheese, eggs, powder sugar, British spirits and green tea, as well as the price of hiring carpenters and servants. The servant costs applied only to English ones. "Canadians are not near so high prised," he explained, "but the English have verry few of them."

Molson's general optimism encouraged him to make one of his few observations on his life in the new country: "I find nothing disagreeable here neither in the Summer or Winters, for in the Severest weather we do keep our Houses so Hot with stoves yet we very often strip in our Shirts, & when we travel (which is in a Cariole)* we rap our Selves up in furs that make it far more agreeable traveling here than in England in ye Winter season."

---

* *Cariole:* A one-horse carriage equipped with skis.

By then a new wrinkle had appeared in the short history of Thomas Loid's brewery, through an advertisement that appeared September 4 in the *Quebec Gazette*—an issue dominated by an address by the victorious George Washington:

BARLEY

Notice is hereby given to all persons who have any Barley to dispose of that by producing a sample thereof to Mr. Thomas Loid, or Mr. Levy Soloman, of Montreal, they may sell the same at a good price, according to quality, at any time during the course of the next eight months.

Quebec, August 23, 1783

This "Soloman" most certainly was Lucius Levy Solomon (or Solomans), one of the most energetic and diversified Montreal merchants in the first decades of British rule. Believed to have been born about 1730, Solomon had left the fur-trading post of Albany, New York, for Montreal soon after the town fell in 1760, making him one of the first contractors to service the British Army in Montreal. As a leading member of Montreal's small Jewish community, he helped found the Shearith Israel synagogue in 1768. When Loid took out his joint advertisement with him, Solomon was presiding over an increasingly elaborate operation on a large property containing several buildings north of rue St-Paul, between St-Nicolas and St-Pierre. A two-storey stone structure contained a bakery, part of which Solomon converted into a tobacco processing operation. In 1787, with the construction of a new three-storey stone building, he would diversify into the production of starch and hair powder, in addition to creating a bakery with two large ovens.

Solomon's enterprises were pertinent to Loid, because the ambitious merchant also had a grain mill that produced feed for the local beasts of burden (along with a stable that could board ten horses). Barley is a feed grain, not just a brewer's key ingredient, and both Solomon and Loid were sufficiently desperate to acquire some to place an advertisement together so late in the growing season.

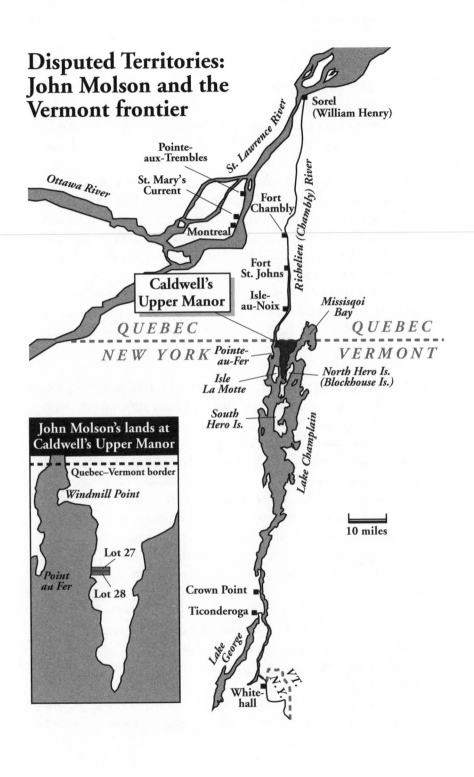

Disputed Territories: John Molson and the Vermont frontier

Ottawa River

St. Lawrence River

Sorel (William Henry)

Pointe-aux-Trembles

St. Mary's Current

Fort Chambly

Montreal

Richelieu (Chambly) River

Fort St. Johns

Caldwell's Upper Manor

Isle-au-Noix

Missisqoi Bay

QUEBEC

QUEBEC

NEW YORK

VERMONT

Pointe-au-Fer

Isle La Motte

North Hero Is. (Blockhouse Is.)

South Hero Is.

Lake Champlain

John Molson's lands at Caldwell's Upper Manor

Quebec–Vermont border

Windmill Point

Point au Fer

Lot 27

Lot 28

10 miles

Crown Point

Ticonderoga

Lake George

N.Y.

VT.

White-hall

A subsequent letter home by Molson would blame a wet harvest for the barley shortage, but a newly established brewer in Montreal like Loid faced a crisis of supply, no matter how good the weather. Local farmers were going to grow the barley he needed only if they were aware that he represented a reliable market. Loid and Solomon may also have been facing market forces beyond their control. The extended embargo on grain exports during the American Revolution had been abruptly removed by the colonial government in Quebec that June. The prosperous habitant farmers of the Richelieu River valley may have been shipping their harvests south into Vermont to fetch the best price, or perhaps they were storing it as a speculative measure.

One solution to the barley shortage was for Loid to grow his own. It may have been in concert with a move to secure the necessary land that, in the fall of 1783, Loid took on a business partner: twenty-year-old John Molson.

In September 1783, soon after the notice by Loid and Solomon appeared in the *Quebec Gazette*, John Molson joined forces with Loid in the fledgling brewery. No contract between them survives, but an account book detailing their joint expenses reveals their new partnership. The earliest dated entry is September 20, 1783, with Molson being credited for a draft on Gosling & Son of £88 18s. (This was the £80 draft Molson requested that summer of Ashley, which Molson appears to have sold at a discount of £8 18s. The discount was then added to the face value of the draft, to arrive at the total expense. Because Molson had sold the bill to Loid, who was his business partner, the discount was included in the ledgers to reflect Loid's profit.)

The first expense credited to Loid on the "contra" side of the ledger was incurred October 20: eight buttons, the cartage of a parcel to Pointe-aux-Trembles and "cash," for a total of 3s 1d. Before November was out, Loid was also being credited for such items as tobacco, a pair of mitts and a pair of "makinsons" (moccasins). The expenses were produced by three distinct yet interrelated activities: the farm Loid occupied, where Molson paid board and lodging of about three and a half pounds per month; the brewery at St. Mary's Current; and a block of land on Lake Champlain.

How much experience Loid had in brewing before going into business at St. Mary's Current is unknowable; how much experience Molson had before joining him is debatable. Loid had been employing a man named John Waite (or Wait) as a maltster, brewer and labourer at 57s 6d per month since at least January 13, 1783. He was probably the same John Waite who had arrived in New York from England around 1774 to lease 150 acres of farmland on the estate of John Johnson in Tryon County. Johnson fled to Canada in 1776 with about 170 of his mainly Scottish tenants, and purchased a farm near the brewery in St. Mary's suburb, but the Waites chose to stay and fight. According to John Waite's claim for relief, filed in Montreal in September 1783, two of his sons were in the King's Royal Regiment of New York—and a subsequent compensation claim filed by his widow in 1787 asserted that three sons and two sons-in-law had served on the British side.[1] Rebels burned the Waites out of their homestead in October 1781, and they escaped to Montreal. Considering Johnson's appointment as superintendent of Loyalist refugees, his former role as Waite's landlord and his proximity to Loid's brewery, he was a natural conduit for introducing Waite to Loid. Waite's claims for losses said nothing about brewing, but he is a good fit for the jack-of-all-trades whom Loid hired.[2]

That he had to pay for specific brewing expertise in such a small operation suggests that Loid lacked it himself, although brewing was so labour-intensive that he would have required assistance regardless of his own knowledge. As for Molson, the brewing craft unquestionably was practised in his family. A maintenance bill for Snake Hall in 1788 included a small repair to thatching on the roof of a "brewhouse" of unknown scale.[3] Rather than being a significant commercial operation, this outbuilding would have been a domestic brewery that required perhaps 100 to 144 square feet of work area and simple equipment to produce beer for household consumption. It's possible it produced enough to serve as a cottage industry for the manor house. Although Molson had left Snake Hall at age eight, after the death of his mother, he may have had more than a vestigial memory of the craft, as it was practised by at least one other family member. The will of his father's cousin John, who died in 1790, included the provision "Also I give and Bequest unto my said Wife Ann Molson . . . brewing Coppers Barrels and other brewing Utensils."

The little brewery at Snake Hall would have provided the staple beverage of the time, for people, as a health rule, avoided drinking water that hadn't been turned into some form of alcohol. Water was generally used only for cooking. Consuming alcohol rather than water that was potentially life-threatening (not to mention brackish, in the case of the Fen Lands) was understandable; but Britons consumed stupendous amounts of alcohol by modern standards—so much that one wonders how anything practical was ever accomplished, or just how sober were the minds that directed global warfare and enacted critical legislation.

Beer—not rum—was the standard drink on eighteenth-century British warships, and sailors (who also drank watered wine and spirits) were allotted a daily ration of one gallon of beer—the equivalent, today, of more than thirteen bottles of Molson Canadian lager. According to the historian N.A.M. Rodger, "The length of time a ship could stay at sea was effectively measured by how long her beer would last." Indeed, a fundamental reason the Pilgrims landed at Plymouth Rock, and not further south as planned, was that the *Mayflower* was running out of beer. As Molson entered the brewery business, it must be remembered that he was about to begin producing a staple good of his time, and not an exclusively recreational beverage.

John Molson had become involved in Thomas Loid's venture just as his second brewing season began. Molson was misleading his family about his activities in letters home, and he never reported his relationship with Loid or his own day-to-day activities in the brewery. Thomas Loid's brewery was the first, but far from the last, subject of evasion and omission for Molson in the new world.

On September 30, 1783, Molson informed his grandfather Samuel Elsdale of a plan to search far afield for agricultural opportunities. "On the Spring [I] shall take [a] tour [of] the United States

& if I find them a better place for to settle in, shall immediately do it; if not, shall return & fall on in good ernest, to clear & settle on. . . ." The continent must have seemed an absurd cornucopia of tillable soil to someone from a cramped island nation who was accustomed to fighting back seawater on reclaimed land. But whether Molson truly intended to search far and wide is debatable, as by then he was firmly associated with Loid—the bill of exchange had been sold to Loid ten days before the letter was written. On the same day he wrote Samuel Elsdale of his travel plans, Molson also composed his letter to his uncle Robinson. He revealed he had already secured four hundred acres in an area that had been attract-ing Loyalists for about seven years, only forty miles south of Montreal, at the north end of Lake Champlain. Without saying anything about Loid being involved, he described the property in letters to his uncle Robinson and Philip Ashley as "fine Rich Land" and "allowed by all Hands as good as any in America."

An advertisement placed in the *Quebec Gazette* of January 1, 1784, aimed largely at Loyalist émigrés, described the property that had caught John Molson's fancy in similarly praiseworthy terms:

> Whereas from the circumstances of the times, there is a proba-bility that many of the Loyalists, who, from principle as well as a laudable attachment to the Sovereign, are obliged to quit their native country, and would now incline to settle in the province:
>
> This is to give notice to all concerned, especially to those who wish to settle together in townships, that HENRY CALDWELL, Esq; of Belmont near Quebec, is possess'd of several large tracts of as good lands as any in this province, sufficient to settle some thousand families, which, from every motive, he is inclined to let out in grants for ever, on the most reasonable terms. . . .

These lands included an old seigneury that Caldwell had renamed Caldwell's Manor, and in the advertisement he pledged the land to be "of a very superior quality, on which there is a great deal of fine Oak timber, with Ash, Beech, Black Birch and Hickory, with large

Pine timber and Cedar, and little or no underwood. The river abounds with fish. . . . "

Molson had already acquired the block of land at Caldwell's Manor by the time the advertisement appeared in the *Quebec Gazette*. Much remains unspoken in this deal. Despite his assertions in letters home that this land was his, entries in the joint account book indicate that expenses in trips to Caldwell's Manor, and possibly for work performed there, were being shared by Molson and Loid. On January 30, 1784, Molson billed the partnership £13 for "Sundries Journeys from Montreal to Manor[,] Articles bought etc."[4] There were also various payments that could have been for services or goods at the Caldwell's Manor acreage. In their final accounting, Molson was credited with paying £4 to "Everard Ostrander as per Order," and Loid was credited with five shillings for "Ostrander & others for board & Liquor." The Ostranders were a family known to be living along the New York shore of Lake Champlain, and one of them could have found his way over to Caldwell's Manor. Molson's "Everard" Ostrander may have been Evert Ostrander, who had served in the King's Loyal Rangers.[5]

Given his pattern of evasion, Molson's assertions in letters home that the Lake Champlain property belonged to him may have omitted the fact that it also belonged to Loid, just as the brewery that he said in letters belonged to Loid also belonged to Molson—if not as real property, at least as an operating venture. But while the acquisition of the Caldwell's Manor land makes sense as the brewery's solution to a chronic barley shortage, it's not clear the land was actually a joint venture. No rental payments, for example, were ever specifically entered in their account book, and while they could have been made from various cash draws, it would have been unusual not to enter an itemized payment. It's possible that at least some of the charges in the joint account were the result of doing business at the Manor, and had nothing to do with land there. The brewery could have been selling its product to the seigneury's Loyalists. Molson was buying grain for the brewery, and some of it could have come from the Manor.

Who owned the land at the beginning of the partnership is open to debate, but at the end of it, when the joint account was settled on March 2, 1785, Molson unequivocally considered it to be his. He wrote on the account summary that he turned over a demand note to Loid for £9 2s 10d "on his relinquishing all Manner of Claim on the Lotts No. 27 & 28, as per McCarthy Survey on siad [sic] Lands." Jeremiah McCarthy (we know from the advertisement in the January 1, 1784, *Quebec Gazette*) was Henry Caldwell's surveyor at the Manor. The lots in question were two hundred acres each, and account for Molson's assertions in 1783 that he had acquired four hundred acres at Lake Champlain.

Twelve days after Molson wrote his uncle Robinson of the newly acquired property, a copy of a covenant between Henry Caldwell and a land agent named James McGlemoyl (or M'Glemoyl) was sent to Thomas Loid. The document passed into the possession of Molson, who noted on it that it came from "Mr. Loids Letters whilst I stayd at Point au Traumble," which suggests that Loid was the prime mover on the Caldwell's Manor front. The covenant between Caldwell and McGlemoyl also suggests that Loid had come to learn of the Caldwell's Manor opportunity through Loyalist connections that he would have made when travelling through Vermont to Montreal in 1781–82.[6]

The covenant identifies McGlemoyl as an agent representing 119 people then located at Danby and Bennington in southwestern Vermont. Caldwell agreed to allow "M'Glemoyl and the above mentioned [119] persons with any others that the said M'Glemoyl shall recommend to settle upon his lands on the South Side of Latitude 45. . . ."

The covenant terms detail how Caldwell's Manor was still operating as a seigneury. Working seigneurial land was far from serfdom, for the tenant enjoyed long-term title to his land that could be bought and sold. The tenants paid rent and provided grain for the seigneur's mills, and in return the seigneur was obliged to build the mill and provide other facilities such as schools and churches. The October 12 covenant reveals that settlers were to pay an annual rent of one guinea per hundred-acre lot. No one but Caldwell was permitted to build a mill, and to this "Manor Mill" his tenants were to pay a toll of one-fourteenth of their harvest.

The rent Molson (or Molson and Loid) paid for four hundred acres should have been four guineas (or £4 4s sterling) per year, had it been arranged through McGlemoyl. But on September 30, 1783, when Molson wrote Philip Ashley and his uncle Robinson, he informed both that the rental rate was thirty shillings per hundred acres. That was about fifty percent higher than the rate Caldwell was permitting McGlemoyl to offer to the Loyalists in Vermont less than two weeks later.

It was not the perfect find for Molson, as it left him a tenant (or co-tenant, if Loid was involved), not a freehold landowner, which he apparently understood, despite his use of the term "purchase." This may have been why he was still considering embarking on a grand tour of the United States. As he added in the margin of his letter to his uncle, "I intend going into the United States in the Spring & if there is probability of doing better for myself, shall settle there, if not, I shall return & begin to clear and cultivate the Land I have already purchased. The Land here is worth about 3L per Acre clear, fit for meadow or arable." Outright purchase of cleared freehold land thus would have cost him £1,200 for the equivalent to the acreage he was leasing at Caldwell's Manor for £6 per year. Molson may have coveted freehold property, but purchasing made no sense when he could lease the same amount of land from Caldwell for two hundred years before reaching the freehold price.

With his letter to Philip Ashley in August 1783, John Molson had formally stated his intention to liquidate his inheritance of Snake Hall and other properties and invest the proceeds in the new world. He was keeping his options wide open, however, as he went from working with the Gibbins in butchering to cooperating with Loid in brewing beer. Renting land at Lake Champlain either widened his options or focused them more tightly on brewing, depending on how one reads his need for the property and its actual ownership. His circumstances were about to be made even more turbid by a traumatic turn of events in his family. But to begin unravelling the critical years from 1783 to 1786, we must first meet his Lake Champlain landlord, Henry Caldwell.

Molson had secured tenancy on the old Foucault seigneury from one of the most prominent, influential and controversial figures in Quebec's colonial history under English rule. Henry Caldwell was the second person in Molson's life to be immortalized in fiction. His uncle Robinson wouldn't become Marryat's Captain Elrington until 1846, but Caldwell had already been cast as Captain Edward "Ned" Rivers in Frances Brooke's 1769 novel *The History of Emily Montague*.

Life in the company of Henry Caldwell and his principal adversary, Ira Allen, would prove to be almost stranger than fiction for John Molson, as the young émigré's decision to lease the Foucault land unwittingly placed him in the midst of one of the most protracted—and at times violent—struggles over private property and political destiny in colonial America. The land did not come complete with angry, dispossessed natives, but Molson could not have chosen a more contentious piece of real estate in which to invest in all of the settled continent. The overlapping claims of political sovereignty and private ownership encapsulated perfectly the untidy history of the colonies in the mid- to late-eighteenth century. The property known as Caldwell's Manor—and the struggle over its destiny—proved fundamental to the futures of Molson, Loid and the Gibbins men.

Henry Caldwell was born about 1735, possibly 1737,[7] in Ireland, the son of Sir John Caldwell, who secured him an ensignship in the British Army's 24th Regiment of Foot in September 1756, at the dawn of the Seven Years War.[8] In April 1758, with Caldwell now a lieutenant, his second division was turned into a new regiment, the 69th, which by strange coincidence would become the South Lincolnshire regiment in 1782, just as John Molson departed Moulton for Montreal. After the capture of Louisbourg in 1758, Caldwell caught the eye of senior officers. Elevated to captain, he was attached to the staff of General James Wolfe at the Battle of the Plains of Abraham.

His charisma promoted him further in fiction than in real life. While he wouldn't achieve a major's rank in America until 1772, when he was about thirty-five, Frances Brooke made him a full colonel at twenty-seven, when she cast him as the romantic lead in her 1769 novel. Caldwell was the very model of the dashing British officer. As Ned Rivers, he is bent on conquering the ladyfolk of Quebec, when he receives a letter from his friend James Temple, who writes:

> Indeed! gone to people the wilds of America, Ned, and multiply the human face divine? tis a project worthy a tall handsome colonel of twenty seven: let me see; five feet, eleven inches, well made, with fine teeth, speaking eyes, a military air, and the look of a man of fashion: spirit, generosity, a good under-standing, some knowledge, an easy address, a compassionate heart, a strong inclination for the ladies, and in short every quality a gentleman could have: excellent all these for colo-nization: prenez garde, mes cheres dames. You have nothing against you, Ned, but your modesty; a very useless virtue on French ground, or indeed on any ground. . . .

Caldwell retired from the army in March 1774, and promptly made a deal for James Murray's Quebec properties. Murray had commanded the left flank of Wolfe's army on the Plains of Abraham, and was named governor of Quebec after the colony capitulated in 1760. Recalled under a political cloud in 1766, Murray never returned to the province; his term as governor for-mally ended in absentia in 1768 with his replacement by another Plains of Abraham veteran, Guy Carleton.

Murray had assembled a real-estate portfolio that included a house in Ste-Foy, in the suburbs to the west of Quebec City's citadel walls, and several seigneuries. One of them was the Foucault seigneury. Its history as a legal tract began with the seigneury assem-bled by François Foucault from his own initial grant of 1733 (not 1740, as Caldwell stated in the covenant with McGlemoyl); this was augmented by neighbouring seigneuries acquired by him in

1743 and 1744.[9] After Quebec became a British colony, Foucault, who lived in Quebec City, turned the seigneury over to Murray in a quit claim deed for £750.

On April 7, 1774, on the eve of passage of the Quebec Act, which would uphold the seigneurial system (it entered the House of Lords on May 2, and passed in the House of Commons in mid-June), Caldwell struck a complex lease-purchase agreement for all of Murray's Quebec properties.[10] Because he was leasing the land, Caldwell himself could not sell it, but he was permitted under the agreement to sublet it. Thus, any assertions by Caldwell that he owned the land outright were false—but in his covenant with agent James McGlemoyl, Caldwell nonetheless asserted, "By title the above lands is by Purchase from General Murray who Purchased from Messrs Foucault who possessed them by Grant from the french King in the year 1740." And any assertion by Caldwell that he could give title to lots from these properties was therefore also false, at least until he himself owned them outright and the seigneurial system (under which all existing Quebec townships were organized) was abolished.

Nevertheless, Henry Caldwell would consistently suggest he could grant clear title. In addition to promising "to give titles to those who are already settled there" (January 1, 1784) and more ambiguously "to let out in grants for ever" (March 4, 1784) in his *Quebec Gazette* advertisements, Caldwell in his covenant with James McGlemoyl stated that he "Doth hereby agree to give the said Settlers Titles & Grants of their Lands forever after they are laid out by his Surveyor or any other Surveyor of knowledge & experience in his possession, provided those settlers are actually residing on their Lands in a year and one day from the date hereof." Caldwell was pitching the merits of his land in the midst of Loyalist unrest about a seigneurial system that denied them clear title. The colonies of Nova Scotia and Cape Breton were free of the feudal system that frustrated the newcomers, and settlement pressure on what would become Upper Canada (and then Ontario) had already begun. Caldwell was promising what he substantially could not deliver.

However, newcomers like John Molson had been prepared for the complexity of the quasi-ownership of seigneurial land by the land-title system back in England. There was still a feudal flavour to property, with owners required to secure tenancy with the lord of the manor (and pay a requisite rent). In the case of John Molson's area of south Lincolnshire, the lord was the baronet Sir Sampson Gideon. After the conquest, the British considered making Quebec a facsimile of England, with a landed gentry complete with hereditary titles who would occupy a House of Lords in the local government. The plan was never carried out, but it would have made the purchasers of seigneuries the new world's equivalent of Sir Sampson. As it stood, the continuing seigneurial system created de facto lords of the manor—hence the renaming of the old Foucault seigneury "Caldwell's Manor." Only in the American colonies, where there was no landed gentry, did true freehold property exist. It was this luxury that Loyalists were accustomed to—and so desired—as they fled the revolution.

About five weeks after Caldwell acquired the Murray properties, he married Ann Hamilton (sister of the bishop of Ossary) in Dublin, and headed for Ste-Foy to begin life as a prosperous landlord, mill operator and speculator. The American Revolution made an untimely intervention; when Benedict Arnold arrived to lay siege to Quebec City in November 1775, he commandeered Caldwell's Ste-Foy home as his headquarters, and in retreat he torched it, destroying its contents.

Although his home was in cinders, Caldwell ultimately profited. Acting with the rank of lieutenant-colonel, Caldwell was instrumental in repulsing Brigadier General Richard Montgomery's attack on the citadel in a snowstorm on the night of December 30/31. He was chosen to carry the dispatches to London, announcing the successful thwarting of the American siege (which cost Montgomery his life), and his performance in the field earned him a five-hundred-guinea bonus. In May 1776 he was appointed to the colony's legislative council, where he became a close associate of Frederick Haldimand, the new governor in 1778. In 1784, Haldimand appointed him deputy receiver-general. When Quebec was divided into Upper and Lower Canada in 1791, Caldwell was named to Lower Canada's legislative council, and held the position until his death.

During and after the revolution, Caldwell continued to increase his property holdings, becoming one of Quebec's largest owners of saw and flour mills. In 1794 he was named the province's receiver-general, and held the post until 1808, when he turned it over to his son, John.

But Caldwell was too charming by half, for he was also a crook, a spectacular embezzler who got away with his looting. Only after his death, in 1810, was it discovered that he had used his power as receiver-general to siphon almost £40,000 from the Crown, and as treasurer of the Jesuit Estates to help himself to nearly £8,000.[11]

The seigneury of Lauson, which lay along the Chaudière River just north of Quebec City, would prove to be Caldwell's most lucrative property, but initially the Foucault seigneury held the most promise. It was positioned perfectly to attract Loyalist settlers streaming north from the rebellious American colonies. While Caldwell's efforts to develop it would be stymied by imperial orders discouraging the settlement of border areas, it was initially a hub of Loyalist relocation, which made much of Quebec's Eastern Townships predominantly anglophone.

The seigneury was, strategically if not agriculturally, prime real estate. Ever since Samuel de Champlain led a Montagnais war party against an Iroquois stronghold on the west shore of Lake Champlain at present-day Crown Point in 1609, the Lake Champlain–Hudson River Valley corridor had played a prominent role in colonial geopolitics. The corridor ran north-south between the crucial Atlantic port of New York and the St. Lawrence River. At Albany, near the headwaters of the Hudson, the westward-flowing Mohawk provided a vital east-west corridor across New York State, which in turn allowed access by water and land to the Great Lakes of Erie and Ontario.

About twenty-five miles north of the headwaters of the Hudson was the south shore of Lake Champlain, which drained northward through the Richelieu (or Chambly) River into the St. Lawrence at

Sorel, forty miles downriver from Montreal. The nature of the watershed placed settlers around Lake Champlain, regardless of their politics or nationality, under the economic sway of Montreal. Travellers coming north could journey down the Richelieu River to the British garrison town of Fort St. Johns (the old French Fort St-Jean, now St-Jean-sur-Richelieu) and board a stage for Montreal, or carry on down the Richelieu, running its rapids in a bateau, to reach Sorel, and from there make their way down the St. Lawrence to Quebec City.

The northern extreme of Lake Champlain was divided by a peninsula known as the Missisquoi Tongue. To the east of the peninsula was Missisquoi Bay, a navigational dead end. To the west, the lake emptied north through the Richelieu. This peninsula, overseeing all of Lake Champlain to the south and forming the east shore of the beginning of the Richelieu, fell within the boundaries of the Foucault seigneury.

The seigneury stretched some twenty miles along the east bank of the Richelieu, south into Lake Champlain and west to Missisquoi Bay, encompassing the entire peninsula. For all its strategic importance, however, the peninsula's land was not uniformly suitable for farming. It had originally been part of a seigneury belonging to a Monsieur De l'Isle, who relinquished it to Foucault "at once through the Bad Quality of the Land, among which there is some that may be cultivated, all the remainder being without depth and full of large stones and rocks."[12]

Abandoned after being sacked by English invaders and their native allies in King George's War of 1744–48, the Foucault seigneury appears to have been still unsettled when Caldwell leased it from Murray and, promoting it as Caldwell's Manor, began welcoming Loyalist refugees. In addition to rebuilding a decrepit French mill, Caldwell also helped erect a church and established a manor house. Based on land-compensation claim records, the first Loyalists arrived in 1776, making Molson (and possibly Loid) a latecomer in 1783.

Molson's adjoining lots were superbly placed and probably worth the rent charge, though it exceeded the rates of the McGlemoyl–Caldwell covenant. But they were also part of the

23,000 acres within the 41,000-acre settlement that were known as Caldwell's Upper Manor, which lay south of the forty-fifth parallel, within the boundaries of the republic of Vermont. The lots were on the west side of the Missisquoi Tongue, fronting on Lake Champlain at the southern extreme of Windmill Bay.[13] Pointe-au-Fer, directly across the lake, was home to a British garrison guarding the approaches to the Richelieu; the garrison continued to operate in defiance of the 1783 peace treaty that placed the point well within American territory. For that matter, the British Army still maintained a presence at Blockhouse Island (later North Hero Island), south of the Tongue, and its naval vessels continued to patrol Lake Champlain, using Windmill Bay as an anchorage.

In addition to having invested in lands that fell outside Quebec, Molson had also selected them after a disturbing development: more than two years earlier, the governor of Vermont had granted to Ira Allen and twenty-three associates the very lands Molson was subletting from Caldwell.

To understand the very large mess in which Molson had landed, and from which he would spend several years trying to extricate himself, one must also understand the troubled evolution of Vermont. At the time Molson secured the land at Caldwell's Manor, Vermont was a rogue state that had played a vital if shadowy role in the American Revolution. Not part of the rebel union, it had declared itself an independent republic in 1777.

Vermont was a land-rush gone amok. After being appointed governor of New Hampshire in 1741, Benning Wentworth embarked on the road to personal fortune by selling land across the state's western border, the Connecticut River, in the virgin territory surrounding the Green Mountains (from the French *vert* and *mont*, hence Vermont). These lands, eagerly scooped up by speculators and homesteaders alike, stretched westward to the shores of Lake Champlain and the western slopes of the Green Mountains above Connecticut. Neighbouring New York objected to what it considered an incursion on its territory, as it claimed all of the grant lands east to the Connecticut River as its own, based on a 1764 privy council order. A succession of New York governors, ignoring a 1767 cease-and-desist order issued by the Crown on grants in the disputed territories, began selling land titles as well. Lord Dunmore, who arrived in late 1770 to serve as New York's governor, wasted little time feathering his own nest with grants overlapping those already issued by New Hampshire. Between October 1770 and July 1771, Lord Dunmore turned over about 450,000 acres to speculators.

The dispute over land ownership became a shooting war. Vigilante Vermonters formed a militia known as the Green Mountain Boys to resist incursions by "Yorker" sheriffs and their posses, who were determined to uphold New York grants by evicting and/or arresting homesteaders who had settled on grants previously issued by New Hampshire. Central to the struggle was the mercurial Ethan Allen, brother of Ira, who had moved to the so-called New Hampshire Grants with his family from Connecticut, to both speculate in land and homestead.[14]

In addition to violently resisting New York authority, Ethan Allen helped organize Vermont politically. And when the revolution broke out in 1775, it could be (and was) argued that Vermonters with New Hampshire land grants had a greater argument with New York than they did with Britain. Many farmers, in fact, saw the Crown's authority as their saviour in the land war against New York. While Vermont had no formal standing as a colony—and was not officially part of the rebel union—geography ensured that it was one of the most militarily vital parts of the colonial uprising. The key to controlling the transportation and communications corridor running south from the St. Lawrence was the elongated Lake Champlain, which formed the upper half of breakaway Vermont's western border. In 1776 the British hammered together a small navy just to control the lake. It was up to Vermonters to decide which side, if any, they would take in the cause of furthering their territorial legitimacy.

In the midst of internecine Yankee strife, with the Green Mountain Boys battling sheriffs' posses from New York, Ethan Allen and his armed followers cast their lot with the rebels. They had made a realpolitik decision: by aiding the rebel cause, the legitimacy of Vermont, and the illegitimacy of New York land grants in its territories, could also be won. Vermonters who thought siding with the Crown could achieve the same ends more efficiently were pursued ruthlessly by vigilante rebels, providing some of the first Loyalist arrivals at Caldwell's Manor.

Ethan Allen participated in the American invasion of Quebec in 1775 but was captured in a rash assault he mounted on Montreal in September with Major John Brown, in advance of the main invasion force. Shipped to England, Allen was retrieved in a prisoner exchange in 1778.[15] By the time he was back in America, Vermont had declared its independence. The refusal of Congress to admit it to the union, mainly because of vociferous New York objections, pressed Vermont into a position of neutrality. Ira Allen had been poised to join in the rebels' attack on Burgoyne's troops at Saratoga, New York, with a regiment he had raised. Now Vermont's Committee of Public Safety ordered him and his men to remain within the state's borders. Vermont drew up a proper constitution under Governor Thomas Chittenden, but Congress remained cool to its aspirations.

Vermont's strategists, with the Allen brothers at the forefront, began to play a dangerous game over ultimate fidelity. Perhaps, if Congress wouldn't have it, Vermont should side with Britain. In the spring of 1779, under orders from the colonial secretary, Lord Germain, General Haldimand began to explore an alliance with breakaway Vermont under the cover of prisoner-exchange negotiations between Guy Carleton, Britain's commander-in-chief in New York, and Ira Allen. Talks began in 1780 and continued right until the peace treaty of 1783, after which Haldimand broke them off for fear of interfering in the internal affairs of the United States, now a recognized sovereign nation. The Vermonters, however, would persist in courting the British with flattering proposals of status for the republic as a British province. Haldimand was not blind to Green Mountain duplicity. In June 1780, Governor Chittenden had secured Ira Allen as one of his commissioners to press Congress for Vermont's recognition, even as Allen was conducting secret talks to swing Vermont over to Britain.[16] According to A.L. Burt, "Everything [Haldimand] could learn about the Vermonters led him to regard them as 'profligate banditti,' and he developed a shrewd suspicion of their double game."[17]

Whether or not Vermont was a legitimate political entity, there was no question that more than half of Caldwell's Manor did not fall within Quebec. The Quebec Act of 1774 had reaffirmed the forty-fifth parallel as the dividing line east of the St. Lawrence River between Quebec and the territories of neighbouring colonies. The parallel did not quite exclude Lake Champlain from Quebec: the approaches to the Richelieu and the upper four miles of Missisquoi Bay were above it. But the peninsula between them, encompassed by the old Foucault seigneury, extended below it. Descriptions of the border in Congressional battles over Vermont's legitimacy were explicit in lopping off the small peninsula from Quebec's territory. In a resolution tabled on March 1, 1782, the Vermont border was described as running "along the waters of Lake Champlain to latitude forty-five degrees north, including a neck of land between the Missiskoy bay and the waters of Lake Champlain." It didn't matter to Congress that the 23,000 acres of this "neck of land" were accessible overland only from Quebec.

For Caldwell, the border would not have been a problem if whatever political entity controlling the Missisquoi Tongue remained within the British Empire and recognized the chain of possession from the French Crown to Foucault to Murray to him. But once the Tongue became part of a breakaway state that was busy making its own land grants (and disputing the overlapping grants made by the two neighbouring states), he was in danger of losing his control over it. And anyone who sublet property from him risked eviction. While Caldwell's advertisements in the *Quebec Gazette* of 1784 avoided mentioning that available lands were below the forty-fifth parallel—which would have been a profound disincentive to a Loyalist—this was plainly stated in the covenant with McGlemoyl in 1783. In light of Ira Allen's claim, Caldwell's efforts to settle the portion of Caldwell's Manor below the forty-fifth parallel were a ploy to establish title by force of occupancy. Molson's four hundred acres made him a pawn in what would become a major border dispute.

Apparently, neither New York nor New Hampshire had made land grants for the peninsula when Caldwell leased it from Murray.

But then came the decision, in February 1781, by Vermont's Governor Chittenden, to grant a township to Ira Allen and his associates, called Alburgh (or Alburg) in tribute to the lobbyist/warrior/diplomat, as payment for his ongoing efforts before Congress and the secret negotiations with Haldimand. There were sixty-five original grantees, including Allen, all speculators from Vermont, New Hampshire, New York, Massachusetts and Connecticut, with average holdings of seventy-five acres each. None ever actually settled on his property, in part because Caldwell was settling it first, and the area was under British military control. Between 1781 and 1785, Ira Allen bought up fifty-eight of the sixty-four rights granted to his associates in the original charter, for mere pennies each. But the matter of who owned the peninsula was further complicated by the fact that some of Allen's original associates sold their rights more than once, creating yet another layer of conflicting claims.

Ira Allen

How much time and energy Molson devoted to the disputed property is unclear. The joint account with Loid indicates that there were visits to Caldwell's Manor, and expenditures suggest the possibility of a homesteading effort. Molson's will of March 1785 referred not only to the lands at Caldwell's Manor but also "improvements" thereon. The Montreal diarist Jedidiah Hubbell Dorwin, who became a neighbour of Molson's in St. Mary's suburb, wrote in 1817 that "after going into the State of Vermont for a year or two [Molson] finally settled down in Montreal." But even if Molson never came close to actually living at Caldwell's Manor, he unquestionably valued the property.

In letters home at least, the four hundred acres gave him something to write about while maintaining silence about his involvement with Loid in the brewery. Molson made particular choices about evasion in his communications. A land deal he thought appropriate to reveal, even though he was still a minor and not in control of his own inheritance. (And the fact that he was a minor suggests that Loid must have at least fronted for him in the land deal.) The size of the property certainly impressed his distant relatives; his sister Martha wrote asking for more details about his "estate" on Lake Champlain. While his family, descended from generations of yeomen, could be counted on to appreciate such a tract, Molson didn't have the nerve to mention a brewhouse to them. Either the enterprise itself, or the association with Loid, was too dangerous to reveal. His grandfather may have profoundly disapproved of Molson making a career out of alcohol, as Samuel Elsdale's obituary in *The Gentleman's Magazine* took care to point out that "he was never intoxicated with liquor." Molson felt he could justify requesting more money from his grandfather in the context of land acquisition, but mentioning any involvement in the brewery would get him cut off without a penny and ordered home.

With his statements about the Caldwell's Manor property and his plans to search for better opportunities in the United States camouflaging his increasing involvement in the brewery, Molson appeared to be preparing to take on a far more substantial role. In his September 30, 1783, letter to his uncle Robinson, Molson revealed he had petitioned his grandfather to send a letter of credit on "Finn & Ellis,"[18] or any other principal Canadian merchant or banker in London, as soon as possible "to the amount of L300 sterling payable the 1st of January 85 which will enable me to draw Money here just as I may have Occasion. . . . If my Grandfather cannot get the Money by the first of January 85 it must not exceed the Middle of March following, as it will be too late for these Merchants for to make their payments for that Year." And in his letter to Ashley that same day, Molson emphasized the importance of securing the sum, as it would allow him "to draw money here just as I may have Occasion, only allowing ye discount therefore—By that means my Grandfather will have no Money to advance till after I am at age. But as he is unacquaintd with the method of Obtaining Letters of Credit must beg the favor of you to do that for him."

Molson was also again pressing the issue of removing his grandfather from his supervisory role: "I could wish you to send me a Draft of such a [Power] of Attorney or other Instrument for me to Execute as you shall think necessary for the doing of my Business," he wrote Ashley. "For I cannot do without the *Money*." And he also wanted to be sure his cousin would be turning over his inheritance money from his late uncle Thomas's estate as soon as he turned twenty-one: "Be so kind as to ask Mr. John Molson if he has Rec'd a Letter from me to be in readiness to settle my Account with you or my Grandfather by Christmas 84. PS if not [acquaint] him of my designs. I do not apprehend my Grandfather can run any risk in advancing this Money as I have lived far within my Income since ye the death of my Mother."

In all, Molson was angling to have a large sum of money at his disposal as soon as he came of age, and for his cousin John to make a prompt settlement of inheritance monies, while attempting to arrange the legal means to prevent any interference from his grandfather. More than a year before he would turn twenty-one, Molson appeared to be planning to make a substantial investment—the modern equivalent of £24,000—in North America. It's possible he was thinking of buying freehold land somewhere, as a one-hundred-acre lot would cost precisely £300, at the price of £3 per acre he quoted in his letter to his uncle Robinson on September 30, 1783. But as events proved, Molson was soon on course for an outright purchase of the brewery.

Chapter 7

[A] wise man, without being a Stoic, considers, in all misfortunes that befall him, their best as well as their worst side; and everything has a better and a worse side. . . . I always made the best of the best, and never made bad worse, by fretting.
—Lord Chesterfield, letter to his son, April 27, 1759

THOMAS LOID HAD MADE a very modest effort in his first season of brewing in St. Mary's Current. Writing his uncle Robinson on October 23, 1783, John Molson revealed that Loid had made about fifty hogsheads of ale in 1782–83, which he sold at £7 Halifax or six guineas per hogshead.* If he sold every hogshead, his gross revenues were about £350 Halifax. But he also had to pay for all his ingredients and overheads, not to mention the labourer John Waite, whom he had hired in January 1783. It would soon be evident that Waite had hardly been paid at all. Loid also had not been able to charge nearly as much as he had hoped, based on the inflationary wartime economy, as John Molson's letter to his uncle Robinson in the autumn of 1782 had noted that Loid intended to reap £10 per hogshead.

Loid's solution had been to expand, erecting both a malthouse and brewhouse for the 1783–84 season, as Molson also observed in his letter: "Mr. Loid has now fully completed his Brew house & Malting. . . ." (A legal notice in August 1784 would describe the

---

* The guinea, an English gold coin last minted in 1813, was the equivalent of twenty-one English shillings. With twenty shillings in a pound, the guinea was worth slightly more than one English pound.

property as a lot "with a brew-house, and other buildings thereon erected.") Of course, he had also taken on a partner in Molson, which provided him with additional labour and a necessary cash infusion. (A wage settlement with John Waite, dated October 15, 1784, referred to "Loide and Mosen" and "Loide & Co.")

Having prepared for a more ambitious brewing effort, Loid and Molson were not prepared for a catastrophic shortage in their key brewing ingredient. Molson reported that Loid "has begun to Malt about a fortnight since, tho' I doubt he will not [sic] get Barley enough as we have had a verry wet Harvest. He intends to malt wheat if he cannot get Barley sufficient, which from the experiments he has already made seems to answer verry well."

Molson also observed that Loid was operating a tavern, but he said nothing about being involved in any of it.[1] His familiarity with the brewery's production and sales figures should have betrayed the fact that he had more than a passing acquaintance with it. In fact, Molson was buying all the grain in the new brewing season. His joint account with Loid indicates he paid for eighty bushels of wheat and six bushels of the scarce barley between November 27 and December 19. By the end of January 1784, Molson had contributed almost £45 to supplies for their joint activities, as well as the £80 bill of exchange.

At the same time, Molson was concerned at learning of several deaths within Robinson Elsdale's social circle. He had heard that Captain May "is dead in the W. Indies but hope it is not true. Your old Prentice Jim Brainsby was drowned in Lake Ontario about 3 Years ago, am informed he has 2 or 3 Years wages due, which if proper measures were taken it would be discovered."

The death of a man named Brainsby indicates the south Lincolnshire community's ties to North America predated the exploratory visit by William Haw, Thomas Loid and James Gibbins in 1781. This former apprentice of Elsdale's doubtless was related to the "John Brainsby of Cowbit Yeoman" who appeared in a lease agreement signed by John Molson's grandfather in 1731, as well as in several legal documents involving bonds signed by his great-grandfather around the same time. A 1727 Molson accounts document also included a man named John Brainby, churchwarden of Cowbit.

John Molson's mention of several years' back wages indicates that Brainsby (or Brainby) was serving in the British military, probably the Naval Department, when he drowned. The Naval Department, which oversaw British naval operations on Lake Champlain and the Great Lakes during the American Revolution, created a significant fleet on Lake Ontario, using a base at Carleton Island (where Lake Ontario empties into the St. Lawrence). There, on May 10, 1780, a twenty-two-gun brig-sloop, the *Ontario*, was launched. In the autumn of 1780, the new vessel assisted a reprisal raid on upstate New York by Loyalist forces that included the King's Royal Rangers of New York, which were based at Carleton Island and commanded by Colonel John Johnson, who became John Molson's neighbour in St. Mary's Current.

The Loyalist forces burned an estimated 600,000 bushels of grain, thirteen grist mills, several sawmills and about one thousand barns and houses.[2] When the raiding was over, they retreated to Fort Niagara. Johnson's men and other units from Carleton Island waited for the *Ontario* to arrive to carry them home.

The *Ontario* never appeared, there or anywhere else. A ship's boat, some flotsam and a half-dozen bodies were later discovered along the south shore of the lake. Somewhere in the course of her passage to Fort Niagara, the *Ontario* had been overwhelmed by the tremendous hurricane of 1780. The storm sank forty French ships in Martinique and eleven British ships in the Caribbean on October 12, another fifty ships at Bermuda on October 18, and then veered inland at New England before plowing across Lake Ontario.[3] Circumstantial evidence strongly suggests that Jim Brainsby was one of between twenty-seven and forty sailors who were aboard her when the hurricane drove her under.[4]

But John Molson's comments on the recent deaths of May and Brainsby and the associated news of the lease of the Caldwell's Manor property were never read by his uncle. Nor did Robinson Elsdale ever learn of the progress with Thomas Loid's brewery. Elsdale had died on October 15, 1783, not yet thirty-nine, felled by a vague, lingering illness. Molson's life had just encountered a hurricane of its own. John's sister Martha wrote him to break the news of the loss of "the best and truest Friend we ever had."

Martha reported that Elsdale "lay'd ill abougth a Month of Nervous fever, was exceeding Sencable of his Death, and tooke a very Affecting leave of us all, and I send you his Blessing [and] a little of his Advice, he thought your Affairs could not be settled without you and I hope the innveates [possibly "invitations"] of your Sisters & Brothers will have some weight, we beg you will come and see both your and ours Affairs settled as we have no Friends on earth but you." Martha also revealed that their seventy-eight-year-old grandfather, Samuel Elsdale, was planning to marry again. He and Mary Albin (or Albon) were wed the following March.

Martha confirmed the loss of Captain May, who "has been dead a Twelfmonth he died of Putred fever at port Royal [in Jamaica]." In a rambling summary of social news, she conveyed more unhappy tidings in what became her trademark morbidity as a life of persistent misfortune unspooled for her: "My Uncle Clark [the husband of Father John's sister Martha] is dead . . . Mr. Horton is dead and left no will poor Mrs Horton is very much Distresst. Mr. Muse is dead. Mr. Grundy is dead. . . ."

Martha did not have the chance to mention the death of another old family friend in the letter, which reached her brother with relative speed on December 11. Only days after Martha sent word of Robinson Elsdale's death, the widow Alice Boulton (whom Martha had described as being "so infirm she a cant write") died, and it fell to John's older sister Mary, with whom the widow had been living, to convey this additional sad news in a letter dated January 19, 1784. Miss Boulton had left each of the Molson children £10 (about £800 today). The poverty of the estate, however, would delay any actual payment.

"Apeace in evening we oft talk about you," Mary related, "which she allways expressed a Great Desire to see You Once More at Moulton which poor Woman she had got into her head from what reason I know not that you would come over this December we have lost in her a Sincere Friend which my Dear Brother I am unhappy to say we have very few Left."

The news was catastrophic for John Molson. His uncle Robinson had been a valued mentor, and beyond the emotional devastation wrought by the deaths of his uncle and Alice Boulton, he faced a strategic disaster. Two of the three people he had been relying on to press his case with his grandfather were suddenly lost to him. Only Philip Ashley was left, and the attorney's inherent conservatism did not hold out much hope for bold arguments in Molson's favour. Ashley at best could expedite, but not finesse.

Since the summer, Molson had been striving to arrange his affairs so that he would not have to return to England to settle inheritance matters in person. Stripped of his most persuasive advocates, burdened by siblings who were begging him to come home and rescue them from uncertainty, he was torn between family duty and the opportunities before him. As much as he resisted acting, it would be clear that the two issues were not mutually exclusive. He could not build a future in North America without returning to south Lincolnshire to make the necessary repairs to his past.

For eight months in 1783, Iceland's Laki volcano was in continuous eruption, spewing fourteen cubic kilometres of material into the atmosphere. It was a smouldering, low-energy basaltic eruption, not a Krakatoa-like, silica-rich explosion, but volcanologists believe it created eighty times as much sulphuric acid aerosol as the modern Mount St. Helens blast did. Acid rain destroyed Iceland's crops; fluorine poisoned the grass and wiped out most of the livestock. The resulting famine killed about one-quarter of Icelanders.

The haze from Laki drifted as far east as Syria, and in North America it moved Benjamin Franklin to comment on its effects. The average temperature in the eastern United States for the winter of 1783–84 plunged 4.8°C below the 225-year average. The Laki eruption, whose atmospheric disruptions may have contributed to the poor barley harvest that forced the use of wheat at the brewery, ushered in an especially bitter winter for John Molson, who had to suffer enough with the news of his personal losses back in south Lincolnshire.

As he recalled for Philip Ashley in a May 1785 letter:

Amidst enjoying myself in my future Prospects in this Country there arrived two letters from some female hands, Seal with Black which made me dread the opening of them as it foretold some great alteration in Our family, my Conjectures were but too true. The Letters were from my Sisters informing me of the Death of two of the Greatest friends to the family; my Uncle Robinson Elsdale & Miss Boulton, its easier for you to Guess my Fealings than for me to describe 'em my Orphan Brothers & Sisters left almost to Hands of Providence without any Terestrial Parents except their Grandfather who is arrived at [the] State in Life that rather needs Assistance in his Worldly Affairs than be a father to advice [and] Cherish them in their present Situation.

The letters from his sisters moved him to draft a response. Although he expressed the hope that the souls of his uncle Robinson and Miss Boulton "may the Almighty take into his never ending Regions of Bliss," through the sheen of commiseration we can easily glimpse impatience and exasperation.

My Uncles Blessings give me infinite Satisfaction what a moving & affecting scene must it have been to see a loving Husband & father take his leave in this World of that Amiable Woman his Wife the little Boys & rest of his Relations & Friends. The verry thoughts of it make my Heart run over at my Eyes like a Child yet has received Correction the subject is too melancholy to treat of it more largely.

Dear Martha the Salutation of Brothers and Sisters who are so dear to me is a sufficient inducement to bring me over to the Eastern Side of ye Atlantic (this at ye greatest incon-venience) to see our afairs settled: But am sorry that Martha cannot find one friend in the world besides a Brother who is a distance of 3000 Miles — may ye same be a disgrace a People who call themselves Christians to see Orphans (which must be raised) without any Terestrial Relations but a Grandfather (who needs somebody to help him in his worldly affairs than to be a father to advise & cherish them in their present situation) left entirely to ye Hand of Providence, without giving the least of their Advice which cannot cost any thing but a little Trouble. But hope my Dear Martha you have been too rash in ye Sentence. As I cannot but think our family has some friends [remaining] as Yet. . . .

Having rebuked his siblings for not finding more support within Lincolnshire and for calling on him to make such an admittedly arduous journey, Molson turned his attention to his favourite subject: his own needs. "Am exceedingly sorry I have not Received a Line from Mr. P. Ashley as I wrote . . . Several Times to him & particularly desired it of him as a favour ([I] flatter myself he would have taken the trouble to have given me an Answer). Think his Letters must have miscarried as I wrote them at the same time as I wrote those Letters You Received."

He asked his sisters to "Give my most submissive duty to my Grandfather, for although we parted a little abruptly should consider it as your most unpardonable Crime to be neglectful of my duty to a Terestrial Parent, particularly where the love of Father, Mother & Grandfather is united as in him which may it ever be your Studies to oblige is ardent the wish of one who thinks himself your most Loving & Affectionate Brother." As heartfelt as those sentiments might have been, he was also lobbying for the continued goodwill of his grandfather after the grave miscalculation of the previous summer. With the loss of his uncle and Miss Boulton, it was now even less likely that he could circumvent his grandfather's authority in pursuing his plans in North America.

On February 26, 1784, his cousin John at last replied to his request, written the previous July, that he prepare to settle the portion of Father John's estate that had passed to him through our John's late uncle Thomas. Our John was told that he could "depend on having the Money due to you at the time you mentioned," including interest of £50 recorded by his father, Thomas, when he was our John's guardian. But his cousin also noted that there were "a Bill of 92L not recon'd for and a few more small matters" to be charged against his inheritance, and a sticking point of £100, which involved their fathers and about which Samuel Elsdale "rather makes a dispute." There did not seem to be much promise of an uncomplicated settlement, although cousin John wrote that he "should be glad to hear from you as soon as possible to know from you whether Mr. Ashley is to have the full power of Attorney: to settle between us or whether Mr. Elsdale your Grandfather is to have anything to do with it. I could be glad to have it settled right just between us without any dispute; and always keep friends."

Cousin John also revealed that the news of John Molson's Caldwell's Manor investment had travelled. Molson's grandfather, he wrote, "told me you have purchased 400 Acres of Land. I hope you'll send me the particulars of every thing and the Climate." He then expressed what must have been a widely held sentiment: that John should come home and make his life in south Lincolnshire. "I should be glad for you to settle at Moulton," he wrote, and added in a postscript, "Times are much better than they were when you left us," noting that labour was now cheaper.

Cousin John's invitation to Molson to provide more news on his life in the colony was duly ignored, as was Molson's sisters' eagerness for news. "The giving you a description of this Country by Letter, when I do [hope] Personally to see [you] shortly [I] think unnecessary," he allowed in his letter to Mary and Martha. But he would make no promises about when he would actually appear. He must have dreaded having to return, even beyond the matter of travel expenses, which he indicated to his sisters would require him to draw on Ashley for fifty or sixty pounds—the equivalent of £4,000 to £4,800 today. Once home, the pressure to remain in Lincolnshire likely would be ferocious. If the anticipated imprecations of his relatives to stay on their side of the Atlantic were not enough to discourage him from boarding the first available vessel back to England, he found other reasons to avoid the voyage. He stayed in Quebec for another year, striving to settle three compelling issues on two continents: his inheritance of the bulk of his late father's estate, his lease of the Caldwell's Manor property and the ownership of Thomas Loid's brewery.

While Molson was paying for wheat and barley over the winter of 1783–84, Loid (in addition to making unallocated cash contributions) had been spending money on domestic supplies. An initial shopping spree was accounted for in one entry, dated October 31, 1783: a barrel of pork, one hundred pounds of biscuit and one hundred pounds of flour, four axes and a spade, twenty-seven gallons of rum, a stove and lengths of chimney pipe, five hundred nails, two pounds of tea, twenty-eight pounds of sugar, a grinding stone, a frying pan, two kettles, some tins, a teapot, sixty-six pounds of butter, soap, candles, three padlocks and three files. An entry for Loid on January 31, 1784, detailed more supplies, including four panes of glass and frames, ten yards of cloth, overalls, "1 buckskin," a saw, pork, biscuit, another grinding stone, three axes and six loaves of bread.

These goods may have represented, at least in part, a homesteading effort at Caldwell's Manor. But within the expenditures can be found traces of a brewery. In addition to Molson's grain purchases, there were Loid's ten yards of cloth (possibly haircloth used in malting) and the grinding stones, which could have been meant for milling malt rather than sharpening axes and knives. Three loads of wood paid for by Molson in February 1784 would have been useful for making barrels, and Molson recorded a single payment of wages to John Waite on March 30. While there were no purchases of hops, Loid could already have received some before the partnership was formed—or they might not have been using hops at all in brewing a traditional ale.

Molson's purchases suggest he and Loid had been able to secure almost no barley, which makes it difficult to imagine what they were brewing that winter. While we know they were planning to make wheat beer, recipes generally call for almost equal measures of barley and wheat, and one German recipe specifies barley for seventy-five percent of the malt.

The barley shortage crushed Loid and Molson's brewery efforts over that bitterly cold winter. The partners also may have been devastated by the demobilization of the British military in the wake of peace. By January 1784, all of the provincial regiments around Montreal had been disbanded, likely erasing many brewery customers. Waite had been paid only once, and not enough at that.

The joint-account entry noted that Molson had given him three half Johannes, or slightly less than six pounds, but was "wanting 9 Guineas."

In June 1784, the brewing venture between Loid and Molson dramatically disintegrated. Molson sued Loid in the Court of Common Pleas of the District of Montreal for the stated debt of £150.

The suit filed by Molson against Loid ushered in several months of curious, even improbable, manoeuvres that were designed not to settle an alleged debt but to steer the brewery into Molson's hands and out of the reach of creditors. The suit apparently was conducted on friendly terms; Molson may have continued to live with Loid, and goodwill was evident long after the suit was settled. The process was probably rigged from the moment all parties gathered to hear Molson's case.

Loid's £150 debt was presented to the court as "so much Money lent him." It may have been based on the expenditures not yet credited to Molson in the joint account. Just before the suit was heard, they made an interim settlement of the account—the last credit to Molson being 2s 6d for butter on May 28. According to the ledgers, by this point Molson had spent £71 17s 6³/₄d and was trailing Loid by £14 12s 9¹/₄d, which was entered on Loid's side of the ledger as a credit. But there were three other major expenditures on Molson's part, which, for some reason, would not be entered in the joint-account's pages until later, even though they were given dates that preceded the interim settlement. One was the £80 bill of exchange sold by Molson to Loid in September 1783. The two other outstanding expenses totalled £79 4s 8d.[5] (Loid for his part would be credited after the interim settlement with expenditures of more than £189, all backdated to February 2, 1784.)

Molson and Loid's accounting was atrocious, and their motives virtually indecipherable, but perhaps the best explanation for the suit's stated debt, beyond it being an arbitrary fiction, is that Molson was adding up monies he had spent or contributed to the partnership but which, for some reason, had not yet been credited to him in the account ledgers. We have no idea how, or even if,

Molson and Loid shared revenues, or what mechanism they might have been using for Molson to acquire equity in the brewery. It may be that the Molson credits not yet entered in the books stood to be converted into equity. (In 1809, when he entered into a partnership to operate his first steamboat, his partners were permitted to convert the value of their wages into equity.) The two outstanding expenses, totalling £79 4s 8d, when combined with the bill of exchange's discounted sale of £71 2s, came to £150 6s 8d.[6]

Of course, this "debt," if based on Molson's unclaimed credits, overlooked entirely Loid's own considerable credits, which would be logged in the joint account, and in the final summary he would still show more credits than Molson. Thus, if the joint account was the source of the sum owed Molson in the suit against Loid, it was a fictitious obligation designed to give Molson the dominant claim to Loid's property. But as we shall see, there were still more curiosities in the joint accounts themselves.

The only other possible source for the debt was profits from the brewery that Loid had failed to share, but there was very little to go around after the winter of 1783–84. Molson's purchases of eighty bushels of wheat and six bushels of barley would only have made about eighteen hogsheads of wheat beer, perhaps more if they stretched the malt.[7] If used in a typical recipe, the six bushels of barley, combined with another six of wheat, would have produced only about three hogsheads of true wheat beer. A wheat-beer recipe, followed correctly, would have resulted in a distinctively hazy brew, owing to the proteins in the wheat malt. Despite Molson's assurances in his letter to his uncle Robinson that Loid's experiments with wheat had been successful, without sufficient barley they would, in reality, have been turning out a suspiciously murky concoction sure to offend most potential customers.

The wheat beer would not have commanded a top price. If they had been able to charge £5 per barrel, their maximum revenues would have been between £115 and £150. But the partners had not come close to selling their full production. At the subsequent auction of Loid's movables, exactly eighteen barrels (including two half-barrels) were sold, which coincidentally is all the beer that could have been brewed from Molson's grain purchases. But there were also sixty bushels[8] of what the movables inventory called "Blee germay" (*blé germé*), which indicates it was germinated (malted) but never brewed. Malted wheat increases in volume because it absorbs water during germination, but it can still be said that the malted wheat in the inventory was the equivalent of about three-quarters of the wheat that Molson purchased in 1783–84. Either Molson and Loid never actually brewed all of the wheat that Molson bought—which would suggest that at least some of the beer sold at the auction was left over from Loid's previous efforts—or Loid had built up a large inventory of malted wheat before Molson made his additional purchases in the joint account. In either case, a substantial amount of malt was never turned into beer.

The auction figures reveal a brewery that had experienced an utterly disastrous season: there wasn't enough barley to brew a proper wheat beer; a significant quantity of malted wheat never made it to the brewing stage; and most of the beer they did make had probably gone unsold. Saddled with unwanted inventory and minimal revenues, Molson and Loid appear to have abandoned their brewing efforts altogether. Thus, there could not have been enough unshared revenues to account for Loid's indebtedness to Molson.

A collusive chain of events stretched from the June 5 judgment against Loid to the final sale of the brewery property to Molson the following January. The main character on the judicial side of the process was Edward William Gray, the forty-one-year-old sheriff who was responsible for disposing of Loid's property and overseeing the disbursement of the proceeds. Gray, however, was also, at various times, a notary and an attorney. And from 1777 to 1788, he was a justice of the peace in Montreal. It's very possible he oversaw the entirety of Molson's case—ruling on the suit as a justice, and then seizing and auctioning off Loid's property as a sheriff.

Justices in colonial Quebec were seldom formally trained in law. Of forty-two active justices in Quebec between 1764 and 1787, only one was a lawyer and another a notary. In general, from 1764 to 1830, about forty to fifty percent of justices were merchants and another fifteen to twenty percent were landowners.[9] Of the twelve justices in Montreal at the time of Molson's suit, five were anglo-phone and three of those were prominent members of the North West Company: James Finlay, Benjamin Frobisher and James McGill. Gray was not one of the justices considered "active,"[10] but he had the vested authority to carry out the entire legal ruse that unfolded. Even if Gray was not the justice to rule on Molson's claim, Molson would have found friendly faces among the other justices, for Benjamin Frobisher's brother Joseph, and James McGill's brother John, would appear in Molson's brewery sales records in 1788 (and they too would serve as justices). With a civil system overseen by appointed judges who were drawn largely from the merchant and landowning ranks, Molson had every right to expect an accommodating response to the plan to convey the brewery to him.

As was generally the practice in England, justices in Quebec held court in their own homes. In October 1783, Gray had purchased a large property on rue Saint-Vincent in Montreal, and it is likely that the necessary parties met here to decide the case. Loid wasn't in attendance: he had granted power of attorney to a lawyer named Debonne. Molson may not have shown up either, as he was represented by James Walker. The thirty-year-old lawyer had been active locally since about 1780 and would secure a judicial appointment in 1790, serving mainly in Sorel from 1794 to 1811. He would also represent Montreal in the first elected assembly of Lower Canada, from 1792 to 1796. Further evidence that this was a friendly suit is the fact that on November 15, 1783, Thomas "Loyd" used Walker as his lawyer in successfully suing a man named Henry Bolton for £27 in unpaid board and lodging in the Court of Common Pleas.

No trial was necessary—one seldom was in these matters. Debonne "confessed the Said Sum to be Justly due." Loid was ordered to pay Molson the full amount plus suit costs of £5 2s 10d. Walker would have known his way around the compromised and easily manipulated process of the Quebec civil legal system. With Debonne agreeably capitulating, and Gray placing the official stamp on the proceedings, Walker could finesse the transfer of Loid's assets to Molson without risking their loss to another claimant.

Loid and Molson's main concern would have been Pierre Monarque, who held the mortgage on the property he sold to Loid. It was a debt that Loid had scarcely, if at all, addressed. But the threat that did emerge was posed instead by brewery employee John Waite, who was owed considerable back pay—more than £51—and appears to have launched a suit of his own against Loid and Molson. Under the province's civil law, a writ of *saisie* (seizure) could be used to impound the assets of a defendant in a suit over a debt before the case went to trial. Should Loid and Molson attempt to defend themselves against Waite's suit, the brewery could be taken from them until after the case was heard. At the least, if they bowed to Waite's claim, all of Loid's movables would have been auctioned off to satisfy it.

Broke and defeated, Loid was probably willing to give up the brewery. Molson wanted to persist with it, having more funds to invest once he gained control of his inheritance. With Walker's help and Gray's cooperation, Loid and Molson were able to satisfy Waite's claim and steer the brewery in Molson's direction.

And so the suit served two purposes. First, the so-called debt Loid owed Molson was the means by which his property was seized by the sheriff and kept away from anyone with a serious claim against it. Second, the auctions of Loid's assets would deliver the brewery safely into the hands of Molson, provided the sales were rigged and the principal counterclaimants were kept happy. The use of the auction process was especially important in this case, because it allowed the brewery property to be parked in Sheriff Gray's legal possession until Molson reached the age of majority and could bid for it himself. Until Molson turned twenty-one on December 28, 1784, he was unable to sign an indenture of sale.

The convoluted strategy may have been the best Molson and Loid could make of a bad situation. A straightforward sale of the brewery to Molson does appear to have been the initial strategy, explaining Molson's request in his letters to Uncle Robinson and Philip Ashley on September 30, 1783, to receive £300 in January 1785. Molson evidently had been planning well in advance to have a large sum of money in order to purchase the brewery soon after he

turned twenty-one. The amount he requested was probably roughly what the brewery operation was worth, based on combining the
outstanding £100 mortgage issued by Monarque, the £150 debt said
to be owed Molson by Loid and the potential value of the movables.

Molson's claim to his grandfather—that having one large sum in
January 1785 from which he could draw would be more convenient—
was a lame cover for his actual needs. Although he could not have
known his grandson's real intentions for the money, Grandfather
Samuel wasn't playing along. In a July 5, 1784, letter, Philip Ashley
reported that Molson's grandfather would honour a draw of only
£50 to £60—to pay for his voyage home. "But I cannot get leave to
consent to accept your Draw for so large a sum as 300L payable in
January 1785." If Molson wanted that kind of cash, he would have
to turn twenty-one first, receive his inheritance, and either mortgage the estate or sell it outright. The only money Samuel Elsdale
was prepared to advance was that required to ship Molson back to
Lincolnshire.

The course taken by Loid and Molson through the courts must
have been launched as a Plan B to the outright purchase of Plan A.
It explains why Molson was so anxious at not having heard from
Ashley when he wrote his sisters in early 1784. He couldn't be
bothered scribbling them a dutiful line or two about life in Quebec,
but he found the energy to spill a stream of ink about Ashley's failure to answer his mail. Because Ashley's response to the request for
£300 was not written until July 5, 1784, after the chain of legal
actions in Montreal had begun, the alternate strategy must have
been launched in the face of the brewery's genuine financial problems, with no known hope of funds arriving from Lincolnshire in
time to rescue the situation. Coincidentally, the same day that
Ashley wrote Molson of Grandfather Samuel's refusal, Sheriff Gray
held the auction of Loid's movables to address the claims of both
Molson and Waite. At this point, Molson was the primary
claimant, his so-called debt being about triple that of Waite.

With Loid declining to contest Molson's and Waite's actions,
custom prescribed that he first be given an opportunity to make
amends before his property was seized. It was impossible for Loid to

come up with more than £150 for Molson alone—and in any event, the scheme never expected him to do so. Thus the next step had been to seize Loid's movables for auction. Gray was issued the order (presumably by himself) to seize the movables on June 22, and he did so the following day.

An inventory of all of Loid's assets, both the movables and the brewery property (which had not yet been seized), was prepared on June 29 and signed by Jean Baptiste Flamand, Gray's clerk. Flamand's inventory indicated the movables had been seized to satisfy the claims of both Molson and Waite. The auction proceeds would be used first to satisfy Waite's claim. The sheriff would then determine if the brewery property would also have to be auctioned to satisfy all of Molson's claim. But everyone understood that seizure and auction of the property was the whole point of the lawsuit.

The movables auction, held July 5, was such a muddle that it reinforces the theory that the entire suit was an elaborate contrivance. Flamand produced an accounting of the auction on July 8, listing all items sold, with the buyers and winning bids, but the numbers would never add up. Flamand's sales tally amounted to £102 11s 13d. Yet Sheriff Gray's accounting of the monies collected on Molson's behalf indicated that the movables sale amounted to only £85 9s 8¹/₂d. And while Flamand's inventory of the items sold indicates Molson personally spent £10 10s 15d, Gray's November 29 statement deducted £15 17s 8¹/₂d for "goods bought at the sale" by Molson.

Auctions under Quebec's justice system did not necessarily unfold along predictable lines. They could be exploited to many ends. Friends of a debtor could turn out en masse and buy back his property from the sheriff—and return it to the debtor. A malicious prosecution over a debt could pack the auction with sympathizers who grossly underbid for all items, making the proceeds so low that they could not satisfy the debt for which they'd been seized.[11] In Loid's case, the auction was a matter conducted between friends, in collusion with the merchant-dominated judicial system, and most or all of the bidding was probably done on Molson's behalf.

Among the bidders was Molson's own lawyer, who spent thirty-five shillings on an odd assortment of items: three books, a tin cooking pot and tongs, and some porcelain plates. What need a prominent man like Walker would suddenly have felt for a second-hand tin pot is difficult to imagine. Walker's clerk, Flamand, also bought a number of items. About two-thirds of the auction proceeds were accounted for by one bidder, a Mr. Tourneau, whose identity is unknown but who was also probably fronting for Molson. Under his own name Molson bought five "Barils," or hogsheads of beer, for prices ranging from twenty-four to thirty-six shillings, as well as a table and some bottles.

Flamand's cramped script and eccentric French spelling make it challenging to identify every item in the sale, but Molson must not have been concerned about losing any important brewing equipment if the beer, the table and the bottles were all he bought at the auction. The principal brewing equipment would have been considered part of the immovables. In any event, Molson probably ended up with most or all of the items sold, regardless of who actually bid for them.

As part of the order to seize the movables, Gray was required to prepare an audit for the Court of Common Pleas on October 23. This statement, as well as the one prepared for Walker on November 29, confirms that Waite's claim for back wages had been satisfied from the proceeds of the sale. He had claimed £51 15s 10d for eighteen months' wages, dating from January 13, 1783, to July 13, 1784—eight days after the movables auction.[12] Why Waite should have been entitled to wages after the brewery ceased to be a going concern is unanswerable, but after deductions for various expenses shouldered on his behalf by Loid, Waite received £20 10d on October 15 and was sent on his way. He didn't enjoy the money for long—Waite died on January 31, 1785, according to the records of Christ Church.

By Gray's accounting, which was submitted to Walker in the November 29 statement, after the deductions for his own fees and charges, Waite's wage settlement and Molson's own purchases, Molson was left with £43 8s 11d from the movables sale. This was turned over to Walker by Gray that day, to be given to Molson. It left him more than £100 short of having his claim against Loid satisfied. Gray had already published the announcement of the auction of the brewery property[13] on August 19, by displaying it on the door of the local church (he didn't say which one) for four consecutive Sundays, and by paying £2 10s to have this notice appear in the August 26 edition of the *Quebec Gazette*:

> By virtue of a Writ of Execution issued out of his Majesty's Court of Common Pleas for the said district [of Montreal], at the suit of John Molson, against the goods and chattels, lands and tenements of Thomas Pelgrave Loid, to me directed, I have seized and taken in execution, as belonging to the said Thomas Pelgrave Loid, a lot or piece of land, situate in St. Mary's suburbs, near the town of Montreal . . . with a brewhouse, and other buildings thereon erected: Now this is to give notice, that I shall expose the said premises to sale by public vendue, at my office in the city of Montreal, on Friday the thirty first day of December next, at eleven o'clock in the forenoon. . . .
>
> EDWd. Wm. GRAY, Sheriff

It's significant that Gray waited until the last day of the year for the property auction. It can be explained only by the fact that all parties wanted to postpone the auction until after Molson reached the age of majority on Monday, December 28. But Thursday, December 31, came and went without a sale, owing to "want of Buyers," according to the official court translation of the indenture of sale, as the auction was postponed one week to January 7. It was an odd explanation, as Molson was more than interested in buying the property. The idea that Sheriff Gray wished to wait for more bidders to appear is absurd. Molson was the ultimate beneficiary of the sale. It was being held to allow him to make a legal purchase of the property, now that the debt to Waite had been settled and Molson was old enough to bid for it. The reason for the postponement could have been something as mundane as bad weather. We don't know where Molson was living after May 1784, but because no further payments to Loid for room and board appeared in the joint accounts after the interim settlement, Molson could have gone to the Missisquoi. Impassable roads, then, might have delayed his arrival for the auction. It's also possible that the postponement was the result of a financing problem. Before he could complete the purchase, even at a rigged auction, Molson (through Sheriff Gray) had to settle two *oppositions*, or counterclaims, against the proceeds of the sale.

One *opposition* was filed by the Sulpicians, the seigneurs of the island of Montreal, who were owed *lods et vents* by Loid on the property. But the outstanding amount—£8 6s 8d—was not overwhelming, and Molson should have been able to settle this easily. Far more worrisome was the main *opposition*—that of Pierre Monarque, who was owed more than £108 in principal and interest for the mortgage granted to Loid in September 1782.

The process of transferring the brewery to Molson by using the civil courts and a rigged auction produced a bewildering flow of funds, with several hairpin turns. If Molson's suit had been a conventional one—that is, if Molson had been an arm's-length plaintiff legitimately owed money by Loid—then the brewery auction would have been fairly straightforward. Molson had already received about £43 from the immovables sale, leaving unsatisfied £112 of the judgment he had secured against Loid. When the movables auction was held, someone other than Molson likely would have been the purchaser. The sheriff would collect the bid funds and deduct the total costs of the two *oppositions* as well as his own costs and charges. The *opposition* filers would be reimbursed, and the remaining funds would be turned over to Molson.

But Molson was playing two roles in the brewery auction. He was both the purchaser and the beneficiary, the source of the funds that were to satisfy his own claim against Loid. Had there been no significant *oppositions*, the auction would have involved almost no actual money, because any funds he paid for the brewery, less the sheriff's fee, would have come right back to him as the beneficiary—and he would have owned the brewery as well. But this auction was complicated by the large sum represented by the *oppositions*.

When the "auction" finally went ahead on January 7, Molson agreed to pay £131 5s for the brewery property. He assumed the outstanding £100 mortgage on the property at six percent interest—and an initial reluctance on Monarque's part to grant the mortgage could have been the cause of the auction delay. But Molson was still short of the auction price. While the movables auction had delivered Molson more than £43 at the end of November, much or all of the bidding likely had been conducted on his behalf, and so it's possible no significant funds ever actually changed hands. It could have been a paper shuffle, with "purchased" items turned over to Molson. It isn't known how short he was of the purchase price for the brewery property, but he borrowed at least some of the necessary funds from James Walker.

After signing the mortgage agreement with Monarque on January 29, Molson spent several days earnestly trying to repay Walker for the bridge loan. "Another week is passed without anything being done towards settling the Acct between us," Molson wrote him on January 29. "I do most earnestly desire of you to make it convenient by tomorrow (Saturday 30th Instant) or Monday following at farthest—as time is more than expired. That I should have paid the money that [I] borowed settling with Sheriff."

Molson was acutely conscious of the effect an unsettled debt would have on his reputation, even though his attorney did not seem particularly concerned about the obligation. He reminded Walker how attention "ought to be payed to a person's word in Business & doubly so by a young man and a stranger entering into life without friends, or any person to speak a word in his favor. Mr. Walker duly considering these circumstances that I labor under at present, cannot but flatter myself; he'll endeavour to retrieve a young man's character (who himself Esteems is the greatest Acquisition Attainable)." This, in mangled form, was the wisdom of Chesterfield, for whom preservation of one's character was a relentless subject.[14]

On the following Monday, the last day of January, the indenture of sale was drawn up by Gray. It reported that Molson had been "the last and highest bidder" for the brewery property. The phrase would suggest Molson had competition at the January 7 sale, but this was probably either standard boilerplate or an outright fiction. Gray deducted from the sale price his costs and fees (£6 10s 7¹/₂d) and the distributions (£116 7s 13d) for the two *oppositions*, leaving £8 6s 3¹/₂d for Molson.

Molson now had only to settle with Loid their joint expenses. There's no good explanation for the mess that the joint-account ledgers were in. Both men were credited in the ledgers with far more spending after the interim settlement than before it, even though most of this subsequent spending was recorded in the ledgers as having actually occurred before the interim settlement.[15] Their accounting was so slipshod that they ended up with two irreconcilable sets of sums. In the summary that accounted for the spending logged after the interim settlement, Molson was credited with more than £180 in new credits. In the revised single-page summary that accounted for all spending since September 1783, Molson's credit was more than £234.[16] Based on the interim settlement, the difference in the totals should have been about £72; instead it was £54. Regardless of the inconsistency, Molson and Loid were able to make the figures agree that Loid's spending was ahead of Molson's by £9 2s 10d.

On March 2, as the account summaries recorded, Molson gave Loid a demand note for the amount of the difference. The note probably was used because Molson did not receive the net proceeds of the auction from Gray until March 25. But instead of calling the note, Loid chipped away at Molson's obligation by submitting expenses for him to pay, which Molson began to log anew in the joint account. That note, and the monies Molson continued to provide Loid against it, would resurface in the controversial fate of the Caldwell's Manor land.

It has long been suspected that the entire suit and auction process camouflaged a property swap, that Loid agreed to let Molson have the brewery in exchange for the lands at Caldwell's

Manor. But the account summary of their joint spending quashes any notion that Molson surrendered title. On the contrary, Molson specifically wrote at the end of the account summary that he agreed to turn over the demand note "on [Loid's] relinquishing all Manner of Claim" on the lots surveyed by McCarthy, which we know represented the four hundred acres at Caldwell's Manor. Loid did come to live on Molson's lands, and the credit Loid consumed against the demand note was dedicated largely to his relocation to Caldwell's Manor. It's not certain, however, that the lands Loid initially occupied on the Missisquoi were Molson's. He may have gone to live with James Gibbins or on some other property first. More than two years after the account between Molson and Loid was settled, Molson firmly believed that the four hundred acres were still his.

Any doubt that Loid and Molson were still on good terms is erased by the will Molson drew up one week after settling with Loid, as he prepared to return to Lincolnshire to settle his inheritance. He bequeathed to "my Friend Thomas Loid all my Interest & Improvements made on [a] Certain Tract of Land known by the name of the Tongue or Caldwell's Manor Situate in Vermont State"—and Molson chose to leave the brewery to James Gibbins Senior.

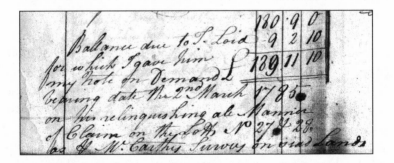

When John Molson and Thomas Loid settled their joint account on March 2, 1785, Molson agreed to pay Loid £9 2s 10d "on his relinquishing all Manner of Claim on the Lotts No. 27 & 28 as per McCarthy Survey on siad [sic] Lands." These lots represented Molson's four hundred acres at Caldwell's Manor. (Collection: The Molson Archives/National Archives of Canada)

But the circumstances surrounding the Caldwell's Manor property were becoming more convoluted. In early 1785, as Molson was assuming ownership of Thomas Loid's brewery and settling their joint account (with the provision that the four hundred acres were unequivocally his), Henry Caldwell was meeting with Ira Allen in an effort to determine who owned the peninsula lands known both as Caldwell's Upper Manor and Alburgh. The meeting was cordial, as might be expected of one between Quebec's deputy receiver-general and a state commissioner who had drawn a new assignment in late 1784: negotiating free trade between the province and his rogue state.

The two men must have met in Quebec while Allen was furthering the free-trade cause. On March 29, Caldwell wrote Governor Chittenden of Vermont to inform him that he and Allen

> had frequent conversations respecting my property to the Southward of this province, his Claim he tells me is founded on a late Grant from Vermont State in Consideration of his service & the Expences he has been at on Account of the State, that he had asked for that land in preference to any other from liking its Situation, & the goodness of the Soil, not Knowing any thing of my Claim to it, that however he is very willing to relinquish his Claim provided he gets an Equivalent from your State elsewhere, & I believe he is very well Satisfy'd of the justice of your Adopting that measure. . . .

Caldwell's letter was read before the Vermont General Assembly on June 14, and the matter was held over to the October session. But an alternative compensation for Allen could not be arranged, and the issue of the ownership of Caldwell's Upper Manor was doomed to drag on through the courts into the new century, with the dispute becoming increasingly heated. It's doubtful that Allen really was interested in giving up his claim to Caldwell's Upper Manor. Were his free-trade negotiations to prove successful, the Alburgh property would occupy a major trade corridor. The same day that Caldwell was writing to Governor Chittenden with the apparently misguided notion that Allen was willing to surrender Alburgh, Allen was writing Quebec's lieutenant-governor, Henry Hamilton, with the idea of having a road built from the border at the forty-fifth parallel to St. Johns (the British garrison town on the upper Richelieu) and a canal dug to bypass the Chambly rapids. As a landowner who could benefit directly from the transportation and trade initiatives, Allen could not have been seriously entertaining the notion of turning away from Caldwell's Upper Manor.

Molson met at least once with Ira Allen before departing Quebec for south Lincolnshire in the spring of 1785. And at some point, he also had heated words with Henry Caldwell at the Lake Champlain property, for in a letter sent to James Gibbins, Sr., while he was in England, Molson alluded to "our little altercation at the time he was up at the Lake." As he set out for England, more than eighteen months after learning of the death of his uncle Robinson, John Molson had no idea whether the four hundred acres were his. At least initially, Allen is believed to have attempted to settle civilly with Caldwell's tenants, and Molson would have had reasonable hope of coming to some arrangement with Allen, if the struggle swung in the Vermonter's favour.

In May 1785, Molson was in New York, waiting to depart for London aboard the *Triumph*. He was twenty-one now; he no longer had to answer to his grandfather or anyone else. He now owned a brewery, an estate in Lincolnshire, and—if the squabble between Henry Caldwell and Ira Allen could be settled favourably—four hundred acres of prime waterfront property at the north end of Lake Champlain. For all his apparent wealth, however, he had no money. He had been forced to draw on the Gosling account for a ten-guinea bill of exchange to pay his passage, which the ship's master, Jacob Stout, insisted be payable on sight—no standard grace of thirty days. Stout expected to be able to march into the Gosling office on Fleet Street in London and be given ten guineas upon presentation of the bill. Molson wrote Ashley on the eve of his departure from New York to warn him of the bill, trusting that the mail packet would beat him to London.

In July, with the *Triumph* anchored safely in the Thames, John Molson was back in England for the first time in three years, no longer a boy but a man in the eyes of the law. He had left in war and returned in a window of peace, which renewed hostilities between France and Britain would slam shut in 1793. It would be his last visit for twenty-five years.

Chapter 8

*Pleasure is the rock which most young people split upon; they
launch out with crowded sails in quest of it, but without a compass
to direct their course, or reason sufficient to steer the vessel; for
want of which, pain and shame, instead of pleasure, are the returns
of their voyage.*
—Lord Chesterfield, letter to his son, March 27, 1747

NO SOONER WAS JOHN MOLSON back in England than he was
hatching another scheme to advance his prosperity. He wrote an
acquaintance named John Wilson in Yorkshire on August 21, 1785,
outlining an unexpected development. "In respect to our buying a
Ship or Brig jointly (as we were talking) I remain firmly in the same
mind," Molson penned. "If you are inclined to purchase & willing
to accept me in the co-partnership [you] may rely on me to the
amount of £800 sterling—whether you have or not any Intentions
of purchasing (Ship or Brig) on accepting me in co-partnership
hope you'll not delay in giving me an Answer."

Where did this idea come from, and where did Molson think he
could raise £800 sterling—about £64,000 today? And how did he
imagine the brewery fitting into it all?

Molson must have intended to liquidate Snake Hall and his
other inherited properties as soon as possible, so that he could
invest in a transatlantic shipping venture while still running the
brewery—or after selling all or part of it. He had left the brewery
property under the care of James Gibbins, Sr., while he was in
England, although no brewing appears to have been undertaken

in the 1785–86 season. The idea had already formed that Gibbins could become a brewery partner.

Molson was aggressively preparing to diversify, but as it turned out, there was no ship in his immediate future. John Wilson wrote him back promptly, begging off the initiative: "In respect to Ship buying we [John Wilson and his father] have entirely lain all thoughts of that aside in consequence of some intelligence from America of a nature we did not expect or we should have been very happy in such a partner."

The nature of the intelligence from America isn't known,[1] but beyond Molson's commercial ambitions, the exchange of letters was more important in revealing where—more important, with whom—he was staying. He had moved in with his late uncle Robinson's widow, Ann—informally known as Nancy—Gibbins, at the Elsdale estate in Surfleet.

The Elsdale estate became his base of operations for tidying up his inheritance, and he hoped to stay only a month or two before returning to Montreal. He wrote Thomas Loid on August 29, informing him that he "shall be out if possible this Autumn; if not, shall take the first opportunity in the Spring." Despite having acquired Loid's brewery through the convoluted auction process, it seems he had only recently decided to commit himself fully to it, as he informed Loid that "[I] continue in the mind that Brewing must be verry lucrative in Canada therefore shall make the necessary provision for entering into that Business."

He did not make it back to Montreal that autumn; the return voyage would have to wait until the spring of 1786. The postponement was due to delays in settling his estate, but the longer he stayed at Surfleet, the more apparent it became that he was falling in love with his dead uncle's bride, the woman of beauty and intelligence who was only six years older than himself.

John Molson's slate was full of estate business that autumn. The legacies from Alice Boulton had to be settled for all the Molson children, and Philip Ashley wrote the family heir, the attorney Henry Boulton, Jr., on September 5 to bring matters to a close.

Boulton informed him the next day that he had sold the estate at Moulton and that the deal would be concluded on October 6, after which John Molson and his siblings could have their money. He warned Ashley, however, that "the Estate that she left to pay her Legacies & Debts does not amount to enough to pay the Legacies in full."

Molson was also pursuing a final accounting of his inheritance with his cousin John and grandfather Samuel. Settling the proportion of his father's estate that had passed on to his cousin John was achieved on October 8. Cousin John owed him precisely £248 14s 11d. Molson presented his cousin with a demand note for the pounds, leaving the shillings and pence to be settled out of pocket.

That same day, Molson moved to acquire unencumbered title to Snake Hall and its properties by filing a conveyance known as a Common Recovery, which probably was intended to defeat the rights of tenants so that the properties could be sold easily. In filing the conveyance, Molson alleged that he had resettled in England, identifying himself as being "late of Montreal . . . but now of Surfleet." One week later, the Alice Boulton legacy was tidied up. As Boulton had warned, there was very little to go around. Ashley delivered Molson £34 11s to distribute, and on November 10 Molson turned over to his brother Thomas £8 10s 3d. All that was left for John Molson to achieve was the very considerable business of getting the majority of his estate turned over by his grandfather. There was no rushing the process; John Molson was stuck in England for the winter of 1785–86.

The family had scattered to various households. No Molsons were at Snake Hall, which was still rented out. Martha, eighteen, was at the Elsdale estate in Surfleet with John. Mary, nineteen, and Samuel, twenty-one, were with their grandfather in a house he had taken in Spalding with his new wife, Mary Albin, while Thomas, seventeen, had been staying for the past two years with a local family named Clayton.

In late November and early December, Molson wrote two letters to James Gibbins, Sr.—the second prompted by a letter from Gibbins that arrived soon after Molson posted the first one.

Molson's letters were the most voluble, personable and frank he had yet written. As he confided to Gibbins in the first letter, written at eleven at night on November 29, "I am now come to a full Resolution of Conquoring that foolish & absurd Timidity & Bashfulness (that [I am] ashamed to own) which in a great measure prevents me from communicating my nonsense to a friend."

Molson had been enjoying himself thoroughly in the company of Gibbins's daughter, carrying on like a young Regency dandy. In addition to receipts that indicate extensive purchases of clothing (as well as a fine saddle the following spring), his notebook detailed money spent on hair powder and tobacco, and several fines paid to "Nancy" for swearing. He informed Gibbins that on November 26, he drank "a buffer of grog" in honour of Gibbins's birthday in the company of Nancy, her young boys "Sam & Robin" and the boy Luke Gibbins, related in some way to James, Sr. Two days later "I had the pleasure of paying Nancy the same compliment. I forget to tell you I smoaked two or 3 Pipes on either of the days."

Molson informed Gibbins that he intended to be in London "in a fortnight or three weeks," and if he met with any of the Canadian merchants Gibbins had previously mentioned to him, he would use them to remit to Gibbins one hundred pounds to retire the mortgage held by Pierre Monarque. But the financial news from south Lincolnshire was not as bright as he had hoped, and he confessed that he had "not settled with my Grandfather yet & what is more ye Money in his Hands & J Molson has fallen short of my expectations."

Molson had "given over all thoughts coming over till the Spring & then shall embrace the first opportunity." In the meantime, he was preparing for a return to brewing, and for having Gibbins as his partner. In his will of March 1785, Molson, as noted, had left the brewery to Gibbins (named "Pell" in the will), while his Lincolnshire properties were to be divided among his siblings. He reminded Gibbins of the bequest to him, and affirmed: "if I live intend taking you in partnership with me & as to mony to carry on the Business till I come you told me you believed you could muster [money] in Montreal on a scheme of that kind." What "kind" of scheme Molson did not say, but he counselled Gibbins on what should be done in his absence: "The Old Beer suppose you have sold it before now if not dispose of it as you think fit & make such use of the brewhouse as you think most to our advantage. If you should have altered your opinion in respect to the brewing business, thinking it will not answer give me an answer soon as possible & the particular Reasons why not."

Molson confessed he was reluctant to settle down as yet. "[I] feel in myself as great a desire to Ramble as ever or more so there fore when you see me with you I am not to be depen[d]ed upon when in staying with you but as I informed you in my last if I could fall in an eligible way of trading from port to port shall embrace an opportunity of that kind." The letter indicated he had not given up on going into the shipping business and was considering actually sailing aboard a vessel, despite the Wilsons' reluctance to form a partnership. And while he was away on voyages, he would expect Gibbins to run the brewery to both their benefit. "I may be blamable for such Notions," he allowed, "but however when my wild oats are sown shall then become steady & settle to Business perhaps with the Wise Man's reflection all is vanity & vexation of spirit."

Within a day or two of Molson's sending his first letter to James Gibbins, Gibbins's letter to him, written October 15, arrived at the Elsdale house. "I have no particular news but Jim is settled at Misisque Bay, Bill at Montreal & George, at St. Johns. Each man for himself, and you'll find me at Mrs. Jacobs."[2] With one sentence, Gibbins painted a broad picture for us of how domestic affairs had progressed since the Atlantic crossing of 1782. James Senior was living with and considering marrying a widow named Jacobs, who had also emigrated from England, possibly even from south Lincolnshire. (In Molson's second letter, written December 2, Gibbins was informed: "Give my kindest Compliments to Mrs. Pell or if there be no such Lady to Mrs. Jacob & tell her I delivered her Letters personally.") William (Bill) was living in Montreal; George was at St. Johns; and James Junior, now at "Misisque Bay," was near his brother George in the vicinity of Caldwell's Manor. James Junior could have been living on property that belonged to his father, as a reference to James Senior's title to lands at Missisquoi Bay would surface in October 1786. Having taken shelter under the roof of James Gibbins's daughter Ann while in England, John Molson's life was becoming firmly rooted among the Gibbins clan on both sides of the Atlantic. Molson approved heartily of the Diaspora among the Gibbins men, responding December 2: "Very glad to here [*sic*] you & sons are parted & every one become his own Master which in my opinion is by far the most eligible Scheme."

"We all should be glad to see you this fall," Gibbins wrote in response, "but we rather expect you not be able to get your matters settled till the Spring." Gibbins suggested he use Captain George Featonby "if you have any cash to remit he will take it from you and be accountable for it, at Montreal." Gibbins must have known already that Molson wanted to pay down the Monarque mortgage once he had funds from his estate, and he thought it important that Molson send actual specie and not try to rely on bills of exchange, in large part because of the number of merchants levelled by the burst credit bubble and the downturn of the peacetime economy. "I think it's the safest chanel it can come," Gibbins explained, "as there has been a greater fall amongst the merchants since you left Montreal. Messrs Fowlace, Hunter,[3] & all the Airds, Burn and a number amore to the amount of Fifteen." Replied Molson: "Sorry to hear such a Number of Merchants stoping Business it shows a great scarcity of Money & Consequently Trade." Molson would decide not to ship specie to Montreal in advance of his return, but he did choose Featonby and his ship, the *Everetta*, for his own pas-sage. She was owned by James Phyn of the merchant house Phyn & Ellice, which was a partner in the North West Company.[4]

The credit disaster had dragged most of the prominent Montreal merchants into court in an untidy battle involving them with the colonial government and the bubble's unrepen-tant burster, the exchange agent John Cochrane. Governor Haldimand had been moved to sue the defiant Cochrane, an unwinnable strategy, and the mess ultimately precipitated Haldimand's withdrawal from Quebec and his replacement by Henry Hamilton as governor in 1786.

If the ugly financial news was not enough to give John Molson pause, Gibbins then revealed that the brewery had been robbed. "You have had the Brewhouse broke since you left us," was the semantically clever way Gibbins reported the lapse in his responsibility for overseeing the property while Molson was overseas. Gibbins wrote that a group of Dutchmen had stolen a millstone (no easy or inconspicuous thing to carry off) and some haircloth. (By "Dutchmen" Loid may not have meant men from the Netherlands, but ne'er-do-wells from the large Dutch population that had first settled New York, Albany, and the Hudson River valley.) None of the stolen goods could be recovered, but Gibbins was pleased to note that "there has been three of them hanged lately and several more in Prison." Going to the gallows for stealing a millstone and some haircloth made the lashes received by the sailors on the *Assistance* for theft seem, in hindsight, a fairly light punishment.

Gibbins also gave no indication of an inclination to do any brewing or to pay much attention to the inventory. It was the second time Molson had been seriously let down by the elder Gibbins—the first having been the poor selection of the *Dispatch* for the near-disastrous 1782 passage. If his disappointment made Molson reconsider his relationship with the slightly roguish character, however, it was not apparent. "As you have not mentioned about your Ale . . . in ye Brewhouse [cellar] suppose you have not sold it," Molson replied, gently urging, "If you have not, sell it, if it be worth selling & take what care you can of the Rascals of dutchmen or any other people from stealing any thing for the future."

Molson was also depending on Gibbins to act in his interest in any new developments in the struggle between Henry Caldwell and Ira Allen. "[Y]ou will by this time know to whom the Land belong," Molson had instructed on November 29. Molson must have been privy to the discourse between Caldwell and Allen, specifically Caldwell's letter to Governor Chittenden. "[I]f to Ira Allen remind him of his promise & tell him as I told him by Letter as when I wrote to you before that I shall be out as early in the

Spring as possible, if Caldwell conquers then use your Interest on my behalf as most likely to turn to my greatest advantage."

From this cryptic statement it is difficult to know what Molson was up to. Evidently he had written Allen a letter for which no draft survives, and the Vermonter had made some kind of promise to him. The statement regarding Caldwell is ambiguous—either he wished Gibbins to act on his behalf with Caldwell in a way that would be to Molson's greatest advantage, or he thought that a successful claim to the property by Caldwell would be to his greatest advantage. Molson's second letter, on December 2, revisited the land dispute: "And my Lands by arival of this you'll know to whom they belong—if to Allen remind him of his Promise—& if Caldwell do what you can for me till I come." Now, however, Molson indicated that Thomas Loid might also be involved: "If Mr. Loid cannot or wou'd rather than take any other Land but mine will let him have 1 or 200 Acres on a Lease—that however may as well wait till my coming. . . ." Two years before Molson's involvement with Caldwell's Manor came to a spectacularly volatile end, he, Thomas Loid and James Gibbins, Sr., were all involved with properties on or around the seigneury.

Despite his many concerns—settling the inheritance, planning a future in brewing and possibly in shipping, trying to imagine how the Caldwell's Manor fiasco would play out—Molson was managing to enjoy himself in Surfleet. "Have been very happy since my Arrival in England," he informed Gibbins on November 29, "tho' have not made myself popular by entering into every fools company to be teased with their Nonsense." But the loss of Robinson Elsdale was deeply felt. "Now do I miss that worthy man our friend on whom I always considered as my confident & teacher having nobody to advise with in my future prospects & intentions—nobody that I can pour out my Heart to as a Friend, or at least nobody that can judge of the eligibility or uneligibility of my schemes. I have this reflection however left me there are two fine little Boy[s], & his one much beloved & affectionate wife on whom every encomium my pen can bestow will fall infinitely short of her Merit & Qualifications."

Molson's future, if not his mind, was becoming seriously clouded by his feelings for the widow Elsdale. On December 2, Molson wrote Gibbins:

> Nancy and me being by ourselves this evening our Conversation fell upon the manner of my Uncle's taking his leave of friends & his particular desire to see us before his death drew tears from the Worthy Little Woman's Eyes to a very great degree, it caused some involuntary Tears to flow from mine tho' ashamed of such a weakness cou'd not suppress 'em—if it is a weakness is what the greatest of statesmen & Philosophers are sometimes guilty of—tho' I have no claim to either distinction, still there's a Satisfaction in seeing or knowing our Superiors not able to suppress the feminine Qualities on similar occasions. . . .

In the postscript to the December 2 letter, Molson allowed that "your injunctions on me In Respect to Nancy were obey'd," but we don't know what these injunctions were or when they were made. By the time Molson wrote Gibbins the second letter, he had been living in the widow's house for five months—and, in the conveyance he filed on Snake Hall on October 8, he had asserted that he was now a Surfleet resident. How far their relationship had progressed is pure speculation, but there can be no doubt that Molson had fallen in love. His letters to James Gibbins were no longer to a friend and proposed business partner; they were to someone who might become his father-in-law. And by bequeathing the brewery to Gibbins "and his Heirs and Assigns forever" in the March 1785 will, Molson made Ann Elsdale and the children among the ultimate beneficiaries of his estate. He felt some shame at the boisterousness of his earlier letter to Gibbins, for which he apologized in the second missive. "I talked rather wildly about sowing my wild oats—can assure you have been since I have been here more sober & solid than any young fellow in the Country; perhaps sounding my own Trumpet in a Matter of this kind will not prove the veracity of it to my Friend."

On December 18, Molson at last settled with his grandfather Samuel what he recorded in his notebook as "the whole of his disbursments & receivings for & on my Acct: my Brother Thomas's, Mary's & Martha's Accts being Included." Molson's notes are ambiguous on what was due to him from his grandfather and cousin John, but on December 21, in settling his "general account" with Philip Ashley, he noted he was owed "344 pounds, 1 shilling nine pence and a half penny."

Two days later, on December 23, he was boarding the stage to London. A childhood friend, Jack Baxter, surely related to the Boaz Baxter whom Father John had named one of John Molson's guardians, had arranged lodgings for him. Writing Molson on December 14, he instructed him, "As soon as you arrive in London leave your things at The Inn [and] call upon me in Fenhurst Street ... then we will talk more large on the Subject." The "subject" was not elaborated upon, but it could well have been Molson's feelings for his aunt. Typically, Molson was disappointing those close to him with his extreme economy in letters. "I must confess I thought Implements of writing scarce at Surfleet," Baxter chided him, "but knowing you was not far from a Market Town, supposed you would soon supply that Defect and that I should have been honor'd with a few lines from Mrs. Elsdale['s]."

Molson intended to visit with his grandfather as well, for in early November Samuel Elsdale and his wife had taken a house in London, where they were "to remain during the Winter for Sam's health." In his December 2 letter to James Gibbins, Molson proclaimed his grandfather to be "as hearty as ever," and reported how Samuel's wife, Mary,

> says he has very much improved for the better since his leaving Spalding; what he is better in cannot justly say (leave that for you to determine as you are a better Judge in matters where Women give merit than myself) but this am sure of whether he is praised by Man or Woman he is an Original; and as Dr. Rodgerson observes it can be no Idolatry in falling down to Worship him as there is not his likeness in Heaven above or in

the Earth beneath therefore you may conclude he remains the same kind of being still.

Martha wrote her brother on Christmas Day—the date (not even a formal day of rest) did not become a significant social event until the Victorian era, and Martha was more concerned with not being able to celebrate Molson's twenty-second birthday with him on the twenty-eighth than with missing his company on the twenty-fifth. Martha's offer of "compliments for the approaching season" was a reference to the social whirl that seized London every winter, as the gentry relocated to the city (as Samuel Elsdale had) from their country estates. The Prince of Wales, the most dandified of dandies, had taken his seat in the House of Lords in 1783, and London, especially now in peacetime, was far more amusing and exciting—and expensive—than provincial Spalding. On Christmas Day, Molson delivered from Ashley to Robert Gosling & Son a letter that allowed him to open an account of £200.

By February Molson was back in Surfleet, intervening on Jack Baxter's behalf with Baxter's mother, in Spalding. Baxter was entertaining thoughts of marriage, but unlike the freshly endowed Molson, he had no means of funding it. No mention is ever made of what Baxter was doing for a living in London, but judging by the reference to the expense of his education, he may have been studying there at some point. Molson reported back to Baxter that he told his mother

> I had every reason in the World to support you had a favorite Girl in View . . . but ye believed it was also necessary for an advance of something handsome on your part: to which she with a shake of her head replyd wished she had it in her power; but that she had already been at great expenses in your Education etc etc. . . . And that your present line of Life was but a bare Maintenance with Economy & without any future prospects & in a Married State would not support a bare existence & therefore you cannot be so mad as to marry in your unsettled state.

Particularly mentioned your wish for entering into the farming & Grazing Line—& to be situated near one or both of your Friends Squires or Pilgrim for to consult and advise with—to which she answered in the Negative with seeming regret but Money which will be wanted—was the grand Cause.

Mother is satisfied in her Opinion that your Sedentary employment is the Cause of your indisposition—& that change of place without altering your employment will be of no Service . . . took every possible pains to convince her . . . you who know her better than I will sense the event more clearly—however think every Nerve will be strained in your favor.

It appears from this letter that Baxter was considering not only marriage, but joining Molson in the new world. The friend named "Pilgrim" must have been Thomas Loid, as the same nickname would be used for Loid in a letter to Molson in 1796. If Loid was Pilgrim, then James Gibbins or one of his sons (or possibly Molson himself) was Squires. Baxter was seeking more than an advance from his mother to make himself eligible husband material—he also required the funds to set up as a farmer around his two pseudonymous friends, which would have brought him to the Missisquoi area.

The letter is an important relic of John Molson's years as a young man, for it encapsulates Molson's basic character as a friend. On practical matters, he was prudent and thorough; the business of friendship had no greater practitioner. While there is obvious warmth in the letters between Molson and Baxter—they made sly references to prescriptions written by "Dr. Vice" and "Dr. Blather"—when it came to the maintenance of actual intimacy, Molson often appeared at a loss or uninterested, or was accused of being so.

After intervening on Baxter's behalf, Molson spent some time in Surfleet before heading to London to prepare for his return to Quebec. On March 11, Philip Ashley provided him with a summary of monies still owed him. Much of it was back rent, but his grandfather Samuel still owed £61 9s 10d from the estate settlement.

His departure for Quebec aboard the *Everetta* was only two weeks away, and the enormity of it was beginning to weigh on him. This withdrawal had an air of permanence. He realized he would not be back in England for some time. He wrote his grandfather from aboard the *Everetta,* on the eve of sailing, with his hope "that you continue that Vigor of Constitution which you have been blessed with—that your seven Grandchildren may meet on the Anniversary of your birth 85 or 86 at which time I purpose being in England with the permission of God." At the earliest, then, Molson did not foresee being back in south Lincolnshire until 1793 or 1794, in seven or eight years' time, when he would be approaching thirty. As it turned out, his estimation was off by about fifteen years. War resumed between Britain and France in 1793 and continued for thirteen years, with only a thirteen-month truce as an interruption. The Atlantic became a war zone, off limits to all but the most determined travellers. Molson's departure, for many people in his life, including his grandfather, was final.[5]

As for his relationship with his aunt, the widow Ann Elsdale, Molson left behind no clues to what had transpired—if his feelings for "Nancy" were mutual, if he had imagined any future for them, in England or Quebec. It was as if John Molson had planned to take inheritance to the extreme: now possessing most of his late father's property, he would next possess his late uncle's wife and children. It would have been a socially and economically powerful union, binding together the principal inheritances of the Elsdale and Molson families. With his departure aboard the *Everetta* set for April 8, however, there was no conceivable future for him and his young aunt. Molson had mentioned in one of his letters to James Gibbins that there had been some thought given to his brother Thomas coming to Quebec with him, but never a word was mentioned in writing of Ann Elsdale and the boys joining him in Montreal. A union, for whatever reason, had not and would not come to pass. Molson sailed for Quebec with his heart still very much with the widow.

He wrote his sisters, before his departure, from the Guildhall Coffee House in London. A "coffee house" generally sold much stronger beverages than its name suggested, and Molson seemed close to drowning his sorrows as he penned a farewell to Mary and Martha. For the normally taciturn Molson, the letter verged on hysterical. Molson wrote:

> As the separation of us once [more] is unavoidable at present, [I] therefore hope you arm yourselves with all the fortitude in your powers—the fewness of your Friends who would take any interesting part in your affairs—demands the greatest Attentions to be paid to those few existing. If I am any judge of the human heart from my little knowledge of the world & if my advice would be acceptable, shall here take the liberty of pointing out such as I think would be willing do you a service if required.

He recommended to them both James and Philip Ashley. The Reverend Ashley in particular "would do almost any service that may lie in his power," a noteworthy endorsement in light of the considerable tumult that lay ahead in Lincolnshire for the Molsons—tumult that would find the poor reverend at its epicentre. He reserved his greatest endorsement for the woman he was leaving behind:

> [T]here is another friend I have not mentioned yet who perhaps may be the best friend you have;—in every respect, that lies in her power; think you cannot think other ways of her from her being the choice of one who was the greatest friend we ever had & who was as good a Judge of human heart as most men that ever exist & when you consider that, that good opinion which at first rather sprung from external appearance, was still more strongly confirmed by a Connecting which of all others is the most likely to find the True Jewel of the Soul—think of his choice & his ever after happy in that choice, & then you need not have a dread of entering into the most open & Generous Friendship with the worthiest of Women—if what I have stated does not confirm you in your

good opinion of her, can scarce think of informing you how worthy I think her of your Friendship & Confidence considered as a female, there's nothing but what you may impart— the advantages are too numerous & sure for to escape your notice.... [I] think you need not any further discussion from me only let me add that with that friendship you may be as happy as circumstances will admit, but without it, tis my opinion you'l fall infinitely short of the happiness attainable in your union.... Dear Sisters how much it hurts me to part with you for so long a time—nor the almost impossibility of your accompanying me....

More than an endorsement of Ann Elsdale's goodness, the letter indicates that friction had grown between the widow and Molson's sisters, as he reminded them of how no less a person than Robinson Elsdale had chosen and been made happy by her, argued that they "need not dread entering into the most open and Generous Friendship" with her, and expressed close to exasperation that they might not be convinced of her worthiness. He also committed a proto-Freudian slip, informing them if they did not take the "worthiest of Women" to heart, they would "fall infinitely short of the happiness attainable in your union." By "union" he could only have meant marriage—an impossible arrangement between Ann Elsdale and the Molson sisters, but plausible (if ultimately impractical) between the widow and John Molson. It was as if, in advising his sisters on the merits of a close friendship with the widow, he had stumbled into mourning his own failure to achieve a treasured union.

Having reached a crescendo of despair over the consequences of his imminent departure, Molson left England two weeks later, on April 8. He reached Quebec on May 25. Now in control of his inheritance, he could direct his future as he pleased. The number of changes looming in his life—and the extent of their repercussions—was nothing less than stunning. It would have astonished those who knew him that the John Molson of the next few years was the same young man who had lived in such bliss at Surfleet with Ann Elsdale and penned her father such wordy and good-humoured letters. As if confronting the wormy wood in the British warships of his day, Molson would pick at and condemn the rot he purported to find at the core of his greatest friendships. His life did not merely change after he left England in the spring of 1786. It turned upside down.

Chapter 9

People at your age are in a state of natural [in]ebriety; they want rails, and gardefous, wherever they go, to hinder them from breaking their necks. This drunkenness of youth is not only tolerated, but even pleases if kept within certain bounds of direction and decency. Those bounds are the point which it is difficult for the drunken man himself to find out; and there it is that the experience of a friend may not only serve, but save him.
—Lord Chesterfield, letter to his son, October 29, 1748

JOHN MOLSON PREPARED CAREFULLY for his return to Quebec. His life was entirely his own responsibility now, and while he would continue to depend considerably on Philip Ashley, he took every measure to ensure a reasonable amount of self-sufficiency in the new world.

Two days before sailing, he sent to James Gibbins, Sr., two bills of lading—one for the *London*, which was bound for Quebec, and another for the *Fame*, headed for Montreal. Molson had been busy in March rounding up various supplies for his little brewery: casks of barley, sacks of hops, haircloth, corks, malt baskets, nails, shovels, screening and more. He needed to make up for lost time at the brewery, idle and robbed during his year-long absence. Despite the appearance of shipping coals to Newcastle, Molson was sending English barley to Quebec because he wanted to get to work on his initial production as soon as possible. After the wheat-beer debacle of 1783–84, he feared that locally grown barley would not be available soon enough. More important, he would have been importing the two-row

"Maritime" barley favoured for brewing. North American farmers were growing only six-row "big" barley, which produced a harsher beer. As Molson had observed in one of his first letters home, in the fall of 1782, "the Barley is all Barley Big here, I believe at Present."

Philip Dormer Stanhope, fourth Earl of Chesterfield. Portrait by Allan Ramsay, 1765.
(Collection: National Portrait Gallery, London)

In his letter accompanying the bills of lading to Gibbins, Molson revealed that he was travelling with £250, and that neither it nor the cargo on the *London* and the *Fame* were insured against loss. "The News of this Country shall omit relating as shall be defered till we meet by your friendly fireside—If you have changed your state may you & yours be as happy as the state will admit." Molson didn't know if Gibbins had married the widow Jacobs, because Gibbins had not bothered writing anything after informing Molson that the brewery had been ransacked by Dutchmen, despite Molson's specific request for Gibbins's opinion on becoming a partner. Molson added: "Have been much disappointed in not hearing from you since last Autumn." In his new-found independence, Molson found his patience for inattention rapidly wearing thin. The pleading for the good favour of friends was soon eclipsed by blunt and damning words. Where he had once relied on friends in areas of business, the presence of business came to press all considerations of friendship firmly aside.

John Molson's return to Quebec in the spring of 1786 unfolded with almost unrelieved urgency. Despite having been in England for a year, he spent his last days chasing too many details and obligations—with too few hours to accommodate them. "I know not how to apologize for my later apparent disrespect," Molson wrote his friend and attorney, Philip Ashley, from aboard the *Everetta* at Gravesend on April 6, as he awaited departure,

> first for my not having call'd on you before my leaving Lincolnshire—second for not having taken up my pen to excuse myself for that part of my conduct which it was impossible to avoid—the day appointed for waiting on Mr. Ashley was the Saturday before my leaving Surfleet—that purpose was frustrated—the Sunday was obliged to dine with my Grandfather & on Monday I took coach for London—Business has been so pressing that nare a Minute has intervened that I could call my own. After every apology for my past conduct I still rely on a matchless Generosity to forgive. Returning you my most grateful thanks, for every favor conferred & particularly for your expression of kind wishes for my future welfare. . . .

Molson's letter to Ashley was one of his last acknowledgments of his own shortcomings, however excusable in the pell-mell rush to take his leave of family and friends and arrange for the shipment of every necessary good to Quebec on separate ships. Already that day he had jotted a quick note to Ashley, announcing his boarding of the *Everetta* and warning him of his intention to draw on Gosling for £500 after reaching Montreal.

Molson was carrying with him two other noteworthy items, both manuals of a kind. One was the third edition of the Hull brewer John Richardson's seventy-four-page *Theoretic Hints on an Improved Practice of Brewing*, published in 1777.[1] The other was a four-volume set of the collected letters of Lord Chesterfield, published in 1774. The former would explain to Molson how to run his brewery, the latter how to conduct his life.

Lord Chesterfield's letters were favourite reading for Molson and his friend Jack Baxter. The volumes had been purchased for twelve shillings on Baxter's account from the London bookseller John French in January 1786, and Baxter first made reference to Chesterfield in a letter to Molson on February 15. Molson evidently had also been attempting to further his own short formal education with the purchase of a grammar book from French in August 1785.

The idea of the orphaned John Molson stepping ashore at Quebec on May 25 with the volumes of Chesterfield under one arm and Richardson's brewing manual under the other provides one of the most poignant images of his young life. The brewing guide testified to the admirable depth of Molson's initiative. He had turned his back on life on a middle-class estate, preparing to sell it off in favour of a new enterprise on another continent for which he required printed instructions. And with no family member left to guide him—his parents long dead, his beloved uncle Robinson lost, his contrary grandfather, though grudgingly admired, now both distant and undesired as a source of wisdom—Molson was reduced to relying on the published advice of the late Lord Chesterfield to mould his character and guide his behaviour.

And what an extraordinary mentor he chose, for Philip Dormer Stanhope, fourth Earl of Chesterfield, had been subject to both praise and vilification when his letters were published by Edward Gibbon in 1774, the year after the Earl's death. Lord Chesterfield had not written the letters for any eyes but their recipients'. Most were addressed to his illegitimate son, whom he advised extensively on manners, morals and professional and social advancement as he strove to carve a career, as his father had, in public life. There was much admirable common sense in the letters, even on the subject of common sense. "Common sense (which in truth, is very uncommon) is the best sense I know of; abide by it; it will counsel you best," he advised his son on September 27, 1748. But some of Lord Chesterfield's directions and musings scandalized critics. Where many saw a worthy education distilled into a series of posted discourses, Samuel Johnson decried a collection that would impart "the morals of a whore and the manners of a dancing master."

The forty-seven-day passage to Quebec would have given Molson time to explore Chesterfield's letters and Richardson's brewing guide and to mourn the missed opportunity for bliss with his widowed aunt, Ann Elsdale. Awaiting favourable winds in the St. Lawrence to complete the journey, Molson wrote a brief letter to James Gibbins, Sr., reminding him (in case his letter from England had not arrived) that ten bushels of barley were coming to Montreal aboard the *London*. He was keen for some news about the Caldwell's Manor dispute between Henry Caldwell and Ira Allen, which Gibbins had never provided:

> There's one thing which I want to be particularly inform'd of: that is, in respect to my Lands on the Tongue, whether or no, Caldwell retains all them Lands to himself—if it apears he is the Legal proprietor, how you wou'd have [me] act, while I have an opportunity of transacting Business with him personally. I need not inform [you] of our little altercation at the time he was up at the Lake—be particular in your advice if there's any necessary in respect to him—Suppose my stay in Quebec will be about 6 or 7 days, to wait an Answer.

Molson must not have stayed in Quebec City more than a day or two, however, as he arrived there on the twenty-fifth and was in Montreal on the thirty-first after an overland journey that would have taken about four days. If Molson ever met with Caldwell at Quebec City in those final days of May, no record remains.

Soon after his return to Montreal, Molson appears to have made up his mind to rid himself of the Caldwell's Manor property. "My Lands on Lake Champlain [I] believe [I] shall dispose of they are too great a distance from this, & are attended with loss of time & expense, in going & return," he informed Philip Ashley on June 8. Whether or not this was an honest intention, Molson made no practical effort we know of to be rid of them.

Allen, meanwhile, had engineered some trappings of legitimacy for his title. Though still unorganized as a town, Alburgh nonetheless had been granted a seat in the Vermont state legislature (though the state remained unrecognized by Congress) in 1786. The first person to hold it was a man identified in state records[2] as Thomas P. Lloyd, who is unquestionably Thomas Pelgrave Loid, friend and erstwhile brewery partner of John Molson. Stratton reasoned that because the town was unorganized, this "Lloyd," who was also justice of the peace, owed his positions to direct appointments by Ira Allen.

Loid had probably been living on some or all of Molson's lands in Caldwell's Upper Manor since 1785, with James Gibbins perhaps having acted on Molson's directions to allow Loid to lease one hundred or two hundred acres of his property. Perhaps after returning from England, Molson allowed Thomas Loid to lease all of the Caldwell's Manor property, and not just the one hundred or two hundred acres proposed the previous autumn. Molson noted in his record book on June 26, 1786: "Sent by Mr. Pell about 8 lb of white 8 lb green turnips & half a peck of rape to leave on my lands opposite Point au Fair with T.P.L." Loid thus was settled at Caldwell's Upper Manor no later than the summer of 1786, on lands Molson considered still to be his own. Gibbins evidently also was settled around Caldwell's Manor, or at least had title to land there, as on October 13 Molson noted in his record book: "Lent Mr. P. four pounds & thirteen [shillings] & four pence—made me except [*sic*] deed of his lands on Missisque Bay Lake Champlain."[3]

Molson's record book indicates that James Gibbins, Sr., was becoming increasingly indebted to him—in addition to the small loan made October 13, 1786, Gibbins had borrowed from Molson more than £30 on June 9, a little more than a week after Molson was back in Montreal. The mounting debt thus had moved Gibbins to pledge the deed to a Missisquoi Bay property. At the same time, as noted, Thomas Loid was living on John Molson's Caldwell's Manor lands. The two older men, who had become guardians of a sort for Molson with his 1782 crossing, were now conspicuously dependent on the industrious young man. At the same time, Loid had struck a potentially contrary allegiance with Ira Allen, and vio-lence at Caldwell's Manor was just over the horizon.

Loid's close relationship with Ira Allen invites the question of precisely what promise Allen had made to Molson (as alluded to by Molson in his letters to James Gibbins in the autumn of 1785). Perhaps it was nothing more than to give him fair market value for his block of land, or award him title to it at a reasonable price, should Allen carry the day in the title dispute. But it is entirely possible that Molson had expected to fulfill the position of Allen's right-hand man at Alburgh, an honour that fell to Thomas Loid in Molson's absence in England in 1785–86. The trip to Lincolnshire to tidy up his inheritance may have saved Molson a precarious—and even ruinous—detour into upstate Vermont.

On July 6, 1786, Molson wrote several optimistic letters to recipi-ents back in Lincolnshire. "The Brewery which was the principle project of this emigration has the most flattering appearances," he informed his grandfather. "Porter there is very little imported this Season, sells at present £5 Halifax Currency—or £4 10s per Hogshead." He passed along similar news to Philip Ashley: "Brewing at present wears the most favorable aspect. . . . Good ales is all I want, plenty of Customers & Good profits will immediately follow—have not the least doubt about my making Good Ale."

He had reason for optimism. On June 13, he had been able to use the proceeds from his estate settlement to retire the mortgage held by Pierre Monarque, and he was beginning to hire local help. And despite his fears that he would not be able to get enough local barley, he secured eight bushels on July 28. He added to the notation of the barley purchase that day an observation which, like Chesterfield's own writings, would long outlive him:

Commencement on the Grand Stage of the World

Molson's statement moved Alfred Dubuc to remark, "Rarely does the spirit of enterprise find such clear expression. . . ."[4] Molson may have written it with confidence and hubris, but it was likely inspired by a text that was not meant as an endorsement of commercial ambition. The idea of the world being a stage, grand or not, was most famously expressed by William Shakespeare in *As You Like It*. Molson's comment was likely inspired not by a schoolboy memory of the Bard, however, but by his perusal of Chesterfield's letters, which specifically addressed a young man's debut in adult affairs by employing the theatrical allusion best associated with Shakespeare. Chesterfield found the event a cause for caution and concern, not celebration.

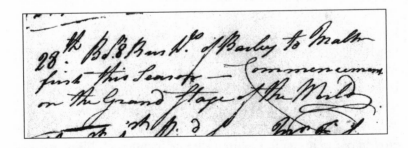

John Molson's journal entry for July 28, 1786: "Bought 8 Bushels of Barley to Malt first this Season—Commencement on the Grand Stage of the World." (Collection: The Molson Archives/National Archives of Canada)

"I cannot help being anxious for your success," Chesterfield wrote his son on December 30, 1748,

> at this your first appearance upon the great stage of the world; for though the spectators are always candid enough to give great allowances, and to show great indulgence to a new actor; yet, from the first impressions which he makes upon them, they are apt to decide, in their own minds at least, whether he will ever be a good one or not: if he seems to understand what he says, by speaking it properly; if he is attentive to his part, instead of staring negligently about; and if, upon the whole, he seems ambitious to please, they willingly pass over little awkwardnesses and inaccuracies, which they ascribe to a commendable modesty in a young and unexperienced actor. They pronounce that he will be a good one in time; and by encouragement which they give him, make him so the sooner.

Now that Molson had taken to the stage, Chesterfield was warning from the grave, the audience was sitting in judgment—indulgent to some degree of a new talent, but likely to draw their conclusions about his character based on their first impression. Molson's notebook entry was a recognition of this dramatic entrance from the wings; how conscious he was of the impression he was about to make is another matter.

On July 6, 1786, John Molson paused in his preparations for the grand stage to jot a brief letter to his sisters, Mary and Martha. In the rough copy he made, Molson wrote that he had "taken up my pen with every pleasure [weighted] by the pleasing Ideas of the welcome reception this will meet with from Sisters who are so dear to me...." He noted that he had hired a housekeeper and, in a section crossed out in his draft, reported that he had rented a vacant house next to the brewhouse "which make it very convenient & in short shall be obliged to have Men to do my Business could not possibly do other way."

Much as he assured both Philip Ashley and his grandfather in letters also written that day, he told his sisters, "The Brewing

Business has the most favorable aspect at present." He then counselled, "Since Dear Sisters we are thus far separated may it be your constant wish & duty to oblige those friends so strongly recommended" in his last letter, "which your good sense makes a further disertation needless." He urged them specifically to turn to the widowed aunt, Ann Elsdale, "the little Woman who believe me I think is worthy of every confidence that can be reposed in her. Listen [to] your affectionate Brother, John Molson."

Molson had also written a hurried note to Jack Baxter soon after his arrival in Montreal, on June 8, when he found a letter (since lost) from his old friend awaiting him. Baxter and a friend named John Morgan had seen Molson off aboard the *Everetta*, and Morgan took care of the barley shipment Molson made to Quebec. Morgan and Baxter had "botanical projects" of some sort in mind—perhaps a reference to relocating in Quebec—and they expected Molson to report back on the availability of land. And they had all developed a poor impression of the *Everetta*'s captain, George Featonby. Molson's reply to Baxter's letter briefly noted an uneventful crossing, confessed that "Our Botanical projects have done nothing with as yet," happily reported that "the mean opinion conceived of Capt Featonby is perfectly obliterated," and provided vague and confusing instructions on how to get mail to him.

Molson's curt, all too businesslike letter encouraged a lengthy response from Baxter. He had received Molson's letter on July 30, but did not find the time or the right words for his reply until September 6.

It appears you had a good Passage & the horrid Idea we conceived of Capt. Featonby was rather too precipitable, but his behavior to my Friend Morgan & I when we were on Board was unparelled disgraceful & totally inconsistent with the Tenets a British Tar should possess. I believe our Botanical Scheme may intirely stand in *Status quo* [meaning, probably, "in limbo"], in 20th June last I had the Misfortune to loose one of the best of Mothers as such I have some property coming to me & am going into Lincolnshire to turn Farmer & Grazier.

As with Molson, Jack Baxter's future had been secured by an inheritance, but unlike Molson, he intended to remain in Lincolnshire. The financial obstacles to a marriage were now behind him—and so, for that matter, was the judgment of his now-deceased mother.

Despite his cheery beginning, Baxter plainly had been offended by the cold brevity of Molson's letter. He had already scolded Molson the previous December for the lack of communication when he was staying at Surfleet.

> I must now accuse you of your very concise mode of writing being so inexplicit. You say there is no regular Post from New York to Montreal but you have a passenger on Board who will forward your Letters from N.Y. to Montreal without saying to whom they are to be addressed to at New York. We have N.Y. ships constantly going from this Port to N.Y. but unless they were addressed to some Person at N.Y. desiring them to be forwarded in all probability they would rest there for some Time.

Fortunately, Baxter was able to turn to a brother Freemason (Molson had probably joined the order with Baxter in 1785–86), who had a friend in New York who could forward this letter to Molson. Baxter had given his name to "Mrs. Elsdale the Needful," as he now slyly termed the Worthy Widow, so that she could send a parcel care of him as well. (If the parcel contained a letter from Ann Elsdale, it no longer exists.)

"I was down in Lincolnshire to attend my Mother's Funeral, being sent for before she died," Baxter continued on the subject of the needful aunt. "They have got in the Country [the impression] you & Mrs. Elsdale are going to make a Match." Molson had apparently said nothing to Baxter about nuptials, but Baxter's intelligence must have been sound. He was staying at Spalding with a man named William Gibbins—possibly the one born at Moulton in 1751, which could have made him an uncle of the purported bride, or at the very least a close relative. Baxter was concerned, if only licentiously, that in the meantime Molson had acquired female hired help. "I see you have commenced Housekeeper," Baxter wrote. Molson had not mentioned this in his brief letter to him of June 8—Baxter must have learned of the development from Molson's sisters. "I commend you but get some Old Woman in the House you do not wish to come within a Yard of," Baxter lectured, "or else you will be wrong; I mean till such Time as you provide yourself with a Rib."

Beneath Baxter's jests lay a broad swath of disappointment with his old friend. He complained:

> I think your Mode of conducting yourself when at Surfleet from what I can learn was acting diametrically opposite to the good Directions laid down by Lord Chesterfield. I am going to be Farmer John & you must excuse my Bluntness, you was called a closr [possibly "cloistered"] & an unsocial Fellow & I must accuse you of being guilty of the first Error & a very gross Error indeed, but my Limits are far too narrow, or else you should have had a good lesson from me, as you have Lord Chesterfield by your side or at least I hope so. I shall leave you to him, peruse him well, you will profit much from him.

After complaining about not hearing any news of "James Gibbins alias Pell" and his sons, Baxter continued in his list of Molson's social transgressions.

> My friend Morgan is much astonished you did not write him. I am sure on my Account he shewed you every kind of Civility & does not deserve such Treatment—If you had no leisure Time I should have excused your short Note, but as I suppose you have plenty of leisure Hours you might have been explicit & more copious. . . . Lincolnshire News shall leave that to the *Little Widow*, who I suppose writes you by this conveyance. . . . Any Commission on this Side the Water shall be happy to execute. . . . I am wishing your every Success. . . . "

The letter from start to finish was almost entirely a rebuke of Molson's recent behaviour. His entrance on the grand stage of the world had been panned by a most valued critic, as Molson scarcely delivered a line worth hearing. Worse, by the evidence of Baxter's accusations, he had been inattentive, uncaring, offensive, and self-absorbed. His actions had been "diametrically opposed" to Chesterfield's instructions, and Molson had been encouraged to "peruse him well."

Chesterfield had, in fact, warned about what Molson had become: the Absent Man. "What is commonly called an absent man, is commonly either a very weak, or a very affected man; but be he which he will, he is, I am sure, a very disagreeable man in company," he wrote his son on October 9, 1746. "He fails in all the common offices of civility; he seems not to know those people to-day, with whom yesterday he appeared to live in intimacy."

Molson certainly had been negligent of the common courtesies of friendship, but Baxter had stumbled in his tirade with his careless observation about Molson's supposedly generous leisure time. By the evidence of his notebook, Molson had, since arriving in Quebec, been moving at a furious pace, as he worked to get his brewery operational and keep abreast of developments at Caldwell's Manor. This did not mean that he would have been unable to spare a few minutes to write more generously to Baxter or to Morgan, but Baxter's notion that he had "plenty of leisure hours" showed how far apart their lives had grown in the rush into adulthood.

Baxter did not have a clue as to Molson's circumstances in Quebec, but ultimately the fault came back to Molson for not explaining what he was up to—least of all when it came to finding a mate. For by the time Baxter conveyed the Lincolnshire wisdom that Molson and the widow Elsdale were to make a match, Molson was in the process of making a different match, about which he had said, and would say, nothing. His rebound from Ann Elsdale was remarkably quick, its mechanics a mystery. Either Molson, realizing such a match was impossible, had set out with deliberation to find a mate as soon as possible, or he had fallen into a long-term relationship that had begun suddenly, if casually. Baxter's letter, with its litany of accusations of poor behaviour and its mention of a possible wedding with Ann Elsdale, pushed the already terse Molson into a lengthy silence. The poor notice posted by Baxter was met with total disregard by the actor. Having made his entrance on the grand stage, he resolved to play his role with his back to the audience.

And long after he left the stage, the audience would still be fascinated by the very identity of his leading lady, who entered stage right—with no warning to be found in the program.

The identity of Sarah Vaughan, John Molson's spouse, has long baffled researchers, and the urge to uncover her origins has never waned. We have long known only her name—or names—but nothing of where she came from, let alone her ancestry. More frustrating is the fact that we still know little of her as a person, for no letters to or from her survive. John Molson exchanged letters with his sons, a brother-in-law, his sisters, his grandfather and his uncle Robinson, to name a few family members, but never with his wife. He also made entries on her behalf in the brewery journal in 1791 and 1792 for cash received for grains and sundries, marking them "Sarah." When it is also noted that she signed her marriage contract with an X, the incontrovertible conclusion is that she was illiterate.

Sarah Vaughan was older than John Molson—the age difference has been presented as anywhere from one year to a dozen. We know she and Molson were together for fifteen years, raising their three children, before they were married at Christ Church in Montreal on April 7, 1801. She may have been married before, and this previous marriage may not have been formally ended by death or divorce before she took up with Molson. Thus, the mystery surrounding Sarah Vaughan is fringed with scandal—an older woman with a foggy past, a hint of bigamy on her part, their children born out of wedlock. All of it, in the shorthand of biography, leaves her sadly, and perhaps unfairly, tainted.

There has long been so little material from which to reconstruct Sarah Vaughan that it seems possible to produce a full spectrum of Sarahs, ranging from a low-born bigamist to a high-born English émigré. To begin, we can determine who she wasn't: a high-born source for Sarah is unlikely, not because of any alleged moral failings, but because of the basic fact of her illiteracy. Her lack of schooling fundamentally discourages associating her with some of England's most prominent Vaughan families. Eighteenth-century women rarely received a university education, but it would have required extraordinary neglect for a girl raised in a manor house not to learn to read and write. The letters written by John Molson's sisters are riddled with spelling and grammatical errors—and the occasional charming malapropism—but there is no question that they were literate, and typically so. The circumstantial evidence that Sarah Vaughan was also, at least initially, John Molson's hired housekeeper further reinforces her modest origins. Another knock against a high-born source is that no inheritance appeared during her lifetime. Had Sarah Vaughan been born to any kind of wealth, the Molson family would have pursued her share of it, and there would have been some recognition of it in her marriage contract with Molson.

In a time of simple names, when English Protestants were generally baptized with only a Christian name and a surname, John Molson's companion and wife was equipped (according to legal documents and brewery records) with no fewer than four names. She and Molson had been together almost a decade when his health began to fail, and the prospect of death compelled him to create a new will on January 1, 1795, to replace his 1785 one. He revised this second will during another serious illness, in June 1797. The 1795 will identified one of his beneficiaries as "Mrs. Sarah Vaughan or Kitley or by whatever other name or names she may be known or called." The revised will of 1797 similarly identified her as "Sarah Vaughan or Kitley, or by whatever other name or names she is or may be called or known, now living with him."

Having been equipped with "Sarah," "Vaughan" and "Kitley," she then acquired another name (and a debt of £30 11s) with her appearance in Molson's brewery account book of 1799–80 as Sarah Insly Vaughan. Their marriage contract of April 7, 1801, then identified her as Sarah "Insleyvaughan," while the marriage record at Christ Church presented her as an Insley Vaughan. In the 1801–2 account book, the debt is carried forward under the name Sarah Ansly Vaughan, and it appears again in 1802–3, this time attributed to

Sarah A. Vaughan. Leaving aside the question of why John Molson was charging his wife such a substantial figure for beer (the equivalent of about £2,400 today), the two wills, the marriage records and the brewery account books added to her basic name the names Insley/Insly/Ansly and Kitley—though never at the same time—with still other names possible, according to the 1795 and 1797 wills.

The Kitley name could be cited as evidence of a previous marriage, even a marriage that had never been formally ended, hence the bigamy charge. "Kitley" may well be a remnant of a previous marriage, but that marriage could easily have ended with the death of her spouse, particularly in revolutionary times.

But some legal impediment to marriage may have existed in the relationship between Sarah Vaughan and John Molson. The fifteen-year wait, with three children left illegitimized, suggests a hidden obstacle to the altar. Were Sarah still legally married to someone else—someone she had abandoned for what may have been very good reasons, or who had abandoned her—she and John may have been forced to wait for news of the absent husband's death before formalizing their own union. Had this Kitley been a soldier or a sailor, years could have been required for word to filter back of his demise, just as it took three years for word of Jim Brainsby's death on Lake Ontario to come to South Lincolnshire via John Molson.

We must also consider the very institution of wedlock at the time. The fact that John and Sarah waited until 1801 to marry at Christ Church does not mean that they were not married earlier in a different church. Christ Church was important for both civil and religious reasons, for only marriages within the Church of England were legally recognized for Protestants in Quebec.

The Protestant congregations in Montreal had been steadily evolving since Molson's arrival. When he reached Montreal in 1782, the English Protestant community was ministered out of the local garrison by David Chabrand Delisle, a Frenchman who had been ordained in the Church of England in London. Delisle had good relations with the English merchant class, and presided over the marriages to Canadian women of the prominent fur traders James McGill, Joseph Frobisher and Simon McTavish.

In 1786, the Scots Presbyterians broke away from the Anglicans and brought in the Reverend John Bethune, who had been chaplain to the 84th Regiment of Foot (Royal Highland Emigrants), a volunteer Loyalist outfit, during the American Revolution. Bethune had settled at Williamstown, Ontario, near the Naval Department base at Carleton Island, ministering at St. Andrew's Church. Bethune remained in Montreal only until 1787, before returning to Williamstown. The Scots Presbyterians didn't find a replacement for him until 1791, when they began building their own church in Montreal, consecrated in 1792. In the meantime, the Anglicans had taken over the city's former Jesuit church in 1789. This Christ Church, where John Molson and Sarah Vaughan were married, burned down in 1803.[5]

It is possible that Molson and Sarah could have previously married in some other Protestant ceremony, perhaps at Montreal's Scots Presbyterian Church, and then underwent the ceremony at Christ Church in 1801 to provide a secure legal framework for their own relationship and the kinship of their children, the eldest of whom was by then fourteen. Civil law in Lower Canada differed from that of England in legitimizing, through marriage, children already born to the couple being wed.

Molson evidently had a religious bent and should have been inclined to formal wedlock: he had contributed to the construction of the Scots Presbyterian church in 1792, and in the last years of his life became involved in plans to establish a Unitarian church in Montreal. But no records of a marriage outside Christ Church have been found, and given the vigorous activity in both Protestant denominations in Montreal since Molson's arrival, there was no shortage of opportunity for a formal marriage.

Circumstances argue against a marriage preceding the one at Christ Church. The marriage contract identified Sarah Vaughan as a "singlewoman," and made no effort to mention an earlier ceremony. Its tone bespeaks a relationship not yet sanctified by any religious denomination, declaring "that a marriage by God's permission is intended to be had and solemnized between them...." For whatever reason, the marriage did not happen until 1801, but such a delay was not without precedent in Molson's life. It took the prospect of imminent death to get him to revise his will in 1795, almost eight years after his first son was born, and more than a year after his last son, so that Sarah and the children were beneficiaries.

Back in Lincolnshire, an unsanctified relationship like the one between John and Sarah would have been unimaginable among the gentry. Morality aside, the pervasive issues of property and inheritance would not have allowed it. The further one moved from England and its constricting property issues, however, the more lax attitudes became to formal marriage. The American colonies were full of casual arrangements. John Johnson's father, William Johnson, who had preceded him as the British superintendent of Indian affairs,[6] was famously informal in his domestic arrangements while in upstate New York. John Johnson was one of three children born to William and a Palatine-German servant named Catharine Weisenberg. "Catharine seems to have been quiet, undemanding, not much given to spending money, and, of course, unnoticed by anybody of consequence," the historian Isabel Thompson Kelly has written[7]—an acceptable description of Sarah Vaughan as well. According to Kelly, Catharine died of tuberculosis in April 1759, and William Johnson is believed to have married her on her deathbed. However, there were also two Johnson children of mixed race from this time, and these point to other assignations. He then entered into another long, informal partnership with Molly Brant, sister of the Mohawk war chief Joseph Brant, and she bore him three more children. They were never formally married, and, in his will, William Johnson identified her as both the mother of several of his children and his housekeeper. William Johnson's familial arrangements were consistent with his frontier life and close relations with the Six Nations tribes, who viewed his relationship with Molly Brant as a legitimate marriage.

John Molson certainly didn't treat his relationship with Sarah Vaughan as a subject of pride or prominence in his correspondence. He never mentioned her or the children in surviving letters home—a fairly glaring oversight. We can rightly presume that volunteering news of an unconsecrated relationship with an older woman—whose personal history was possibly less than pristine—

complete with illegitimate children, would have blackened his name among the Lincolnshire gentry at a time when he was still settling the affairs of his newly inherited estate. Lord Chesterfield was explicit in advising that one would be judged by the company one keeps. In his letter to his son of October 9, 1747, he wrote: "People will, in a great degree, and not without reason, form their opinion of you, upon that which they have of your friends; and there is a Spanish proverb, which says very justly, *Tell me whom you live with, and I will tell you who you are.*"

Yet the illegitimacy of the relationship and of his children does not appear to have harmed Molson socially in Montreal. He became sufficiently allied with the prominent Scottish merchants of the growing town both to contribute to the construction of the Presbyterian church and to play a leading role in St. Paul's Masonic Lodge. Molson was a member of the Masonic order no later than 1786, and he held the office of worshipful master at St. Paul's in Montreal from June to December 1791 and again from June 1795 to June 1796. He also rose to the rank of worshipful sword bearer in the Provincial Grand Lodge of Lower Canada in 1824.[8]

In the end, we know just as little about why John Molson married when he did as we do about who he married. We can only hope he treated Sarah Vaughan with more love and respect than Lord Chesterfield thought appropriate. When John Molson left England for Montreal in the spring of 1786, equipped with four volumes of Chesterfield's letters for moral guidance, he was carrying with him some of the worst advice ever inflicted on a young man who was about to enter into a long-term relationship. How much of it Molson took to heart is entirely open to speculation.

Chesterfield largely held women and the institution of marriage in contempt. Women, for him, were little more than vessels of pleasure, and his own marriage was a political one and presumably loveless. His letters to his illegitimate (though beloved) son are shot through with the low esteem in which he held the opposite sex, and his advice to his son on carnal prospects—championing the educative capabilities of older women and recommending to him some of his own former amours—caused much of the scandal that resulted when the letters were first published. (Chesterfield had also once quipped, in an anonymous contribution to *The Spectator*: "Sex: the pleasure is momentry, the position ridiculous, and the expense damnable.")

On September 5, 1748, Chesterfield advised his son that women

are only children of a larger growth; they have an entertaining tattle, and sometimes wit; but for solid, reasoning good-sense, I never knew in my life one that had it, or who reasoned or acted consequentially for four and twenty hours together. . . . A man of sense only trifles with them, plays with them, honours and flatters them, as he does with a sprightly, forward child. . . .

He also felt they should be steered clear of any business, not having a head for it. And on December 19, 1749, he volunteered

Women are much more like each other than men: they have, in truth, but two passions, vanity and love; these are their universal characteristics. . . . He who flatters them most, pleases them best; and they are most in love with him, who they think is the most in love with them.

His opinion of marriage was equally low. When his cousin Arthur Charles Stanhope wrote him on October 12, 1765,[9] to seek his opinion on a proposed third marriage, Chesterfield blanched.

I may possibly be wrong, but I tell you very sincerely, with all due regard to the sex, that I never thought a woman good company for a man *tete-a-tete*, unless for one purpose, which, I presume, is not yours now. . . . Upon the whole, you will marry or not marry, as you think best; but to take a wife merely as an agreeable and rational companion, will commonly be found to be a grand mistake. Shakespeare seems to be a good deal of my opinion, when he allows them only this department, "To suckle fools and chronicle small beer."[10]

Chesterfield pronounced marriage to be no prescription for a couple's harmony. "Every man and wife hate each other cordially; whatever they may pretend, in public, to the contrary," he informed his son on May 10, 1748.

The husband certainly wishes his wife at the devil, and the wife certainly cuckolds her husband. Whereas, I presume that men and their wives neither love nor hate each other the more, upon account of the form of matrimony which has been said over them. The cohabitation, indeed, which is the consequence of matrimony, makes them either love or hate more, accordingly as they respectively deserve it; but that would be exactly the same, between any man and woman, who lived together without being married.

This Chesterfield opinion—the most important one from the perspective of the relationship between John Molson and Sarah Vaughan—held that marriage was irrelevant to a couple's contentment. Cohabitation, not a licence issued by a church, was the sole source of happiness or despair in a union. Perhaps, as John Molson absorbed Chesterfield, he nodded in agreement. Presumably he was happy with Sarah, and they were not yet married. Did he really need to marry in a church?

But who, after all, did he eventually marry?

Chapter 10

The prudence and necessity of often concealing the truth, insensibly seduces people to violate it. It is the only art of mean capacities, and the only refuge of mean spirits. Whereas, concealing the truth, upon proper occasions, is as prudent, and as innocent, as telling a lie, upon any occasion, is infamous and foolish.
—Lord Chesterfield, letter to his son, January 8, 1750

HER NAME, ACCORDING TO the 1801 marriage contract, was Sarah Insleyvaughan, while the marriage record at Christ Church identified her as "Vaughan, Sarah Insley"; the 1799–1800 brewery accounts had already given Sarah Vaughan the middle name Insly, which was modified to Ansly in 1801–2. And at one time, perhaps, whether by marriage, kinship or alias, according to the 1795 and 1797 wills, she had been Sarah Kitley. The marriage record indicates that she was one year older than John Molson—her age was given as thirty-nine, his as thirty-eight (technically, he was in his thirty-eighth year, with his birthday more than eight months away)—but the difference cannot be substantiated by any other documents. The family tree compiled by Sandwell gave her year of birth as 1759 (without any proof), making her four years older than Molson, but the difference could have been much greater.

Denison alluded to, but declined to elaborate on, "slim" evidence that she came from Caldwell's Manor. In the face of her mysterious arrival in John Molson's life, Sarah Vaughan has often been consigned to the unknown ranks of the Loyalist dispossessed escaping the rebel colonies. The rapidity with which the relationship developed moved Denison to suggest that Molson had known her before he travelled to England in 1785: how else to account for his breakneck rebound from fair Aunt Nancy?

The timing of the relationship's beginning hinges on the fact that John Molson's eldest son, John Junior, was born on October 14, 1787; the meeting between Sarah and John thus must be back-dated at least nine months, to February 1787. Presumably they deserved a little time to get to know one another before Sarah became pregnant, which presses the beginning of the relationship into 1786.

Molson arrived back in Montreal on June 1, 1786. On June 12, he entered into his record book: "Hired Maid Servant for 4 dollars per Month—to come on the 14th at which time her Wages to commence provided said agreement complied with." Two days later, he duly noted: "House keeper entered on her month at 4 Dollars." Where he was living when he hired the housekeeper isn't known; he did not begin to rent the house near the brewery, from a Monsieur Bergevin, until July 21.

In the same letter in which he observed that a housekeeper had been hired, Molson persisted in singing the praises of his widowed aunt to his sisters. He must still have been longing for Ann Elsdale when he hired this woman to tend his house. If she was Sarah Vaughan, she soon made him forget about the Worthy Little Woman back in Surfleet.

Denison privately weighed the circumstantial evidence of the anonymous housekeeper's arrival, factored in the realization that Molson and Sarah Vaughan may well have begun cohabiting in the house rented from Bergevin in late July, and created an unfortunate fairy tale. Without stating that Sarah Vaughan had been the house-keeper, he implicitly drew on the date of the hiring in establishing the beginning of the relationship. He asserted that the couple moved into the rented house "and there John and Sarah began their honeymoon in August, with the Monarques, Barsalous, Bergevins and other Canadian families as friendly neighbours."

Denison was writing complete fiction. We have no idea of how friendly these neighbours were, but more important, there was no honeymoon because there had been no marriage. Denison's account of the relationship, written in the early 1950s under the sponsorship of the Molson family, was pure damage control. Nonetheless, it drew on the high probability that Molson had met his romantic match in his newly hired housekeeper. Jack Baxter's salacious comment in his letter of September 9, 1786—"I commend you but get some Old Woman in the House you do not wish to come within a Yard of"—may have unwittingly scored a direct hit.

This housekeeper is the only hiring from this period who is never named in the account books—in contrast we learn of hirings named James Randall, John and Christopher Cook, Peter Huffman and Thomas Jefferies in 1786 and 1787. The fact that Molson never named this housekeeper suggests that she was soon no longer an employee. On November 11, 1787, about one month after the first-born, John Junior, arrived, Molson hired a woman named Ann Holm (or Holmes) "for six months from 8 Nov to 8 May." Once Sarah Vaughan, if we accept her as the original housekeeper, had a child to raise, Molson must have needed immediate domestic help.

However misleading his prose, Denison had sound instincts: Sarah Vaughan could well have been the housekeeper hired in June 1786. But how she arrived in that position is the enduring mystery.

Hunting for a woman named Sarah Vaughan in records on both sides of the Atlantic is complicated by the fact that the name Vaughan has so many sociocultural sources, not to mention spelling variants. There were Vaughans in the highest ranks of British society, owing in part to the ascent to the British throne of William and Mary of the Netherlands in 1689. There were Vaughans in the counties of East Anglia who had emigrated from Holland in the seventeenth century. In North America, the Vaughans were transplanted Anglo-Dutch, or middle- and upper-class English immigrants, or established landowners from the original Dutch settlements around New York, or Palatine-Germans recruited to settle the American colonies.

As well, searches of birth, marriage and death records in colonial America cannot be considered definitive. While the Declaration of Independence gave a noble sheen to the revolutionary struggle, the actual conflict was waged along old sectarian lines imported from the mother country. Because a large number of American Loyalists were high Anglicans, many Anglican churches were badly damaged by rebels, with the concomitant loss of their records. At the same time, British forces put the torch to Presbyterian churches frequented by the enthusiastically rebellious Ulster-Scot transplants. And where entire graveyards have not disappeared, many aging gravestones can no longer be read. Far more than in Britain, where birth, marriage and death records are generally well preserved (largely because a single entity, the Church of England, was responsible for keeping them), the search for colonial ancestors often relies on privately compiled genealogies drawn from family bibles and amateur sleuthing, augmented by folk memory and what collaborative records survive. Yet even with considerable gaps in the records, numerous Vaughans can be found in Loyalist ranks, and many young women named Sarah Vaughan were born in the American colonies around the mid-eighteenth century.

Although we have no conclusive evidence of where Sarah Vaughan came from, and an infinite supply of possible sources, we can nonetheless reduce the field to four different Sarahs. We can call them Sarah of Bolam, Sarah of Lincolnshire, Sarah of the Upper Country and Sarah of Caldwell's Manor.

Sarah of Bolam is one of the most enduring candidates. No one has ever been able to find a Sarah Insley Vaughan in genealogical records anywhere in the world, but England's Northumberland County has come the closest. Denison attempted to confirm that a woman named Sarah Insley Vaughan had been born in the parish of Morpeth, north of Newcastle upon Tyne, in 1759. He wrote the town clerk on July 31, 1952, seeking confirmation of her birth and any evidence of a marriage to a man named Kitley (as Molson's 1795 and 1797 wills suggested), but he received a negative reply on September 11. Then, on June 14, 1955, just as *The Barley and the Stream* was being published, Denison received belated news from Morpeth. A marriage had turned up in the parish register for July

16, 1775, between "David Totchley Batch. & Sarah Vaughan Spinster[1] both of this Parish by Banns."*

The information came too late for Denison, but was it even of any use? Such a marriage would make Sarah Vaughan considerably older than the marriage record at Christ Church indicated. This Sarah would probably have been at least seven years Molson's senior. And could "Kitley" be considered an acceptable corruption of "Totchley" (which has been reinterpreted as "Tetchley")?

The lead turned up by Denison nonetheless fuelled further research, and a christening turned up for one Sarah Aynsley Vaughan—a name tantalizingly close to the brewery records entry of Sarah Ansly Vaughan—in Bolam, Northumberland, on February 13, 1752. Bolam was a small rural parish of fewer than five hundred souls near Morpeth, in the heart of the great northeast coal district. The father's name was Thomas, and because the parish priest in Bolam was named Thomas Vaughan, it is thought plausible that Sarah was his daughter. But the 1752 birthdate is even earlier than the 1759 date proposed by Sandwell, producing an age difference between this Sarah and John Molson of about twelve years. It would make Sarah forty-nine, not thirty-nine, when she married Molson at Christ Church.

Yet for some people interested in the Molsons' history, Sarah Vaughan's Bolam heritage appears a closed case. A thorough genealogy of the Canadian Molsons, produced by Richard Carruthers in 1995, states: "The Hon. John Molson, The Elder . . . married 1801 Sarah Aynsley VAUGHAN alias KITLEY daughter of the Rev. Thos. Vaughan, of Bolam & Morpeth, Northumberland, and sometime the wife of David Tetchley (1752–1829)." But there are abundant problems with Sarah of Bolam. No mother was recorded in her christening record—highly unusual for the daughter of an Anglican priest, which means Rev. Thomas Vaughan was by no means her father. And while it might seem reasonable to presume that the Sarah Aynsley Vaughan born in Bolam in 1752 was

---

* *Banns:* The proclamation made in a church, usually on three successive Sundays, of an intent to marry.

also the Sarah Vaughan who married David Tetchley in nearby Morpeth in 1775, when Sarah of Bolam would have been twenty-three, the "Aynsley" is not recorded in the marriage record.

The Tetchley marriage appeals on the "Kitley" front, as "Kitley" could be interpreted as a corruption of "Tetchley." It does, however, seem a stretch. While some variance in spelling of the name in a Molson will would be understandable, as it was probably written down on oral evidence from Sarah Vaughan, we would expect her to be able to pronounce her first husband's name better than to mangle Kitley into Tetchley. (On the other hand, the mangling may have been the fault of Molson, who could have misstated the name for the notary, without confirming it with Sarah.)

In all, Sarah Aynsley Vaughan of Bolam and Sarah Vaughan, bride of Totchley/Tetchley at Morpeth, are fraught with internal inconsistencies. It should be remembered that the name Insley and its variants were grafted onto Sarah Vaughan's name several years after she was first recognized in John Molson's will, and thus she may not even have been born with it. Nothing known about Sarah Vaughan and David Tetchley after the 1775 marriage, or about Sarah Aynsley Vaughan after the 1752 birth, would place them in America. The best guess—and that is all it is—in support of Sarah of Bolam as John Molson's wife has been that Sarah separated from Tetchley at some point, perhaps after they emigrated to America, and found her way into John Molson's life.

Our second candidate from England is Sarah of Lincolnshire. If Sarah was another Lincolnshire émigré—even crossing the Atlantic with Molson in the summer of 1786—it would help explain why they so quickly set up house after his arrival back in Montreal. We know very little about what he was up to in the final months of his 1785–86 trip home, beyond gathering brewery supplies, and it left him plenty of time to become acquainted with someone new. (That said, one suspects that Jack Baxter, who personally visited him on his ship before departure, would have noticed a female companion and commented on her in a subsequent letter, unless we wish to imagine Molson concealing his companion from view in the best tradition of bedroom farces.)

While no potential bride from Lincolnshire can be absolutely identified in John Molson's generation, genealogical records hold out the possibility that one could have existed. Numerous Vaughans (with typical spelling variants) lived in Lincolnshire in the eighteenth century, and inevitably the Vaughans in the county produced their share of Sarahs, a popular girl's name. In 1766 a Sarah "Vawghan" married a Robert Howden at Wainfleet-All-Saints, twenty-five miles from Spalding, at the mouth of the Wash, while in 1734, a Sarah "Vaughn" had married a man named Richard Manton about five miles north, at Irby-in-the-Marsh; and in 1770 and 1771, children were christened by a couple at Bicker named Joseph and Sarah Vaughan.

While none of these Sarahs could be considered "the" Sarah, they establish that a number of Vaughans living not far from the Molsons in Lincolnshire were naming their daughters Sarah in the eighteenth century. And it may be more than coincidence that a John Moulson was christened at Wainfleet-All-Saints in 1733. If the Moulsons of Wainfleet-All-Saints knew the Molsons of Moulton, then a bridge may have been built between our John Molson and the Vaughans of south Lincolnshire. It should be remembered that John Molson's great-great-grandfather Thomas, who left Cantley for Crowland in the middle to late seventeenth century, spelled his last name "Moulson," as did many of his Cantley ancestors.

The possibility that the names Kitley and Insley were attached to Sarah Vaughan in legal documents to strengthen inheritance claims supports a Sarah of Lincolnshire, for the two names are tantalizingly close to affluent ones in John Molson's past. Snake Hall probably came into the possession of the Molsons through the marriage, in 1691, of Thomas of Peakhill to Mary Wincely, and this Mary, for whom no birth record can be found, could have been Marie Winsley, born at Holbeach in 1668. "Insley" is close enough to "Winsley" to be considered a variant. As for "Kitley," the Boulton family of Moulton, to whom the Molsons were close enough to inherit money from them, were allied with the high-born Knightleys of Northamptonshire in ownership of the "Fenland" estate. "Knightley" is certainly much closer to "Kitley" than is "Tetchley." Kitley (or variants such as Kitely and Keightley) was an uncommon name in England, and it appears only sporadically around England in the eighteenth century, never occurring in Northumberland or Lincolnshire. The name, however, does appear in Liverpool, in the territory of the Knightley family, which somewhat reinforces its association with Molson's past through the Knightley-allied Boultons. Kitley in fact may be a corruption of Knightley.

Through his will and his marriage, then, John Molson could have been trying to stake claims, however slight or difficult to prove, to the fortunes of the Knightleys and Winsleys, on behalf of his Lincolnshire-born wife. All of this is speculation, of course, however worthwhile. No Sarah Vaughan from Lincolnshire precisely fits the bill of John Molson's spouse, and so we have to continue our search for her in the American colonies.

The hunt for a Loyalist source for Sarah Vaughan brings us to Sarah of the Upper Country (west of Montreal). It's possible she came into Molson's life through John Johnson, his St. Mary's suburb neighbour and the superintendent in charge of Loyalist refugees. As noted in connection with the death of Jim Brainsby, John Johnson was prominent in Loyalist military activities during the American Revolution, commanding the King's Royal Regiment of New York from the Naval Department base at Carleton Island. Wives and children of Loyalist soldiers gathered at Carleton Island during the revolution, and Sarah Vaughan could have been among the spouses or relatives. But of the twelve soldiers named Vaughan (or Vaughen) who appear in Loyalist regiments in the British Military and Naval Records (Series C), none appear in a regiment associated with Carleton Island.[2] (The Naval Department did employ a shipwright named William Vaughan, but the only reference to him in the payroll places him at the Detroit base.) Perhaps Sarah Vaughan came to Carleton Island on her own, to escape the strife in upstate New York.

If she did, she might then have moved on to the nearby Williamstown settlement founded by Johnson. And as we have seen, in 1786 the Reverend John Bethune, the former chaplain to the Royal Highland Emigrants regiment, left his position at St. Andrew's Church in Williamstown to spend a year ministering to the new Scots-Presbyterian congregation in Montreal. If Sarah Vaughan encountered Bethune at Williamstown, perhaps taking employment with him, his appearance in Montreal in 1786 was perfectly timed for a meeting between her and Molson.

But Carleton Island, Williamstown, Reverend Bethune and John Johnson present only a pathway along which Sarah Vaughan *could* have travelled, and provide no real evidence for her. Given what was known in the 1950s, Denison was prudent in proposing that she probably came into John Molson's life through Caldwell's Manor. And the strongest evidence is still found there.

The most obvious source for her would be the well-known Vaughans who settled in and around Henry Caldwell's seigneury. They were Palatine-Germans who had come to the American colonies well before the revolution. Genealogical records indicate that Josephus Vaughan, born at New Fairfield, Connecticut, owned an estate there valued at about £3,000.[3] All nine children of Josephus Vaughan and Rebecca Towner were born there between about 1757 and 1776. New Fairfield was a high Anglican, Loyalist stronghold; the Vaughans' sympathies for the Crown forced them to take refuge in Long Island in 1777, and the New Fairfield property was seized by the state of Connecticut in 1778. Two sons, Wait and Benjamin, served in the British regular army during the revolution.

In 1783, their seventeen-year-old son, Josephus the younger, settled at the sixth concession of Caldwell's Manor (present-day Clarenceville, Quebec). His parents soon joined him. In 1804, Josephus the younger swapped properties with Enoch Salls (a Loyalist from New York) at Noyan, and established the first ferry service to cross the Richelieu to Lacolle. Their large home and tavern and indispensable ferry service were well known to travellers moving between Montreal and Lake Champlain.

The Vaughans, in short, were a prominent Loyalist family in and around Caldwell's Manor from 1783 onwards. But placing among them a Sarah Vaughan with whom John Molson could fall in love is difficult. To be the right age to form a relationship with John Molson, she would have to have been a sister of Josephus the younger, but none of his eight siblings was named Sarah. And the Vaughans who settled at Caldwell's Manor are also a problematic source for Sarah because they were an educated middle-class family. Rebecca Towner was remembered by her grandson Amos Hawley Vaughan as "very intelligent and well educated,"[4] according to the local historian and genealogist David M. Bell. Her son Wait received a university education. It wasn't the right environment to produce an illiterate woman. If these Vaughans were the source of Sarah, she must have been from another branch of the Connecticut Vaughans (one of which did have slight Insley connections by marriage)[5] and come to live at Caldwell's Manor with relatives after the revolution.

But there is another source for Sarah in Caldwell's Manor—or perhaps more accurately, in Alburgh. And this may present the most persuasive case for the origins of the woman who married John Molson.

The connection begins not with a family named Vaughan, but with one named Sweet. On November 9, 1763, Stephen Sweet was born in North Kingston, Rhode Island, less than two months before John Molson was born on the other side of the Atlantic. In April 1777, as Molson was being educated by Mr. Whitehead in south Lincolnshire, the fourteen-year-old Sweet became a Revolutionary soldier at Boston Neck. Stephen Sweet repeatedly re-enlisted before receiving a final discharge around November 1779, just as he turned sixteen. Sometime after that, his father, Sylvester, moved the family to Little Hoosick, New York, across the Vermont border from Bennington. Stephen probably went along, but, before turning twenty-one, he married his cousin Anna Sweet. Stephen and Anna Sweet next appeared, without warning, in Alburgh, where their first child, George, was born on June 1, 1783.

At least three months before John Molson announced in letters home that he had acquired four hundred acres at Caldwell's Manor, the precocious Revolutionary soldier Stephen Sweet was home-steading on the disputed Missisquoi Tongue with his young family. His father and brothers also moved to Alburgh at some point, prob-ably before the decade was out, and together they became notable landowners, accumulating about 350 acres around the settlement of Alburgh Springs, which was on the east side of the Tongue, near Missisquoi Bay. Their property may have made them neighbours of James Gibbins, Sr., as Molson had noted in October 1786 that the deed Gibbins presented to him as collateral for his debts was for land "on Missisque Bay."

In the Sweets we may have the strongest case for Sarah Vaughan's origins, and for how she could have met John Molson. Stephen and Anna Sweet were descended from the brothers John and James Sweet, two of the purchasers of four thousand acres from the natives at Warwick, Rhode Island, in 1662. And in 1719, John Sweet's granddaughter Joanna had married a man named Robert Vaughan. These Vaughans and Sweets were two of the oldest families in colonial America, and had been moving through time on parallel paths since the 1630s, until the marriage of Joanna Sweet and Robert Vaughan finally united them.

The Massachusetts Bay Colony received its royal charter in 1628, and in 1630 the first flotilla of settlers arrived to establish the new Puritan settlement of Salem, north of the original Plymouth colony. The early genealogy of the Sweets and Vaughans is far from absolute, but both families were established in Salem in the early 1630s. John Sweet arrived with his wife and children in December 1630 aboard a supply ship named the *Lyon*. John Vaughan, the other patriarch, may not have been far behind him. It's possible that when he arrived, he was known as Johan Vahan, and that either he or his son Johan anglicized the name. One privately com-piled lineage identifies him as the Johan Vahan christened in St. Edmund's parish within the great medieval walled city of Norwich on April 14, 1617. Since the first son of the Johan Vahan/John Vaughan who lived in Massachusetts, and later Rhode Island, was not born until 1644, the Norwich birthdate is a reasonable one. If this Johan was indeed Sarah Vaughan's ancestor, it means that her

English roots were less than sixty miles to the east of John Molson's birthplace of Moulton.

That Vahan could have come from Norwich is not surprising, as East Anglia was the source of so many of the participants in what became known as the great migration of the 1630s to the Puritan colonies. Seeking either religious freedom or new economic opportunities (or both), they streamed onto migrant ships and made for America. Like John Molson, Johan Vahan was only a teenager when he made the crossing to North America. He may have been as young as fifteen, perhaps travelling (as Molson did) with older companions, as there's no indication his parents came with him.[6]

Because there were a number of men named John Vaughan (or some variant) in the early Massachusetts colony, it may be unfair to heap a number of crimes attributed to "John Vaughan" onto Sarah Vaughan's potential ancestor. Nonetheless, a John Vaughan was fined on March 4, 1633, for "drinking strong waters," and on March 4, 1634, convictions were handed down to one John Vaughan and several others for "misspending their time, drinking strong waters and selling contrary to law."

Whatever John Vaughan's legal problems, the Massachusetts Bay Colony was seething with religious factionalism. Having fled England to free themselves from the oppression of the state-sponsored Church of England, the Puritans turned against their own dissidents and banished them as they moulded the colony into a rigid theocracy. Several spurned groups struck out for Narragansett Bay, which would become Rhode Island. And because these factions wanted nothing to do with each other, they ended up settling in four separate towns.

John Sweet was an ardent follower of Roger Williams, having arrived with him in Massachusetts aboard the *Lyon* in 1630. Williams preached the gospel of antimonianism, which held that once baptized or saved, a person, regardless of his conduct during his mortal life, could not suffer damnation. This naturally led to charges that the antimonians were advocating every form of debauchery humankind could imagine. Williams's teachings got him banished from the Massachusetts Bay Colony in 1635. After an initial 1636 stop in the Plymouth colony, where they were asked to move on, Williams led his followers to Narragansett Bay, where he established the settlement of Providence. John Sweet's son John was granted property there by Williams in 1638.

Back in England, concern was growing about the independence of the Massachusetts Bay Colony and its republican enthusiasms at a time when Parliament and the Crown were heading towards civil war. Charles I revoked the colony's charter in 1638, placing it under his own administration, and the Vaughans followed the Sweets in striking out for Rhode Island. John Vaughan the younger appeared on a list of inhabitants who had been admitted to Rhode Island (then known as the Narragansett Bay Colony) since May 20, 1638. He had probably followed another banished religious leader, Anne Hutchinson, who had been excommunicated by the church in Massachusetts Bay in March 1638. That same month, Hutchinson and her adherents established a settlement at what became Portsmouth, at the north end of Aquidneck Island. A year later came a schism in the Portsmouth religious community, and William Coddington led his believers to the other end of the island to found Newport. John Vaughan the younger must have been a Coddington acolyte, as he was granted a lot in Newport that year.

In 1662, the brothers John and James Sweet and several other men made their successful petition to the local court to be permitted to purchase four thousand acres from the natives—it was Roger Williams's tenet that settlers should purchase lands directly from tribes and not expect grants from the Crown based on Britain's own negotiations with the natives. The land was around Warwick, in the northwest corner of Narragansett Bay, and John Sweet built a grist mill there. When it was burned down by raiding natives during King Philip's War in 1675, he and his family removed to Newport, where the Vaughans were well established.

The families doubtless met each other in Newport, but neither was to remain there. In 1677, George Vaughan, of the family's third generation in colonial America, was one of forty-eight men to receive a five-thousand-acre grant in East Greenwich, just south of Warwick. The Sweets presumably returned to their own plantation at Warwick after the hostilities. In 1719, Joanna Sweet and Robert Vaughan united the family bloodlines by marrying at East Greenwich.

Less is known about the Sweets who descended from John's brother James, but four generations later, Sylvester Sweet, who was born around 1741 at North Kingston, south of East Greenwich, married Patience Congdon. They were the parents of Benjamin, the teenaged Revolutionary soldier who married his cousin Anna and appeared in Alburgh in 1783.

Over in the Sweet branch descended from plantation investor John Sweet, Joanna Sweet and Robert Vaughan raised a family of eight children, one of whom was also called Benjamin, born in 1730. He married Catherine Godfrey in 1751, and they had seven children. The fourth, born in East Greenwich on February 17, 1761, was christened Sarah in honour of her aunt, Sarah Susannah Vaughan, who had died the previous May. This Sarah Vaughan was only a year older than the woman of the same name who married John Molson in Montreal in 1801, and since Molson's age was misstated in the marriage record, we can consider her, age-wise, a perfect fit.

But was she *the* Sarah Vaughan? Virtually nothing is known about her beyond her date of birth.[7] Whether Molson's wife was the Sarah Vaughan born in 1761 or was another member of the sprawling family tree of the Rhode Island Vaughans related to the Sweets (and the full Vaughan genealogy is still being sorted out), a logical path to Alburgh can be drawn for her.

A number of the 1761 Sarah Vaughan's siblings relocated to New York State, which suggests a general movement in the family that could have involved her or another Sarah as well. They all came of age in the years framing the American Revolution, and it is easy to picture them, like so many others of their generation, being set in motion by the turbulence stirred up by the war. Loyalists were not the only ones in transit during and after the conflict; as peace returned, many rebels young and old, now citizens of a new nation, left the towns and farms that had been their homes for generations to pursue opportunities on the colonial frontier that had been denied them through eight years of fighting. We can see this Sarah Vaughan joining the northwesterly migration that carried relatives into New York—and, the Sweets among them, on to the Missisquoi Tongue of northern Vermont.

The suggestions in Molson's early wills that Sarah Vaughan may have had a relationship with someone named Kitley supports a colonial American source for her. Several Kitleys appear in the rolls of Massachusetts Revolutionary soldiers, and there are more listings under the names Keitly, Ketley, Kettelly, Kettly, Kitly, Kittely and Kittley. As well, Insley (or Inslee) was a well-established family name in colonial America, with some branches able to trace their roots back to the early 1600s in Maryland. Some were also Loyalists. Records of the Loyalist regiment known as the New Jersey Volunteers indicate that a John Insley was taken prisoner on February 18, 1777, and recovered in a prisoner exchange on September 1, 1780.

But looking for a literal Insley or Kitley in England or colonial America may be a mistake. Molson's 1795 will identified Sarah Vaughan as a Kitley "or by whatever other name or names she may be known or called." The phrasing indicates that Kitley was an alias with a number of variants. And a root source for all the Insley variants to Sarah's name, and even the Kitley reference in Molson's early wills, can be found with one family who had the opportunity to meet Sarah through the Sweets in both northern Vermont and around Little Hoosick, New York.

Their name was Kinsley—and it wasn't. The actual surname was Kingsley,[8] but tradition has it that as arch-patriots of the American Revolution, the Kingsleys so despised the "king" in their name that they did away with it in daily usage. But if they were willing to pass themselves off as Kinsleys, one has to wonder how many other name variations different family members tried—and if it had anything to do with patriotic fervour. If one were to pick a common ground for "Kitley" and "Insley," one could not do better than "Kinsley."

Like the Vaughans and the Sweets, the Kingsleys were an old American colonial family; they had been in Connecticut since the 1630s, and Stephen Kingsley and his wife, Mary Elizabeth

Spaulding, were among the first settlers at Dorchester. Mary Packard, wife of Stephen's great-grandson Samuel, could trace her ancestry to Mary Chilton, who, tradition has it, was the first person to step off the *Mayflower* onto Plymouth Rock in 1620.

The Kingsleys had a traumatic beginning in America. Hanna Brackett, the wife of Stephen Kingsley's son Samuel, was killed in an Indian raid in 1706, and the succeeding generations were filled with soldiers. The family begat numerous Minutemen in different generations. Among them were the brothers Nathan and Daniel Kingsley. Nathan was sixty-two and Daniel forty-six when they fought together at the Battle of Bennington, at Vermont's capital, in 1777.

Daniel Kingsley had already seen action in the French and Indian (or Seven Years) War; he appeared in the muster roll of the Third Connecticut Regiment in 1758. In 1753, Daniel had married Eunice Bingham at Norwich, Connecticut, about twenty-five miles west of the Rhode Island homes of the Sweets and Vaughans. Eunice Bingham's family members must have been among the homesteaders and speculators who received land grants from New Hampshire in what became Vermont, as the town of Binghamville was named for them. The settlement was at the north end of the state, about twenty-five miles southeast of the Missisquoi Tongue.

Daniel Kingsley is thought to have moved his wife and seven children to Bennington, at the south end of the state, around 1780, although his presence at the Battle of Bennington suggests he was there sooner. But sometime during the next decade, the family headed north, settling only a few miles from Binghamville, at Cambridge, where Daniel appeared in the first United States census of 1790.

Like Daniel, their father, the sons Stephen, Daniel Junior and Nathan all served in the Revolutionary War, and all ended up living at the north end of Lake Champlain. Stephen, the eldest, settled on North Hero Island no later than 1800. Their sister Eunice, who was a few months younger than John Molson, married James Butler, whose family owned Butlers Island near North Hero. Eunice was probably settled there by 1787, as her first child was born in 1788. Daniel Junior was on North Hero by 1810, with seven children and an unknown wife.

The youngest son, Nathan, had become a Revolutionary soldier in 1781. He was thought to have been born about 1765 in Massachusetts, but when he entered Canada to trade in the early 1800s, he swore that he was born in 1767—if so, he was only fourteen when he took up arms against the English. He married, at an unknown date, a woman named Lydia Pearl, who may have been born in 1767 as well. We don't know where she came from, but her name provides a potential link to Ira Allen and Alburgh: one of the original seventy-five grantees of the Alburgh lands in 1781 was a man from New Hampshire named Noble Pearl, who sold his right back to Ira Allen in 1785. Nathan and Lydia's son, Nathan Junior, born at Cambridge in 1790, was married at North Hero in 1816 and eventually settled at Alburgh, where he and his wife were buried.

With the lives of the Vaughans, the Sweets and the Kingsleys sketched in, we can envision the path Sarah Vaughan of Rhode Island followed to a meeting with John Molson. She probably joined her relatives the Sweets who moved to Little Hoosick, New York, around 1780, seeking fresh opportunities of her own, as her age of majority approached. The Kingsleys who fought at the Battle of Bennington were living in Bennington, just across the state border from Little Hoosick, by 1780. Both the Sweets and the Kingsleys boasted their quota of Revolutionary soldiers, had come west from the same general area of New England, and could have fraternized. In addition, the Kingsleys had ties by marriage to land in northern Vermont, within twenty-five miles of Alburgh and the nearby islands. At the same time, Stephen and Anna Sweet made a connection with Caldwell's Manor/Alburgh. Perhaps it was through Ira Allen, who lived just north of Bennington, at Sunderland, and in any event was regularly in the state capital. Or it might have been through Henry Caldwell's agent, William McGlemoyl, who was active in southern Vermont in the fall of 1783, and perhaps earlier. We know Stephen and Anna Sweet were in Alburgh by June 1783, just before John Molson acquired his four hundred acres from Henry Caldwell. We know the Sweets settled next to Missisquoi Bay, where James Gibbins, Sr., held land by 1786. We also know the Kingsleys moved on to northern Vermont sometime after 1780 and before 1790, settling first at Cambridge. Through marriage, many of the Kingsley children made their way to North Hero Island.

And we know nothing about what went on in the lives of these young Kingsley men between their arrival in Bennington, around 1777–80, and their eventual marriages at unknown dates. All but Nathan would have been the right age for a relationship with Sarah Vaughan, which could have begun in Bennington or blossomed later when she followed the Sweets to Alburgh in 1783. Through a liaison with one of the Kingsleys, Sarah Vaughan could have been known as a Kinsley, an Insley, a Kitley, "or by whatever other name or names she may be known or called."

When would this Sarah Vaughan and John Molson have met? Perhaps in 1783–84, when he was making his first visits to Caldwell's Manor. Or perhaps the encounter waited until he was back from England in the summer of 1786, when he was hiring help and everyone was in place on the Missisquoi Tongue: the Sweets at Alburgh Springs and James Gibbins, Sr., somewhere close by.

It is a scenario built out of circumstantial evidence from the lives of common people that the eighteenth century tends to leave for us. But the facts produce a hypothesis with more breadth and depth than previously offered. The Sarah Vaughan currently in vogue is a woman named Sarah Aynsley Vaughan, who was born in Bolam, Northumberland, to an Anglican priest and an as yet unknown mother; who despite her middle-class surroundings failed to learn to read and write; who then married a man named Tetchley, lost him somehow and made her way to North America somehow; who met John Molson somehow, had her first child with him when she was thirty-five and he was not yet twenty-four, and then married him in 1801, when she was forty-nine and he was thirty-seven, even though the marriage record asserted they were only one year apart in age.

To a large degree, identifying Sarah Vaughan is an exercise in narrative. She encourages a wishfulness about who she might have been, even a well-meaning desire to raise her above the ranks of an illiterate servant, to place her on an equal footing with her now famous husband. If nothing else, the Sarah of Caldwell's Manor who came from Rhode Island gives John Molson's spouse a gravity and dignity otherwise denied her.

This Sarah Vaughan was an American—not a Loyalist but a woman surrounded by fierce patriots—with deep roots in the continent that lured Molson out of Snake Hall. The head start that Sarah of Rhode Island enjoyed in the journey to St. Mary's Current was staggering. The founding of Montreal by an obscure French religious order was still about a decade away when Johan Vahan arrived in Massachusetts. Her family had beaten the Molsons to the continent by about 150 years. Through Sarah Vaughan, the sons of John Molson had roots in North America that stretched back almost to the dawn of organized European settlement—and they never realized it.

Chapter 11

Whatever is worth doing at all, is worth doing well.
　　　—Lord Chesterfield, letter to his son, March 10, 1746

A LETTER FROM JOHN MOLSON to Philip Ashley on June 25, 1786, a few weeks after his return to Quebec, spelled out for the attorney his looming financial requirements. As he reviewed for Ashley, he had spent more than £300 on hops and other supplies before leaving London. We know he left London with £250 sterling; after retiring the mortgage held by Pierre Monarque, Molson reported he was left with only £100 sterling, and with no hope of generating any revenue from the brewery for four or five months. He did not mention to Ashley the loans he made to James Gibbins, Sr. Molson emphasized that "£500 more will be the least sum that I can carry on the Brewing Business." Raising such an amount would require Ashley to mortgage Snake Hall, and Molson was concerned that Ashley send him the necessary legal instruments so that he could return the executed paperwork by the close of autumnal shipping in October. If Ashley couldn't arrange the mortgage right away, then Molson wanted to be able to sell a bill of exchange for £100.

By failing to keep his scheduled appointment with Philip Ashley before leaving England, Molson had precipitated an almost immediate crisis. Obviously, he had not worked through his cash-flow requirements very thoroughly before boarding the *Everetta*, and in a matter of weeks was confronting the possibility of running out of money. He may have taken false comfort in the considerable monies still owing him, as tabulated by Philip Ashley in the summary delivered to him on March 11. Much of it was back rent, but his grandfather Samuel had also given a note for £61 9s 10d for the remainder of the monies owed him from the estate.

His decision to retire the mortgage on the brewery property at the first opportunity may have been in keeping with the advice of the wise Lord Chesterfield, who counselled "Never run in debt, for it is neither honest nor prudent." But for the sake of avoiding £6 in interest over the next year, Molson had surrendered £100 of his cash on hand. His generosity towards James Gibbins, Sr., had further depleted his specie. An unspoken relationship with Sarah Vaughan would soon develop, and by early in the new year she would be pregnant. His increasing anxiety was understandable, but John Molson's frustrations, unfortunately, would be taken out on Philip Ashley through some of the most mean-spirited letters he ever penned.

He wrote Ashley a follow-up letter on July 6, revisiting the themes of money spent and required. Although he may have been sending a second letter only in case the first went missing, it was becoming Molson's habit to pound away at Ashley before the attorney had a reasonable chance to respond. By July 30, when he wrote Ashley again, Molson had given up hope of getting the £500 mortgage arranged before the close of shipping. Instead he proposed writing a bill of exchange for £60, payable six weeks after sight, in hope that Ashley could collect some of the Lincolnshire rents due to him in the meantime.

Samuel Elsdale had first leased the lands of John and Thomas Molson to William Cannington in 1773, and made a subsequent lease arrangement with Edward Pavey. Molson was owed about £100 from a bond posted by Cannington; Pavey still owed him four years' back rent totalling £44. On October 8, 1784, Elsdale had replaced the delinquent Cannington and Pavey with a new lessee named Thomas Waddington at the annual rate of £120, beginning April 5, 1785. Waddington was proving to be no better a risk. "There will be nearly three half years Rent due from Mr Wadington & perhaps you'l get something from Pavey," Molson instructed

Ashley on July 30. But Molson also owed the handyman William Bennett for repairs to Snake Hall, and he was hoping Ashley could hold him off—"perhaps he would wait till you had acquired a sufficiency, believe me he could not do me a more singular service."

Molson now was openly afraid of falling afoul of Quebec civil law, should his bill of exchange not be accepted by Gosling: "if draft is not answered will do me a great disservice as well as there is a particular *Act* of province *here* to recover large damages on a protested Bill." He was acutely sensitive to the hazards of doing business in a province where the Protestant merchants did not enjoy the full protection of English commercial law. An effort by reformers in the 1785 session had failed to extinguish the hated writ of *saisie*. Molson was abundantly familiar with it, as the collusive lawsuit he filed against Loid in 1784 was probably meant to avoid the brewery being seized under such a writ to satisfy a suit by John Waite over unpaid wages. Molson had left Montreal for New York in May 1785, just after the legislative session closed, to board the *Triumph* for his passage to London, and likely did not hear of the defeat of the reform initiative until he was back in Quebec in 1786. He knew then that the entire brewery could be lost if one sufficiently large bill of exchange, written on the Gosling account, was not honoured by Ashley.

A haughty bitterness made its first appearance in Molson's communications with Ashley, whose "matchless generosity to forgive" would be sorely tested. "My dear Sir excuse my importunities," he continued in the July 6 letter, "but as with the old proverb; necessity is the Mother of invention—so at present it makes me strain goodness & generosity of an already experienced friendship beyond its limits—tho' the unspeakable service it will do me & the certainty of your ever finding me Grateful has urged me to these Lengths."

The prospect for immediate success with his brewing efforts must have fed Molson's anxiety and impatience. His only competition was the porter imported by ship, which sold at £5 Halifax. A heavy, dark brown beer, one of its advantages for brewers was that it required less barley than a standard English ale, relying instead on the strength of the charred malt, in addition to hops, for flavouring. It could also keep for years in the right conditions. Until India Pale Ale was developed, primarily to solve the problem of beer going sour on tropical passages, porter practically defined exported British beer.

As the fall of 1786 approached, Molson concentrated on preparing the little brewery at the foot of St. Mary's Current for its first production season under his ownership. Whatever discussion there had been between Molson and James Gibbins about a partnership had not produced anything concrete. But since there were no letters of incorporation or stock, it's impossible to dismiss the possibility that Gibbins was involved to some degree as a silent partner. Gibbins's presence in Molson's business affairs continued into 1787, and it is difficult to distinguish between the actions of a friend and those of a partner. Whatever role Gibbins played in creating the first batch of ale in 1786, however, was at best minimal.

Brewing, even at the modest scale Molson first practised it, was a proto-industrial process. The brewer had more in common with the metallurgist than the baker, despite the common ingredients of cereal grains and yeast. He was operating a small, multi-facility factory, employing a variety of machines, tools and techniques to transform a cereal crop into a potable beverage. As the industrial revolution progressed, many elements of the process would be mechanized, and the science of biochemistry (not yet in hand when Molson entered the business) would greatly quantify the brewing art. But in the fall of 1786, in a corner of the world where he was both the new brewer and the only brewer, Molson was simply making the best of whatever equipment he had inherited from Loid.

Brewing not only required precision and hard-earned wisdom; it was also laborious and prone to utter failure. Molson would spend more than a month creating his first batch of beer, and he would not know if it was marketable until he sipped the finished product. If the batch failed—as the wheat beer of 1783–84 had—time and precious ingredients would be lost. Winter was setting in; he wouldn't be able to replace the hops he'd used until the next crop became available in England, and the local barley had long since been harvested and was possibly in short supply. At twenty-two, John Molson was single-handedly taking on perhaps the most complex agri-industrial process of his time. He was his own maltster and brewmaster, with only casual labour to assist him. His ambition and nerve were impressive and, ultimately, rewarded.

All of which makes one wonder just how inexperienced Molson was. The more we understand the brewing methods of his time, the more astonishing it seems that a relative neophyte like Molson took them on so successfully. How much he had learned back in Lincolnshire as a boy is unknown. The 1783–84 fiasco with Loid must have taught him some hard-earned lessons—foremost, to stick with time-honoured processes and avoid being caught short of a vital ingredient like barley. If John Waite had been a truly experienced maltster and brewer, he could have imparted some valuable knowledge in what little time he worked for Loid. Perhaps Molson had hoped to rehire him when he returned from his trip to south Lincolnshire. But Waite had died while he was away, leaving Molson to tackle the fall brewing season essentially alone.

We are left with the image of a young man preoccupied with reviving a brewery that had been idle for two seasons and robbed in his absence. Before he could do anything else, he would have to repair whatever damage had been done by the thieving Dutchmen, and adapt the rudimentary operation's equipment as best he could to meet the demands of Richardson's authoritative guide, all the while absorbing the almost impenetrably dense prose of one of the most systematic brewers of his time. (Richardson's guide is so hostile to the norms of prose that it will not be quoted.) Molson's success would lie in his fastidiousness, his commitment to methodology. Surrounded by alcohol, he could not have been more sober in his approach to the business before him.

Brewing was linked to the change in seasons by the barley harvest and the need for cool weather for fermentation. By late September, Molson was ready to begin. We know little about the brewery property Molson acquired from Loid, beyond the fact that construction was from squared four-inch logs and that more than one building was standing by the fall of 1783.[1] Two structures would have been expected, to accommodate the distinct phases involved in making beer. He would begin in the malthouse, where the barley seeds had to be coaxed into germination. Germination releases enzymes that convert starch in the seeds into the sugars necessary for plant growth. The maltster encouraged the creation of these sugars for fermenting, then arrested the growth of the seed. While descriptions of brewing often ignore the malting stage, it consumed the most time in the historic process and commanded a fair quantity of the skill. The quality of the beer depended enormously on the ability of the maltster, as he made critical decisions based on intuition and experience throughout the germination process.

Molson took the first step towards his inaugural batch of beer by hiring a labourer named James Randall on September 22, at £6 Halifax per month and "my old cloaths if I have any cast off." Two days later, he gave Randall leave to go into the country and fetch some clothes. But by September 30, he still had not returned. Without help, Molson could not go through the long and labour-intensive malting, and Randall's disappearance was delaying the work. That day Molson arranged for John Cook to work for one month for four (Spanish) dollars, beginning on October 2. At the end of that month, he would be replaced by Christopher Cook.[2]

In preparation for John Cook's arrival on October 2, Molson began steeping the barley, the first stage in the germination process, on September 30.[3] Molson dumped thirty bushels of barley into his cistern, which would have been lined with lead or tiles, and added water until the seeds were submerged four to six inches. The barley was allowed to absorb the excess water for several "tides," each tide being twelve hours. The steeping would have gone on for about four or five tides, or around forty to sixty hours. During this period, Molson carefully examined the steeping barley for its progress, taking sample seeds end-wise between thumb and forefinger and pinching them. Advised the brewer Alexander Morrice in 1827: "If they are in all parts mellow, and the husks open or start a little from the body of the [seed], then it is enough."[4] It was critical not to allow the barley to soak too long, and Molson had ably timed the

Working the barley malt on the malthouse floor. From Charles Tomlinson, ed., *Cyclopedia of Useful Arts*, Vol. 1, 1854. (Courtesy Brewing Archives, Ian Bowering)

steeping so that it would be finished when Cook arrived for the most arduous part of the malting.

With Cook on hand, Molson removed the barley from the cistern and spread it on the floor to continue the germination process. After leaving it still for about a day, they "worked" the malt meticulously around the clock, turning and rearranging it so that its temperature and moisture level remained in the desired range. At first they divided it into several heaps, which were worked every four to eight hours, the exact period depending on the weather. The seed was gradually distributed more thinly until it was arranged into rows to cool. Although we don't know the exact size of Molson's malthouse, it was small and he had limited room for this delicate process. He wanted the barley seeds to begin sprouting, but the root growth had to be arrested; once the seed's shoot (or "spire") appeared, the deep rows had to be turned at least every two hours, more if the weather was warm.

Molson and Cook took care that mould did not set in and that germination did not progress too far. When the malt was thought nearly ready, it was probably left untouched for twelve hours "to heat and mellow," according to Morrice. Then, for another twenty-four hours, it would be turned every six hours, for "if it is overheated, it will become like grease, and be spoiled, or cause the drink to be unwholesome."

It could take three weeks or more for the malt to progress from the steeping in the cistern through the heaping and working on the malthouse floor. The task must have been exhausting for Molson and Cook, as the germinating barley demanded their attention day and night. They might have had some help from James Gibbins, Sr., at this point, as on October 13 he was around for Molson to lend him £4 13s 3d. That same day, Molson wrote Philip Ashley that he had "begun to Malt." Two weeks had passed since he began the steeping and he foresaw another ten to fourteen days before actual brewing would begin. Nonetheless, he was on schedule and doing well.

The next stage was kiln drying. The germinated barley was transferred to a haircloth blanket on the slatted floor of the kiln. How long and how quickly the barley was dried was governed by the type of beer to be brewed. It could take anywhere from four to twelve hours, and the longer the malt was roasted, the darker it made the resulting beer. The fuel for the fire could also affect the brew's flavour. Molson would have been using wood or charcoal, but Irish brewers have long added peat moss to the malting kiln to impart a distinctive taste.

At the time, Molson said, without elaboration, that he was making "ale." While traditional British ales generally were unhopped, we know he was using hops, and the best bet is that he was making a basic amber or "two-penny" (i.e. cheap) beer. (The use of hops technically made it a beer, not an ale.) Morrice described this recipe as "pleasant and wholesome," and the resulting brew was almost as popular as porter in the winter, when it could be consumed at room temperature. It was also easy to make and profitable—because it required little aging, it could be sent quickly to market.

Molson and Cook spread the barley malt for their beer on the haircloth to a depth of several inches, and once it had achieved the desired colour (pale to amber), which would have taken at least several hours, they removed it from the kiln immediately and spread it again for cooling. At this point, the malt could be taken to the next brewing stage or stored for future use; it might keep for six months before spoiling or invasion by weevils.

The kilned malt now had to be milled, to crush the barley husk and free the meal inside, so Molson and Cook trundled it over to the brewhouse, which would have been built to a typical two-storey "tower" design. Before the days of steam-powered pumps (which Molson would not acquire until around 1812), a pioneer brewhouse harnessed gravity to move the raw ingredients through the many stages of the brewing process. The only mechanical assistance came from hand-pumps and horsepower (if available). When all else failed, hand-ladles could transport the ingredients through the gaps in the production flow.

A typical tower brewery that did not have access to water power used a kind of carousel known as a horse wheel to drive the millstones. The animal was harnessed to a great spoke on the ground floor and simply walked in circles, with power from the rotating hub probably delivered directly upward, through the ceiling, on a vertical shaft into the grinding loft on the second floor. The millstones were mounted well above the grinding loft floor, so that as the kiln-dried malt was fed into them from a hopper mounted even higher in the room, the processed malt could be transferred downward to a larger container called the mash-tun.

We know that Molson had at least one horse to drive the mill, because he had a saddle made in England in March 1786, before returning to Montreal. One millstone had been stolen by the Dutchmen in 1785, of course, but presumably it had been replaced by the time the fall 1786 brewing season began. If not, he could have taken the kiln-dried malt to a local mill. When a property adjacent to Molson's was sold in 1816, the indenture noted the presence of a two-storey horse-powered mill. If it was standing thirty years earlier, Molson would have had little difficulty getting the malt milled off-site. The malt had to be milled carefully, however, and not pulverized, as grain was for baking flour.

On October 22, Molson wrote Ashley: "Have got some Malt made shall begin to brew this Week." On October 28 he secured four barrels of charcoal from John Platt, a local ironmonger, which he needed to boil water for the next stages.

The brewhouse kettle, or "copper," towered inside the brewery on a stone furnace foundation like some demonic lighthouse. The structure's design again made the most of gravity in moving liquids around. As Morrice advised, "The Copper should be placed high enough to command every other utensil in the Brewhouse."

The exact size of the copper Molson inherited from Loid is not known, but it may have been tiny. A typical pioneer brewery used a "four hogshead" copper, which meant it could create four hogsheads (about 200 Imperial gallons) of beer in a single day of brewing. But in a letter to Philip Ashley on December 13, Molson said the brewery "will only brew 4 hogsheads a week full employed." A diligent, well-equipped brewer could expect to brew five days in every week. A reference by Molson in the spring of

1787 to brewing twice weekly suggests that the limited production was not due simply to the copper but to the overall scale of the brewing and malting operation.

The brewing day was a long one. It typically began around five or six in the morning, and continued with little respite past sundown. The first task was to pump water into the copper, fire the furnace with Platt's charcoal, and heat the water to about 170°F. (Brewers called the water "liquor," which is why beers and their kin are known generically as malt liquors.) When the water reached the desired temperature, Molson opened the appropriate valve and directed the hot water through a stitched leather hose from the copper down to the mash-tun. The milled barley malt was added to the heated water, and for about an hour Molson and Cook wielded special oars and rakes to turn the malt and water into a mash the consistency of porridge. The oars could be up to fourteen feet long and several inches thick at the mash-tun end. Although Molson stood a good six feet tall, with a strapping build, working the mash would have been taxing even for him.

Mashing converted more of the malt's starches to fermentable sugars, and reduced haze-causing proteins. With the mash ready, Molson captured the sugar-enriched malt extract, called the wort, by filtering it away into a receptacle called the underback. At this point the wort might be sprayed, or sparged, with water to encourage the conversion of any lingering starch into sugar.

The wort was the elixir from which the brewer made his beer. It had taken Molson more than a month to reach this stage, but he had performed flawlessly. After letting grain particles (and grit from the millstones) settle out of the wort where it had collected in the underback, Molson pumped the wort into the copper. For only an hour or so, the wort was boiled, with hops added at the beginning and the end of the process. The hops (actually the flower buds of the vine) added the characteristic bitter flavour of the beer and also acted as a preservative. One historic amber beer recipe also called for molasses (which would have infused the wort with more fermentable sugar), capsicum (pepper), grain of paradise (a west African spice from the ginger family, often used as a pepper substitute) and Leghorn juice (licorice extract).

When the boiling was finished, the wort was flushed through a fresh bed of straw into a container called the hop jack. The hops were captured in the straw and could be used for another brewing, while the wort flowed with gravity into open cooling pans called coolships. The liquor was allowed to cool to around 60 to 65°F. The coolships were located high in the brewery, and sometimes open windows in the second storey helped with the cooling.

At this stage, Molson may have applied the latest tools of the emerging brewing science. He was so successful so quickly in his new trade that it's suspected he must have had both a thermometer and saccharometer to guide him. The saccharometer, which gauged the sugar content of the liquor, had only recently been invented by Richardson; he published a treatise on its use (along with a thermometer) in brewing in 1784. The saccharometer measured the specific gravity of a fluid, and had a scale that differentiated between sugar-enriched wort and water. With the saccharometer, Molson would have been able to judge the sugar content—and ultimate alcoholic strength of the wort—that emerged from the copper and make any necessary adjustments in subsequent batches. Molson left behind no record of having purchased a saccharometer or the treatise while in England in 1785–86. But he also kept no receipt for the purchase of Richardson's 1777 brewing manual, and he definitely owned it when he returned from England in the spring of 1786.

After the desired temperature of the wort was reached in the coolships, gravity was once again called on to direct the liquor to fermenting tuns. Here, yeast was added, or "pitched," and the sugars in the liquor were transformed into alcohol and carbon dioxide. A thermometer would have allowed Molson to gauge the precise moment when the wort needed to be moved from the coolships to the fermenting tuns to prevent spoilage.

The process from mash-tun to fermenting tuns took about fourteen hours. Depending on the capacity of the brewery, several more "charges" of the copper could be made during the day, with every possible amount of fermentable wort extracted from the mash. After several infusions with hot water, the sugar content of the mash would begin to fall off, and the weaker beer produced from the final wort extraction was known as "small" beer.

With the transfer of the liquor to the fermenting tuns, Molson and Cook's day came to an end in darkness. At this point, Molson probably took a well-deserved break. John Cook's employment ended on October 31, and Christopher Cook was hired to replace him on November 4, although he was not expected to start for four days. Molson thus had three or four days of relative leisure while his first batch fermented. Determining when the yeast had run its course was a matter of educated guesswork. If fermentation ended too soon, the beer was attenuated; if too late, it could go stale. Near the end of the fermentation period, the beer was passed into smaller casks, where the yeast frothed out of the bung-holes, cleansing the brew.

The beer then moved into storage vats for aging. For most any kind of malt liquor, whether ale, beer or porter, the period of time from the mash-tun to fermentation was generally the same. It was in the storage vat that the time required for different brewing recipes varied greatly. Porters could not be consumed until at least six months after fermentation. At the other end of the spectrum, amber beer required little aging, a week or less.

With fermentation and storage over, the unpasteurized beer was "racked," or transferred by leather hoses to the hogshead barrels. Molson was also filling bottles, a rare practice for the time. Before a hogshead was bunged, a small quantity of "finings" was placed in the barrel to clarify the contents. This was accomplished with isinglass, a gelatin-like substance collected from the swim bladders of fish, which attracted sediments and other impurities and settled them to the bottom of the barrel.

The resulting amber beer would be a novelty to a modern drinker. "It was less carbonated than today's beers," notes the brewery historian Ian Bowering. "It was brown, likely a dark copper, and while the hops would have added a pleasant bittering aftertaste and astringency and a very light floral accent, the main taste would have been from the malt, and when fresh would have been reminiscent of fresh bread. It also would have been coarser than today's brews—a meal in a bottle."

Once he had his beer in hogsheads or bottles, Molson was ready to deliver it by draywagon to taverners, military barracks and private homes. Among his customers was a Montreal tobacconist,

Designed by W. Tate.   Engraved by S. Belin.

The interior of a small brewery, from Alexander Morrice, A *Practical Treatise on Brewing*, 1827.
LB—liquor back; MT—mash-tun; UB—under back; CB—copper back; C—copper; JB—hop
back or jack back; B—back or cooler; Sq—square or working tun. (Courtesy Brewing
Archives, Ian Bowering)

George Stansfeld, who took a quarter hogshead; the men became close friends.

The day after the sale to Stansfeld, Molson bought sixteen more bushels of barley for malting. "The Speculation now is beginning to show in good Ale & Table Beer—can acquaint my friend that my beer has the readiest Sale order by one half more than [I can] execute," Molson proudly informed Ashley on December 13.

"I know, by my own experience, that the more one works, the more willing one is to work," Lord Chesterfield wrote to his son on September 17, 1757. The winter would have been filled with many fourteen-hour days, as the exhausted but exhilarated Molson raced to satisfy a market that demanded more product than he could supply.

Molson had hired Christopher Cook through to May Day, but on January 29 he was noting, "Cook returned to work[,] last week absent or sick." It is not hard to imagine Molson turning with desperation to his housekeeper, Sarah Vaughan, as Cook failed to show for work. They would have been in the malthouse together at all hours, enslaved to the heaps of malt, tending the mash-tun over in the brewhouse with the great oars and rakes, shovelling the spent ashes out of the copper furnace, pounding bungs into the hogsheads of finished two-penny beer, struggling with a tyrannical success that wore them down and bound them together.

By the time Peter Huffman arrived to replace Christopher Cook on February 28, the new proprietor of the St. Mary's Current brewery was twenty-three years old and clamouring to Philip Ashley for money to expand his operation. He was also the employer of a housekeeper he had probably turned into a maltster and brewer's assistant, and who was now expecting his first child.

Chapter 12

In business be as able as you can, but do not be cunning; cunning is the dark sanctuary of incapacity.

> —Lord Chesterfield, to his godson and heir, to be delivered after his death

JOHN MOLSON'S ENTHUSIASM FOR his brewing venture's success was apparent well before he had racked his first hogshead. "The porter which was imported this season is nearly all consumed," Molson was happy to report to Philip Ashley on October 13, 1786, in the midst of the first malting. "[W]hat remains is very poor & sells at £5 sterling per Hogshead." Molson planned to undercut the imports by retailing his ale at £3 12s and bottles of "table beer" at eighteen shillings per dozen. In addition to being cheaper than the poor-quality porter, Molson's product was priced at almost half of what Thomas Loid had charged for his hogsheads of beer in 1782–83.

We have no idea how much beer Molson produced that first season, but demand proved to be so strong that his price would increase to £4 per hogshead in the spring. Confronting an almost overwhelming—and exclusive—market for a relatively inexpensive domestic brew, before he had even squeezed the first drop of wort from the mash-tun, Molson began to fret that if he didn't expand to meet demand, a competitor surely would arise.

"My expectations grow every day more sanguine on this Speculation & I presume it will in short time prove very lucrative & not without sufficient reason," he assured Ashley on October 22, as he completed the first malting. He emphasized that money

> is the only thing I wants—for to carry it on with a degree of
> spirits & respectability which may in some measure deter any
> other person from entering on same scheme: more especially if
> they see I carried it on in a Languid Manner & if you consider
> the people here are more of an enterprising spirit than at home
> as it is in a great Measure owing to that restlessness, that
> induces them to Quit their Native shore—therefore let these
> considerations urge you the more particularly ye if possible I
> might have a sum of Money remitted by spring shipping from
> London which will be about Middle of March 1787.

Molson's need for money was now largely fuelled by the realization that to exploit the local beer market—indeed to corner it in this colony, shot through with enterprising spirit—he would have to make further investments in equipment and possibly property as well. He had written Gosling & Son on October 10, notifying the banker that he had sold a bill of exchange to a man named P.L. Thompson for £50 (which must have been the bill he had previously proposed selling at £60), payable six weeks after sight. Molson then informed Ashley of the bill on October 13, expecting him to cover it for him.

Now that Molson had his inheritance, his grandfather Samuel appeared to be entirely out of the financial picture. Ashley was exclusively in charge of Molson's finances—collecting overdue rents, paying tradesmen for repairs to Snake Hall, and either guaranteeing Molson's draws on his London banker or arranging satisfactory rates of interest on his outstanding balance. "As my future credits in this place entirely depend on my present probity, hope Mr. Ashley will take the earliest opportunity of giving me Credit to that amount on Mr. Gosling," Molson wrote. He added as a footnote that he was considering an opportunity to acquire one hundred acres adjacent to the house he was renting, "which would grow exceeding good Barley & at a more reasonable rate than can purchase it."

The £50 drawn on Gosling was a bridge to tide him over until his brewing began to deliver revenues. He admitted to Ashley on October 13 that he

> shall be scarce of Money with this £50 drawn but however must make it do if as I expect this speculation will do very great things on a future day—must desire you by all means to hasten in the Business, which have so often mention to procure me £500 sterling on Snake Hall Estate. . . . For that & all favors conferred hope you'll not find me ungrateful.

Nine days later Molson was writing Ashley again, almost compulsively, on the same theme of money.

"There is nothing less required than enlarging the Office which will only brew 4 hogsheads a week full employed," he wrote Ashley on December 13, after he had serviced his first happy customers. "The office is too small to do anything here; when My Ashley considers there is at least 6 or 7 Thousand people & depend on it Canada will continue to improve as long as it belongs to the Crown of Great Britain." Molson was also now considering taking three or four hundred acres of land to grow barley. Though he still considered the block of land at Caldwell's Manor to be his, it was occupied by Thomas Loid and apparently of no use to him for barley production.

Expanding the brewery and buying land required substantial funds, and he implored Ashley to act on securing the mortgage on Snake Hall. He had heard nothing from the attorney since arriving in Quebec, and was adamant about having £500 by March 1787. "Mr. Ashley [I] hope will exert every nerve to accomplish my present wishes," he wrote on December 13. "[I] Shall I expect want £500 more for the following & if as I expect it will answer my present (though not too Sanguine) expectations shall sell out every thing in England & realize in Canada for in point of farming there is no comparison in the advantages on the side of Canada."

Molson asked Ashley to arrange for a new copper kettle with a seven-hogshead capacity and related fittings, as well as sixty yards of haircloth. The willingness to upgrade immediately to a kettle with almost twice the capacity of a typical pioneer brewery underlined his ambition. If Molson had received Jack Baxter's scathing letter of September 6 at this point, it did not discourage him from asking Ashley to turn to Baxter and his friend John Morgan if he needed any assistance. (For that matter, if Molson ever replied to Baxter's list of accusations, no copy has been preserved.) Molson related that he was sending the letter from Montreal the next day, so that it could make the January mail packet from New York, the only line of communication available until shipping resumed to Quebec in May.

Now firmly settled into the Canadian winter with his new companion, Sarah Vaughan, Molson felt his goodwill towards his friend Philip Ashley sour. He was experiencing a taste of his own medicine: the frustration others felt when he communicated little or nothing to them. But Molson's umbrage with the forty-two-year-old attorney was forgivable: he was utterly dependent on Ashley for his survival in business. Determined not to squander the modest fortune he had inherited—by not applying it at the moment of opportunity or by not having his bills of exchange honoured—Molson was close to dropping all pretence of friendship.

"Have wrote since my Leaving Gravesend without receiving a Scrip from you," he complained to Ashley on January 18, 1787.

> To Accuse you of not writing would be more than [I] can justify, but as have received Letters from England—its beyond a doubt, might have received from you.
>
> My continual Theme is *Money & Money* I must have; if I do not enlarge my office this next Summer, shall most certainly meet with an opposition—cannot at present serve half my customers & they [are] increasing—every day—have already served upwards of seventy families.

Molson reiterated that he had written in December about securing the new copper kettle as well as £500— "must have [the money] therefore get it on the best terms you can"—and advised him to commit it to the care of Captain Featonby of the *Everetta* with the first spring shipping. "As shall most certainly sell out everything in England in three years time"—when the properties providing his younger brother Thomas with income would descend to him—he directed Ashley to inform him when he could draw on a further £500: he hoped he could have it by the autumnal shipping, through a bill of exchange payable around Christmas 1787 or New Year's 1788. He also requested that Ashley secure ten hundredweight of hops from his London brewing supplier, H. Townley & Son, which could come out in the fall if it was secured from the 1787 crop. The day before, in fact, Molson had written Townley with his order for the hops and the kettle, instructing the firm to look to Ashley for payment.

These were emphatically critical requests, and Molson, stewing in his attorney's disturbing silence, lectured that "Mr. Ashley Exerting himself in my requests will do me a greater service than will lie in your power afterwards & Consequently more hirt in delay than may lie in your power to me good ever after. . . . Remember to have read in some paper at the Spectators that a Man may do his friend more harm in procrastination than ever lies in his power afterwards to make him amends: that is exactly my case at present."

He wrote George Featonby the same day, informing him of the order placed with Townley and the £500 he expected him to bring to Quebec for him. He asked Featonby to give Ashley whatever assistance he needed, and furthermore, to keep tabs on him: "you'll be so kind as inform him when you sail that he may not disappoint me."

The gulf between the business worlds of Molson and Ashley was as wide as the ocean separating them. Ashley was the leading attorney in the Fen Lands—his brother-in-law was Spalding's mayor—but nothing in his career would have prepared him for the urgency of a young entrepreneur like John Molson, his ambitions frustrated by erratic lines of communication. Molson understood, as he had observed to Ashley, that the merchants in the colony were of a more "enterprising spirit than at home," and he was determined to become one of them, prospering by seizing opportunities in the rapidly evolving and expanding community. South

Lincolnshire, in comparison, was static and entrenched, its rural gentry's wealth atrophying under the "languid" approach to commerce that Molson vowed to avoid.

In the dawning Regency era, money among the gentry was treated with shocking carelessness: gambling impoverished heirs to great estates, and debts routinely went unaddressed for entire lifetimes. Never someone who circulated among the dissolute upper classes, in Montreal Molson was far removed from a social order in which entitlements of birth invested a privileged few with an almost arrogant disregard for obligation; his world was clearly delineated by income and expense and the stern consequences of default.

It was far from the case that no one in Molson's old middle-class circle back in England cared about money; it was more the fact that no one was attempting to employ it with such daring and urgency. The best defence for Philip Ashley's tardiness and reluctance was that he had no real understanding of, or empathy for, Molson's ambition. He could not grasp either the cause of his client and friend's passion or the requirement for swift action to satisfy it. No one was more risk-averse than the ponderous Philip Ashley.

Ashley was at last moved to act on his client's repeated instructions, and his office wrote Molson on February 6, 1787, informing him that in addition to his £50 note having been honoured, a mortgage bond for £500 had been secured on the estate. Copies of the mortgage and bond were enclosed for his signing and return. Three hundred pounds had already been advanced against it, and Ashley had arranged for another £200 to come available on "Lady Day"— the Assumption, or March 25. Molson would not, however, be able to draw on any of it until Ashley had the signed mortgage and bond in his possession as security. As a timely illustration of the fiscal foot-dragging that went on back home, Ashley's office reported that it had been able to collect rent on Molson's land from Waddington only up to Michaelmas (September 29) 1786, through notes payable on Lady Day. The letter did promise, however, that "Mr. Ashley will take care to receive your Rents as Close up as he can." Molson was also informed that his brother Thomas would be occupying Snake Hall on Lady Day, although word of this move reached him by other channels, probably through Gibbins.

The mortgage papers would not come into Molson's hands until June 7, and the delays in communication left him with several more months of fitful worry, which only served to ratchet up both his anxiety and his rhetoric. "Have nothing more to impart than have already communicated," Molson wrote Ashley on February 17, which did not prevent him from revisiting his instructions in more frantic and impatient terms. He concluded the letter by arguing that Ashley should

consider only [that my] Ale [is] selling at £4 per Hhd & my buying barleay at £1 per Quarter [250 pounds] *the highest price: No duties:* Ask any common brewer & Maltster & he can inform how lucrative such a branch of business must be. Enumerating any further advantage of my business would be puerile—the greatest service Mr. Ashley can do me at present will be by complying with my requirements. PS . . . Note have not received one Scrip from *you yet*—whatever you do be particular in informing me every opportunity.

He waited exactly one month, and when the next mail packet brought no fresh news from Ashley, Molson unleashed another reprimand on March 17:

Have wrote till am tired of writing without receiving any Answer which can impute to [no] other reason but you not having wrote any—am confident you must have received my Epistles all or most of them.

Shipping arrived in November in England every person here has Letters regularly every Month by New York packet— here I remain *like a fool* with out being able to determine anything—as have already informed you cannot half supply my customers—every body keeps [buzzing] in my Ears shall make a fortune—have had a person profered to enter £500 in partnership with me—& without enlarging my Office there is not doubt but shall meet with an opposition—'tis already talked on & the only way to prevent it is to carry the business with Spirit—if as I ought to have had power to draw for five

Hundred pounds long since as I have wrote since my leaving Graves-End to that purpose—shall sell out in *three years* therefore Mortgaging can be no Eye sore; be what as it will I do not care.

He also complained to Ashley that his brother Thomas's intention to live at Snake Hall "will be the means of the repairs costing more than I intended. [William Bennett] *told me 60 or 70 would do it* be that as it will the less the better I shall be satisfied." In fact, Bennett's tally would exceed £136 in 1787.

Molson's plans to keep abreast of his under-serviced market hinged on his securing the new copper kettle from Townley and building a new malting house, but he now feared that nothing would happen that summer if Ashley had not yet acted on his instructions. "Mr. Ashley continuing to neglect as *he has apparently* hitherto done will do me a greater disservice than will lie in his power to do me good ever after," he again warned.

Meanwhile, H. Townley & Son had received Molson's order for supplies, including the new kettle. On March 6, the firm informed Molson that the kettle and fittings had been ordered and expected them "to be shipped this week with some Hops ordered at the same Time." As directed, Townley was looking to Ashley for payment. And here the brewing merchant hit a disconcerting snag. Ashley refused to pay the bill.

Samuel Townley had written Ashley, also on March 6, to notify him of Molson's kettle and hops order and to arrange payment. "I have been much acquainted with his Family & esteem myself his Friend," Ashley replied to Townley on March 8, "nevertheless, woud not wish to lose a Considerable Sum by him. Therefore will state to You his Situation with me." Ashley explained how, on February 6, he had left a £500 mortgage bond to be delivered to Molson at the bar of the New York Coffee House in London. As the North West Company partner firm of Phyn & Ellice had established an office at this coffee house in 1774, Ashley intended the bond to be delivered to Molson aboard James Phyn's *Everetta*. Ashley now presumed that the ship had been delayed in sailing. He asked Townley to collect the undelivered papers and forward them to Molson himself.

> [U]ntil I have those deeds returned executed I can not accept any Bills drawn whether by him or his Order but on Receipt thereof will accept Bill, to that amount @ 7 days sight payable at Messes Goslings. My Molson's Property being very consider-able here but I have no Authority from him to charge that Property in Case of Death. I wish You to inform Me if I can be in Time to forward another Deed for the sale of his Effects, in the sum determined to sell the same & if I am in Possession of the Trust I will at all Times answer his Demand.

Ashley's refusal to accept the bill for Molson's order astonished Samuel Townley. He understood what Ashley apparently could not: that Molson's order was fundamental to his survival in the brewery business in Montreal. On April 5, as shipping resumed to Quebec, Townley wrote Ashley, acknowledging receipt of his March 8 letter and noting,

> The contents very much surprizd me, as Mr. Molson informed me when in England that he had given You a proper Power to procure money for him, please to consider what a Detriment it must be to him not to have the Goods, therefore hope you will advance the money for him. I found Capt. Featonby [of the *Everetta*] has sailed, but another Ship will sail the Beginning of next Week, shall be obliged to You for an Answer whether Mr. Molson's request can be complyd with.

A ship named the *Carlton* was about to sail, and although he had no response from Ashley, the brewing merchant decided that he could not abide Molson being left high and dry by his attorney. Townley would send the order without any guarantee of payment and inform Molson of Ashley's failure to cooperate. Most of Molson's order, including the kettle, went aboard the *Carlton*, with the rest consigned to a second ship. Townley wrote Ashley on April 10, informing him that the goods had been shipped, and forwarded the bill, about £150. Townley observed that "by your Assistance" Molson would "meet with Success in his line of Business."

Townley's generosity, and the foolishness of his own intransigence, moved Ashley to reverse his position. He informed Townley on the thirteenth that he would pay the charges after all, and Townley replied that he was "much obliged by your Consent. . . . I was determined Mr. Molson shoud not be disappointed." Unfortunately for Ashley, Townley by then had written to Molson, informing him of Ashley's refusal to pay, and included a transcript of Ashley's March 8 letter.

At the same time that Ashley was having his change of heart, Molson was reaching a crescendo of rage. Another mail packet had called at New York with no word for him from Ashley, just as he was preparing to spend a considerable amount of money. He was in the process of making an offer to a Captain Grant for a property that included a building Molson considered ideal for an expanded brewery operation. The building was thirty-six feet by forty-five feet, four storeys in all (likely a two-storey structure with an attic and a cellar), with stone walls almost three feet thick. All that was required was a kiln to make it a perfect malthouse. On April 16 he offered Grant £1,000 for it, to be divided into three equal payments due October 10, 1787, January 10, 1789, and January 10, 1790.

Molson never made note of where this building was. It was almost certainly south of Montreal, even as far away as Caldwell's Manor. A likely candidate for "Captain Grant" is David Alexander Grant, who had served as a captain in the King's Royal Regiment of New York at Carleton Island under John Johnson's command. In 1781, Grant had married Marie-Charles Le Moyne, the baroness of Longueuil. Her mother, Marie-Anne-Catherine d'Eschambault, was carrying her when her father, the baron Charles Le Moyne, who was also the governor of Montreal, was killed at the battle of Lac Saint-Sacrement in 1755. In 1770, Marie-Charles's mother married the prominent Montreal Scots merchant, politician and deputy receiver-general William Grant, who was David Alexander's uncle.

David Alexander Grant's marriage to Marie-Charles, who had ascended to the baronetcy in 1770, gave him joint title to the Longueuil seigneury, which was an extensive property south and east of Montreal that included Fort St. Johns. By the time Molson made the purchase offer, about two hundred Loyalists had been settled around the post by Grant, who would rename it Dorchester in honour of the governor general, Lord Dorchester, in 1790. The massive stone construction (in the *ancien régime* style) and the presence of a tenant farmer named De Shaumboc suggest that the property was somewhere on the Longueuil seigneury.

But Molson's Captain Grant could also have been Captain John Grant, an American veteran of the Revolutionary War who served with the Green Mountain Boys. Born in Scotland in 1755, Grant was an "artificer," or skilled mechanic, during his military service. After the war he spent some time building houses and mills in Pawlet, in southern Vermont, where he married Eunice Stark on April 17, 1786. Exactly when Grant came to the Missisquoi area is uncertain, as he does not appear in the first Alburgh census of 1790. Grant is known to have settled at nearby South Hero Island around 1800, when his wife's family also moved there from Pawlet, and Grant was still in the construction trade when he built the first frame house for Jabez Rockwell at South Hero Island in 1806. But the presence of Grant's name in transaction records that survive from the 1790s indicates he was already speculating in lands on the Missisquoi Tongue before he actually lived in the area. In 1795, Grant would purchase two hundred acres at Windmill Point, just north of where Molson had leased his property from Henry Caldwell. Molson's letter to a Captain Grant in the spring of 1787 makes it possible that John Grant had become involved in Alburgh-area land deals soon after his marriage.

Molson's letter suggests that, whichever Grant it was, he was acting on behalf of someone named "Mr. Wm," and members of a family named Williams were among Alburgh's earliest residents. A woman named Margaret Williams was the wife of Samuel Mott, who settled in the vicinity of Molson's property at Caldwell's Upper Manor in 1787 and whose clan figured prominently in the fate of those lands. In fact, the abbreviated name in Molson's letter could be interpreted as Margaret Williams rather than Mr. Williams. That the property Molson was prepared to buy could have been on the Missisquoi Tongue is reinforced by his nominating James Gibbins, Sr., who owned land at the Missisquoi, to represent him in any further negotiations: "My Friend Mr. Pell can explain to you [that] any alterations he shall make with you will strictly [be] abided by." At the least, Molson's nomination of Gibbins suggests that the property, if instead on the Longueuil seigneury, was well removed from Montreal, probably around Fort St. Johns.

Having acquired the St. Mary's Current property from Pierre Monarque in the summer of 1786, Molson was now on the verge of quitting it. He complained in a letter home that the present brewery was too far from his market—evidently Montreal was not the source of the majority of his business at the time.[1] Instead, he must have been focused on the British military bases at the north end of Lake Champlain and along the Richelieu, and on the many Loyalists gathering in the area, although he could have been sending beer into the new Royal Townships of the upper St. Lawrence as well. Molson would count among his brewery customers Captain Grant in 1788, as well as Captain John Savage, Caldwell's effective aide-de-camp at the seigneury, and Captain Francis Dechambault, commander of the British forces at Pointe-au-Fer. The majority of Alburgh's residents around 1786 appear to have been Loyalists who owed their tenure to Caldwell. At least seventy Loyalist men and their families are known to have been living within or around Caldwell's Upper Manor in 1786, with ten having borne arms for the Crown during the rebellion.[2] They were a natural market for Molson's beer. The influence of Sarah Vaughan, who probably came into Molson's life through Alburgh, might also have been an important factor in his sudden desire to relocate. And we know that various Gibbins men and Thomas Loid were also in and around Caldwell's Manor, and thus would have been a ready-made community to welcome him.

If Molson in fact was planning to purchase the property through Captain Grant of Vermont, he may have seen the Missisquoi

Tongue as a refuge from the disagreeable commercial environment of Quebec. In addition to his displeasure with the tyranny of the writ of *saisie*, which gave the justice system draconian power over debtors, he was also unhappy with the availability and price of grain in the province. Securing a more reliable and cheaper source of barley was a priority, and that was why he considered purchasing several hundred acres of farmland in 1786. Grain dealers purchased from one habitant household at a time, rather than from a public market, and that allegedly made the grain more expensive and the quality less consistent. In 1787 the legislative council ignored reports from the merchants' committees of Quebec City and Montreal on how the province's grain collection system should be overhauled.[3] An Alburgh property would not only give Molson a brewery outside the legal reach of Quebec, but it could also secure him a personal supply of cheap barley, as it came with a tenant farmer.

Molson also may have caught wind of Ira Allen's successful lobbying efforts for free trade, for only two days after he wrote Captain Grant with his purchase offer, Quebec's new governor, Lord Dorchester (who was the newly titled former governor, Guy Carleton), ordered the province's customs collector to permit the free import, through the Lake Champlain corridor, of lumber, naval stores, hemp, flax, grain and provisions, as well as the produce of the lake's neighbouring states. The free export of British goods (except furs) through the lake was also permitted. A few days later, the free import of leaf tobacco and pot and pearl ashes was also sanctioned.[4]

The negotiations with a Vermont Captain Grant would suggest that Molson was as much in Ira Allen's camp as Thomas Loid, who was settled on Molson's land. While Molson was forming his plan to buy the Grant property, Loid left a rare trace of his existence in his own hand. He was in Bennington, where the state legislature was in session. A petition presented to the general assembly on February 28, 1787, calling for improved mail service, features T.P. Loid as the last of nine signatories. The signature is attributed in the Vermont State Papers to "Thomas P. Loid, Representative for Mosiske Tongue (Alburg[h])."[5]

Was John Molson harbouring secret republican sentiments if he was preparing for a move to Alburgh, where his former brewery partner held political and judicial postings conferred by Ira Allen? It's an intriguing question, but the act of relocating below the forty-fifth parallel would not automatically have made Molson an American, since Caldwell's Upper Manor/Alburgh was such a hopeless tangle of allegiances, and the very status of Vermont remained unresolved. Both Henry Caldwell and Ira Allen, of course, thought they had the right to settle the land, and while the Missisquoi Tongue was undisputably outside Quebec, no one could decide what it was *in*. Lord Dorchester had managed to sidestep a home-government ordnance forbidding free trade with the United States in part by reasoning that Vermont wasn't officially part of the new republic. At the time, Vermont's entire destiny hung in the balance between potential statehood in the breakaway republic and status as a new province in British North America. The idea of a politically neutral Vermont, a Switzerland of North America, would catch the fancy in 1789 of Colonel John Graves Simcoe, who became lieutenant-governor of the new province of Upper Canada in 1791.

As Molson contemplated a move that might have been to the Missisquoi, British troops still occupied the Pointe-au-Fer post opposite Molson's four-hundred-acre holding, and the British schooner Lady Maria still patrolled Lake Champlain from an anchorage near his property in Windmill Bay, harassing local shipping at will. The British military presence continued inside territories ceded to the United States in 1783, on the purported grounds that they would not relinquish the forts until Loyalists received proper compensation for their losses. But the occupation and harassment probably owed as much to sheer obstinacy in a military force unhappy to withdraw from territories it never surrendered in battle. British forces would not agree to relinquish all posts inside American territory until Jay's Treaty was signed in 1794, and even at that they were permitted to continue occupying western posts until June 1796.

But if the Missisquoi Tongue followed the rest of Vermont into the United States, Molson probably would not have been compelled to retreat to Quebec. In an imminent tirade against the odious laws of the province, Molson would identify himself as an "English Man," but this was an Englishman whose nationalism was inspired by English commercial law, which had yet to come to Quebec. An Englishman like Molson would be happier in the United States, where the laws were closer in spirit to those of Westminster than they were in Montreal. Molson's politics were defined narrowly by his commercial aspirations—as they were for most members of the merchant class. He had not hidden his desire to explore the American colonies when he first arrived in Quebec, and relocating across the border to the Missisquoi in 1787 would have been a business initiative, not a political statement.

Nothing, however, could come of Molson's plans to purchase the land offered by Captain Grant, wherever it was, without money from Philip Ashley. Unaware that Ashley had finally acted on the mortgage (or of how close he had come to not receiving any of the brewery supplies on which his business's survival counted), Molson wrote him a scathing letter on April 14, venting fully his frustrations and suspicions of the reasons for Ashley's apparent failure to heed his instructions. The circumstances had flushed out Molson's own lingering suspicions about Lincolnshire opinions. The disapproval that he must have feared when he failed to reveal his involvement in Loid's brewery in 1783–84 came tumbling out in bitter accusation.

"Shall be very concise with this Epistle as my prolixity avails nothing," he began, then proceeded to go on for more than three pages. He explained that he was about to buy the property from Grant and that he required £1,500, as "it will not come for much less—five hundred pounds must [be] paid next October at least." Either Molson was lying about the true price or the £1,000 offer he made to Grant two days later was a low-ball gambit. Nonetheless, he was "determined of having it." He had calculated the costs of the alternatives, and as he explained to Ashley, the existing log building would cost three or four hundred pounds to expand and would not last as long as the stone building Grant was offering. Building new from stone at the scale of the Grant property would cost £3,000, he alleged.

He expected Ashley to arrange for the money on credit from Gosling, and appended the direction with a stern condemnation of Ashley's behaviour. "Am sorry to say I think Mr. Ashley has used [me] *verry ill*[. H]ere I remain with my hand tied—with a fortune in England which would in a few years provided I had it here render me independent. For Mr. Ashley to think it a pity for the paternal estate to be sold is altogether *puerile*[. E]ven for a Father to wish a Son to keep anything of the kind contrary to his real interests is altogether repugnant to the duty of a Father to a Son—whatever I have said is barely to convince Mr. Ashley I have a will of *my own*." He ventured that Ashley "has neglected giving me Scrip [not] through any ill design but rather that he does not wish me to become a resident in this Country—which is altogether impossible to prevent & your not complying with my request will be my immediate ruin. Therefore when I return let me have the pleasure to say that Mr. Ashley's ready compliance with my request has been the means of the Ale Brewery being brought to perfection in *Canada*— think not this the Chimera of mad brain—for depend upon it tis the only road to advance my self in Life.

"If My Ashley does not acquiese with my demand," he concluded, "[I] shall be obliged to come to England myself which will cost at least £150 and the loss of Business £500 more—the other ill effect have not room to must[er]. ..." Molson confessed that he had "gone above the limits which intended giving myself"—his angry script had now moved onto the outside of the letter—"but on Mr. Ashley complying or not depends my future good fortune or ruin."

He signed the letter "from one who would wish to be favoured with your correspondence & friendship as has been the case." It was a faint attempt to mitigate whatever damage he had done to the "friendship" he purportedly cherished and depended on. Molson's assault on Ashley's non-compliance and Ashley's compliance were to pass each other on the Atlantic.

Chapter 13

*In the mass of mankind, I fear, there is too great a majority of fools
and knaves; who, simply from their number, must to a certain
degree be respected, though they are by no means respectable. And
a man who will show every knave or fool that he thinks him such,
will engage in a most ruinous war, against numbers much superior
to those that he and his allies can bring into the field.*

—Lord Chesterfield, letter to his son, December 20, 1748

ON MAY 21, JAMES GIBBINS, SR., wrote John Molson in
Montreal to report that he had met the *Carlton* at Quebec City,
and after some confusion over the waybill—it was mistakenly
made out to Townley in Montreal, instead of from Townley in
London—he was able to locate the new copper kettle and seven
of the ten packets of hops, as well as some barley. The rest of the
shipment was evidently still inbound, and Gibbins was arranging
to ship everything upriver. Because Gibbins went to considerable
effort to travel to Quebec City to meet the shipment, we must
again consider the possibility that he was involved with Molson
at some level of partnership.

"I examined the Post Office and found a double letter for you
which I hope will answer all your wishes," Gibbins added. Some of
the documents from Philip Ashley had at last arrived; the mortgage,
posted March 6, would not reach Molson until June 7. By then,
Molson also had the incriminating copy of Ashley's initial letter to
Townley, indicating that he would not accept the bill for any shipments until Molson signed the mortgage papers.

Molson could not help ridiculing Ashley for refusing to accept the bill on the grounds that if Molson died without first executing the documents, Ashley would be saddled with the debt. As he signed the necessary papers and posted them back on June 10, he acidly observed how "in *Case of Death* it will be attended with less Trouble to prove," and added that he was now sending Townley a bill of exchange to pay for the brewery goods "for which he was so kind as to give *me Credit*."

Molson's mood was uniformly bitter. How much of it was due to genuine setbacks, and how much to the fact that Sarah Vaughan would have been about five months into a possibly unexpected pregnancy, is unknown. But he had begun to turn on those, and the very country, around him.

The list of once close family and friends by whom he felt "ill used" was growing. Ashley had been the first to cross him; now he confessed to anger with his grandfather over the way the estate had been settled. "Think my Grandfather has used me ill," he informed Ashley as he complained that the sum of about £61 left over from the settlement had not yet reached him, "at a time when I want money so much." He asked Ashley "to get a full discharge on my Account" with his grandfather, for (as he could not resist remarking) while "there is a chance of *my Death* [I] think there is a still great one of his Death & do not wish to have any dispute with his executor."

Ashley's arrangements to collect back rent on his Lincolnshire properties did not impress him, nor was he happy with the expenses he was incurring maintaining Snake Hall while his brother Thomas occupied it: "Am sorry to see rent paid with Notes at a long date & likewise that the repairs has run so high. Tom's taking that farm is premature. . . . Will not be at any extraordinary expense on account of Tom's taking the farm. Nothing but what is absolutely necessary."

And having been so outraged by the possibility that Ashley would not arrange the money he so needed to purchase the Grant property, he now allowed that he had decided against buying it. Instead, he would build a new malthouse on his existing property for about £400—not the £3,000 he had promised Ashley such a structure would cost. The old malthouse, which evidently was bigger than the original brewhouse, would now become the brewhouse and storage cellar. His notebook indicates the new malthouse was already underway when he wrote Ashley; he had begun sinking the cellar for the new stone building on May 9.

Molson gave no reason for changing his mind about the Grant property. It's possible he and Grant could not agree on a price, and Molson had resorted to a cheap alternative on his existing property at St. Mary's Current, even though he was unhappy with its location. His dissatisfaction was accumulating; the year was appearing to unfold as a series of vexing miscalculations. The nature and strength of the relationship with Sarah Vaughan is beyond speculation; we know only that a child was on the way. Having convinced himself that he had to purchase the Grant property, Molson had abandoned the deal, by choice or necessity, to build in a location that did not suit him. And now he threw another twist at Ashley: he was suddenly no longer sure he even wanted to stay in Quebec. As he allowed to Ashley: "for the selling out entirely believe shall not do that: at least not at present . . . for there has been some laws made this Spring which is repugnant to the Constitution of an English Man to think of settling for Life."

He had reversed his position so many times in a matter of weeks that it became almost impossible to gauge his true intentions. On April 14, just two days before making the offer to Captain Grant for a property that might have been within northern Vermont, Molson had railed at Ashley about the necessity of his cooperation so that the brewery could be "brought to perfection in *Canada*." Was he concealing, as was his habit, his intention to relocate to Vermont? Or did the ambiguous statehood of Vermont make him consider the Grant property to be within Canada? Geographic niceties probably weren't called for—Molson's point was that he and the brewery were not in England, and he had no intention of returning to live there, whatever friends and family back in Lincolnshire wished. But then, having decided that he would be better off building on the St. Mary's Current property after all, he was suddenly reconsidering selling off his inheritance in Lincolnshire, which, as he had relentlessly emphasized, was the means to his success in Quebec. One can hear Philip Ashley's exasperation exhaling across the centuries.

And what were the "laws made this Spring" that so offended Molson? Dorchester's decision, in April, to open trade through Lake Champlain could not have been a mortifying development. If anything, free trade in Vermont grain would have been an incentive for Molson to remain at St. Mary's Current. Molson was probably making an imperfect reference to a momentous and ongoing confrontation between the British merchant class and entrenched Canadian interests over the future of civil law in the province. The merchants had been making a concerted push for judicial and legal reforms that would see the English civil law system fully implemented, but the effort failed utterly that spring. By the time Molson wrote Ashley on June 10, Lord Dorchester had given the highly partial chief justice William Smith, an advocate of the merchants, the task of holding hearings into legal reform—they began the day after Molson wrote Ashley, and ran into November. Molson may have been writing with unspoken apprehension that nothing would come of the impending hearings; if so, he was absolutely correct, for Smith's thirteen-volume report was essentially ignored.

Though the height of summer was less than two weeks away, Molson's character was still chilled by the financial frustrations that had built through the past winter. For all his protests over his right to make his own way in life, he condemned Ashley's alleged obstructions and the burdens imposed by his grandfather and brother with the air of someone indecently put upon, his entitlements denied him. He had not lost Ashley through his outbursts—and Ashley was obliged to feel some amount of guilt for his tardiness— but the number of people Molson could count as being close to him without any attendant financial obligations, encumbrances or resentments was narrowing rapidly. His family and friends—those he still retained—were all bound to him in some way by money. He was not, in his own mind, receiving enough—and he was spending too much at the same time. Molson was almost predestined to plunge into the crisis that both expanded around him and drew him into deeper isolation.

It had all begun and would end with Caldwell's Manor: with the grants that could not be granted forever by Henry Caldwell; with the land that was or was not in the United States, which was or was not legally part of Vermont or New York, which did or did not belong to Caldwell or Ira Allen. With a border that was not a border, pointedly ignored by the British military. With a family named Pell that was actually named Gibbins. With a man named Loid, who was both a British subject and a justice of the peace and legislator in a state recognized by no other state—a self-described republic that aspired to American statehood while negotiating a future as a British colony. A place that likely introduced Molson to the woman named Vaughan, who was his wife with no marriage to prove it, who may have used the names Kitley and Insley, which may have been variations on Kinsley, which itself was an alias for Kingsley. The Missisquoi was a sinkhole of ambiguities, misrepresentations and contradictions that could not remain unresolved. Tensions built within the terrain in lockstep with the ones within Molson's life, and they converged in that bleak summer of 1787.

The summer unfolded industriously for Molson, whatever his discouragement. The new malthouse was begun, and he distributed the two-row barley seed favoured in brewing among several growers. To men named Maburn and Kerby, as well as James Gibbins, Jr., he gave four and a half bushels each of barley seed, on the condition that he receive two bushels of the harvested barley for free and would pay two shillings six pence for each additional bushel he required. Later in May, he struck an arrangement with "Mr. Logan Jr." to give him any barley mash he could spare, "he only allowing me to give a pint or quart to friend." The identity of these men is not known, but some could have been from around the Missisquoi.[1]

In June came the papers from Ashley; on July 10 Molson was borrowing almost £90 from his friend the tobacconist George Stansfeld. Six days later came a substantial, unspecified transaction with James Gibbins, Sr.—"amounted to Sixty four pounds Eighteen Shillings & Ten pence exclusive of Seven pounds, of shingle nails"—which suggests Molson paid him for something, probably using the money borrowed from Stansfeld.

On the final day of August, Molson composed an explosive letter; the recipient was not named in the surviving draft, but the content indicates it was Thomas Loid. "I receive a strange Account from two Men," Molson wrote, "who tell me they are come from you—that Savage has sold my Lots to one Joseph Mott for two half Joes—which proceeding, you must have known; as they likewise tell me that they were a going turning you off—& further; that you were a going to quit entirely: all which you did not turn to give me the least advice of."

"Savage" would have been the close associate of Henry Caldwell, Captain John Savage. A former British Army regular who had spent four years as a prisoner of war during the revolution, he had settled around 1784 in the same area as Molson's land, at a place duly named Savage's Point. Molson understood that "they"—the two men who visited Molson—were evicting Loid from the property, but that he had been planning to give up the land anyway.

The "half Joes" referred to half Johannes, the Portuguese gold coin. And the purchaser, the thirty-five-year-old Joseph Mott, was a duplicitous and at times unpleasant character. His own family would have him imprisoned from 1821 to 1825 in a dispute over ownership of lands at Alburgh. Mott and Savage could not have made a more unlikely pair, for Savage was dealing with a man whose allegiances had flipped at least once during the American Revolution and swung with whatever opportunity presented itself. Although Mott was associated with Savage in the 1787 purchase, he switched to the Ira Allen camp, serving as Alburgh's tax collector in the 1790s. But then, in 1802, he signed a petition for a Loyalist land grant in the town of Sutton, Quebec.

Mott may have been a Loyalist as he claimed, but by the most narrow definition. An undated estimate of personal losses sustained by members of the King's Royal Regiment of New York did include a farmer from Tryon County, New York, named Joseph Mott. A Joseph Mott also shows up as a private in the pay lists of the Loyal American Regiment in November and December 1777, only to be listed as a deserter on February 24, 1778.[2] But at the age of eighty-two, Mott would make a successful application for a military pension of $30 per year for his services as a Revolutionary soldier.

Like the brewery employee John Waite, Mott hailed from a region that witnessed some of the most vicious internecine warfare of the Revolution. Tryon County took in the Mohawk Valley settlements west of Albany. John Johnson had returned to it with both Loyalist troops and Mohawk warriors (led by Joseph Brant) in reprisal raids that included an outright massacre at Cherry Valley. Loyalists like John Waite, in turn, had been burned out of their homes. When the supervisors of Tryon County attempted to assess the impact of the war for a report made on December 20, 1780, they found, after only a partial review, that at least 1,200 farms were uncultivated, that 354 families had abandoned their farms and left the county, and that in communities like Cherry Valley, Springfield and Harpersfield, no one was left to count.[3]

Mott's testimony at the Grand Isle County courthouse in his pension application indicates he had initially sided with the revolution, enlisting for six months, in June 1775, with Colonel James Clinton's New York regiment. He fought northward with them up Lake Champlain, participating in the siege of Fort St. Johns and the subsequent occupation of Montreal. He renewed his enlistment and took part in the unsuccessful assault on Quebec City under Benedict Arnold before securing his discharge around June 1776 in Albany, New York. Mott switched sides after this adventure to join either the King's Royal Regiment or the King's Loyal Americans— perhaps both, if the enlistees were the same Joseph Mott.[4] He could have been the Joseph Mott listed as a suspected Tory by New York's Committee of the Provincial Congress to Apprehend Tories. For all we know, before Mott swapped allegiances, he and Savage had been shooting at each other.

In the late 1780s, Mott began steadily accumulating land on the Missisquoi Tongue, including Windmill Point, the dispute over which led to his imprisonment in the 1820s. His block of land south of Windmill Point, where a handsome stone house was built on more than 1,000 acres, coincides with Molson's four hundred acres. Molson had specified that he retained ownership of the lots numbered 27 and 28 in the settling of his joint account with Loid in March 1785; Mott is known to have owned lots 25 to 29. The deal overseen by Captain Savage in 1787 for the land

Molson considered to be his may have been the first local acreage Joseph Mott acquired.

But how had it come to be sold without Molson's knowledge or permission? Based on the McGlemoyl covenant of 1783, Caldwell would give title to a tract only if it was occupied within one year and a day. Molson may not ever have really settled at Caldwell's Manor, and his hold on the land was probably tenuous as a result. Molson's letter to Loid referred to "My land, which you have got your living off this Three Years & let me tell you I believe you would have *starved* had not being for my having allowed you to have stayed on them at so easy a rent." Loid may not have been on some or all of the lands three full years, but rather three summers, and it was only through Loid's occupation of it that Molson could continue to claim title. As for the easy rent, Molson was probably not collecting rent himself from Loid, but was allowing him to stay on the land in exchange for paying Caldwell the requisite seigneurial tithe. As Molson conceded in his letter draft, he had little legal ground on which to object to the sale, as "it seems the strongest has the best chance, for any Law you state is distinct at least your part of it."

Molson complained: "You I think might have sent my Note of hand for I sent you more than the Value of & Mr. Ja. Pell Sr. last Summer." Molson was referring to the demand note he had given Loid on settling their joint account in March 1785, against which he had been paying Loid's bills. Molson had continued to list Loid's expenses in the joint-account ledger, and most of Loid's credit was used up in one entry on March 12, 1785, just ten days after the joint account had been settled. Loid had accumulated sundry expenses (thread, tobacco, shoe repairs) that were obviously a result of his relocation to lands at Caldwell's Manor. They included "cash given Thomas Loid to pay Carter to St. Johns & defray his Expences to Manor," and "Tho.'s Butchers Expences at Mr. Pells." On July 5, 1786, Loid made a six-shilling draw on Molson for "Butchers Expences at R. Gilv. as allowed Mr. Pell in his Acct." We don't know who "R. Gilv." was, but Molson's obligations to Loid had become entwined with butchering at the Missisquoi by James Gibbins, Sr.

On August 31, 1787, when Molson wrote his furious message to Loid, the account between the men had been dormant for more than a year, with Loid enjoying an unused credit of 17s 7½d. It certainly was not a large amount—less than a pound—but if Loid was being evicted for failing to pay the seigneurial rent, by presenting the note to Molson for final redemption he would at least have received some cash with which to satisfy Caldwell. Still, since the rent on the lands was thirty shillings per hundred acres, or £6 in total, it would not have been enough to cover even a few months of back rent.

In complaining that he had sent Loid and Gibbins "more than the Value . . . last Summer," Molson was probably arguing that by July 5, 1786, when the last draw was made by Loid in the joint account, Molson had incurred expenses against the demand note which more than exceeded the two "half Joes"—about four pounds—Mott paid for the land. Mott may have simply paid the outstanding rents to get the land from Savage.

While the payments Molson had made on Loid's behalf against the note had nothing to do with the actual sale to Mott, Molson was frustrated that the lands could have been lost for so little when he had sent Loid more than twice the sales price since the spring of 1785. The point for Molson was that he could have afforded the small sum that Mott was able to pay to get the property away from him. After faithfully remitting the expenses Loid had submitted to him, Molson was probably angry that Loid had let the rent payment to Caldwell slip. Molson had been carrying Loid, and his former brewery partner had repaid the favour by allowing the lands to be sold, without calling more than seventeen shillings of his credit on Molson or even notifying him of the trouble.

Loid had returned from his first session in the Vermont legislature to retreat from the Missisquoi Tongue, taking refuge on nearby South Hero Island. A 1790 Vermont census listed "Loyd, Thos. P. Esqr" as the head of a South Hero family comprising four "free white males of 16 and upward." Where three other older males came from isn't known. And with no female over sixteen in the house, Loid was now evidently a widower. He then appeared as "Thos P. Loid," one of two members of a committee named at a

South Hero town meeting on March 14, 1791. And on September 25, 1792, Thomas P. Loid was one of thirty petitioners to ask the Vermont general assembly to divide South Island (South Hero) into two distinct towns. Given that, as Stratton noted, the first twenty signatures (which ended with Loid's name) were all in the same handwriting, the general assembly understandably ignored it.

Loid made a brief reappearance in Molson's life through a letter from Molson's brother-in-law William Rayment. In the letter, written February 23, 1796, Rayment mockingly referred to Loid as "Pilgrim":

> Mr. Boaz Baxter of Helpringham or his wife are interested in some property on the demise of the wife that Pilgrim took out with him to America. Young Chapman* told me that Pilgrim is a Magistrate & situated on one of the Islands in Lake Champlain: cannot you devise means of my ascertaining whether this English wife is yet living—it is not very far from your vicinity. . . . He is called Thomas Lloyd Pilgrim Esquire & was represented as occupying a large room on the ground floor containing the bed & family economy & the Hall of Justice parted off by a curtain.

The information may have been old news, an amalgam of Loid's duties as a justice of the peace at Alburgh and his subsequent residence on South Hero. No political activity can be found for him after the dubious 1792 petition. As one of the poorest property owners on South Hero, appearing in the lowest ranks of the tax rolls in 1793 and 1801, Loid soon faded into poverty.

When Thomas Loid vacated Molson's property in 1787, the position of legislative representative for Alburgh was left unfilled. Although it was assumed by William Coit in 1788, there followed three more years without representation. The lapse was probably because the British Army had invaded Alburgh in 1788.

---

* Probably a former brewery employee of Molson's. See page 282.

Something was already going on, now only half glimpsed, at Caldwell's Upper Manor around 1787, as Molson lost his property. Events soon brought together the residents of the Missisquoi Tongue in an increasingly dangerous confrontation. Joseph Mott had acquired Molson's land there around August 1787, and a man named Benjamin Marvin had moved nearby in June 1787. Marvin and the greater Mott family shortly were at loggerheads with the Caldwell appointees John Savage and Patrick Conroy. What began as a clan feud, superimposed on a clash between the Caldwell and Allen factions, would shortly have Britain and the United States on the brink of war.

Another thread of discord had weaved its way into the events surrounding Molson's loss of the land. About 1786 a man named Cheeseman had arrived from St. Johns to homestead in the vicinity of Molson's property. When he returned to St. Johns in 1787, his brother-in-law John Griggs took over the small farm. The property, at some point, found its way into the hands of Joseph Mott's brother Samuel, but first there was a bloody confrontation in the bellwether year of 1787. A posse of armed men arrived from South Hero to settle a debt with Griggs, and ended up shooting and maiming his fishing companion, Joshua Manning. Griggs eluded arrest and fled to Quebec, but he was not forgotten by his pursuers. It would take twelve years, but the quest for retribution would play out with far more tragic consequences.

Perhaps initially encouraged by Vermont's unresolved status within the breakaway union, the British Army felt free to wade into local disputes and meddle where it saw fit. And so in the summer of 1788, British forces, behaving as a private security firm for Henry Caldwell, marched across the border into Caldwell's Upper Manor and seized control.

The event is described in a petition filed with the state of Vermont on October 13, 1794, by residents of Alburgh, who declared that they had settled between 1780 and 1787 in what they had known as Caldwell's Upper Manor on land acquired from Caldwell. The petition called (successfully) for a new trial to resolve the ownership spat between Caldwell and Allen. In November 1788,

Allen and an associate, John Knickerbacco, had been able to secure a default judgment in the local court of Chittenden County by which "an action of Trespass and ejectment was entered on the Docquet." Allen evidently had somewhat clandestinely finessed the legal means to evict Caldwell's tenants. But the British Army had already rolled in during the summer of 1788, appointing civil officers to run Caldwell's Upper Manor like any other part of Quebec. And when no counterattack or protest from Vermont followed, the petitioners presumed they were beyond the jurisdiction of any Vermont court. The petitioners went on to argue that when Allen and Knickerbacco began their court action, they were afraid to respond to it as they "dare not acknowledge the Jurisdiction of the State of Vermont for fear of Imprisonment by British Authority."

The dispute between Caldwell and Allen dragged on, through litigation and more armed provocation by both sides—and between people for whom no side can firmly be determined. Caldwell fell out of step with the free-trade initiatives championed by Ira Allen and supported by Montreal merchants. When the Quebec legislative council approved the inclusion of pig iron on the list of goods permitted free importation from Vermont, Caldwell, as a member of the council, voiced his objections. And when Vermont was finally admitted to the American union in 1791, Caldwell created a British militia unit that was led by Captains Patrick Conroy and John Savage—the man who had handled the sale of Molson's land. Both lived on the American side of the border, in Caldwell's Upper Manor opposite Pointe-au-Fer. Conroy also served as a justice of the peace.

In the summer of 1792 came a dramatic collision, immortalized as the Alburgh Border Incident. In May 1792, Conroy was summoned to appear before the Vermont Supreme Court in August for enforcing British law as a justice of the peace within American territory. Conroy paid the summons no attention. On June 8, Enos Wood of North Hero, a deputy sheriff of Chittenden County, appeared on the Tongue. He was to serve a writ against Conroy over a £50 debt he owed to Mary Grant, widow of Major John Grant of the Loyalist New York Volunteers, over damages Conroy allegedly committed in trespassing on the Grant property. Expecting trouble, Wood brought along a man named Benjamin Butler to back him up. Conroy, it turned out, was across the border on business in the north manor, but a man named Minard Yeomans was at his house. When Butler attempted to seize some of Conroy's cattle to settle the debt, Yeomans was said to have called for his pistols.[5] Wood attempted to arrest Yeomans but left without him, leading away the livestock. Yeomans ran to Captain Savage's home, and Savage sent word to Captain Francis Dechambault, the commanding officer at the Pointe-au-Fer garrison. Dechambault led a party of British soldiers across the border onto the Tongue, where they overtook Wood and Butler. According to Butler's subsequent testimony, one of the British soldiers "immediately presented to the breast of this deponent a Couple of Pistills & ordered him not to proceed one step or if he did he should fire him through." Wood and Butler were arrested on American soil and taken back to the garrison, where they were briefly held.

On June 11 came the counterattack. Joseph Mott's brother Samuel, an Alburgh justice of the peace appointed under Vermont authority, gave his nephew Joseph Mott, Jr., a local constable, written orders to serve Conroy and Yeomans with a summons to appear at the Chittenden County court in September to answer the charge of "an action of trespass committed in destroying of timber cutting carrying off destroying fences and building and sundry more trespasses. . . ." While serving the summons, Joseph Mott, Jr., appears to have seized some of Conroy's property, including a horse.

The next day, Captain Conroy led a retaliatory raid by British regulars into Alburgh against Benjamin Marvin, a local magistrate who had offended Conroy simply by carrying out the duties given to him by the state of Vermont. Marvin denied to Conroy that he had ordered any legal actions against him, but Conroy commanded the soldiers to escort Marvin to the Alburgh home of Samuel Mott.

Samuel Mott's home was being guarded by more British soldiers under Captain Dechambault when Marvin arrived with his escort. Dechambault had informed Mott he would be taken to the Pointe-au-Fer garrison and then sent to Quebec to stand trial. Conroy, meanwhile, decided to pay a visit to the home of Joseph Mott, Jr., to settle the score from Mott's seizure of his horse and other property. Two of Mott's horses were taken away to Pointe-au-Fer. Marvin was held at Conroy's home, where he and Samuel Mott were warned to clear out of Alburgh within two months or face the consequences. In the end, Dechambault did not make good on his threat to have Samuel Mott sent to Quebec City for trial. He and Marvin were released, having been threatened but not harmed.

The consequences of the arrogant behaviour of Conroy, Savage and Dechambault were felt immediately in the highest political circles. A melodrama of crude threats and livestock snatchings became a diplomatic incident. Vermont's governor, Thomas Chittenden, wrote the country's new president, George Washington, on June 16, and Thomas Jefferson, secretary of state, was soon involved. Negotiations between Britain and the United States over the British military presence at Pointe-au-Fer and other forts within American territory unfolded, with Britain showing no inclination to honour the border recognized in the Treaty of Paris of 1783. A full military confrontation was averted, but when Britain went to war with France again in 1793, belligerent behaviour by the British schooner *Lady Maria*, based at Windmill Bay, almost led to a resumption of hostilities between Britain and America.

This time, Jay's Treaty defused the situation, but the feud around Alburgh continued. In February 1799, a posse of Vermonters led by Deputy Sheriff John Allen of St. Albans made a nighttime raid on the home of Abraham Griggs, just inside the Canadian border, to snatch his brother John and settle the matter of the 1787 debt. On the raiders' way back over the frozen lake, their sleigh fell through the ice and Griggs was drowned. Allen and his companions were charged with murder at Montreal, and diplomatic negotiations were required to avert a trial. Governor Isaac Tichenor of Vermont formally apologized for the incident, and relations on the Missisquoi began to approach normalcy.

Around the turn of the century, Ira Allen's long-standing efforts at eviction were thwarted, and Henry Caldwell's property rights were upheld in the Vermont courts. After Caldwell acquired outright ownership of his leased Murray properties in 1801, his tenants at Lake Champlain received full possession of their lands, and the unoccupied remainder was eventually sold by Caldwell's son John to another Allen clan member, "for whom the price paid," Stratton observed, "with consequent expenses in suits, proved to be a bad investment."

The mysterious sale of Molson's Caldwell's Manor property and his decision not to purchase a ready-made malthouse property from Captain Grant that might have been in Alburgh had spared him from becoming enmeshed in decades of enmity in a corner of the world displaying all the charms of a Balkan blood feud. However, Molson's own world was generating enough enmity to sustain him. Having severed ties with Thomas Loid on August 31, 1787, Molson broke with James Gibbins, Sr., only weeks later.

Molson never gave a reason for the break—it's not clear if it had anything to do with the loss of the Caldwell's Manor property, an unpaid debt, services paid for but never rendered, or some final disappointment in Gibbins's behaviour. Gibbins had made several appearances in the joint account between Molson and Loid after the March 2, 1785, settlement, and he could have had some complicity in the loss of Molson's property. There is a faint suggestion that Gibbins might also have been maintaining a credit account with Molson, as Loid did, for the final payment Molson made to Loid on July 5, 1786, for butcher's expenses was "as allowed Mr. Pell in his Acct." Perhaps Gibbins had decided to quit the Missisquoi, and sold his land there without regard to the fact that he had pledged the property as security to Molson for the loans he had accumulated in 1786.

Molson revealed the schism with Gibbins in a letter to Philip Ashley on October 21, 1787. He first reported that the stone malthouse at St. Mary's Current was complete—much bigger than the one on the Grant property: eighty feet long, thirty-nine feet wide. He had been malting barley in the new building for the past three weeks, and hoped to begin brewing in the new copper kettle in another week. Molson also must have been busy that summer with a major transformation of the old malthouse, where he installed the larger copper kettle and all the apparatus from the original brew-house. With the porter off the ships selling at £5 per hogshead, he noted he would keep his prices the same as in 1786. And then, without warning or elaboration, he added, "Mr. Gibbins has used me very ill. I [have] parted with him."

The charade was over. Mr. Gibbins was Mr. Pell no longer.

Since April, the number of people Molson had accused of hav-ing treated him ill had grown from Ashley alone to include his grandfather Samuel and now James Gibbins. And while he never used the words in any letter, Molson thought he had been treated very ill indeed by Thomas Loid.

James Gibbins, Sr., skulked back to south Lincolnshire, to make occasional cameo appearances in letters to Molson from his rela-tives. James Gibbins, Jr., apparently remained around the Missisquoi as James Gibbins Pell, and William may have stayed as well.[6] But if Molson ever had anything to do with the Gibbins sons after the break with James Senior in October 1787, his surviving papers do not indicate it. He had carved away the closest people in his life from his Lincolnshire past, and those with whom he remained civil he was keeping in the dark. One week before Molson wrote Ashley, Sarah Vaughan gave birth to John Molson, Jr., on October 14. He said nothing about the event—having said nothing even about Sarah Vaughan—to Ashley, or to anyone else in his old life.[7]

"Have very little time to my self at presents," he wrote Ashley. "Therefore shall conclude with desiring you to make my duty & love as due & accept dear sir the sincere thanks of your most obliged & humble Servt, John Molson." The warmth had returned to his correspondence with Ashley. But his accusations of ill-use were about to spread to the most unexpected quarter.

Chapter 14

I have often thought, and still think, that there are few things which people in general know less, than how to love and how to hate. They hurt those they love, by a mistaken indulgence, by a blindness, nay, often a partiality to their faults: where they hate, they hurt themselves, by ill-timed passion and rage.
— Lord Chesterfield, letter to his son, November 26, 1749

WITH THE FALL BREWING season of 1787, John Molson was firmly established in his chosen trade. Samuel Townley's determination not to allow Molson to be left in the lurch by his cautious attorney had ensured his receipt of the equipment and supplies he needed to exploit properly the colony's unsated beer market. "Your kind letter now lies before me dated Oct. 22 1787," Townley wrote Molson on January 4, 1788. "It gives me great Pleasure to hear your Business succeeds be assurd I shall be happy to contribute my poor assistance for your Welfare."

The customer base for his brewery ran the gamut of colonial society. In addition to his former landlord Pierre Monarque and the ship's captain George Featonby, Molson was soon supplying the governor general, Lord Dorchester, the prominent merchants Joseph Frobisher and John McGill, and the local British Army barrack house, to name but a few customers from the 1788–89 ledgers. He had made himself indispensable as his product met with the success he had predicted. He was not entirely clear of hardship, but John Molson was irreversibly established; the brewery and its cash flow became the foundation for other enterprises that would follow.

John Molson marked his twenty-fourth birthday on December 28, 1787, as a new father, although he was determined not to share any news of the milestone with his own family back in England. With the new malting house, he had built himself a means to prosperity that also served as a stone keep. Thomas Loid and James Gibbins, Sr., had been banished from his life, and he had washed his hands of Henry Caldwell and Ira Allen and their fractious tongue of land. However, the duplicity of his life had not departed with the last sight of Mr. Gibbins/Pell or his own inelegant removal from the quagmire of Caldwell's Manor. Appearance and experience had become their own cultivated realities in John Molson's life. The exchange of letters with family members, a routine opportunity for gossip and good cheer, became for Molson the most carefully weighed transactions. Like some deft import-export merchant, he chose to reveal far less than he learned, as he surrendered only the information that he felt motivated to provide. ("Nobody can be more willing or ready to obey orders than I am," wrote Lord Chesterfield on October 11, 1769, "but then I must like the orders and the orderer.") Molson's motto for the business of life evidently was, "Disclose as little as one must and learn as much as one can."

Two days after his birthday, he received (by the New York mail packet) a potent challenge to his isolation and to the balance of trade in family intelligence. It was a letter written by his sister Martha the previous summer, on July 21. Her script routinely was riven with misspellings, grammatical errors and malapropisms—she wrote on this occasion that the issue plaguing her had been "revolting in my own mind" (she plainly meant "revolving"). It is all too tempting, given what transpired, to view Martha as ill-educated, covetous and destructively calculating. But poor Martha, obsessed at times with mortality, the financial gains of others and her own limited opportunities, made clear the consequences of being the youngest female in a family that showered the first-born male with the lion's share of its inheritance.

Martha confessed she had been deliberating over the issue for the year that had passed since she had last seen her elder brother, and had finally "determined to acquaint you with it, as I think it absolutely necessary not only with regard to my health, which I find suffers of my Life." Martha would come of age on March 31, 1788, and as she wrote, "I find my *Fortune insufficient* to appear in measure [in]dependent. . . . Oh! Brother tis impossible, which has made me determine to extricate myself out of this difficulty, or my health would be the Forfeiture. I am far from being well and I can assign no other cause for ill health, than the continual agitation of mind, which I have experienced since you left England."

The only solution Martha could find to her financial predicament was to apprentice in London as a milliner—the trade practised by their grandfather Samuel's new wife, Mary Albin. As John was a man of commerce, his opinion was important to his sister: "I earnestly intreat you to take this matter into serious consideration and if it meets with your approbation I will immediately adopt it," unless her brother came up with something better. "I hope my dear Brother [will] consider this a laudiable motive—rather to [throw] myself in Business, however disagreeable—than by living Genteel be a Burden to my Relations."

Martha then alluded to what seems a particularly heartless directive made by her brother at some unknown time: that he wished to receive letters concerned only with business, not with personal matters:

> As my *Happiness* greatly depend upon the subject of this letter, I hope that will be a sufficient *Apology* for adressing these lines. I think they also come under the denomination of Business, or I should not have troubled you as you desire I sure would not, on any other head.
>
> I feel myself at this Moment capable of [writing on other subjects]. But as you desire only Business, and I will not deviate from the rules prescribed. Oh! Brother! I have a mind . . . to complaint, yet I cannot help wishing your answer may contain a little more then as what I aludes to [in] the first part of this letter. If it bring Information of your health and happiness it will be considered A Treasure. Mary does not [know] of my writing nor any of the subject it contains for if it meats [sic] with

your approbation it will then be time to acquaint the rest of my friend's with Instructions. I imagine it's needless.

Why would John Molson have cruelly instructed his sisters to lower a cone of silence around their personal lives? (Almost pathetically, Martha stole the chance to add the simple but apparently illicit news that "my Brother Tom live at Snake Hall—and Mary keeps his House.") One cannot help suspecting that if Molson made the directive after he returned to Montreal in 1786 in a now lost letter, its purpose was to shield him from having to share and share alike. If his relatives were forbidden to forward the basic news of their lives, then he would be under no obligation to surrender his own news of Sarah Vaughan and the child born in October 1787.

To his everlasting credit, Molson gave his distraught sister a full and considerate reply, while at the same time removing the business-only directive. "You mention several times my desire of you & your sister Mary, not writing to me without Business," he added to his reply. "If I said tis more than I know—however for the future you [are] under no such restrictions." But the removal of the directive did not mean that John Molson intended to respect it with his own letters. He declined to provide the most important personal news he could share—a fairly remarkable decision, given the contents of his reply.

"I take this first opportunity of giving you my opinion of your intentions," Molson wrote in a surviving draft of the letter sent January 21.

> Your decision of rendering yourself independent of your friends obligations are truly laudible—for of all situations in life dependencies on; or obligations to one's friends is the most uncomfortable. The only way to obviate that dependency is to enter into some kind of Business which for a Woman is more difficult than for a Man. Your Idea of a Millinary Business is the only one that I can see practicable for you & as you observe your fortune would enable [you] to set up in that & with tolerable success you might get a living.

Molson had only one alternative for her—that she come to Montreal and serve as his housekeeper.

> I should be able to give you twenty pounds this Currency per year equals Eighteen pounds sterling that is Eighteen English pounds. Do not think Martha because I am putting a stipulated price that you would be considered as an ordinary servant or hirling—but to shew you that as there is a consideration given that of the two I am the obligated party—your passage hither will cost thirty guineas which I mean to be included in the allowance [i.e., added to the salary].

Molson could not see his sister settling her affairs and making the Atlantic crossing before 1789, and he volunteered to guide her through the necessary steps to prepare for the voyage if she so chose. He warned her, however, of a life in social isolation:

> If you come here you must not expect to keep much company for in the first instance I live on a street plan of economy & in the second ye Gentlemen & Ladies here are so much adicted to pleasure dress that to come into their way would be ruinous to a persons circumstances—tho' at the same time the assemblies might be attended without any great expense & the riding in a Cariole on the Snow is very agreeble in the Winter season & a Caleche in the Summer. Those things we can effect without any ruinous tendency.[1]

He skimmed past the basic facts of his existence like the sleighs and carriages he offered up as superficial details of his life at St. Mary's Current. He offered nothing more than the passing panorama beyond the window, not daring to turn around and reveal who was gathered at the hearth. The housekeeping proposal was a daring offer by Molson, as it meant that inevitably he would have to reveal to his sister the relationship with Sarah Vaughan and the very existence of a male heir, John Junior, then three months old. And once Martha knew, everyone else back home would learn by the first available packet. It does raise the question of how serious Molson considered the relationship with Sarah Vaughan when he wrote Martha to offer the position that originally might have been Sarah's—even if he envisioned the relationship lasting into 1789.

The same day he wrote Martha, Molson addressed another letter to Philip Ashley, apprising him of the employment offer he had made to his sister. He admitted that "this is a very distant Idea of mine." If she agreed to the proposal, Molson wished Ashley to aid her with her finances: "your assistance to help her settle her affairs will be esteemed a favour from her am sure; as well as from your most obliged humble servant. PS I have intelligence of War in Europe tho not officially yet. That may prevent Martha thinking of coming here for it would be a cursed thing for a Woman to fall in to the hands of the French. . . ."

War with the French did not come, at least not in 1788 or 1789. Nor did Martha, to keep his house. In the months that had passed since she had written her plaintive letter, Martha's troubles had been resolved by a most practical, if predictable, route: she had found a husband.

The news was set down in a letter dated March 2, 1788, which did not reach Molson until October 25. It may have been the most momentous communiqué ever to reach him, eclipsing even the disastrous 1783 message from Martha relating the news of Robinson Elsdale's death. The latest letter propelled the consequences of his uncle's death—Molson's frustrated romance or infatuation with the widow—into dark and disruptive terrain. Its reverberations would be felt for years.

The correspondent, William Rayment, gamely began, "You may possibly recollect my being once in Company with you at the Fleet Rectory—Tom & the widow were there also I think on a Sunday." By way of introduction, Rayment had coincidentally gathered on the stage most of the main characters in the coming melodrama: himself, Martha, John, Thomas, the widow Elsdale and, by implication, the rector at Fleet, the Reverend James Ashley. (The relationship between James and Philip Ashley is not certain, but they were likely brothers or cousins.) "I then little thought I should ever stand in my present *happy situation*, as (tho'

I do not now recollect the time I speak of) I was not then acquainted with my dear Martha."

After explaining at meandering length his opportunity to post Molson the letter in the Wednesday mail packet, Rayment broke from the news of his imminent marriage to Martha to deliver bluntly a second bulletin: "The news I have to communicate is the decease of your Grandfather Monday Feb 7 88 the funeral the proceeding Friday."

Samuel Elsdale's passing warranted an obituary in *The Gentleman's Magazine*, published in London,[2] which noted he had died in his eighty-fourth year and declared him to have been

> much esteemed, and sincerely lamented . . . formerly a considerable farmer and grazier in that parish [of Surfleet], but had many years retired from business. This gentleman was a remarkable instance of health and spirits, almost to example. He lived to be nearly 80 years old without having ever experienced pain or sickness. Until that age he had never taken a dose of physic, or been confined to the house by indisposition for a single hour; and, till his death, was never let blood, or suffered any other medical operation.

With Samuel Elsdale dead, the melodrama now had a plot. What followed in the letter from Rayment must have been so disturbing to Molson and so freighted with consequence that it should be absorbed as it was by its recipient:

> To explain my first paragraph, I may cut the matter short, by saying, I shall shortly be your brother by the marriage of your dear sister Martha. We are most happy in each other's Love, & our present prospects are as fair as we ought to wish them. Pat [Martha's nickname] tells me there is a striking likeness between you & myself, as to our mode of thinking, principles of action, possible she sees with too partial eyes.
>
> However, as I have the happiness of being in the entire, & perfect confidence of Mary, Martha & [Samuel Elsdale] Molson, I am pretty intimately acquainted with the affairs

of the family, & will now give you a plain unvarnished account of circumstances, of which you ought not to be ignorant. I will say nothing, but what I can prove & as to the illiberal and jesuitical principle of some people I hold myself above it.

The dispatches you will receive from Surfleet if they do not forget to write, will carry a different face or I am much mistaken—beware my dear Sir of giving too implicit credit to accounts from that quarter. I am happy I can so certainly anticipate their information. . . .

I most sincerely congratulate you on the escaping a connexion with the little widow:—I have but too much reason to say point blank, I know her to be, & can prove it:—she is a bad woman.

Mrs. Elsdale has used me, you, & Martha very ill [and Martha and I] have parted with her as to any connection [but] that of cold civility. Phil Ashley who knows me & my family very well though not so well as he does yours, will tell you my evidence may be taken in a court of Honour.

I long since saw & felt that an accursed spirit of malice & envy from whence I did not then know was the moving cause of that coldness which poor Martha used to lament she experienced from her Brother John. I for a length of time did not entirely credit my dear Pat's account of her aunt's heart & consciences. I am too convinced she did not asperse her Aunt.

. . . As I saw through a deep line of secret influence, & back stairs business, for the purpose of prejudicing the old Gentleman [Samuel Elsdale] against *all the Molsons* I tried & succeeded in counter acting the schemes of the Bridge Party but not so effectively as I could have done had I known then, what I do know now. Yourself & your Brother Tom are left out of old Sir's Will—Sam is scantily provided for—your Uncle Sam has only a £50 legacy & your Uncle John of Ipswich is left as sole Executor in trust for Mary, Martha & the widow's two Boys—who at his death are to share equally what may remain of the old Gentleman's Estates & effects after all dues & demands thereon are fully satisfied. The Executor being in a bad state of health could not come over neither before nor since Mr E's decease—but intends being with us in a few weeks. Interim he has put the management of the concern into the hands of Parson Ashley. I should suppose you must be aware of it, that this Gentleman is not much of a man of business.

I design to offer the Executor my assistance by tomorrow's post—5 years in a Counting House should & I believe has given me a taste for mercantile regularity & correctness. I trust I shall not be denied your correspondence. You may command my services as to any assistance in my power for your own concerns. Previous to your return to England which I have heard talked of, if I mistake not, but I should be far happier to take you by the Hand of the Brother of my Martha—she expects to hear that I so wrote to you as I promised by the Packet. She sends you her Love & I may safely venture to do the like for my Sister Mary & Brother Sam for such I must esteem them. Tom's an oddity.

... The account in this business will be found complicated enough—your Uncle Samuel is gone to reside in London & has been to Surfleet. I chanced on him for a companion to Town in the Boston Coach last Monday.

I call him a queer fellow.

I hope & trust my dear Sir I may be in some measure the means of reconciling all jarrings among the Molsons & that I shall be esteemed by you as I am very truly your friend & brother.

In this innuendo-filled letter, Rayment also included news of James Gibbins, Sr.:

Your guardian Companion Gibbins is among us & doing God only knows what. His account of yourself was a vast deal longer than that you gave P Ashley of him. Gibbins is a very

free spoken plausible genius. I rather more than suspect him to
be an hypocrite & that he is not over & above addicted to the
crime of veracity.

Rayment's comments on Gibbins strongly imply that Molson's
former friend had been spreading interesting stories about him back
in Lincolnshire, no doubt including eyebrow-raising details about
Sarah Vaughan. Molson had entertained Gibbins in a fall 1785 letter with the news that Luke Gibbins's mother had married a man
who turned out to have an illegitimate child with his housekeeper,
with another on the way. Gibbins (who had boisterously written in
verse to his future son-in-law, Robinson Elsdale, in 1769: "Ah
[Rough] Enough the Weomen are Kinde/There's the thing, Capt,
Capt, there's the Thing. . . .") may now have been having a good
laugh with his Lincolnshire cronies at John Molson's expense.
Rayment was delicately warning Molson about the gossip in circulation without actually repeating it. By suggesting that Gibbins
might be lying, Rayment was inviting Molson to provide the truth.

All of the intrigue conveyed by Rayment had no chance to reach
Molson before he decided that he would indeed liquidate his holdings in Lincolnshire and commit to Quebec. On March 20, he
informed Ashley: "Am come to a final determination to sell the
whole of my Estate in the parishes of Moulton Peakhill & Cowbit
& therefore wish you immediately after the receipt of this to proceed in that Business."

This letter and one to Martha on January 21 had reached
Lincolnshire by the time William Rayment penned a second letter
to his future brother-in-law, on May 24. Rayment noted that since
he last wrote Molson, "Martha has received your very acceptable
favour of 21 January [it arrived March 27]: which brought the pleasing intelligence that she had still a Brother not unmindful of her,
though at so great a distance. I am commissioned to answer your
Letter now before me. . . ." He regretted to report that their wedding
had not yet taken place: "it has been unavoidably postponed,
through some very unpleasant differences with my friends"—an
obstruction he declined to explain. "Whether these obstacles will

be removed or not, is impossible to say, but I am firmly of opinion they can make no difference in our mutual attachment."

Rayment then revealed that he and Martha were considering emigrating to Canada as early as the spring of 1789, and he invited Molson's advice on opportunities—"whether there is a fair probability of starting in a respectable line of business either in the mercantile line (to which I have been most accustomed) or in the retirement of a farm or plantation, which best suits my ideas & wishes, as my aim will be chiefly at the quiet enjoyments of domestic happiness."

Philip Ashley now had Molson's instructions to sell off all his property, which would leave homeless his brothers Thomas and Samuel and his sister Mary, who were all at Snake Hall. (Martha was staying with an aunt at Wisbeach.) Ashley asked Rayment to give Thomas the news that Snake Hall was to be sold. There was some thought of Thomas purchasing it, but according to Rayment, "Thomas has since said he finds the purchase above his ideas, & therefore rather thinks of quitting at Lady Day next." Rayment also informed Molson that Philip Ashley's wife had died. If John Molson ever sent his condolences, no draft or copy survives.

The estate of Samuel Elsdale was the chief concern of Rayment, who had either insinuated himself into the proceedings or been drawn in through his fiscal experience. The most uncharitable rendering of Rayment's character would colour him a gold-digger among gold-diggers, showing up suddenly in Martha Molson's life just before she came of age and just around the time Samuel Elsdale died and left a large estate to be fought over. Everything known about Rayment is revealed in his own letters; and, in addition to the counting-house experience already cited, a letter written in 1795, which indicated he had been in the army twenty years earlier, suggests he was about thirty years old when he became engaged to Martha. His writing also suggested he had enjoyed a much greater formal education than John Molson, and he seemed well connected with many of the principal characters in the brewer's life. Rayment was never less than thorough in advancing the cause of the Molson children, but he was also presumptuous, judgmental, probably libellous, fond of breathlessly escalating innuendo, and well in over his head. His arrival on the scene in 1788 precipitated nearly a decade of enmity, just as John Molson was shrugging off the calamity of Caldwell's Manor and the break with Thomas Loid and James Gibbins, Sr. It was as if Molson barely had the chance to draw his breath before considering the next crop of people to do him ill.

As outlined by Rayment in his March 4 letter, John Molson and his brother Thomas had been left out of Grandfather Samuel's will. Their brother Samuel Elsdale Molson, who had been left only £100 by his own father on the understanding that grandfather Samuel would take care of his needs, had been "scantily provided for." Martha and Mary were to share equally with their late uncle Robinson's two children, Robinson and Samuel, in the proceeds of Grandfather Samuel's estate. Grandfather Samuel's son John, the tanner in Ipswich, had been named executor of the estate, but there was some doubt as to whether his health would permit him to take on the task. In the meantime, the estate's affairs had fallen into the hands of the Reverend James Ashley, rector at Fleet, who was already the guardian of the late uncle Robinson's two boys.

Puffing himself up with his counting-house experience, Rayment initially doubted Reverend Ashley's abilities to oversee matters of business, but he would increasingly—and sensationally—cast him as an ally of the widow Ann Elsdale in a grand effort to deny the Molson children what was rightfully theirs. Rayment had already placed the widow—and a social circle known as the Bridge Club—in opposition to the Molsons' interests. As time passed, he inserted conniving deceit and compromising adultery into his conspiratorial tableau. It was a fantastic effort that would have captured the narrative interest of Thomas Hardy, but for now it was only important for Rayment that it fascinate John Molson.

Rayment elaborated on the estate dispute in his second letter, dated May 24. He advised John Molson that he had persuaded Samuel, as a principal legatee of the estate, to secure a copy of the will from the Reverend Ashley, and, as a result, Samuel was formally attempting to determine if his uncle John Elsdale was going to fulfill the role of executor. "Really, my dear Sir," Rayment complained to

Molson with self-satisfaction, "these good relations of yours, are a kind of body without a head in their business, & not a little in want of their elder Mother to inspect into this business & manage for them. I can do no more and am at present circumstanced, than give my opinion."

Whatever limits Rayment felt at the moment, however, he was prepared to become as fully involved as possible in the name of his soon-to-be wife and her put-upon siblings. "Samuel, Thomas, Martha & Mary all concur in thinking that the affairs are at present in improper hands," Rayment related, "Mr. James Ashley who is Guardian to the Widow's children, being the factotum in every step that has been taken, both before & after the Old Gentleman's departure. He is the particular friend of the widow, & they have no doubt of her being by no means the friend of the Molsons. I thought it right to give you this information, as I make no doubt but that you interest yourself in the welfare of the family."

Martha made her own contribution to the growing estate controversy, writing to John Molson on March 29, the same day she received his letter of January 21. John's letter "gave me real pleasure but particularly at a time when I was very much depresd by the loss of my Grandfather who quitted this Vale of Memory the 10th of February but doubtless you have heard of that event long before this reaches Montreal with all the particulars of his *Will etc*. My Uncle John refuses to act as Executor in consequence of which tis supposed all the Estate will be spent in Chancery."

Martha professed to be

extremely obliged to my Dear Brother for his kind offer [of the housekeeper's position] and should most gladly have accepted it if this Connection had not taken place—but I still retain the wish of fixing in America & as Mr. Rayment tries to oblige me in every thing that lays in his power he said he had mentioned that I . . . consult with you in what line we should be most like to succeed whether in the Planting or Mercantile if there is any prospect of doing well in either—would like to quit England and be out [next] Spring, as his father does not approve of his son marrying a Woman with so small a fortune. I am happy to find that makes no alternation [*sic*] in his son['s] sentiments with regard to me, I think on this account it would not be pleasent to fix in this part. . . .

Martha volunteered that "we mean to be quite domestic people there fore our plan must chime in with yours exactly." It was the closest Martha came to acknowledging that she had learned of Sarah Vaughan and the boy via James Gibbins's gossip. If that was her intent, she did not have the nerve to press the issue further. "I wish to hear from you immediately after you *receive this* as we shall not look out for any situation till we hear from you; if you approve of our moving to America beg you will be very Particular in your directions about the Voyage etc you will hear more on that subject when we know your opinion."

Almost the entire Molson clan was in the grip of wedding plans, as Martha announced that Tom was going to marry a woman named Miss Cooling, while Mary "I think will have Mr. Hannings, his wife [their cousin] Martha Clark has been dead six months[;] I believe they were not married when you left England." John Molson's siblings were in a frantic race to secure their futures through wedlock as their brother prepared to sell Snake Hall out from under them. Neither wedding forecast by Martha, however, actually occurred; Mary rapidly moved on to Abraham Whitsed, whom she married on December 26, but it took more than two years for Tom to find a suitable mate.

Martha also reported that Jack Baxter had come into an inheritance of £3,000, "at least report gives him it but for my own part I do not give it much Credit as the gentleman which they say has left it has a family, it is OW Morgan whose son you may remember seeing with Baxter at Surfleet when you was last in England." There was also another sighting of James Gibbins, Sr.: "Mr. Gibbins has fixed in London since he left you but not finding it answer he is now trying to Butcher at Boston."

Within all the social news was the essential matter that would plague so many lives for so many years. "At my Grandfathers decease you may recollect there was an Estate at Stickney which we all suppose whent to my Uncle R Elsdale," Martha wrote. "It was given to my Aunt Nancy for life." Aunt Nancy was their sickly late aunt, Ann Elsdale, who died before any of them could know her and is all too easily confused in these letters with Robinson Elsdale's widow. Martha's reasoning in the ensuing paragraph is difficult for us to follow, but her brother readily grasped it. She understood that when the Reverend Ashley inspected the will, he discovered one of those brain-teasing inheritance puzzles endemic to eighteenth-century bequests. Samuel Elsdale had set the Stickney estate aside under a trust to provide for Nancy. But if Nancy died after coming of age, unmarried and childless, the Stickney estate would devolve equally to two of her siblings: John and Martha's mother, Mary, and their uncle Robinson.

Despite its name, which to some modern ears might suggest an elegant country retreat in which the widow Ann Elsdale lived in genteel splendour, "Stickney Estate" was an unremarkable property, consisting of three separate parcels of pasture totalling twenty acres, two of which featured a "messuage"—some kind of building. Ann Elsdale never occupied it; the pastures, when rented out, were simply meant to generate income. Edward Pavey had been renting the thirty-eight acres attached to Snake Hall in the 1780s for £11 per annum. Thus we can imagine that the annul rental income from Stickney might have come to all of £6, although the presence of what might have been houses would have increased the return. However modest its income potential, any amount of land was too coveted to ignore.

"[I] mention this circumstance as [I] know you to be my Mother's heir with [regard to the] Estate," Martha explained. "If you wish to claim it you [can most] certainly have it as Nancy was near three and twenty when she died." Thus, by Martha's understanding of the will, the estate north of Boston, at Stickney, was one-half her brother John's. Already Rayment had implied that the Reverend Ashley was blatantly favouring the widow Ann and the two boys— a theme on which he would later enthusiastically expand. Rayment and Martha were building a case that John Molson was being cheated out of a substantial inheritance by his uncle's widow and a conniving parson.[3]

Molson did not receive Rayment's first letter of March 2 until October 10,[4] while Martha's letter of March 29 reached him by early October. He was in the process of composing his response to Rayment, dated October 25, when Rayment's May 24 letter also arrived. Although occupied with the fall brewing season and the first birthday of his son, Molson nonetheless took time to compose a lengthy and carefully considered reply.

On the matter of resettling in Canada, Molson provided a generous amount of advice, much of it discouraging. Regarding "the mercantile line," Molson wrote that

> there are complaints of the great quantities of goods in the Country & a Scarcity of Money I can vouch for—to be on respectable footing requires a good support from home & believe it would be a difficult Matter to get any considerable share in the Fur Trade (by the Way believe it a very indifferent one at present) in a retail way see some do very well & others do ill—perhaps conduct regulates that—to the particular goods suiting this Market can not take upon me to say, but it is generally overstocked or a scarcity prevails of some sort of Merchandise or other—for instance a Gentleman of the place has last Week made a Speculation in Rum perhaps it may Answer & next year in all probability we shall be over stocked with ye article—believe 'tis allowed in general ye Cash in this Country can be turned to the best advantage by a Person who has talents for speculation or who takes care to apply [it] to those who want Money.

Farming was no more appealing. Quebec was in the grip of two successive summers of disastrous harvests, although Molson never made any specific reference to the failures. While bread was in short supply in Montreal, it has been suspected that the worst losses were suffered by the francophone Canadians, with little damage done to the Loyalist farmers. Molson provided a long accounting of produce and meat prices as well as land costs, but concluded "the farming & grazing line . . . will not answer." In his opinion, the best bet was to purchase a seigneury, which Molson hazarded would cost two to six thousand pounds. Although the advice was dissuasive, it was fair, and the state of the merchant community was well presented.

Most important, Molson turned a sober eye in his reply to the overheated allegations of his soon-to-be brother-in-law. He first welcomed Rayment into the Molson midst: "tho' [I am] a stranger to you only from the circumstances you Mention make no doubt but the intended connexion does honor to my family." He also acknowledged that there were hostile sentiments in the Lincolnshire countryside when it came to Molson affairs, and thanked Rayment for playing the white-knight role: "Am extremely obliged to you for generous kind respects—the Bridge Party—& for your trouble in trying to Counter Act their Malavolence."

All the same, Molson made an admirable effort to disabuse Rayment of the bulk of his conspiratorial notions. "I do not see any real impropriety in the Old Gentlemans Will only that he has not been generous enough to Sam. Tom & me had above our Quantum of my fathers Estate—for my part never expected a Six pence from Old Sir—& I suppose he thought Tom had sufficient with care & industry. . . . [M]y Sister's having equal shares with S & R Elsdale is I think as much as they could expect. . . ."

Molson agreed that "an executor in ye Country might have been better—perhaps the malynity of the Bridge party may have other tendencies—wish you had been more explicit on ye head," which suggests Molson was wondering if the Reverend James Ashley's wife or the widow Ann was playing the leading role. But Molson would not accept Rayment's casting of Reverend Ashley or his wife as villains: "my good friend your *inestimable friend the Rectoress* was an inveterate incorrigable & declared Enemy to Robinson Elsdale deceased therefore I conceive no friend to his Widow or children. The Rector is diametrically opposite & I believe he would render any service to the Molson's on account of the friendship that existed between them." In fact, at some point (possibly already) the poor abused rector had given shelter both to Martha, after she was turned out by an aunt in Wisbeach, and to Rayment, after he was ejected by his father. James Ashley would come to be justifiably enraged by the abuse Martha and her beau steadily heaped upon him.

John Molson's letter was precisely the sort of sane advice required to suppress the hysteria of wrongdoing being marshalled by Rayment. Unfortunately, according to references to letters sent and received, this letter never reached him.

John Molson's interest in the Stickney estate had been piqued, however, by Martha's letter. He had written Philip Ashley on October 19 and was back to registering his disappointment with Ashley's tardiness. (The Ashley men would brook a surfeit of indignation from maligned Molsons.) "Am sorry & surprised at my not having received any Answer to mine of March wherein I desired you to proceed immediately in the sale of my Estate. I fully expected the Deed of Trust by laterly Shipping—but not a scrip— for we had the last dispatches from England yesterday can have this season."

The delay meant that Molson could not proceed with selling his Lincolnshire properties until 1789, and his need for cash had not waned. To pay Townley for brewery supplies, he had drawn on Gosling for £125, which he needed Ashley to cover, and he scolded: "your delay [with the property sale] will embarrass me a great deal as I regulated my affairs in a full dependance of receiving a deed of trust this Autumn to be filled up. . . . Hope after receipt of this you'll proceed to the selling [of] my Estate as you think it will fetch the nearest its Value—it would cost me at least One Hundred Guineas to come to England myself & not only that but I cannot leave my Business—Let me once more desire you to use the utmost dispatch. . . . " In a postscript, Molson mentioned, as an almost casual aside, that he had been informed that "[the] Estate at Stickney which was Nancy Elsdale's desends [sic] to me as heir at Law—please enquire into that matter."

One cannot blame John Molson for wanting to prove or disprove his sister's allegations regarding the Stickney property, but any legal action would have major consequences. The estate now belonged to the widow Ann Elsdale. Should Molson prevail and Stickney be proven to be at least half his, the security of the widow with whom he once imagined a perfect union would be seriously affected. With Rayment (and Martha) casting her in the role of arch-nemesis to the Molson children, John was given little reason to consider her welfare. Having broken with James Gibbins, Sr., Molson apparently had given up all sentimental attachment to the former friend's daughter as well, having pointedly made no effort to defend her in the letter to Rayment. An inheritance was an inheritance, and Molson could certainly use the money Stickney would raise when sold.

Once Rayment knew that Molson had directed Ashley to look into the Stickney matter, he moved forward with self-righteous fervour. Never having received the calming advice of Molson's October 25 letter, he was confident he had the full backing of John Molson in his crusade against the worthy widow, the Bridge Club, the rector and rectoress, and anyone else who would deny him his complete satisfaction on all matters concerning Samuel Elsdale's disputed estate. With Philip Ashley largely inactive or inattentive, Rayment developed a momentum that swept up even John Molson. It would take the much maligned Reverend Ashley seven years to fend off Rayment's most strident and wrong-headed claims, while Molson watched from a safe distance in Montreal, the silence on his own personal affairs carefully maintained.

Chapter 15

Wrongs are often forgiven, but contempt never is. Our pride remembers it forever.
—Lord Chesterfield, letter to his son, July 1, 1748

ON JULY 4, 1789, the eve of the French Revolution (the Bastille would be stormed ten days later), John Molson placed the deed of ownership for Snake Hall and various surrenders for his Lincolnshire properties in a box and shipped them back to Philip Ashley. A buyer had been found for Snake Hall—a Moulton grazier named Samuel Wood—and the indenture witnessing the sale by "John Molson of Montreal common brewer" had been completed on June 11. Because Molson had already mortgaged Snake Hall and was drawing from Gosling against its value, it's not clear how much money he netted from the sale, but one estimate has placed the total proceeds realized from his inherited properties around £10,000.[1]

Whatever the gain, Molson had at last been able to liquidate his inheritance and devote all his monies to the brewery. In addition to drawing on Ashley for £100, Molson informed him that he would sell a bill of exchange for £900 in the fall, payable on thirty days' sight. This he did on October 20, placing the bill with the tobacconist George Stansfeld. Writing to remind Philip Ashley of the large bill on October 21, Molson noted: "[I] particularly hope there has been no miscarriages in deeds & Surrenders to prevent your accepting my Bills for the consequence would be terible. All Bills returned back protested to Canada pay sixteen & half per cent damages."

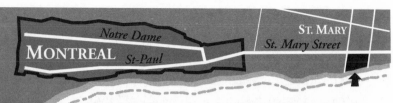

John Molson in St. Mary's Suburb

The Molson brewery was established in St. Mary's suburb, less than a mile from the old walled city of Montreal.

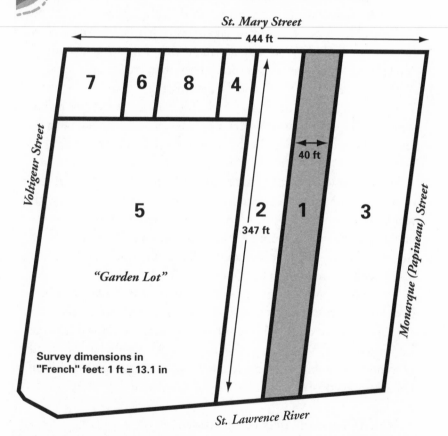

1. Original brewery lot, purchased by Thomas Loid from Pierre Monarque, 1782. Purchased by John Molson from sheriff's auction, January 7, 1785
2. Purchased from Pierre Monarque, 1788
3. Purchased from Pierre Monarque, 1789
4. Purchased from François Desautels, 1799
5. Purchased from J.P. Leprohon, 1799
6. Purchased from Paul La Fleur, 1801
7. Purchased from J.P. Leprohon, 1808
8. Purchased from Pierre Desautels, 1811

Molson was in the midst of expanding his land holdings in the St. Mary's suburb. Already in 1788 he had bought from Pierre Monarque the adjoining lot to the west of the brewery property. After returning the deed for Snake Hall to Ashley, Molson hired a contractor named Joseph Perreault to build him a stone house on the new lot. On the same day that he sold the bill of exchange to Stansfeld, he bought the lot on the opposite side of the original brewery property from Monarque as well. He now had 206 "French" feet of frontage on St. Mary Street, and in the spring of 1790 he built a stable for delivery horses, a barn and what may have been an ice house. His beer production, which included "strong," "mild," "table" and "small," as well as spruce beer, increased from 11,000 to 30,000 gallons in 1791.[2] To help pay for the expansion, Molson secured a five-year mortgage with Monarque, which probably heightened his interest in William Rayment's ongoing campaign to expose the chicanery of the Reverend Ashley and the scheming widow.

Having gone through a succession of hirings in his first winter of brewing, Molson continued to experience problems with employees. At some point, he hired a man named Chapman. He could have been the "Young Chapman" who would be referred to in a letter from William Rayment in 1796, in which case he may also have been related to George Chapman, one of the signatories to the raucous celebratory letter sent to Robinson Elsdale in 1769. Like Jim Brainsby, he was probably another man from Molson's old Lincolnshire circle who spent time in Canada. However long he worked for Molson, by February 1789 his behaviour had become intolerable. Molson left behind a short memo detailing his transgressions:

Feb 26 Chapman drunk & impertinent
Feb 27 Dr[unk]—fell down into lower floor—hurt his back & arm—would have nothing apply'd—after dinner went out without leave or acquaintg me
March 2 Came in the Morng—3 P.M. asked leave to go to Coltmans for Quarter of an hour returned not that night.

3rd Returned drunk & impertinent demanding his Wages & acquittance

6th Came & settled with him in full & he took away his cloaths—gave me receipt in full of all demand & an acquittance from our agreemt. . . .

Having to make ledger entries on behalf of the illiterate Sarah Vaughan must have helped convince Molson to take on a bookkeeper, but the work of a man named Charles Lilly gave him more headaches. (He was probably related to the prominent Montreal merchant John Lilly, whose daughter Elizabeth married Molson acquaintance Francis Badgley in 1795.) Molson hired Charles Lilly on June 6, 1793, for an annual salary of £26. But as Molson pored over his cash-book entries from June 29, 1793, to May 4, 1794, he found a rash of errors, some of which he charged were "errors wilful": overcharges on postage and barley, "false additions" and "money taken out of grain box." Lilly must have been dismissed, but he was not considered an outright thief, as on Monday, November 10, 1794, Molson wrote a note to a man named McArthur, informing him: "Mr Lilly called on me on Saturday respecting entering into my employ—you can inform him if he thinks proper, can come at £20 per annum." Whether Lilly ever agreed to come back to work at the reduced salary is unknown.

Martha Molson and William Rayment had at last married, at Crowland Abbey, on May 31, 1790. Two weeks earlier, the late Robinson Elsdale's half-brother John, who had declined the position of executor of Samuel Elsdale's estate in August 1788, had died at Ipswich at the age of sixty-four. Authority over the estate passed to the Reverend Ashley, who was consulting with the late Robinson's other half-brother, Samuel, who lived in Pimlico and was the eldest surviving male in the Elsdale family. The parson thus was still very much in the picture and very much under siege.

Now a fully vested member of the Molson family, Rayment had adopted a new strategy in his estate mining. Initially, he had presented his interest in the grandfather's estate as chivalrous—indeed, the only person who would seem able to benefit from his crusade with respect to the Stickney property was the distant John Molson. But once married to Martha, Rayment shifted tactics: he was working himself into a counting-house lather over interest charges on unremitted income from the disputed property—creating a more expansive scenario of estate indebtedness that would benefit all the Molson children and, by extension, himself.

On August 10, 1790, Rayment (who was living with Martha in London, where he was a partner in a cabinetry business) wrote Philip Ashley with an update on his investigations and suppositions. He had concluded that, on Ann Elsdale's death around 1766, the rents from the Stickney estate should have been passed on to her purported heirs—Mary (Elsdale) Molson and her brother, Robinson. Mary had died in 1772; thus Rayment now argued that there were six years of rental income from Stickney that should be divided equally among the five children of Mary and the two of Robinson. Of course, there would also be interest accrued on the unremitted revenues that had become part of the Samuel Elsdale estate.

Rayment could not pursue this line of reasoning without engaging in further character assassination:

Let the Reverend James Ashley pretend as much as he pleases to the character of a conscientious guardian & a man of probity yet I am bold enough to charge him (on the supposition that my statement is near the facts[)] 1st with inattention to the interest of his wards the 2 fatherless children [of the late Robinson Elsdale] whose claim I think I have not even wished to slur over, 2ndly with something very like a positive injustice to the 5 more fatherless children the Molsons, 2 of whom being under age at the time of making the Old Gentleman's Last Will....

If I am wrong informed as to the claim of the 7 grandchildren & have drawn my conclusions wrong in consequence, nobody shall sooner retract either or both of these 2 points; for I am well aware that the Reverend James Ashley['s] inattention or inability as a professional man may have innocently & ignorantly led him into error in these points.

3rdly However these things may be I do most unequivocally charge the Reverend James Ashley with a positive injustice in withholding from Mr. John Molson of Montreal the information he derived from the Deeds which are or lately were in the possession of the former; & with having connived at least at the receipt of the Rents of said Estate for these two years last past. . . .

As I have no intention but to avow what I write, so have I no objection to this letter being shewn to all or any of the friends of the parties herein named, or even at a proper time to the public in Lincolnshire.

Rayment was now engaged in libellous attacks on the parson, and his accounts of the monies owed the Molsons (he was now also pursuing bequests in the will of the deceased John Elsdale of Ipswich) and the actions of all the parties involved became so convoluted as to be nearly impossible to untangle. It was clear at least that Rayment (along with the other protesting Molson siblings and spouses) had made an enemy not only of the Reverend Ashley but of Samuel Elsdale of Pimlico.

Having heard nothing from his brother-in-law, Rayment wrote Molson an update on September 1, 1790, compelled to keep him apprised of his actions. He confessed: "To say the truth from about the time of Old Sir's death, [I have had] a very shabby opinion of the Priest's honesty & fair dealing, proof of which I shall give you 'ere I close this Epistle." Reverend Ashley's crimes were multiplying:

Without going into all the particulars, I will only say, the Parson is endeavouring to cheat your Brother Samuel out of £100 left him by his father's will . . . & you are aware that Samuel is but scantily provided for. . . . [I]t is beyond a doubt that the Reverend James Ashley has destroyed a great quantity of your Grandfathers papers. . . . [H]e has blackened the family in the most gross & abusive language, & been moving heaven & earth to embroil them with their Uncles. . . . So effectually has the Priest poisoned the mind of Mr. [Samuel Elsdale] against us all by falsities & worked upon the tender part of his feelings by representing it as an intention to injure the young Elsdales (though nothing is more foreign to our wishes) that Mr. S.E. will hear no reason nor correspond with any one of us, & the affairs now stand out in a very unpleasant unsettled state. Such a friend to the Molsons has this man proved: he is really duplicity, implausibility itself, & turns out, if possible, worse than I have long suspected he would do.

Rayment was now also beginning to suggest that there was something more going on between the Reverend Ashley and the widow Ann Elsdale. He alleged the parson had *"roguishly with his friend the Widow* connived at smuggling the rest of the Rents" from the Stickney estate.

Rayment paused in his evidence of chicanery to pass along the latest news of James Gibbins, Sr.: "we hear [he] is banished [from] his daughters House: it is a melancholy truth that he has been an enormous trouble & expence to her. She allows him about 1 shilling per day & he keeps at Boston." Rayment also noted that John's brother Thomas, the youngest of the Molson children, was a tenant farmer at Surfleet "& appearances lead us to believe he will be shortly united to Miss Ann Atkinson, Martha's particular friend." The wedding took place on December 8. All siblings except Samuel were now married—or at least, as in John's case, firmly attached. John had still given the family no word about Sarah Vaughan and John Junior; in fact, he had not written at all. Rayment noted: "Martha bids me say she has been much hurt at not hearing from you."

Molson was soon writing, however, at least on the business matters of family, for Rayment, amidst all his confused allegations about Stickney, had made one observation that caused Molson to pay firm attention. According to Rayment, Philip Ashley had caught James Ashley in the act of transferring, to either the widow or the two children, a small piece of copyhold land—a little more than an acre—at Pinchbeck belonging to John Molson: "Your agent Mr. P. Ashley (who *is the friend* of the M family which his namesake has pretended to be) noted it down, & will take it up for you."

Molson received Rayment's September 1 letter on November 3, and wrote an immediate reply, which has been lost. The next day Molson also wrote Philip Ashley. He had become convinced of the justness of Rayment's crusade on all fronts. He informed his attorney that Rayment had provided

a Concise History of family affairs[. I] find myself extremely obliged to you for the active part you have taken in my family Business & hope you continue to frustrate every attempt made by the Rector to the injury of any of my Brothers & Sisters. . . . [As] Malignity with its attendant Companions be ever so powerful[,] Honesty & Integrity must withstand them[. I] understand my Grandfather has left Sam but a poor pittance . . . [I] shall remain in full confidence that upright intentions will defeat all Malevolence.

"Stickney Estate," Molson declared, "appears clearly to belong to me & doubt not but you will take the proper steps therein." Molson also thanked Ashley for his attentiveness in the matter of the small property at Pinchbeck. In defence of the poor parson, the various bits of copyhold land floating in the complex estates of the Molsons and Elsdales would have made his mistake all too understandable, and the tiny acreage was hardly worth misappropriating. Molson nonetheless urged Ashley to "be kind enough to write particulars of my affair with that of family [at] first opportunity." Molson directed Ashley to write him care of Rayment, who was now also overseeing business matters for Molson in London.

Rayment's efforts to seek justice for the Molson siblings cannot be dismissed as entirely misguided. The Stickney inheritance, beyond any allegations of malice, was a muddle. To his credit, Rayment also succeeded in convincing Samuel Elsdale to pay from Grandfather Samuel's estate the outstanding £61 10s due to John Molson from his inheritance that had remained unsettled since

1785. But Rayment also presented the case that John Molson owed about £47 to his sister Mary (demanded on her behalf by Abraham Whitsed) and about £34 to his brother Thomas due to oversights in the way rents were accounted for on their behalf during the trusteeship of their uncle Thomas in 1770–71. Molson was initially apologetic about the debts, but as time passed, he became less convinced of the validity of the claims, and he would take years to settle them.

But at the same time, Rayment's struggles with the Reverend Ashley had become deeply personal and outrageously malicious. In a letter to Philip Ashley on December 13, 1790, Rayment observed that the reverend "favoured me with a ridiculous Letter [on December 4] with the Form of a Recantation of mine & my wife['s] calumnies on his immaculate Character for our signature, which was passed over with silent contempt. This Letter is a curiosity of its kind which I may shew you when I have the pleasure of seeing you in Town."

The reverend had had enough of Rayment and his wife's attacks upon his good name, which had apparently been made public, as Rayment had promised. Reverend Ashley wrote Philip Ashley on January 4, 1791, in a fruitless attempt to end the slander and lay the Stickney Estate controversy to rest:

> When I was lately in London I understood from Rayment and Tom Molson that you are employed to institute a Suit in order to recover for Mr. John Molson of Montreal a part of the Estate now in the possession of Mrs. Elsdale of Surfleet as Tenant for Life under her late Husband's Will.
>
> Tom Molson also informed me that this Suit is grounded upon an opinion said to have been given by me in favour of Mr. John Molson's Right to the Estate in Question. I recollect nothing of giving such an Opinion; which I certainly should not forget if it was so. And therefore I conclude that like Thousands of other Things from the same Quarter it has no Foundation in Truth. Be that as it may, if Mr. John Molson has the Shadow of a Right to the Estate in Question,

God forbid that I should Countenance Mrs. E, or any person, in withholding their Right from another; however hard in her particular case it may be to restore it. I promised Rayment and Tom Molson that so far from countenancing such a piece of Injustice, I wou'd most readily and willingly furnish you with every information in my power to explain the Matter. I now write to repeat that promise and therefore need only add: if you will point out to me what Information you want to make out your Client's Case: if it be in my power to furnish you with it; I will do so immediately.

I will as readily and cheerfully do the same in the Business of Rayment and his Wife; as soon as they have honestly and properly contradicted a number of the most scandalous aspersions and basest falsest Calumnies they have invented and propagated against me in order I suppose to show their Gratitude for my being a father to them both in taking them into my House when his own Father and her Aunt had turned them out of Doors. . . . If Rayment will show (that is if he can show) that any One of the many vile Things he & his Wife have written and said of me have the slightest Foundation in Truth, or that I ever justly provoked such ungrateful Conduct from them, I will (as I ought) give up my Expectation of having them contradicted & recanted. If not I will sacrifice the last Shilling I have in the World before I will do such people any more unmerited Favours.

Rayment pressed on regardless, emboldened by the confidence placed in him by John Molson. On March 25, 1791, he wrote Molson with an accounting of the latest skulduggery. Rayment's story grew more elaborate with every passing month. He now asserted that he had succeeded in turning around Samuel Elsdale, the surviving son of the deceased grandfather who had power over the Reverend Ashley. Rayment said he had managed this by using a Mrs. Wright, who not only knew the late grandfather and his widow, Mary Albin, but "was also, from a temporary intimacy with the Rector so perfectly well acquainted with the whole of [James

Ashley's] knavery, & its too successful effect with the now remaining head of the family." Mrs. Wright had convinced the eldest surviving Elsdale to order the reverend "to instantly give up his trust & the possession of every scrap of paper thereto belonging."

What should have set the stage for Rayment's triumph by his own evidence accomplished nothing. He had a difficult time explaining to Molson what went wrong when he joined Tom Molson for a meeting with the Reverend Ashley. "We found he had gained strong ground against us," he vaguely asserted,

> [and] that opposition would only answer the very purpose the enemy wished, of breaking us with [Samuel Elsdale] forever. We found it therefore good policy to wink at small matters. In short the Priest carried most of his points, except getting over the glaring inconsistency of extolling myself to a very high degree in one Letter, having a few days after vilifying me in the grossest Terms in another. His knowledge of quirk & quibble . . . enabled him to keep beyond ye reach of the Law in his abuse of the family in common with myself.

Rayment's claims that John Molson's brother Samuel had been left destitute by his grandfather's will were proved hollow. He was obliged to report that "to be sure [Grandfather Samuel] kept and maintained [Samuel Molson] during his life, & by his will left him £200 in Cash, a life Estate in land at Pinchbeck, Gosberton etc. then let at about 21£ per annum net Rent; & a copy hold Cottage of 40 shillings [per annum rent] in [Langtoft]."

Yet Rayment—and, one supposes, Samuel—remained unsatisfied with this bequest. They appeared to be expecting the original £100 legacy that Samuel had been left by his father (and which had been held in trust by Grandfather Samuel), in addition to the total bequest Grandfather Samuel had made to him. "Professional people are clearly of opinion the claim is a good one," Rayment ventured. "The Reverend J.A. insists on the contrary position, & Mr. [Samuel Elsdale,] who stands in no small awe of this quondam pettifogger, seems uninclined to do anything pro or con in the affair. Here then is Sam's positive situation. The only alternatives are to submit to the Loss, or to proceed against the Executor, who will not discriminate in that event but resent it against us all without exception."

Samuel Molson's general prospects were apparently narrow: he was unmarried and evidently disabled, and perhaps even suffering from epilepsy. "The poor fellow's situation is melancholy in other respects," Rayment advised John Molson. "Besides his natural lameness, he is exceedingly nervous, & has frequent serious attacks of the Gout etc. I say serious from ocular proof. He came to London a few weeks since with Whitsed, & remained behind him. The Gout appeared in his foot & thence removed to the Head & Stomach so as to render him blind for a time & light headed, besides having alarming fits etc." The sickly Samuel would die in 1792.

Rayment could not resist heaping further abuse on the widow Elsdale, portraying her as a woman perpetually on the prowl for some new conquest. He wrote:

Jack Baxter has at last obtained Miss Gynn of Wisbeck [Wisbeach], so that the widow has no hopes left in that quarter, nor in any other that we can devine. . . . [N]ot content with estranging the Priest from his rib, she keeps her hands in as to coquetry etc. with a former Townsman but now (from just provocations) [an] avowed enemy of the Parson[,] Captain Wilson[,] a married man also[,] resident in Pinchbeck parsonage, when she cannot have her factotum J.A.'s good company.

Whether Rayment wrote the truth, half-truth or slander about the widow's character, it made no difference to Molson's chances of taking the Stickney Estate away from his once-beloved worthy little woman and her two adorable children. Rayment at last revealed the crumbling foundation to the legitimacy of John Molson's claim. It all depended on what Samuel Molson allegedly had heard the Reverend Ashley say in a meeting at which the only other person present was the widow. Rayment wrote:

It may be now a proper season to tell you whence the discovery originated if, as I think, I have not done it already. After J.A. got possession of [the estate] Title Deed ex officio as Executor's agent, he was perusing it carefully at the widow's. Samuel, the Lady & himself only being present & unthinkingly exclaimed, "Good God! Why, if Nancy E. died above 21 half this Estate is John Molson's." Here he recollected Sam was present & dropped the subject. This matter was you may be sure soon imparted to us.

Rayment asserted that the inheritance terms were then "strongly corroborated" by a letter from the wife of the Reverend John Theed, who had been trustee of the property for Nancy Elsdale, but it is absolutely extraordinary that so much damage had been done to reputations and relationships over this single anecdote.

It took John Molson more than a year to reply to Rayment's lengthy and confused account of the struggle over his grandfather's estate and the Stickney property. "Am very sorry for the Difficulties you have met with & hope you may get better through than you think," was the sum of his commiseration on June 12, 1792, although he did apologize at length for the debts it appeared he owed from his father's estate settlement.

In tending to shipments of hops for Molson in August 1791, Rayment had announced that "our sister Mary has honoured you and others with the title of Uncle by the birth of a son on the 30th April who is named Isaac," and he also passed on word that Martha was expecting. Molson replied in his June 1792 letter: "Congratulate Mrs. R. from me of her son or daughter which ever it may be on the arrival of this & she has my full liberty of making me sponsor."

And that is all John Molson would say on the subject of family, for about his own affairs he remained close-lipped. His second son, Thomas, had been born to Sarah Vaughan on September 1, 1791, and his family had not been able to draw him out on his domestic circumstances, despite more broad hints of general knowledge. "We have been something disappointed at not receiving your expected dispatches [with the] January packet," Rayment had written in his March 25, 1791, letter, "but look for the same every day.... We are made very happy in the accounts given of your situation by Mr. Platt & young Badgley & impatiently expect the promised History of your proceedings in Montreal to confirm the same...."

Despite the span of geography separating John Molson from his family in England, it could be a remarkably small world. The Badgley family is believed to have been established in Montreal since 1764, although the "young Badgley" to whom Rayment referred, Francis Badgley, was born in London in March 1767. Like Molson, he was about eighteen when he immigrated to Montreal in 1785, and he was probably related to a local merchant named James Badgley. When he came of age in 1788, he formed a partnership with Richard Dobie to outfit fur traders (his parents may have been London fur dealers), and he was evidently in London tending to business when Rayment met him in 1791. The following spring, Badgley was paddling to Grand Portage, the overwintering station of the North West Company on western Lake Superior, to perform surveying work for the fur giant.[3]

"Mr. Platt" would have been from the Platt family of Montreal. Molson had purchased charcoal from John Platt in making his first batch of amber beer in October 1786, and he appeared among brewery customers in the 1788 sales records. A Loyalist who lived near Lake George at the south end of Lake Champlain, John Platt spied for General Burgoyne and raised men for Major James Rogers's King's American Rangers. Lieutenant Platt then settled in Montreal and, as a hardware merchant, was an active importer of goods from England. He established an ironmonger's operation within the walls of Montreal in 1794; the fact that he had so much charcoal for Molson to borrow suggests he was already working iron locally in 1786. He had two sons, John and George, a machinist who would figure in John Molson's steamboat venture. The import business must have caused one of the Platt men to cross paths in London with Rayment.

Molson's isolation was evidently illusory: his private life in Montreal was in plain view of people in touch with his own family back in England. Yet he resolutely continued to hold his tongue about his own affairs. On November 5, 1793, his third and final child, William, was born. As with Sarah, as with John Junior, as with Thomas, John Molson told no one in England of this new arrival.

In 1793, John Molson's efforts to wrest ownership of the Stickney estate from his aunt Ann were sidetracked by a daunting series of setbacks in William Rayment's life. The first was a plunge into madness for Rayment, and a consequential plunge into isolation and impoverishment for his wife, Martha.

John Molson had already decided to do what he could for Martha by signing over to her a small piece of copyhold land at Wigtoft left to him by his brother Samuel. Its buildings were in near ruin, and Molson couldn't be bothered putting any money into the little property. When Martha wrote him on March 17, 1793, to express her gratitude, she revealed her alarming situation. Martha explained how the previous May she

> came down to visit my friends in Lincolnshire with an intention of spending the summer with them for the first time after our marriage, when I was sent for to Town again on account of Mr. Rayment's being very ill. But judge my astonishment on my return to find him in a state of frenzy hardly to be equalled. I was oblige[d] to have him confined at home as I could not afford to have him in a private Mad House this I also found very expensive & very troublesome as he took such a dislike to me which was little short of Hatred. I was therefore oblige[d] under such circumstances to apply to Bethlem Hospital[4] & get him admitted a patient in that House[. In] about two months after the application he was removed to the House.

At the time, Martha was raising a young son and expecting another child. (Despite the animosity surrounding the Old Gent's estate, Martha's boys were reverently named Samuel and Elsdale.) Martha and John's brother Tom took her and the boy in.

Rayment was obviously an intelligent man who was either prone to episodes of instability or, in this case, had suffered a nervous breakdown. A business partnership had soured for him, and his losses could not be settled without a lawsuit, which he couldn't afford but which appeared to be ongoing. Martha reported in her March 1793 letter:

Mr Rayment is so much recover'd as to be able to take a Secretary place [with] the house of Franklin—but it's not thought prudent for me to live with him again at present for fear of an Elapse & indeed if that had not been the case he could not have maintained me for any length of time for he had not been discharged above a month before an inflammation took place in his leg which he Broke the preceding spring, an abscess formed at the Bone & he was again confined for more than two months & I do not at present know whether he is out again.

Though estranged from him, Martha held Rayment blameless for his troubles and praised his qualities as a husband and father. But until he was well enough for them to live together again, she was planning to find employment "as intendent to a Lady or something of that nature."

Rayment proclaimed himself recovered in a letter written April 2, 1794, although it does not appear he and Martha were reunited—Rayment wrote from London and noted that Martha was staying in Spalding. He was faithfully attending to John Molson's business, trying to secure for him "a pair of Rollers to be worked by one Man, for grinding Malt," which Molson had requested in a letter of October 21, 1793.

Whether he was concerned about Rayment's capabilities or simply taking advantage of a timely opportunity, Molson decided to give power of attorney to his friend George Stansfeld, who was travelling to England in 1794, so that all the papers relevant to his properties and inheritance could be collected and brought to Montreal. When he left England in 1786, Molson had suggested he might return for another visit around 1793. But the outbreak of war between Britain and France, combined with the arrival of his third child in 1793 and difficulties he would have faced in finding reliable help to oversee the brewery in his absence, probably discouraged him. When Stansfeld attempted to collect some of Molson's papers from Rayment, however, he ran into a fresh misadventure: Molson's brother-in-law was about to go to prison.

Stansfeld had already been to Spalding on Molson's behalf when Rayment wrote the tobacconist in December 1794, promising to collect the necessary documents for him. But on February 14, 1795, Rayment wrote Stansfeld from Exeter, explaining he had been unable to complete the task, in part because of a lack of time but also because of "certain occurrences in my eventful history."

Rayment had decided to seek refuge from his life's ordeals in the British Army, to which he had belonged twenty years earlier, by enlisting at Exeter on January 1. As he explained to Stansfeld, he had several motives for the enlistment. He wanted to secure a pension that could provide for his family in the event of his death, and he hoped to "shew myself so useful as to merit & obtain [an officer's] commission without purchase through parliamentary & other influence." Perhaps most important, he somehow imagined that the enlistment "would simplify if not wind up an Exchequer Suit which I have on foot with a bad man who has aimed at my ruin"—a reference to his old business partner. There was also a hint of a death wish in Rayment's motives: enlisting in the army as war raged between Britain and France presented him with the opportunity to provide for his family by being killed in battle and leaving them a pension. As he put it, "Should I die in the field, [it would aid in] repairing the injury my family has sustained from an unhappy connexion"—the "connexion" being either himself, as he had failed to provide for Martha and the two boys, or his litigious business partner.

Whatever Rayment's ambition for a glorious and profitable death, it was quickly denied him. What he had failed to inform Stansfeld, as he admitted in an April 2 letter, was that when he wrote him on February 14, he was marking his fourth day as a prisoner, awaiting trial "on a pretended charge of 'Depreciating the characters of three officers,' though the truth is, I am the victim of the malice & self interest of certain mercenary plunderers, through my zeal for the service, in opposing abuses highly prejudicial thereto, & to the military character."

Rayment's penchant for self-righteous crusading had landed him in serious trouble almost from the moment of his enlistment in the army. The exchequer suit and his arrest on military charges may have been related—in his partnership, Rayment could have been involved as a military contractor, and allegations of bribes paid to officers would explain the charge he faced. He may have had the notion that he could right all wrongs in the situation if he was shielded by a uniform. On the contrary, as it turned out, Rayment explained that he had been mistreated by the regimental colonel, Thomas Stribling, who "knowing his reputation was very particularly connected with what would come out if he brought me to trial at Exeter, his native place, removed me Feb. 17 with 13 others, his prisoners, to Plymouth."

Rayment argued it had been Colonel Stribling's plan to have him and the other men drafted into other regiments, so that they could face charges far from Exeter—in Rayment's case at Plymouth, where he was held prisoner at the garrison. "It was here that he made his unmanly attempt to try me 40 miles distant from every means of defence, which Exeter would have abundantly afforded me." Rayment appealed to Lord George Lenox, "notwithstanding I was close prisoner & expressly forbidden pen, ink & paper, unless I procured them by stealth." His appeal foiled an immediate trial, but Colonel Stribling had responded by locking Rayment away in a prison ship, the *Cambridge*, in Plymouth harbour, on February 27. He had been awaiting his fate in this hulk for thirty-four days when he wrote Stansfeld on April 2.

Rayment had written the attorney William Bolton, hoping to enlist his aid. In his April 2 letter to Stansfeld, he pleaded: "May I beg the favour of your calling on him (as perhaps that letter among others has been intercepted) & endeavouring to concert with him some means of [my] release from this confinement & the hazard of being banished to some distant country by the influence of my oppressors."

Rayment was almost poignant in his promises to Stansfeld to do whatever he could for John Molson's Stickney claim, even as he lay penniless in the gloomy *Cambridge*, with permanent exile to Australia an eventual possibility—Britain had begun shipping criminals there in 1788. He also provided Stansfeld with a list of "hints," written April 17, that might be used to flush out the documents that allegedly would prove the Stickney property's true owner.

Beyond any familial obligation he might have felt, Rayment viewed the Stickney affair as an opportunity to seek a craved revenge against the hated Reverend Ashley, whom he blamed for virtually all his present misery. In his letter to Stansfeld on April 23, he observed: "The clerical Gentleman you mention, is I firmly believe, a very bad man. I have to impute to him in a great measure my misfortunes, as arising from his practices & influence in my late partnership, with a man in many respects his own counterpart."

Whatever Stansfeld was able to do for him, Rayment did not have to face life in exile Down Under. He was freed from the prison ship in September 1795 and resumed his duties in London with the house of Franklin. He reported his "compleat victory over all my adversaries" in a letter to Molson on February 23, 1796—a letter which revealed that his self-esteem was intact, even brightly polished. "My time was not entirely lost while in HMS *Cambridge*, as my active services envinced, both as the advocate of the distressed, & the detecter of imposters & cheats; & I believe my departure was rather regretted than otherwise."

By then, the Stickney case had lost all momentum, and Philip Ashley had died. Rayment suspected that the late attorney "had some particular objection to this matter," and that since 1788 he had been "a material impediment." Given that Philip Ashley was likely a close relation of the vilified Reverend Ashley, his lack of interest is understandable. But Ashley's death did not move Molson's case rapidly forward. Ashley's practice was taken over by his nephew Thomas Foster, who almost immediately extinguished a substantial part of Rayment's long-standing allegations. He had collected an explanatory letter written by the Reverend Ashley on April 15, 1795, a copy of which was provided to Stansfeld. "On the other side," the Reverend Ashley wrote Foster,

> I send you an Abstract of the Deed settling the Estate at Stickney, which contains all the necessary Information respecting Mr. John Molson's supposed claim to that Estate. I should have sent it sooner but expected being at Spalding today.
>
> Independent of my general wish to do every Person Justice for its own sake; I could have no desire to withhold from Mr. John Molson any Information in my Power to serve him: because exclusive of the Esteem I feel for his Character as a worthy and respectable man; he is the only one of that Family from whom I have not experienced most rude and ungrateful Treatment in return for a world of Labour as well as Expence to serve and oblige them all.

According to the transcription, in April 1753 Samuel Elsdale and his wife Mary drew up an indenture "for the purpose of making a better provision for said Mary his wife and their younger Daughter Ann Elsdale." The indenture placed what became known as the Stickney Estate in the possession of the Reverend John Theed of Carlwitch and his heirs, to hold in trust, with Ann Elsdale the chief beneficiary. The trust was created so that Ann could be supported by incomes from the estate. If Ann Elsdale died under the age of twenty-one and unmarried, the property would pass to Robinson Elsdale and Mary Elsdale—John Molson's mother—in joint tenancy.

Samuel Elsdale Molson had heard incorrectly in his meeting with the Reverend Ashley and the widow. The Stickney estate would go to Robinson and Mary Elsdale only if Ann died unmarried *before* she turned twenty-one, not after. Ann Elsdale had died unmarried on March 31, 1765, in her twenty-second year. Wrote the Reverend Ashley: "Mr. John Molson could take nothing as Heir of his Mother under a limitation that never took effect."

The entire dispute, it was now clear, had been touched off by the late Samuel Molson's mistakenly thinking he heard the Reverend James Ashley say "after" when he actually said "before." And the assertion that Ashley exclaimed that this meant half the estate belonged to John Molson was a complete fiction.

The matter was not entirely closed. It still wasn't clear how the Stickney property had passed into the hands of Robinson Elsdale before being bequeathed to his widow, although even Rayment came to suspect that some arrangement had been made between the privateer and his father when Ann died after she came of age. While plainly satisfied with the reverend's explanation, Foster allowed to Molson that "I think it necessary that copies of the Lease & Release shou'd be had, but I will not request them of Mr. Ashley without your consent." Foster evidently thought it imprudent to move forward. Molson did not pursue the inheritance any further—for now.[5]

John Molson must have, should have, realized what the Reverend Ashley's letter of April 15, 1795, meant. Molson had abetted William Rayment's abusive crusade against Ashley, and had said nothing in defence of the worthy widow as his brother-in-law blackened her reputation. But with a new mortgage to service on the expanded brewery property, John Molson had reduced the business of family relations to the point where all sentiment was obliterated. If it had ever concerned him that his suit might impoverish his late uncle's widow and two children, no record survives. He had pressed forward, based on hearsay, with an unsupported claim against a woman he had once considered the ideal friend to his sisters, if not the ideal bride for himself. It is at least a testament to the esteem in which he was still held that Molson was never blamed by the besieged Reverend Ashley for his miserable treatment. Yet John Molson had done Reverend James Ashley and the widow Ann Elsdale very ill.

Know all men by these presents That on the first day of January in the Year of our Lord one thousand seven hundred and ninety five Before me John Gerbrand Beek Notary Public dwelling in the City of Montreal in the Province of Lower Canada duly admitted and Sworn, and in the presence of the hereinafter named witnesses personally was present John Molson of the Quebec or St. Mary Suburbs near the City of Montreal Brewer Lying in his bed at his House in the said Suburbs Wick and Sick of Body though of Sound Mind, Memory and understanding as to us the said notary and witnesses appeared. And declared the said John Molson that having considered the uncertainty of this life and Certainty of Death, It was his Request That I the said Notary should take and set down in writing this his Last Will and Testament which he directed me in manner following. . . .

John Molson, lying on what he considered his deathbed—as George Stansfeld collected his papers in England and attempted to sort out the Stickney Estate mess with the incarcerated William Rayment—dictated the will that recognized the new-world family he had kept hidden from his old-world siblings and associates.

To his eldest son, John, he bequeathed his books, except for any with the name of Robinson Elsdale in them, which he directed to be turned over to the widow Ann. All the silver plate was to go to Sarah Vaughan. And the rest of his property, including the brewery, was to be apportioned equally among Sarah and the three children—"to be by them shared and divided Share and Share alike." If Sarah happened to be pregnant when he died, then the property would be divided into five equal parts rather than four, to accommodate the child he would never know.

There would be no favouring first-borns over second- or third-borns, or even an unknown fourth-born—and children would not be favoured over mother, nor mother over children. John Molson had made a profound break with the long and at times bitter history of inheritance and primogeniture in his family. He was determined to leave behind a family of equals, not one of haves and have nots. He must have understood the inherent unfairness of the way his father's estate had been parcelled out, how unusually well favoured he had been in receiving the bulk of several generations' worth of accumulated Lincolnshire property. For all the recognition he deserved for demonstrating the energy and daring to establish himself in Montreal, none of it would have been possible without the inheritance. His brother Thomas might have been equally clever, but he could never attempt to achieve what John had. When their father died, his will had predestined most of their opportunities—if not their lives. Kismet. John Molson, certain of death in Montreal at the age of thirty-one, had resolved to give his boys an equal start in life on the grand stage.

Yet this equanimity evidenced a new fervour for the imperative of lineage, and it promised confinement for the benefactors. In contrast, primogeniture was, in some respects, liberating. When the lion's share went to the first-born male, his siblings received what amounted to an enforced exile, a push to find their own way through industriousness or careful marriage to fresh wealth. John Molson's departure from Lincolnshire, his selling of Snake Hall and his abandonment of the first-born principle were not a disavowal of his fundamental roots. He was absolutely committed to the idea of the Molsons becoming, in a new place with a new enterprise, a family of wealth and power. Molson's determination to make his children equal owners of his possessions, which in 1795 were fundamentally his brewery, would serve to bind them together as partners. There was an enforced interdependence at the heart of this bequest, and the primacy of the Molson bloodline would become entwined with the inherited enterprise.

John Molson's determination to keep the fruits of his labours within the family was underscored by a provision in the will that allowed for an alternative set of beneficiaries should all of his children die before they reached the age of majority—or could marry and leave a lawful descendant. In this case, Molson decided that Sarah Vaughan would have her equal portion of the estate set aside for her, and the children's share would be passed down to John Molson's three surviving siblings: Thomas, Mary and Martha. And this portion was to be shared equally among them.

To this provision he attached an important limitation: "It is the absolute will of the said Testator that in such Case the Husbands of the two last named Mary and Martha shall have no manner of right or disposal of the abovesaid Property. But that the same shall be vested solely in the said two above named Mary Whiteside [*sic*] & Martha Rayment and either of them, their & either of their heirs and assigns and at their free disposal."

Molson was explicit that his brothers-in-law, William Rayment and Abraham Whitsed, would have no control over the inheritance. Rayment and Whitsed were allied with the Molsons by marriage, not by kinship. If their foreign blood had not made them unworthy, then Rayment's bout of madness (Molson would not yet have learned of his detention in a prison ship) and Whitsed's annoying persistence in wresting some of Father John's inheritance from John Molson (on his wife's behalf) undoubtedly moved them to the margins of the bequest.

John Molson had missed a golden opportunity to merge estates and family branches when a marriage to Ann Elsdale eluded him. When he survived the brush with death that provoked the 1795 will and carried on with overseeing the brewery's growth, it was left to two members of the next generation to achieve fusions within the bloodline. Ironically, one of Molson's sons would enter a marriage that threatened to tear the family apart even as it bound it together.

Chapter 16

*A fool squanders away, without credit or advantage to himself,
more than a man of sense spends with both. The latter employs his
money as he does his time, and never spends a shilling of the one,
nor a minute of the other, but in something that is either useful or
rationally pleasing to himself or others. The former buys whatever
he does not want, and does not pay for what he does want.*
—Lord Chesterfield, letter to his son, January 10, 1749

MONTREAL IN THE 1790S began to turn away from its fundamental status as a fur-trading hub, becoming a commercial centre
for Canada's developing interior. Land grants in Upper Canada—
which predated the division of Quebec into two provinces in
1791—were transforming present-day Ontario from a pelt resource
into a new agricultural frontier. As the highest navigable point from
the Atlantic, Montreal afforded its established merchants the
opportunity to exploit the economy of the new province by acting
as shipping agents for both inbound and outbound goods or by
establishing agents in Upper Canada for their own commercial
activities. Other merchants used their established businesses and
personal wealth to become financiers in a colony that still did not
have banks. The city grew to the point that its crumbling stone
defensive works had to go, and when their dismantling finally
began in 1804, settlement had long since spilled beyond the
redoubts.

Molson's stature within the community was solidified in the last
decade of the eighteenth century, thanks especially to his prominent

role in the local Masonic chapter, his contribution to the construction of the Scots Presbyterian Church in 1792, and the general success of the brewery. In 1793, he drafted a letter to the London hop merchants Sanderson, Roxby & Co. (through whom William Rayment had secured for Molson a machine for crushing malt with metal rollers rather than between grindstones). He wrote, then crossed out, a bold assurance of his financial health: "not owing in Canada ten pounds, my malting, brewhouse & dwelling house with lot on which they stand, having cost upwards of two thousand pounds, all built by myself & all payed for you may rely on—should not have mentioned the above had I not been a perfect stranger to you."

And yet the monies Molson still owed his brother Thomas and his brother-in-law Abraham Whitsed from his father's estate continued to go unpaid. In a letter drafted to Rayment in October 1793, Molson promised that he "shall make provisions for Mr. Whitside's [sic] demand on me." He was giving Tom's claim another look, having received a patiently, if densely, argued letter his brother had written Rayment, spelling out the source of the debt from old estate revenues. Molson told his brother-in-law that Tom's letter required careful review because, as he noted with amusement and admiration, "one part seems to have been made out by [a] lawyer[. H]as it been himself its a pity his Talent in that profession should be lost in the Farmer & Grazier." Beneath that remark must have been some appreciation that the youngest male had been denied the resources that could have made him so much more than the farmer and grazier he had become.

It took years for Molson to settle with Whitsed and his brother, as he became convinced there was in fact no obligation. In February 1796, Rayment urged him to "think of finishing the business of Mr. Whitsed's claimed arrear Rent & the like of your Brother's: the former party is I know impatient." Molson's foot-dragging with Whitsed may have been provoked by the loss of Whitsed's wife, Molson's sister Mary, who died from complications in childbirth in January 1796, leaving behind Whitsed and two children, Isaac and Mary.[1] With no family connection to Whitsed any more (although the children should have engendered some attachment) Molson was loath to settle with him. With thirteen years of interest, the original sum of what was finally agreed to be £15 had grown to £23 15s 6d, which Molson at last remitted in the fall of 1798. As he explained curtly to Whitsed in a letter written October 20, 1799, the £15 was "*said* to be received by me." Molson had concluded that he had never been overpaid by the estate, "however as I gave you reason to expect it in a former letter & particularly as you have had the misfortune of loosing poor Mary [I] consider myself more in honour bound to pay it."

To be sure, £23 and change was a trifling amount for Molson by 1798. He was so well established that, in 1796, he was involved in a proposal with the distillers McBeath & Sheppard at L'Assomption to divide the Quebec barley market with John Young, a prominent Quebec merchant who was a member of the province's appointed legislative council from 1794 until his death in 1819. Molson could have been supplying McBeath & Sheppard with malt for their distilling.

What became of the proposal to divvy the barley market isn't known, but by 1799 Molson was moving towards absorbing McBeath & Sheppard. Late that year he bought a still from them, and he hired William Sheppard as his "brewer, malster and distiller." Molson had moved beyond casual labour with this hiring. Under the five-year contract, which began November 18 and paid $400 per year,[2] Sheppard agreed "to enter into his service for conducting in the best manner he the said William Sheppard can, the Brewing, Malting, and also, if by the said John Molson on the remits required, the Distilling Business; in the last of which the said William Sheppard shall keep no secrets from the said John Molson, and shall and will carry on the two former thereof under the inspection and subject to the orders and directions of the said John Molson."

Molson erected a still-house on the brewery property, but the venture into spirits evidently was speculative: sales of whiskey and "high wines" were less than £34 by the end of 1802. In 1803, total whiskey sales to date reached about £628, but more than half the revenue came from one sale, of over £334, on July 21, 1803, to McTavish, Frobisher & Co., one of the partner firms in the North

West Company. The fur trade had been in decline since the 1790s, and Molson's involvement in supplying its most notorious trade good (a ban on trading spirits with natives had been rescinded in 1794) was short-lived.

Molson had probably attempted to take advantage of heightened competition between the North West and XY Companies, which greatly increased the North Westers' requirements for rum and other spirits. The trading partnership's use of alcohol increased from 10,000 to 16,000 gallons from 1799 to 1803. It was a mean business for Molson to have entered—the effects of alcohol on the native populations was catastrophic. Wrote the trader Alexander Henry in his journal while among the Saulteaux in 1803, "What a different Sett of people they would be, were there not a drop of liquor introduced into the Country . . . We may in truth say that Liquor is the Mother of all evil even in the North west." The amalgamation of 1804, which saw the XY partners join the North West Company, clipped the latter's use of spirits back to about 12,000 gallons.While no brewery accounts survive from 1804 to 1807, Molson's only non-beer sales in 1808–9 were £50 in high wines.

Molson also branched out into lumber. Britain's war with France had deprived her of the traditional Baltic lumber supply, which opened a new export opportunity for Canada. Financial records from John Molson's activities in the 1790s are thin,[3] but he was prosperous enough to have the cash flow to diversify into the burgeoning lumber business no later than 1797, although his focus was entirely local. No account book survives from that year, but in the 1798 book the business of "planks and boards" is fully formed, with expenditures carried forward from 1797 of £324 16s. It was the beginning of several years of purchasing log rafts and lumber, and the employment contract with Sheppard also called on him to run a lumber (or "deal") yard in the summer. By the end of 1800, Molson had spent more than £4,000 on wood, while his sales of a comfortable inventory neared £2,900. He was likely buying the wood from all over—from Upper Canada via the St. Lawrence, from the Ottawa River, even from Lake Champlain. Some of the lumber was coming in rafts from Philemon Wright, an American merchant who founded Hull in 1800. A rudimentary sawmill must have been operating on the brewery property to rip the logs into dimensional lumber.

Denison suggests that, based on the very small markups, Molson may have been in the lumber business as a public-spirited gesture, to aid the continued growth of Montreal and the island parishes at a time of dimensional lumber shortages. This may have been the case in 1797, but by 1799 Molson was probably anticipating his own needs for building materials. Another round of expansion had begun as Molson rapidly bought up the properties to the west of the brewery in St. Mary's suburb. They formed a parcel almost 240 feet wide—larger than the holding Molson already owned. (Survey dimensions were all in "French" feet, which measured about 13.1 inches.) Molson's first purchase, from François Desautels in January 1799, was a forty-foot-wide streetfront lot that abutted his existing property. The eighty-foot-wide lot next door to it, owned by Pierre Desautels, was the last acquired, in July 1811. In the intervening years, Molson purchased a large parcel called the Garden Lot in September 1799, another forty-foot streetfront parcel in July 1801, and the eighty-foot-square corner lot at St. Mary and Voltigeur in July 1808.

But as with the whiskey, the revenue flow from softwood lumber was temporary. After 1800 Molson bought almost no new lumber, and was content to sell from the inventory he had mainly built up in 1799 and 1800. The only purchase expense he noted thereafter was some £56 in 1802–3, by which time he was coming close to breaking even: his expenses totalled £4,088, while his revenues had reached £3,800. Clearly this was not a way to make money, if it was ever intended to be. Molson seems to have hoarded lumber up to 1800, then gradually sold off the inventory or put it to his own uses. "Planks and boards" were only an incidental entry in the 1808–9 ledgers, with expenditures of about £345 having been carried forward from the missing ledgers. David Munn established a lumber operation and shipyard next door to the Molson property in 1806, and Molson may have bowed out of the business in Munn's favour, if he hadn't already decided to wind down the venture earlier in the decade.

In the meantime, Molson had made his entry into the banking world that would prove so important to the family's future. With the brewery operating on a cash basis and sales increasing, he had long been able to make small loans. His account book detailed a number of very modest loans in 1790— £11 8d to Rosseter Hoyle, a guinea to James Porter, and about £95 to George Stansfeld. But these were short-term favours repaid within a week or two. By the turn of the century, Molson was positioned to make more ambitious deals. A ledger entry in 1802 noting a credit of almost £1,980 to Parker, Gerrard, Ogilvy & Co. indicates he was purchasing bills of exchange on discount and remitting them at profits of up to twenty percent.[4]

But Molson's financial dealings were far more ambitious than the exchange bill purchases would indicate. The "farm book," an accounting record of expenses for his agricultural holdings from 1799 to 1818, reveals a portfolio of rural properties and related financing around Montreal and far beyond.

Molson owned sixteen shares in the Montreal Water Works, a private venture that brought water down from Mount Royal to the city in wooden pipes; his first accounting entry for that investment was made in the farm book on October 19, 1799. On February 18, 1801, he noted the receipt of £50, being "so much allowed me for the water on my farm on mountain purchased from Burton & McCulloch." Evidently Molson had acquired a farm on Mount Royal. Four more local rural properties also appeared in the farm book accounts.[5]

At the same time, Molson was investing in real estate within the city of Montreal. An income property containing two houses was acquired on rue Capital near the market, and in March 1799 Molson leased it for three years to a man named John Teasdall, who operated a coffee house there; in 1807 Molson contracted Isaac Shay to build a new house on the rue Capital property. He also bought—probably after 1805[6]—a home and several lots on rue Saint-François-Xavier, as the farm book notes that he sold them to Colonel Fleury Deschambault for £1,500 in 1807.

Montreal merchants were slow to warm to the possibilities of large-scale real-estate speculation. The persistence of the seigneurial system effectively suppressed it in Lower Canada, although, at the time of Molson's farm purchases, entire town plans were being granted to Loyalists in the Eastern Townships, which were settled by a wave of American émigrés and attracted Yankee speculators.[7] While Creighton has argued that opportunities in Upper Canada did not initially capture the imagination of Lower Canadian investors, Molson's activities indicate that within a decade of the division of Quebec, the opportunity to act as a private banker in the Upper Country was being exploited in Montreal. As Molson had already observed to William Rayment in 1788, "Cash in this Country can be turned to the best advantage by a Person who has talents for speculation or who takes care to apply to those who want Money."

Molson was active in Upper Canada property no later than 1800, becoming a financier for cash-strapped and distressed speculators. The Montreal merchant John Gray proved to be an important connection in Molson's investment activities. He was the brother of Edward William Gray, the sheriff who oversaw the auction of the brewery property in 1786, and of Jonathan Gray, one of two notaries who prepared Molson's marriage contract in 1801. But Molson was probably introduced to the opportunities above the Lachine Rapids by William Berczy. The artist, architect and would-be land baron arrived in Montreal from Upper Canada in 1798, facing complete ruin.

John Molson's list of assets, drawn up in April 1809, reveals his extensive activities in property and personal financing in Upper Canada. This portion of the list itemizes some of his dealings with Samuel Heron and William Berczy. (The Molson Archives/National Archives of Canada)

One hardly knows where to begin with Berczy, who lived most of his life under a pseudonym.[8] Born Johann Albrecht Ulrich Moll in Germany in 1744, he changed his name to Albert-Guillame Berczy after business difficulties in his native land compelled him to move to Florence in the late 1770s to work as a miniaturist. The name was anglicized to William Berczy after he relocated to London in 1791. He became a paid promoter of a land tract on the Genesee River in New York State; the British speculators who hired him hoped he could persuade Germans (who were thought hard-working and inexpensive) to relocate. He attracted more than two hundred settlers, but they (and Berczy) encountered so many difficulties with the land company—including what amounted to indentured servitude—that they abandoned the Genesee tract, arriving at Newark, Ontario (present-day Niagara-on-the-Lake), in 1794 in search of a less odious grant in Upper Canada. Lieutenant-Governor John Graves Simcoe, eager to settle the wilderness north of his new capital at York (now Toronto), persuaded Berczy's German Company to settle its 186 émigrés on a 64,000-acre grant at Markham Township, and to finish cutting Yonge Street north from York to Lake Simcoe in exchange for four additional lots.

The Germans arrived in Markham Township in late 1794 and worked diligently on the road, but delays gave unsympathetic and probably prejudicial administrators the excuse not to grant Berczy his promised tracts after Simcoe's term ended in 1796. At the same time, Berczy became deeply indebted in support of his settlers.

Berczy spent the rest of his life trying to get the lands he'd been promised and warding off creditors. He drew up two petitions to George III in March 1798 and arrived in Lower Canada, preparing to cross the Atlantic to argue his case. Here he became embroiled in the efforts of other claimants to win back their expropriated townships, and added more enemies in the ranks of the appointed council of Lower Canada to the ones he had already made in Upper Canada.

Berczy might have reminded Molson of his brother-in-law. Like Rayment, he was self-aggrandizing and prone to evasion and hyperbole, but he was also badly treated, as Rayment had been when unjustly locked up in the prison ship. Berczy's situation attracted sympathy among elite Montreal merchants. His wife, Charlotte, and their sons, William Bent and Charles Albert, relocated to Montreal in 1798, while Berczy spent the winter in Quebec City, earning money painting portraits so he could pay for his passage to London to argue for his land.

The Berczy sons were eight and four when they arrived in Montreal in 1798; the Molson sons, John, Thomas and William, were eleven, seven and five. According to Berczy biographer John Andre, the Berczy children "were now playmates with the Molson boys." Charles and Thomas, in particular, became friends, and Thomas was taught languages and art, including architectural rendering, by William Berczy. The influence is evident in the numerous precise drawings of brewing and distilling machinery Thomas Molson left behind in his notebooks.

During his time in Lower Canada, Berczy produced portraits of such prominent citizens as William McGillivray, Louis Genevay, Governor General Robert Prescott, Jean-Marie Mondelet, Pierre-Amable De Bonne and James McGill. He is remembered as the finest portrait painter active in the Canadas in these years. (He also designed grave monuments and produced the winning design for the new Christ Church in Montreal in 1803, after the one in which John Molson and Sarah Vaughan were married burned down.) No Berczy drawings or paintings of Molson family members survive, but Molson's farm book left behind ample evidence of the brewer's involvement in the debt-ridden affairs of Berczy and the Upper Canadian speculators he knew. Where Molson's commiseration ended and opportunism began is open to debate. A single page in the farm book, on which Molson tallied his assets in April 1809, provides an impressive survey of Upper Canada investments, involving some of the province's best-known figures. By 1800, the brewer was deeply involved in the land business in both Canadian provinces.

After Berczy, the foremost figure to appear in Molson's records is John Small, born in Cirencester, England, in 1746. Named clerk to the executive council of Upper Canada in 1792, he had been involved in Simcoe's grant to Berczy, and he augmented his £100 annual salary by speculating in land in York Township.[9] In late 1799, Small and the province's solicitor-general, John White, became involved in a ridiculous exchange of insults over their

William Berczy, self-portrait, circa 1798–99. (Collection: Art Gallery of Ontario)

wives and marriages, which prompted Small to challenge White to a duel. Berczy's pistols were borrowed for the occasion, and on January 3, 1800, Small shot White dead. While Small eluded a murder charge, his name was blackened; however, he continued to speculate in land in York, an avocation that eventually made him wealthy. How Molson came to Small's financial aid in the dark days of 1800 isn't known, but Molson's farm book entries indicate he issued him a nine-year mortgage bond for £340 that year, and he paid Upper Canada's new solicitor-general, Robert Isaac Dey Gray, to draw up the document.

Small was the only successful speculator in the rogues' gallery that appears in Molson's farm book accounting. More typical was William Willcocks, a good friend of Berczy, who went from one disaster to another. Born about 1735 in Ireland, Willcocks was bankrupted by the loss of two ships in 1782. By working connections in the executive council of Upper Canada, he was able to acquire a valuable streetfront lot in York, and two hundred acres elsewhere in the township, in 1792. At the end of the year, Willcocks and some associates wrested a grant for Norwich (later Whitby and East Whitby) Township. Willcocks personally received one thousand acres, and he earned an additional two hundred for each settler he brought to the land. When he crossed the Atlantic in 1792 to collect homesteaders in Ireland and Wales, however, the outbreak of war between France and Britain trapped him on the wrong side of the ocean. After serving as mayor of Cork, he recrossed the Atlantic in 1795 with only thirty-three settlers, all of whom deserted him in New York. A second load of settlers on their way over were carried off by French privateers. Then he lost the grant altogether in May 1796 after advertising its lots "on moderate terms" when all granted lands were supposed to be given freely to settlers.

Instead of becoming a land baron, Willcocks had to settle for being a shopkeeper and postmaster in York. He did manage to be appointed a judge in January 1800, just as Small was killing the solicitor-general, despite the fact that he wasn't an attorney. Willcocks then ran against Small, Judge Henry Allcock and Provincial Secretary William Jarvis in an 1800 election. After Allcock won by only two votes, the result was quashed because of polling irregularities, and a new election was held, which was won by a new candidate, Angus MacDonnell. Things might have turned out all right for Willcocks if he hadn't gone back into land speculation, acquiring fifteen thousand acres in present-day Oxford County in 1799. The investment ruined him, and John Gray foreclosed on his mortgages in 1803.

Willcocks was not free of Gray, however. Elizabeth Russell of York wrote in her diary on January 24, 1806:

> Willcocks came at dinner time. . . . After tea was over Mr. St. George came and sat the evening. Willcocks & him were talking about the former's debt to Mr. Gray of Montreal. Willcocks thought that St. George took Mr. Gray's part and began to grow in a passion with St. George, and had he been let go on he would have been in a violent rage & insulted St. George, but I put a check to his going on by speaking a little sharp and telling him that there was quite enough of it. He had got primed with his grog which he often is.—He drinks a great quantity of brandy wine & water mixed together.— However they went away good friends together—St. George was not in fault at all.[10]

Willcocks soon must have been cursing John Molson, instead. It appears that Gray sold some of Willcocks's debt to the brewer, as in his April 1809 tally of assets he noted a debt payable by "W. Willcocks with Interest" worth £1,750.

Then there was Scottish-born Samuel Heron, who settled on two hundred acres near present-day Ashbridges Bay in east Toronto in 1793, marrying Sarah Ashbridge in 1794. He quickly began pleading for free land, petitioning the executive council for a town lot in York, and had to be satisfied with a less valuable back lot. While operating a general store in York, he supplied goods to Berczy's German Company settlers in Markham Township, and in 1795–96 became Berczy's partner in a grist mill on the Don River, as well as his mortgagee. When Berczy left the area to argue for his land grant, Heron served as his business agent.

Heron diversified into shipping on Lake Ontario with a partner in 1796, and by the turn of the century, he had a tavern in York and a shop housing two tailors. He also worked as a small-scale financier for settlers, and worked his own speculations, which proved as disastrous as those of Willcocks—who was also a creditor of Berczy. Strapped for cash, he advertised three thousand acres for sale in Scarborough, Vaughan and Norwich townships. But like Willcocks, he had mortgaged his properties with John Gray, and Gray fore-closed on him too in 1803. To recover the funds, Gray put up for sale more than 2,500 acres of Heron's properties in York, Scarborough, Vaughan, York, Crowland and Norwich townships.

While it's possible Molson acquired lands directly from Heron, he probably picked them up from Gray in the 1803 sell-off. His 1809 list of assets included 500 acres in Scarborough, 400 in Vaughan, 300 in York and 1,000 in Norwich, all marked "from Heron," as well as "Heron House in York," valued at £250. Another 600 acres in Markham were labelled "from Berczy by Heron." Molson also possessed "Berczy's Mills and Lands" through an assignment worth more than £800, about £577 of which had come from Berczy's indebtedness to Heron and about £226 "for self," which must have represented Molson's own efforts to finance the impoverished Berczy.

And there was still more to Molson's Upper Canadian portfolio: an obligation of Heron's to which Molson assigned a present value of £250; another two hundred acres in Markham labelled "for self"; "More lands & houses in U.C." valued at £250; and a £60 obliga-tion (probably a mortgage) attributed to a man in Detroit named Alex Harrow. In all, Molson's Upper Canadian investments totalled £4,821 7s in April 1809.

The final character in Molson's adventures in Upper Canadian investment was an old neighbour from Moulton, D'Arcy Boulton, a refugee of the family's misfortunes in England.

The Boultons were an old south Lincolnshire family; the main estate of Fenland at Moulton (not the one sold to settle Alice Boulton's legacies) had been purchased by Henry Senior in 1751. With his wife, Mary Preston, Henry Senior had two sons, Henry Junior and D'Arcy. Born in 1759, D'Arcy had married Elizabeth Forster in December 1782, while John Molson was away on his exploratory journey to Quebec.

Legal documents in Britain's Public Record Office indicate that Fenland was jointly owned by Henry Boulton, Jr., and Lucy Knightley (a man), a prominent member of a Northamptonshire family who was probably related to Henry's mother, Mary Preston.

In 1791, Fenland was sold by Henry Junior and Lucy Knightley's widow, Elizabeth, to Samuel Wood—who coincidentally also acquired Snake Hall from John Molson in 1789. D'Arcy Boulton, meanwhile, followed in his brother's footsteps by enrolling in law school at the Middle Temple in 1788. He was not, however, admitted to the English bar at this time, and he became a partner in the Woollen Yarn Company. What role the sale of Fenland might have played in the wool-industry venture is unknown, but by 1793 the business was bankrupt. In 1797, D'Arcy was forced to look to North America to make a fresh start with Elizabeth and their eight children.

Boulton's first years in North America are sketchy, but he may have served as a lowly oarsman on a lumber raft on Lake Champlain, and perhaps his path crossed with John Molson as the brewer diversified into lumber. By 1802, Boulton was settled at Augusta County, one of the original Royal Townships that had been laid out on the upper St. Lawrence in 1784.

Molson evidently provided Boulton with £20 (an oddly small sum) to invest in land on his behalf in Upper Canada—a sum that grew with interest as Boulton failed to put it to use. At some point in early 1802, Boulton wrote Molson, explaining that "The badness of the sleighing" had prevented him from sending him a receipt for the money. On October 25, 1802, a receipt was signed by Boulton acknowledging the money (now £20 11s 6d) he had been given by Molson "for the purchase of Land in the Province of Upper Canada & which I am accountable for the Application of on demand." Three years later, on July 15, 1805, Boulton wrote:

> I received your favour of the 2d Inst. . . . With respect to the account, £22, 12s, 7d, I have only to observe that I undertook the expenditure of that sum in land, but if you recollect, I particularly cautioned you not to think of investing money in land, if you had any thoughts of wanting the money again suddenly. I made a purchase of 400 acres soon after the time I had your instructions but from the usual delay in land business I have not even yet got out the Deeds. I long ago intimated this to you, but have never been favoured by any Answer,

neither have I received any Letter from you since my departure from Montreal, except the one above mentioned. I expect to be at Montreal before I repair to York, in which case I shall resume, with your permission my old Quarters. I am highly gratified to hear from all my friends your great success in your brewery.

I presume you have heard I am appointed his Majesty's Solicitor General for this province: having established a Court of Chancery here the office is important. I have not been idle this winter be assured, tho' I have not paid you a visit.

Boulton's rise through the ranks of Upper Canadian society was truly meteoric. Although still not a member of the English bar, in 1803 he became an accredited attorney, as the lieutenant-governor was empowered to license them in response to a shortage in the Upper Country. Next came a fortuitous calamity: in October 1804, the *Speedy* was lost with all hands on Lake Ontario while en route from York to Presqu'isle for a murder trial. Among those aboard was the province's solicitor-general, Robert Isaac Dey Gray, who had handled the paperwork for Molson in the Small mortgage. Molson was close enough to Gray to serve as guardian for his son John and oversee his legacy.

As Boulton noted in his letter to Molson, he had succeeded to Gray's position. The plum job came to him after some judicious lobbying, for as he went on to note in the letter, he had "pressed my English Int[erests] for the above Vacancy." Gray's death also left his parliamentary seat vacant in the Stormont and Russell riding, and Boulton rushed to fill it as well. In reporting his successful election in the letter, Boulton observed that he "stood a warm Contest for one of our Counties & to conclude as the parson says, carried every point."

Judging by his admonition in the 1805 letter, Boulton found Molson's lack of communication as frustrating as so many others had. A letter from Boulton to Molson on July 21, 1806, however, indicates that the effort by Molson to invest in Upper Canadian land had been thwarted by misadventures at Boulton's end.

In regard to your Land purchase, I made the same long ago, but owing to my taking the promise of a Man I had had considerable dealings with, in regard to the title, I have been deceived. I hope on this Circuit to compleat the business tho' I feel mortified at the Delay—the Land is improving in value; in short I am personally responsible & must take the whole blame on my own shoulders. If I am again deceived I shall make another purchase & submit to the Loss of the first, if I cannot do better.

Whether this purchase effort ever came to anything is unknown, although it could have become part of Molson's list of miscellaneous holdings in the province. Boulton's letter indicates, however, that Molson's ambitions in Upper Canada went beyond property investments:

My son reminds me that you wished for hints respecting this place in the brewery line. There is a great quantity of beer consumed here. We have two little Breweries—neither of them good—one under the management of a person of some capital, the other the reverse. This is a growing place & in a short time a brewery may be of great importance. No doubt if you were to establish Works here, you would command the trade from your superior Science in the Line. The Land around [is] well calculated for Barley & Hops appear spontaneous. I trust it is needless for me to say that if you attempt an establishment here, you may command at all times any services within the compass of my power.

In contemplating an expansion into Upper Canada, John Molson may have been thinking of his three sons' futures, for by 1806 the eldest, John Junior, was about to turn nineteen. And Boulton, who was becoming one of the most vilified members of the province's ruling elite—known as the Family Compact—would have smoothed the way. But before anything could be done about brewing in the neighbouring province, commercially viable steam power in shipping suddenly hove into view.

Chapter 17

Your moral character must be not only pure, but, like Caesar's wife, unsuspected. . . . There is nothing so delicate as your moral character, and nothing which it is your interest so much to preserve pure. Should you be suspected of injustice, malignity, perfidy, lying, etc., all parts and knowledge in the world will never procure you esteem, friendship, or respect.

—Lord Chesterfield, letter to his son, January 8, 1750

AT ONE O'CLOCK on the afternoon of August 17, 1807, a nameless vessel—more a machine than a proper ship—made a historic journey that was to change the course of the Molson family's fortunes. About forty people were on board, none of them Molsons, but as the vessel left its dock on the North River near New York City to journey some 150 miles up the Hudson River to the state capital at Albany, it described a course that would extend deep into the Molsons' affairs.

The vessel was the property of the North River Steam Boat Company, and so was known unsentimentally as the *North River Steam Boat*. Modifications in 1808 caused her to be re-registered as the *North River of Clermont*, but the press reduced this to the *Clermont*, the name by which the vessel would be forever remembered. She was the culmination of more than a decade of perseverance by a failed American painter of miniatures turned civil engineer named Robert Fulton. On that August day, Fulton overcame widespread scepticism and derision through the twenty modest horsepower generated by a Boulton & Watt steam engine,

320

which was animated by no more than three feeble pounds of pressure per square inch in its twin cylinders. Burning oak and pine to fire the boiler, the boxy 150-foot vessel belched frightening clouds of cindery smoke, and even flames were seen licking from the funnel. She must have seemed by turns absurd, appalling and impressive. Driving a pair of side-mounted paddlewheels, the engine pressed the vessel up the river to Albany in thirty hours, and returned her to New York in thirty-two, thus averaging a leisurely yet dependable rate of almost five miles per hour—a rate clocked without regard to the wind's fickle strength or direction and with no oars in sight.

"The power of propelling boats by steam is now fully proved," Fulton wrote to his friend Joel Barlow after the triumphant demonstration. "The morning I left New York, there were not perhaps thirty persons in the city who believed that the boat would ever move one mile an hour, or be of the least utility, and while we were putting off from the wharf, which was crowded with spectators, I heard a number of sarcastic remarks. This is the way in which ignorant men compliment what they call philosophers and projectors."

Steam-powered vessels had been a subject of serious experiment for decades on both sides of the Atlantic, with some in America even entering commercial use before Fulton's effort. There is no evidence that John Molson took any special notice of Fulton's successful demonstration, but his North River Steam Boat Company quickly became hard to ignore. It placed an advertisement in the *Albany Gazette* on September 2, 1807, announcing the beginning of commercial service between New York and Albany in two days.

The next year, the novelty of steam service migrated to Lake Champlain, as the *Clermont's* pilot, James Winans, established a new venture with his brother John, a carpenter who may have helped build Fulton's vessel. They formed a partnership with a foundry operator, Joseph Lough, and at their new shipyard at Burlington, Vermont, the Winanses began building a 120-foot steamboat called the *Vermont* to carry the revolutionary momentum of the *Clermont* still further north. Because the *Vermont* called at

St. Johns, north of the Canadian-American border, when it began plying the lake in June 1809 the Winanses officially became the first steamboat operators in Canadian waters, in addition to laying claim to the first international service. Her first visit to Canada drew the interest of the *Montreal Gazette,* which published an account of her arrival on July 3, 1809. However, John Molson was close behind the Winanses in launching a truly Canadian operation, and it tackled the St. Lawrence between Montreal and Quebec City, a stretch of water longer and far more challenging than those faced by Fulton or the Winanses.

That Molson launched his shipping venture at all is a marvel, as he had none of the practical experience of the Winanses or the long-standing determination of Fulton. While his debut as a brewer in Montreal was impressive, there was at least some initial experience with Thomas Loid and a small brewery at Snake Hall as precedents. His nautical heritage, so heroically contained within the career of his late uncle Robinson Elsdale, might have provided an emotional impulse, but it offered no practical knowledge. A commercial shipping venture had briefly surfaced as a possibility in 1786, when he proposed the partnership with the Wilsons of Yorkshire, but since then nothing like it had arisen.

But not even a solid background in commercial shipping would have prepared Molson fully for the enterprise he took on, for going from sail to steam was nothing like a brewer diversifying from beer into whiskey. One could find published material on the nature and construction of steam engines, but the steamboat was so new that whoever wanted one was on his own in working through every imaginable detail. What he could not imagine himself he would have to master by observing the work of others, and Fulton had been adept at studying (some would say stealing) the experiments of the truly ingenious.

We don't know if Molson even initiated his St. Lawrence steamboat venture; he may well have stepped in to serve as a financier for a project already in the planning stages, for he didn't sign a contract with his ultimate partners until the ship was nearing completion. The three principal participants in the construction of the vessel were the mechanic John Jackson, the boatbuilder John Bruce and the cabinetmaker John Kay.[1]

Virtually nothing is known otherwise about the origins of these three men. Kay left the project before the boat was completed and is of only incidental interest. Bruce was a Scotsman, and would become better known to history as he participated in a number of steamboat projects in Canada. Jackson did not stay around long enough to leave a biographical impression. The name Jackson appears several times in earlier Molson affairs—Paul Jackson chartered Robinson Elsdale's *Duke of Ancaster* in 1770, and a servant named Dan Jackson was paid by Samuel Elsdale in 1771 in the course of managing the Molson inheritance—but none of them suggests a definitive heritage for John Jackson. It is worth noting that someone named Jackson was associated with Fulton's Hudson River venture. In a letter to Andrew Brink, the captain of his new steamboat, on October 9, 1807, Fulton advised, "As she is strongly man'd and every one except Jackson [is] under your command, you must insist on each one doing his duty or turn him on shore and put another in his place." Perhaps, like the Winans brothers, John Jackson had been associated with Fulton's steamboat initiative and struck out on his own as soon as Fulton's venture proved viable.

Between his recent lumber activities, selling beer and buying hops, Molson was sufficiently active commercially in the Lake Champlain region to have tapped into the news of the Winanses' work in progress by late 1808. His St. Lawrence service, whether he initiated it or not, was in lockstep with the Winanses in threading a revolutionary transportation system through a historically important corridor. Fulton's service took travellers (and goods) from New York up the Hudson to Albany, where they could board a stage at Troy that delivered them to the Winanses' wharf at Whitehall, New York, at the southern end of Lake Champlain. The *Vermont* then carried them the length of the lake and into the Richelieu River to St. Johns. A forty-mile stage trip could then deliver travellers to Montreal. If Molson could launch his own steamboat, he could carry them on to Quebec City. Each independently operated steamboat venture was viable in its own right, but together they could create an integrated transportation link unlike anything on the planet.

Whether or not Molson was involved at the conceptual stage of the project, he was the financier from the beginning of construction. Six months before a partnership contract was signed between Molson, Jackson and Bruce, work began on the steamboat, with Molson paying all expenses. A new brewery account book was opened on December 27, 1808, and Molson wrote on the flyleaf the names of Jackson and Bruce, which marked their debut in his affairs. Jackson would have overseen the engine's design and construction, but a large role was played by the Montreal machinist George Platt, the son of the ironmonger John Platt. Platt was in charge of producing the mechanical components, and he outsourced the castings and forgings to the St. Maurice Forges in Trois-Rivières while finishing items with another machinist named Ezekiel Cutter.

Two very different models of the *Accommodation*: at top, one built around the time of the 125th anniversary of her launch; at bottom, one built in 1959 to commemorate the 150th anniversary. Neither are correct. The top model wrongly shows paddlewheels at the bow and stern and a covered passenger area, but it has the right utilitarian flavour. The one at the bottom is too shiplike in shape and detailing, more closely resembling later Molson steamboats such as the *Malsham* or the *Swiftsure*. (National Archives of Canada/A-42585; The Molson Archives Collection/National Archives of Canada/PA-139120)

The Forges dated back to 1733 and the French regime, when the facility was established to take advantage of the considerable iron ore deposits around Trois-Rivières. Production in the first few decades was mainly composed of bar, which was shipped to the French arsenal at Rochefort to create the weaponry required for the relentless campaigns against Britain. Since the conquest, the Forges had been the property of the British Crown and were leased out to entrepreneurs. At the time of the Molson steamboat's construction, the Forges were under lease to David Munro and Matthew Bell.

The first entry on the Forges account, made on January 25, 1809, was a modest order for some files, a rasp, two sheets of sandpaper and a hundred brads (a type of wire nail). Molson made his first of many compensations of Platt's expenses on February 11, and thereafter paid wages for four to six men, rented them a house (but charged them for beer) and bought materials on his own. While Molson had no contract yet between himself and the men building the steamboat, he was marshalling their efforts. A statement from the attorney Benjamin Beaubien summarizing work performed for Molson between January 27 and March 22, 1809, included a ten-shilling fee for "a consultation concerning a certain agreement between Kay, Jackson & Bruce." The charge must have been due to Kay's withdrawal from the partnership on March 22—the last day in the Beaubien account summary. In a notarized agreement that day, Kay surrendered his share of the partnership to Jackson and Bruce for £26. It was a buy-out financed by Molson, as the very same day he loaned Jackson and Bruce £30. From that point forward, Molson was effectively Jackson and Bruce's new partner, in addition to carrying on as the project's financier, as the contract the trio finally signed on June 5 was backdated to April 1.

At the same time, Molson was keeping Isaac Shay busy with carpentry work on multiple fronts. On February 21, Molson paid Shay's bills for construction on a "new house," probably the one he was contracted to build in 1807 at rue Capital, and for work on a gallery at the rue Capital coffee house; there were also charges by Shay for "brewhouse work" and a "summer house." Molson was also still actively dealing with speculations in bills of exchange through the London banking firm of Parker, Gerrard, Ogilvy & Co., as he made ledger entries in March for interest received from them on sums of £2,000 and £3,000.

On March 29, Molson paid for "17 Knees & 6 Crooked pieces for Steam Boat as per Bruce's order." The framing of the hull was underway. In April, Molson made his summary of assets, exclusive of the brewery properties, in the farm book. He appeared to be pausing to assess his net worth before plunging ahead with the steamboat venture. He must have found the calculations reassuring. His non-brewery assets in Upper and Lower Canada came to £17,040 3s 8d.[2] After factoring in accounts payable and receivable, he arrived at a total of £15,259.

The summary of assets of April 1809 indicates that Molson was a wealthy man, even without taking into account the thriving brewery. These assets came to the modern equivalent of £660,000. His ability to finance the expansion into steamboats has puzzled some, but the asset list tucked away in the farm book shows he had deep reserves on which to draw without endangering the core business of brewing.

On June 5, just before the Winanses' *Vermont* went into service on Lake Champlain, Molson signed the contract with Jackson and Bruce, cementing a partnership to operate a steamboat service on the St. Lawrence between Montreal and Quebec City. The back-dated agreement provided for an equal partnership, with Molson serving as treasurer. Molson agreed to fund the completion of the vessel and to allot Jackson and Bruce a daily credit of 7s 6d for their efforts in building the ship, which would be converted into equivalent company stock in their name.

Jackson and Bruce probably deserve credit—or blame—for the initiative's practical details, as it is impossible to imagine Molson conceiving either a ship or a propulsion system on his own. He certainly had experience with the mechanics of brewing (and he would turn to steam power in improving the process), but his own accomplishments were built on the expertise of others. A steamboat, as noted, was essentially something to be invented—Fulton in fact made an American patent application on January 1, 1809, for "improvements in steamboats," which was granted in February 1810. No commercial steamboat venture existed in Europe at the time. Molson was steering into waters only recently charted by Fulton and other American innovators on a more modest scale. And Fulton's charting was not flawless for, despite his preparedness, he still experienced mechanical difficulties with the *Clermont;* the Winans brothers, for their part, kept a pot of molten lead handy to fill any cracks that appeared in the *Vermont's* engine while under-way, and the *Vermont* would eventually sink in the Richelieu River in October 1815 when one of the engine's connecting rods broke away and punched a hole in the hull.

Molson left behind no drawings or dimensions of his first steam-boat, although shipwrights at the time tended to work from models and experience and not from formal plans. No drawings survive of Fulton's *Clermont,* either, but we know her basic dimensions and general shape. Fulton made careful note of the latest studies in resistance experienced by ships' hulls—a science in its infancy—and drew on them to create an un-ship-like ship. The *Clermont* was not simply a general sailing hull outfitted with paddlewheels. She had a boxy cross-section midships, where the paddlewheels were mounted, and was fairly V-shaped in her deck view at the bow and stern. She was also double-ended, so that she could travel with equal efficiency in "forward" or "reverse" without having to be turned around in a narrow river. Some speculative models and art depicting Molson's first steamboat have tended to show her, for no particular reason, as traditionally ship-like in shape. But it's sus-pected that she was fundamentally a scaled-down imitation of the *Clermont*—or of the *Vermont's* imitation of the *Clermont:* no cabin superstructure and a spartan appearance, with few efforts to impart a ship-like grace.

As for her name, *Accommodation* may have been a signal by Molson that this venture was almost philanthropic, a gesture of his willingness to do favours or service to his fellow Quebecers, in the spirit of his unprofitable lumberyard. More mundanely, "accommo-dation" refers to berths or seats on ships, and the *Accommodation* certainly strove to be accommodating, offering quality food and drink (including, naturally, Molson's own beer) during a passage.

An account of the *Accommodation*'s first trip from Montreal to Quebec, published in the *Quebec Mercury* on November 6, 1809, provides the basic facts about her. She was about seventy-five feet long on the keel and eighty-five feet on the deck, considerably smaller than Fulton's and the Winanses' ships, but like them she used a pair of side-mounted paddlewheels. Belowdecks were berths for twenty passengers. A mast and sail were planned to assist the steam power, but they weren't present in 1809. The purchase of a sail in 1810 indicates that a simple rig was installed for the second season.

We do know one more extraordinary fact about her: she was built entirely in Quebec, from wooden hull to mechanical systems, including, almost inconceivably, her engine. Fulton was not so brave as to attempt to build a steam engine—his genius was to focus on practicality, employing proven technology and not trying to innovate in all directions. He ordered from the pioneering Birmingham engineering firm Boulton & Watt the power plants that drove the *Clermont* and his subsequent ships. The exact source of the engine for the *Vermont* isn't known, but the Winanses didn't attempt to build it; it was acquired second-hand from someone on the Hudson. Molson, Jackson and Bruce, in contrast, built their engine from scratch.

It's possible Jackson fancied himself a steam-engine designer, as in 1798 a man named John Jackson of Dockhead, England, was awarded a patent "for his mode of constructing Steam Engines."[3] If the hubris of Jackson was not the cause, only desperation could have compelled the partners to build their own engine. Molson appears to have relied consistently on "off-the-shelf" components sourced in England for his brewery, and the mechanical components of a brewery were far simpler than a steam engine. Even the engines produced by Boulton & Watt, as much as they were based on proven technology, were not truly "off the shelf." Each hand-crafted engine had to be ordered from the firm with specific dimensions, to meet the power requirements of a particular application, and there was a lengthy wait for the finished product. The engine that Fulton installed in the *Clermont* in 1807 had been built for him by Boulton & Watt back in 1804. Molson and his partners may have realized they could neither find a second-hand engine like the Winans brothers nor order one from Boulton & Watt without a delivery schedule that would keep them off the river while a competitor arose.

The *Accommodation's* success depended entirely on whether Jackson, Bruce, Platt and Cutter, working with the St. Maurice Forges, were capable of designing and executing a functioning propulsion system for the boat. It all must have seemed a strange twist on the brewery business to Molson. Instead of the copper kettle feeding hot water to the mash-tun and boiling the wort, he now had an iron boiler producing steam that was delivered to a single cylinder, which drove a piston, which in turn provided the motion that turned the paddlewheels. But how large should the paddlewheels be? How wide and long the paddle boards—and how many? How large the boiler? How long the stroke of the piston and the diameter of the cylinder?

The engine cylinder was completed relatively early, as the Molson accounts noted a payment for transporting it on April 12. But there must have been problems getting the other components manufactured, as the boat was close to completion when the rest of the machinery for the propulsion system began to show up in Molson's accounts. The boiler had already been paid for on June 29 when the first serious work on the engine parts (since the cylinder delivery) appeared in the account entries. On June 30, the account book noted, "1 Large Piston Rod to be turned 70 lbs." The substantial proportion of the engine components came in July; when the partners were buying mattresses and chintz for the cabins, the *Accommodation* still had no engine.

The *Accommodation* was launched unceremoniously sometime around August 19, 1809, but was not ready to attempt her first passage to Quebec City until November 1, narrowly entering service before the close of shipping. The long shakedown bespoke fundamental problems. She was grossly underpowered. While no drawings or specifications survive, it's believed her engine produced about six horsepower from two pounds per square inch of steam pressure. She operated from Molson's brewery property, below St. Mary's Current, which, apart from the convenience of the location for Molson, underscored her inability to defeat the current and reach the city of Montreal.

Ten passengers braved the first trip (although there were berths for twenty), which according to the *Quebec Mercury* took sixty-six hours, of which thirty were spent at anchor. While some of this time would have been spent waiting for favourable winds and tide, there were also delays due to refuelling stops for wood to fire the boiler. Molson left behind no account of the voyage, but the novelty attracted the attention of both the *Quebec Mercury* and *Quebec Gazette*, as well as many pier-side visitors at her destination.

The inaugural performance was less than satisfactory. While the *Mercury* was enthusiastic after the *Accommodation*'s arrival in Quebec City, declaring "no wind or tide can stop her," the *Gazette* was more realistic in observing three days later that "her progress was very slow" specifically against wind and tide. "It is obvious her machinery, at present, has not sufficient force for this River," the *Gazette* concluded.

On the way back to Montreal, the *Accommodation* put in at Trois-Rivières, probably both to refuel and to arrange for new parts or repairs at the St. Maurice Forges. A second, and final, return passage for the season was made on November 15. For some reason, the fares reported in the *Mercury* on November 6 were in dollars (eight from Montreal to Quebec City, nine to return), but Molson recorded the revenues in pounds. The upbound passage, which often frustrated sail-powered vessels, was the more popular one on those first two round trips: the total upbound revenues from Quebec City were £45 5s, while the downbound runs brought only £18. Total revenues for the brief season were £76 4s 7^1/2d, which included all fares collected, cash received from the steward and sales of six dozen bottles of beer. It left the venture with a loss to carry forward in the ledgers in February 1810 of £1,364 12s 2^1/2d.

Despite the *Gazette*'s reservations about the *Accommodation*'s performance, the newspaper was encouraging, allowing that "there can be no doubt of the possibility of perfectionating it, so as to answer every purpose for which it is intended; and it would be a public loss should the proprietors be discouraged in their undertaking." But scepticism must have been such that three passengers — Will Tudor Hall, Alphonso Pilgrim and Thomas Tuzo—from the first season wrote a laudatory letter to the Canadian *Courant:*

> As the Public may be biassed to the prejudice of the STEAM BOAT in consequence of the length of her passage from Quebec, we do hereby give it as our opinion, that the reason of it is attributable only to an error in the calculation of the quantity of fuel she would require, to contend with and make way against the rapid tide of the St. Lawrence, by which means, nearly half of the time was consumed in the delays to procure supplies and to the impossibility of obtaining coal (except a small quantity at Three Rivers) which is indispensably necessary to produce the full effect of her machinery.
>
> From her progress during the use of the coal, when compared with the steam from the wood, we believe she will generally perform a voyage to Quebec in thirty-six hours, and return in seventy-two.
>
> We feel a pleasure in acknowledging that the accommodations are excellent—the entertainment [food and beverages] good, and well served, and that the others on board evinced the greatest [effort] to render the passengers comfortable and happy—and we, therefore, wish most complete success to an undertaking, on which much labour and money have been expended, and which ensures to both Ladies and Gentlemen, a cheap, comfortable, and expeditious mode of travelling between Quebec and Montreal.

But a shortage of coal plainly was not fuelling the *Accommodation*'s problems. Molson and his partners toiled through the winter of 1809–10 to improve the boat, focusing much of their efforts—and expenditures—on overhauling the troublesome engine and machinery. More than £350 was spent at the Montreal shipyard of David Munn, and £54 10s 7d was logged on April 11 in payment for sixty-one pieces of cast iron from the St. Maurice Forges—evidence of a major rebuild. A "cambouse," probably an on-deck cookhouse, was added for the second season, in addition to a mast and sail for auxiliary power.

The partners also moved to protect their investment by preparing a petition for a provincial monopoly on steam navigation. The three men published a notice of their intention to apply to the provincial legislature in the upcoming session "for a law giving them the exclusive rights and privileges of constructing and navigating STEAM BOATS or of causing Steam boats to be constructed and navigated within the limits of this Province for the space of fifteen years, to be computed from the first day of May next." The partners were seeking a monopoly not only for the St. Lawrence but for all waters within the province. This implied a ban on the Winans brothers' service to St. Johns with the *Vermont,* and also would have touched on the Ottawa River, which was shared with Upper Canada.

Joseph Papineau, a notary public and Montreal politician, wrote his son Louis-Joseph, an emerging political star who had been first elected to the lower assembly for the 1808 session, on February 22. The elder Papineau remarked favourably on the petition of "Mr. Molson, notre brasseur de bierre." However, the petition never came before the 1810 session. Perhaps, as George H. Wilson has suggested, time ran out before it could be tabled.[4] But the petition was likely too ambitious in its geographical scope to survive scrutiny, and may have been withdrawn by Molson. Passing it would have invited all kinds of territorial squabbles between Quebec and its neighbours.

Before the 1810 season could begin, and perhaps because of the stillborn petition, the partnership between Molson, Jackson and Bruce dissolved. Neither Jackson nor Bruce could withstand the losses the steamboat venture would continue to sustain until the enterprise was perfected. But there had also been a falling-out between Jackson and the boat's engineer, James Clark, who wrote to John Bruce on March 25 to tell him he couldn't serve on the *Accommodation* if Jackson was involved. Molson probably sided with Clark in the course of dismissing Jackson and assuming complete control of the steamboat venture, while Bruce remained with the operation.

Molson's involvement in the steamboat venture echoed his entry into the brewery business in Montreal. The steamboat initiative lay with others—Jackson, Bruce, Kay, and possibly William Horner (see endnote 1), just as the brewery had begun with Loid. The brewery and then the steamboat had caught Molson's fancy in their infancies, and in both cases he moved into partnerships with the founders. After a setback was encountered—the disastrous 1783–84 brewing season, the unsatisfactory 1809 debut of the *Accommodation*—Molson acquired outright ownership. In both cases, he was able to do so because he had the money where his partners did not. With the brewery, the funds came from his inherited properties in Lincolnshire. With the steamboat, more than two decades of brewery profits, much of it invested in real estate and loans, gave Molson alone the means to proceed and prosper.

On May 15, 1810, Samuel Bridge wrote in his journal: "In the Evening, walking by the water Side saw the Steam Boat just going to make an experiment of her powers before setting off for Quebec—went on Board with several others & she went out into the River for abt. 1^1/$_2$ hours & then retd. She has been built by Mr. Molson the Brewer . . . if she succeeds will no doubt pay well from the increasing intercourse between this [city] and Quebec."[5]

An advertisement was placed in the *Courant* on June 4, announcing that the first passage of the season to Quebec City would depart at nine o'clock the next morning. How many runs she made that season isn't known, but the *Accommodation* continued to hemorrhage money. By the end of the 1810 season, the accumulated losses had reached £1,908 16s 3^1/$_2$d.

The *Accommodation* had been built on an experimental scale, and as an experiment she was a failure. Her main shortcoming was her propulsion system. Attempting to build an engine in Montreal had proved to be folly. The technical expertise did not exist to produce components with the narrow tolerances a cylinder and piston required when working under the limited pressure the boiler produced. Platt and Cutter were using a metal lathe to finish components, given the numerous references in the account books to items that had been "turned." This meant a piston casting could have been machined to reasonable tolerances, but boring the cylinder casting to a precise fit was probably beyond them. It's believed that the *Accommodation*'s cylinder had a sixteen-inch diameter and a three-foot stroke. The cylinder amounted to a small cannon, too large for an early metal lathe to bore. The engines of Boulton & Watt had been made practical by James Wilkinson's invention of a horizontal boring machine in 1775. (Wilkinson showed the French how to use one to bore cannons out of solid castings.) But it's very doubtful that such a tool existed in George Platt's shop or at the St. Maurice Forges, as no previous work would have called for precision-machining such large dimensions.

The failure of the *Accommodation* could at best be called brave in the attempt. W.R. Riddell, a passenger aboard her on a run to Quebec City in September 1810, dismissed the vessel as a "clumsy, ill-constructed thing and the power of the works, which were out of order, was by no means adequate to its magnitude."[6] One of her last passengers was the diarist Samuel Bridge, who met Molson on the street on October 2, 1810, and learned that the *Accommodation* would make a run to Quebec City at nine o'clock the next morning. He was one of only nine passengers, and recorded a sour impression: "The boat is very small & owing to useing coal when [there is] a Head wind the smoke is an intolerable nuisance & makes Ye boat very dirty."[7]

By then, Molson had washed his hands of the filthy contraption. Even before the season was over, Molson had turned to the world's leading expert on steamboats, in New York, to determine how to replace her.

Robert Fulton's claim to a pioneering role in steamboat development has long been controversial. He certainly didn't invent the first practical one, nor was he a great innovator. He benefitted enormously from the patronage of Robert Livingston (whose niece Fulton married in 1808), a wealthy New Yorker with an estate on the Hudson at Clermont (the port of registry for the first Fulton vessel), forty-five miles south of Albany. As a prominent lawyer, Livingston had helped draft the Declaration of Independence, and had served as chancellor (or chief justice) of New York from 1777 to 1801. Long after his duties had ended, he was still referred to as "Chancellor Livingston." While serving as the American minister to France from 1801 to 1804, Livingston met Fulton, who had emigrated to England (from the U.S.) in 1794 to try his luck as a miniaturist, only to turn to civil engineering when his artistic talents met with indifference. Fulton was a marine-engineering dynamo, investigating canal schemes, submarines and other weapons of war (which he attempted to sell to the warring French and British), as well as, almost incidentally, steamboats.

An excoriating portrait of Fulton was contained in Thompson Westcott's 1857 biography of the American steamboat innovator John Fitch.[8] As Westcott wrote, Fitch had secured an exclusive right to steamboat navigation on the Hudson, but in 1798 Chancellor Livingston, who had been closely following steamboat developments in America since at least 1793, convinced the state legislature to terminate Fitch's right (by arguing that Fitch was dead, when he was not) and turn it over to him. Livingston used the monopoly to encourage the experiments of Nicholas Rooseveldt, but abandoned Rooseveldt when he received his diplomatic posting to France. After meeting Fulton there, Livingston was able to secure another steamboat monopoly on the Hudson from the legislature, for a twenty-year period, and used it to cultivate Fulton's efforts, while warding off such talented rivals as John Cox Stevens, who had demonstrated a stern-wheel model on the Hudson in 1804. Westcott tabled considerable evidence (or at least serious allegations) that Fulton, in addition to benefitting from Livingston's original poaching of Fitch's Hudson River rights, further benefitted by poaching the technology of Fitch and other innovators.[9]

While Fulton's ingenuity has been mocked,[10] he assuredly deserves credit for achieving what others like Molson did not: a synergy of components that resulted in a practical design that could also be commercially viable. As Fulton's biographer H.W. Dickinson argued: "Fulton had done what every engineer would do in like circumstances. He had availed himself of all practical information that he could find bearing on the subject he was dealing with, and had applied also to it the results of theoretical investigations. He was the first to treat the elementary factors in steamship design: dimensions, form, horse-power, and speed in a scientific spirit; to him belongs the credit of having coupled the boat and the engine as a working unit."[11]

Fulton was a man of Molson's methodology: a gatherer of necessary knowledge rather than a purblind pioneer, a true entrepreneur of the emerging industrial age. When the *Accommodation* was proving an unequivocal failure in 1810, the forty-six-year-old Molson naturally turned to the forty-five-year-old Fulton for advice and assistance.

Molson went to New York to meet with Fulton in August 1810. We can imagine him making the pilgrimage by travelling the length of Lake Champlain on the Winanses' *Vermont* and then down the Hudson on Fulton's *Clermont* or her new sister ship, the *Car of Neptune*, shrewdly assessing the enterprises in the process. That Molson might have hoped to pry free advice from Fulton is not impossible, for he was a firm believer in gathering intelligence. When his son Thomas was sent to England in December 1815 to expand his horizons, Molson, concerned he was wasting valuable opportunities, wrote him with advice on how best to make use of his time:

John [Junior] tells me it was with the greatest difficulty that he could get you to see & sail in the steam boats [in New York]; I should have thought you would not have lost a moment in seeing every thing that was worth seeing & hearing—manners & knowledge are to be acquired most particularly by traveling [and] on that principle I let you take so long and expensive a journey; I can assure you [I] shall have no objection to any reasonable expense . . . as you profit by all the circumstances that present themselves; on the contrary, shall be much dis-apointed & angry if it is not the case. . . . By all means loose [*sic*] not an opportunity of seeing all kinds of machinery that you can get to see, even should it cost a trifle for in seeing nothing, it will cost you a great deal; take your time and money is lost for a few dollars or pounds spent on proper objects will repay the whole expense. . . . Mr. Grayhurst is the person to show or get somebody to show you everything about London[. T]he Brewhouses and Machinery are well worth seeing. There and every town and place endeavour to get some person to introduce you to such places—in the Manufacturing Towns neglect not to see such Manufacturers as that you can get at. The Steam Boats in England or Scotland be particular in seeing and sailing; on some occasions it may be necessary to let know that you are from Canada to strangers; will ease their minds from any fear of you stealing anything from them to their prejudice and when necessary let know that I have built three Steam Boats; two of which are running—that will draw questions from them; your answers will convince them of your knowledge; & at last some of them will be more communicative. . . .

John Molson made his New York visit as Fulton was preparing an unsuccessful demonstration for the U.S. Navy of his "torpedo" (actually a floating mine), along with a cable-cutting invention meant to cleave enemy ships from their moorings. Fulton and Livingston were also in the midst of negotiating an exclusive right to steamship navigation on the Mississippi from the state of Louisiana, which had been created by the massive Louisiana Purchase (which Livingston had helped negotiate) of 1803.

After the successful 1807 trial of his first steamboat on the Hudson, Fulton had predicted to his friend Barlow that the technology "will give a cheap and quick conveyance to the merchants on the Mississippi, Missouri, and other great rivers which are now laying open their treasures to the enterprise of our countrymen." An agreement with Molson for the St. Lawrence would secure him a formidable stranglehold on three major commercial rivers.

Molson was back in Montreal by September 15, and he brought with him a proposal drawn up by Fulton on September 7. Fulton outlined the basic plan for a cooperative venture between himself and Molson for a St. Lawrence steamboat service. If Molson ever

thought he could get out of New York with free advice, the proposal made it clear Fulton believed his expertise had considerable
commercial value.

The proposal illuminates a fundamental reason for Fulton's success on the Hudson, beyond the monopoly finessed by Livingston.
His plan was concerned with commerce, not engineering. Fulton
had carefully crafted (presumably with the input of basic facts from
Molson) a detailed business venture for a St. Lawrence operation—
an exercise Molson probably never conducted before wading in
with the *Accommodation*.

Fulton's plan exposed the inadequacies of Molson's simplistic
bookkeeping, a symptom of his naive approach to business. By the
late 1790s, the brewery was generating so much profit that Molson
had diversified into other ventures without bothering to impose an
accounting system to manage or justify them properly. For every
separate undertaking, such as the steamboat, whiskey and "planks
and boards," Molson kept running tallies of expenditures and revenues within the brewery ledgers, carrying forward the net profit or
loss from one ledger to the next. His bookkeeping methods hadn't
improved much from the scrawled ledgers of the joint account with
Thomas Loid of 1783–84. The ledgers were neater, but they did
nothing but log money spent and money earned on an item-by-item
basis. While it was all meticulously indexed according to business
areas and individual customers, the books were never properly
balanced. There was no attempt to track capital expenditures or
depreciation, no effort to assess inventory. No such thing as a
quantifiable annual statement of profits or losses existed. As with
the lumber business, the steamboat venture simply built up a head
of steam of debits against which Molson recorded revenues, with
the running tallies carried forward ad infinitum. The debits made
no distinction between wages, which were seasonal operating
expenses, and construction costs for the ship, a long-term investment that should have been depreciated over the projected life of
the vessel. It would be left to Molson's sons to bring fiscal order to
the family enterprises.

Compared with Molson's efforts, Fulton's steamboat technology
and business acumen belonged to another age of entrepreneurial

sophistication. He began by determining the frequency of service, based on the length of the passage between Montreal and Quebec, the currents and tides, and the anticipated vessel speed. He concluded it would take thirty hours to descend the river, fifty-four to ascend. Thus a single-boat service could make two round trips a week. "Were a boat established so as to be certain in her operations and commodious to passengers," Fulton advised, "the probability is she would average 50 passengers a trip or 100 a week at 10 dollars each equal for 6 months to 24,000 dollars."

Against this revenue, Fulton calculated a thorough and authoritative list of expenses: crew, provisions, washing of and wear on linen and furniture, fuel, vessel maintenance and depreciation ("to be rebuilt in 10 years"), repairs to boiler and machinery, insurance costs and contingencies. He arrived at a total annual expense of $9,570—"Leaving a profit of 14,430 dollars . . . which is near 60 per cent."

Based on these calculations and the generous profit margin, Fulton proposed to design and oversee the construction of a boat that would run at least $4^3/4$ miles an hour in still water, accommodating fifty to seventy passengers. He would relinquish any patent rights

> which I might as Inventor attain and transfer it to Mr. Molson. Of course I will not encourage opposition or rivalry to him which I might do by a free gift of my invention to any other person; I will use my best endeavors to obtain for him through the British government an exclusive right to Navigate the river St. Lawrence by vessels moved by fire or steam for 15 or 20 years. For which aid and assistance I will take one fourth of the neat profits of the boat or boats which may be built by Mr. Molson or grow out of his establishment.

The shrewd methodology of Fulton's business plan must have been a revelation to a brewer whose own core business plan was based on purchasing barley for a little and selling beer for a lot. And only someone with the hands-on experience of Fulton could have drawn up such an impressive scheme. Indeed, Fulton's only serious rival in experience was the very modest single-ship operation of the Winans brothers on Lake Champlain. For Molson, it was an invaluable blueprint for success. Fulton concluded by requesting that Molson "will please to return an answer to these proposals as soon as possible."

On September 15, as Molson logged his expenses from the New York trip in his primitive accounting ledger, Fulton wrote Boulton & Watt, reporting the success of the North River operation on the Hudson. He announced that "profits have also been such as to induce me to form similar establishments on some of our other rivers. I will therefore esteem it a favour if you will have the goodness to make for me another engine as soon as possible. . . ."

Fulton might have had his new venture on the Mississippi in mind when ordering the engine, but exclusive rights to the river wouldn't be secured from Louisiana until the following April. In light of the proposal made to Molson only days earlier, it is reasonable to suppose that Fulton was getting an engine underway for an anticipated joint venture with the Montreal brewer.

But Molson left the anxious entrepreneur dangling. On October 7, Fulton supplied his brother-in-law with a letter of introduction to present to Molson in Montreal. "On his return," Fulton wrote in it to Molson, "please to let me know your decision on the establishing of the contemplated steam boat."

John Molson replied to Fulton on the nineteenth. "The certainty of precuring [an] exclusive priviledge [on the St. Lawrence] is at present but very faint. I am on eve of my departure for England. I have left the business in the hands of those whom I have the greatest confidence in. I believe [they] are the only Gentlemen who are likely to effect any thing; if any thing is done will advise you."

Rather than formalize a partnership, Molson had brushed off Fulton with a vague promise that the matter was in the hands of "the only Gentlemen" who were in a position to advise him of any agreement—namely, his young sons. But the sons were not inclined to strike a deal with Fulton. The day that Molson wrote Fulton, he left for England aboard the *Everetta,* with no intention of ever forming a partnership with the American. When Samuel Bridge met John Molson on October 2, the brewer's plans for his steamboat venture, in the wake of the *Accommodation*'s failure, were already set. "Mr. Molson intends building a larger Steamboat next year & is going home to get out material—the Power of the present one not being sufficiently extensive particularly in coming up Ye River," Bridge wrote in his diary. "She has several time been more than a week making her voyage from Quebec [City]."[12]

Molson intended to visit Boulton & Watt in Birmingham and order an engine of his own before racing home to get to work on a newer, larger and ultimately profitable steamboat. And while he had indicated to Fulton that the possibility of securing a monopoly on the St. Lawrence was "but very faint," he nonetheless immediately began preparing to secure that very thing. Molson set his attorney, Beaubien, to the task of drawing up a new petition to the provincial legislature, which asked for a fifteen-year monopoly on the St. Lawrence, not on the waters of the entire province as he, Jackson and Bruce had requested the previous February. An advertisement in the *Quebec Gazette* was prepared, announcing Molson's intention, which because of delays did not appear until November 26.

In Molson's defence, Fulton's partnership proposal contained a fatal flaw that a keen-eyed businessman would have noticed. "Of course I will not encourage opposition or rivalry to him which I might do by a free gift of my invention to any other person," Fulton had promised, but the words "by a free gift" would have sounded alarms. They meant that Fulton could still *sell* his technology and expertise to a rival of Molson's without violating their arrangement. In other words, if Fulton failed to secure Molson a monopoly on the river, he could help a competitor start up and still collect twenty-five percent of Molson's profits. And his demand for one-quarter of the profits from any boats "which may be built by Mr. Molson or grow out of his establishment" suggested a perpetual obligation to Fulton. But that does not excuse the fact that in pocketing Fulton's invaluable business plan and his general advice without a penny of compensation, Molson ruthlessly took advantage of the American steamboat pioneer in the fall of 1810.

Chapter 18

My object is to have you fit to live; which, if you are not, I do not desire that you should live at all.

— Lord Chesterfield, letter to his son, December 18, 1747

MOLSON BOARDED THE *Everetta* at Montreal on October 19, 1810, to make his first visit to England in almost twenty-five years.[1] The voyage was potentially as dangerous as his 1782 passage to Quebec had been, as this one too was conducted in wartime. Except for a thirteen-month truce in 1802–3, France and Britain had been at war since 1793. Molson's friend D'Arcy Boulton also attempted an Atlantic crossing in 1810, only to be captured by a French privateer and imprisoned for three years.

Molson had the most perfunctory journey planned: out in the fall of 1810 and back in the spring of 1811, with time enough for visits with what remained of his family in Lincolnshire when business was taken care of. The family enterprises and the task of lobbying for a steam-navigation monopoly on the St. Lawrence had been left largely to the care of twenty-three-year-old John Junior.

The eldest son wrote his father in England on January 6, 1811, with a variety of news, personal and professional. "The business (Thank God) is going on as well as possibly can be expected, and everything is agreeable in the house, my dear Mother wishes you the greatest prosperity in your undertaking, and every success in your voyage. She complains of being very lonesome on acct of your absence.... Thomas is industrious & healthy, William is still at school & I believe he can go the whole season as we will endeavour to do without him, he is growing fast & is nearly as tall as I am."

The application for the monopoly had been delayed in coming before the elected assembly, but John Junior assured his father that "Mr. Sewel promises faithfully to do his best for you and Mr. Papineau the same." These elected members, Stephen Sewell of Huntingdon and Louis Joseph Papineau of Kent, were both from Richelieu County. They agreed with Molson's argument (as expressed in his petition to the legislature) that the steamboat service provided a "utility that will accrue to the public from having such a vehicle for the conveyance of passengers from Quebec to Montreal." The *Quebec Gazette*, in its November 6, 1809, report on the *Accommodation*'s inaugural voyage, had already argued that it would be "a public loss should the proprietors be discouraged in their undertaking." To make this public service possible, Molson was arguing for a fifteen-year monopoly on the river to shield him from further losses, pointing out that he was the sole investor in the scheme since the original partners, Jackson and Bruce, could not afford the red ink.

In return for the monopoly, Molson promised to put the *Accommodation* back in service for 1811 while he built a larger vessel. In fact, the *Accommodation*, which had been laid up for the winter at Île Boucherville, just downriver from the brewery, never returned to service, and was probably cannibalized to build the second boat.

Meanwhile, there was fresh news of Robert Fulton: "Fulton & Livingston intend to build two boats on Lake Champlain, to raise 50,000 dollars by subscription for the purpose," John Junior reported. The rumour never bore fruit: Fulton's ambitions were thwarted by the War of 1812, and the Winans brothers' *Vermont* continued to serve the lake until her sinking in 1815, the same year that Fulton died of a fever.

There was much more news: of improvements to the home on the property next door to the brewery, on the brewery itself and on the barley crop. "I shall now conclude with my most ernest wishes of you having had a safe, speedy & pleasant voyage," John Junior wrote. "Thomas & William join me in their love and affection towards you, & pray for your safe return home to your family."

Father and son were enjoying a kind of generational resonance as John Senior returned to England. John Junior was twenty-three, John Senior's age when his first child was born, and so the elder Molson understood that he was not leaving a boy in charge of the brewery and its associated ventures. It had been a time in his own life when he was isolated in Montreal, far from family and freshly estranged from Thomas Loid and James Gibbins, Sr.

John Junior was now the family's designated heir apparent, the chief beneficiary of his father's retrograde revisions of his last will and testament. Before leaving for England, John Molson had drawn up a new will to replace the one he drafted in June 1797 on what he thought (as he had in 1795) was his deathbed. Much had changed in the thirteen intervening years: the expansion of the business, the maturation of the three boys (Thomas was now nineteen and William seventeen), and the marriage to Sarah Vaughan in 1801.

The 1797 will, which survives only in draft form, was substantially the same as the one created in 1795, which had Sarah Vaughan and the three children sharing equally in the bulk of the estate, including the brewery property. But in 1797 Molson placed limitations on the benefits his common-law spouse would enjoy. Initially he wrote that she should have power, through her own last will and testament, to dispose of her share of the estate after her death "as she may think proper." This would have provided Sarah with a dower, her own inherited property, to do with as she wished.

But this provision was struck out while the will was being dictated to the notary John Gerbrand Beek. One can almost picture the pause in the proceedings as Molson considered advice from an unknown party, perhaps Beek himself. Molson now prescribed that Sarah Vaughan "shall only be entitled to the interest or annual produce of such her share for and during her natural life." The share, then, would never actually be hers, and would pass to the children after her death. Should Molson die before her, she would be left without any property whatsoever and a modest allowance.

The marriage on April 7, 1801, was likely designed to legitimize the three children, as this was the main thrust of the marriage contract John and Sarah signed that afternoon at Molson's house. As noted, unlike English law, the civil law in Lower Canada allowed existing children to be legitimized by their parents' marriage. John and Sarah pledged in the contract that "they are desirous to recognize the mutual affection they have long had for each other by reason whereof and in contemplation of their future marriage they have had issue three Children. . . ." After listing the boys and their dates of birth, the couple stated that they "do hereby legitimate [them] as their lawful Children and Heirs which with all legal and heriditary [sic] rights as fully amply and effectually as if the said three Children had been born in lawful wedlock or after the present intended marriage between the said parties."

But the marriage to Sarah Vaughan exposed John Molson to some worrying consequences. A fundamental principle of marriage law in the province was the concept of "community of property." All "movables"—furniture and the like—became jointly owned, while "immovables" were treated with careful distinction. (Immovables consisted principally of land and buildings, although a barley crop still growing in the field was considered an immovable, while one that had been harvested was a movable.) Any immovables a woman brought to a marriage automatically came under the control of her husband. His was essentially a managerial role, however, as he could not sell these immovables without her consent. (In England, in contrast, the woman's property automatically became the husband's, to do with as he saw fit.) As for the husband, under the law of Lower Canada, all of his immovables, except for those he inherited before the marriage, became communal property.

English common law did prescribe that, unless she was sufficiently provided for by a dower, a widow was to receive at least one-third of her husband's property—half if there were no children. But the common-law prescription for bequest permitted the husband to select which assets he chose to leave his wife. If his estate was worth £18,000, he could leave his wife £6,000 in real estate and reserve

£12,000 in business assets for his eldest son. Under the province's civil code, all immovables were jointly held. The wife owned half of everything; the husband could not decide that after his death she was entitled to a farm but not a brewery. Marriage contracts under English civil law could set property and inheritance terms that overrode traditional provisions for the widow, and this was the regular practice among the Molsons of the eighteenth century. The law of Lower Canada similarly permitted a marriage contract to defeat the community-of-property principle. And so, after stating their intention to legitimize the children, John and Sarah's marriage contract moved promptly to the issue of property and inheritance. Without the contract, the marriage would have been unthinkable for John Molson.

Had Sarah Vaughan refused to sign the 1801 marriage contract, on her wedding she might have been able to make the case that she was entitled to half of all John Molson's properties, including the brewery. Molson presumably would have argued that the brewery qualified as a premarital inheritance, because his equity in it had been converted from Snake Hall and the other bequests from his father. Sarah would have countered that the property was not an inheritance, but rather was the result of ongoing investment on his part, in which case half of John Molson's immovables (which would be valued at £63,550 in 1816) would have been hers, and an annuity based on a return of five percent would have brought her £1,588 15s per annum if he had died at that time.

Instead, under the marriage contract, the new Mrs. Molson waived all matrimonial rights. The contract stated that "there shall be no Communauté or community of property whatsoever either personal or real between the said John Molson and the said Sarah Insleyvaughan his intended wife." In the event that she outlived him, she would receive a slender annuity of £60 and "have two Rooms and one Kitchen furnished to her." But neither this apartment nor its furnishings would be her property. When she died, they would revert to John Molson's estate and be passed on to his heirs.

Any interest in the brewery and in Molson's increasing portfolio of investments was thus denied her. If Sarah had been contributing her labour to the brewery since she met Molson in 1786, it now amounted to nothing. Rather than giving Sarah Vaughan greater security, the 1801 marriage diminished it. She was left with only the promise of a small annuity and no personal property. One hopes the illiterate Ms. Vaughan understood what she was agreeing to.

With his trip to England in the fall of 1810, Molson abandoned any inclination to provide his wife and children with an equitable division of property, as expressed so generously in the 1795 will. He reiterated in the 1810 will that his wife was limited to the £60 annuity, though he now enhanced it with the provision that she could occupy the stone house and the associated property he had purchased from François Desautels. His estate would also be charged with "the expence of putting the same in good & sufficient repair, for the convenient and comfortable accommodation of my said wife." She would receive no more than £300 with which to furnish it. The furnishings (technically movables) would be her only dower, hers to dispose of as she wished; on her death the home would pass to their eldest son, John Junior. This bequest, a slight improvement over what had been promised in the 1801 marriage contract, would be valid only if she agreed not to pursue any further claims on his estate to which rights of marriage or dower would otherwise entitle her.

The severe limitations Molson placed on Sarah's inheritance in the 1797 will, the 1801 marriage contract and the 1810 will might be interpreted as evidence of his deep concern for her past—a still-legal husband named Kingsley/Kinsley, perhaps, who might resurface from northern Vermont after Molson's death and make off with a large part of his estate, to the detriment of his sons. But there was no legal risk of this actually happening. Any previous marriage that had not come to some legitimate end would have made void Sarah's marriage to Molson—and defeated any effort by a stranger to help himself to Molson's estate.

Instead, the marriage contract and evolving wills demonstrated Molson's gradual determination to channel his wealth along a long-standing family path, for the benefit of the eldest male (as his own father's will had done). Having diminished Sarah's entitlements, he also limited Thomas and William Molson, in the 1810 will, to an "annuity or yearly rent charge" of £250 each, payable from the incomes of his properties. And those properties, including the brewery, would become the possession of the eldest son, John Junior.

It was a profound reversal of the 1795 will, marginalizing the (ironically now legitimate) spouse Sarah and championing the old custom of primogeniture that John Molson had appeared to leave behind him in Lincolnshire. He made clear the importance of hierarchy in birth by prescribing, according to traditions of English common law, that if John Junior died before his father, Thomas would step forward to enjoy the majority of the estate, and that if both John Junior and Thomas died, William would then be the prime beneficiary. (He made no inheritance provision in the event of the deaths of all three sons before his own.)

Bequeathing the brewery property to the first-born was probably the most practical solution. The brewery was an enterprise that could not withstand being subdivided into increasingly smaller shares as beneficiaries multiplied over the generations. It made more sense to keep the property under the control of a single individual and hold him to providing his siblings with income from it. But there was no reason, except overt favouritism, for Molson to grant all of his properties to his eldest son. It would be fair to say that, when Molson drew up the 1810 will, the brewery accounted for about half of his net worth; by late 1816 the brewery represented less than one-third of his estate. Yet all of it was going to the eldest son.

Most interesting is a provision regarding the brewery's future that didn't make it from the draft of the final 1810 will. He had instructed that John Junior "shall teach [to his brothers] the whole Knowledge he possesses in the brewing Business to the best of his Skill & Knowledge & give them board Lodging & Washing during the time of their Minority or being under the age of Twenty one years." Molson had also instructed that John Junior take his brothers in as partners in the brewery and any other business in which the family was involved "as soon as one or both of them become of age." The partnership was to last no more than five years, however, during which the younger brothers were to split one-quarter of the brewery profits, instead of receiving the annual stipend. Molson added, near the end of the draft, "'Tis always understood that Thomas & William Molsons take that active & labouring part that they are now a doing." Molson's provisions seemed to anticipate that after the probationary period for the partnership ended, the brothers would reach their own terms in an operating partnership, although the actual underlying property would still belong to John Junior. But in the final will, all mention of John Junior training his brothers in brewing or taking them on as partners was omitted.

In addition to grossly favouring John Junior, the will was a strikingly imperfect document, placing no limitation on John Junior's use of the inherited properties, beyond the fact that he was expected to pay each of his brothers £250 from the revenues every year. A strange perpetuity was imagined, as the individual bequests had been made to each son "and to his heirs and assigns for ever." Implicitly, John Junior (and his heirs and assigns forever) could never dispose of any part of the properties that would prevent the annuities being paid to Thomas and William (and their heirs and assigns forever). It imagined an infinitude of stewardship and profitability, stretching beyond the horizon of conceivable time. John Molson's estate would rest in this surreal stasis for twenty years, until rapidly evolving family dynamics compelled him to invest his will with still more complex provisions.

The will of 1810 mentioned only two other living relatives: John's sister Martha and the widow Ann Elsdale, each of whom was to be left ten guineas to have a mourning ring made in his memory. All his siblings but Martha, who was living with the indomitable William Rayment at Gosberton, were gone. His brother Thomas had died in 1803, leaving behind his widow, Ann, two daughters and a son. Ann Elsdale, who never remarried, was about to turn fifty-four; the two boys, Sammy and Robinson, were now esteemed men, ordained Anglican priests, with families of their own.

The letters from Molson to his relatives had been infrequent and largely guarded over the years of separation, and in those intervening decades had come his potentially acrimonious pursuit of the Stickney Estate, which belonged to Ann Elsdale. The issue, amazingly, was still clinging to life in 1806, when William Rayment, for some reason, wrote an analysis of the tangled affair that gave little hope for resolution in Molson's favour. But Rayment, the old warrior for the trampled rights of Molson orphans, had lost his taste for confrontation. "Blended as the property of Mr. Molson's sister is with that of the Elsdale family," he concluded, "the writer of this requests that his name may not appear in any of the needful proceedings unless it is unavoidable, besides, assertions in prejudice of his intellect may be brought forward to discredit these particulars."

But no proceedings resulted from Rayment's summary of the old issues. We don't know whether Molson approached his old relations, including the widow Elsdale and her children, with joy or trepidation on his 1810–11 visit, but there is no doubt that they welcomed him warmly, even forgivingly.

After Molson left England to return to Montreal in the spring of 1811, Ann Elsdale wrote him a kind and familiar letter. She thanked him for inquiring so anxiously about her health in a letter he wrote before departing. "What a beautiful spring we have had and I often wish you were here to have a stroll with me in the garden," she confessed in the sole surviving expression on her part of any intimacy between them.

The following March, after receiving news that he had returned safely to Canada, the widow penned another gentle letter, full of news from Lincolnshire. "I have heard your name mentioned very little by [any] other family out of my own," she noted, "indeed you know I visit [very] little my pleasures being of a more retired nature & also finding very little friendship out of our own family. Thanks be to God I am most *Happy* in my own family and that you may enjoy the same in full extent & every good this world can give in the sincere wish of your friend A Elsdale." The horrid, promiscuous schemer whom William Rayment had stalked through the Stickney intrigue was nowhere in sight—if indeed she ever existed.

And Molson appears finally to have revealed to his sister Martha the existence of his now legitimate wife and three no-longer-young or illegitimate children. Martha was ecstatic about the news. She wrote him at Surfleet, where he was staying with his cousin Samuel Eldsale, in April 1811, and gushed to her remaining sibling, "I could not suffer you to quit England without writing to wish you a good & prosperous voyage and also to request you would make my best love to my sister[-in-law] & nephews (tho unknown to them)." Only Martha, her life suffused with misfortune, could have written the eccentric best wishes that concluded the letter: "Pray Heaven send that you & they may enjoy a long & happy life without any diminution but if unfortunately a sad reverse should take place may you all meet with as many friends as I have done to comfort assist & alleviate your troubles."

Molson's reunion with his much reduced circle of relatives had been a complete success, and so was his effort to make an end run around Robert Fulton and secure a steamship engine from Boulton & Watt. On February 19, 1811, John Southern, the head of the firm's drawing office at the Birmingham works, wrote James Watt, Jr., who had taken over from his father when the founding partner retired in 1808. Southern was awaiting Watt's return from London, and wrote:

As it is possible from what I learn today from your letter of the 16th that you may get home this evening, I think it right to give you the earliest notice that a Mr. Molson of Montreal in Canada, came here yesterday, recommended by Inglis Ellis & Co. [the successor firm to Phyn, Ellice & Inglis] He wants an engine or two—one for his Brewery, and another for a boat. He is well acquainted with Mr. Fulton & his boats, & with Chancellor Livingston etc. I told him yesterday that I was expecting you, and he came here this morning again in the hopes of seeing you—and determines to wait till tomorrow. He has promised to take his dinner with me today, and if you should return time enough to see him this evening & should be so disposed, you will find him at my house, where I shall be glad to see you.

Whether or not James Watt, Jr., was able to join Southern in entertaining Molson that evening, a strong professional and personal relationship developed between the Molsons and the employees at Boulton & Watt. With his visit to his surviving relatives having also gone so well, Molson returned from England in the spring of 1811 in complete triumph.

Before his visit to England was over, Molson sat for an oil portrait in London. The artist is unknown, but he painted with skill as well as economy. There is a stripped-down severity to the portrait, in part owing to the sitter's opting for an economical rendering. Molson would have minimized the cost by paying essentially for a facial likeness. His clothing was quickly executed as a white cravat and a coat in black silhouette, and the entire background was left as a monochrome wash with an amorphous shadow. Molson's friend William Berczy often created for his colonial subjects elaborate scenarios that expanded on their stature. Had Molson been willing to spend more money, his portrait might have included a fine residential interior with a glimpse through a window of the brewery and the river, with a steamboat defying wind, current and tide.

Molson appears as a merchant of probity and substance, his thinning hair brushed flat, his jaw strong, his cheekbones in rugged relief, his eyes fixed on the viewer in a querying challenge. A smile tugs undeniably at the right corner of his mouth, giving the portrait a warmth that the provincial talents of Berczy could never have conjured. Molson must have charmed the artist. Generally, only women and children smile freely in portraiture of this age, and Berczy would have frozen Molson in the rigor mortis that gripped all his Men of Consequence. (In an inferior copy of the portrait, probably made by Berczy's son William Bent, who was a friend of Thomas Molson, the smile became compressed into an ill-proportioned grimace.)[2] The subtle animation hinted at the good humour that is too easy to lose sight of in the surviving records of John Molson's life, particularly in the manoeuvres surrounding his evolving estate. The smile at least challenges the impression of hard-hearted calculation left by the sadly devolving stature of Sarah Vaughan, even if it does not forgive it.

Like his portrait, Molson seemed somehow unfinished. He had come to enjoy great success in Montreal, but his account books revealed his unsophisticated methods, the product of a too brief education that was forgiven because of the generous returns of his chosen business. He deserved enormous credit for the ambition he displayed in quitting south Lincolnshire for Quebec, and for the skills he learned and applied to making the brewery thrive. His basic intelligence could never be doubted, but he was always working at the limits of his practical knowledge, moving forward on raw entrepreneurial ambition rather than in a calculated pursuit of opportunity.

John Molson was a bridge between the yeomen of south Lincolnshire and the clever and formidably capable entrepreneurs his sons proved to be. The times were partly the cause of the generation gap. When Molson's sons came of age, Montreal and greater Quebec were more established and offered more diverse opportunities, and the world was becoming industrialized. John Senior was one generation removed from a privateer. His son Thomas was one generation away from a sporting Victorian dilettante in a luxury steam-yacht.

This doodle may be the earliest known drawing of a Molson steamboat. The artist (perhaps a child) is unknown; it appears in John Molson's "farm book," whose entries run from 1799 to 1818. It shows a hull with side-mounted paddlewheels, a "cambouse" or deckhouse galley, a funnel with stays, and what may be a boiler on the forward deck. (The Molson Archives/National Archives of Canada)

When John Molson returned from England in 1811, the singular name "Molson" could no longer properly describe the activities centred on the brewery at St. Mary's Current. While Sarah Vaughan's participation has always been inscrutable, by 1810 John Junior was fully involved, with Thomas and William also coming along. The momentum of the enterprise shifted rapidly to the new generation. Although still very much involved, John Molson saw his standing shift from principal to benefactor. His industriousness became the means for his children to succeed, and his authority was rapidly eclipsed without apparent protest. Whether it was because of seniority, initiative or the position of privilege granted him by his father, John Junior would register as the forceful voice of the second Molson generation in Canada in the years following the War of 1812.

While John Junior enjoyed the benefits of a close-knit family and a thriving enterprise, he would not idly take advantage of his circumstances. The eldest Molson son impressed at an early age with his essential sharpness and willingness to drive both himself and those around him to achieve. An entry in the farm book gives a small clue to John Junior's formal education. It notes expenses of £86 7s 9d paid to William Nelson, schoolmaster at Sorel, for "board and schooling for Johnny" from October 20, 1803, to October 20, 1806. For these three years, beginning just after his sixteenth birthday, John Junior had been sent away for what must have been a more advanced education than his father had enjoyed. John Junior was probably fluently bilingual (as his brother William was and his father may have been), and he wrote with far more polish than his father did when he was the same age. The generational difference would become increasingly apparent with the remaining sons. John Senior taught his sons everything he could, and there was so much more to learn. Soon they would be teaching him. John and Sarah had raised a formidable troika of heirs.

Molson was just back in Montreal when John Junior wrote him from Quebec City on July 11, 1811, to welcome him home and inform him that the effort to secure a steamboat monopoly on the St. Lawrence had failed. He had steadfastly monitored the fated bill's progress, expanding his valuable political and bureaucratic contacts in the process. The bill had been passed by the elected assembly 15–4 in February, but it was defeated in the legislative council. Despite presenting petitions again in 1811 and 1813, the Molsons could not secure the monopoly and would have to face direct competition.

When Molson returned from England, he made the final lot purchase, on July 23, from Pierre Desautels, which completed the block of land at St. Mary's Current between Monarque and Voltigeur streets. The Molsons then went to work creating a successor to the *Accommodation*, a much larger vessel called the *Swiftsure*.[3] Her name doubtless was inspired by the seventy-four-gun ship of the line that starred in Nelson's devastation of the French fleet at Aboukir Bay in 1798. A report in the *Montreal Herald* described her as 140 feet overall and 24 feet wide, and praised her machinery as being "superior to any of those established on the Hudson River or Lake Champlain." She offered a total of twenty-two berths for men and eight for women. By the time she made her trial runs in the fall of 1812, Britain and Canada were at war with the United States.

Although war had been in the offing for several years, by the end of 1811 it was approaching inevitability. A British embargo on shipping to French ports had come to enrage the Americans even more than a similar French measure against shipping to British ones. A Republican Congressional majority allied with President James Madison had passed a half-dozen resolutions in November to prepare the union for war against Britain. In June 1812, the opium of Manifest Destiny tipped the decision at the eleventh hour in favour of making Britain the sole official enemy so that Canada could be invaded.

Quebec was considered a priority target; in April 1812, Major General Henry Dearborn had proposed that Montreal be the object of the main thrust of the opening attack by army regulars. Senior commanders like Dearborn were veterans of the American Revolution, and conquering Montreal was seen, as it had been in 1775, as a matter simply of marching. Speaker of the House Henry Clay boasted to Madison that "the militia of Kentucky are alone competent to place Montreal and Upper Canada at your feet."

For many reasons, however, the war largely passed Quebec by. The bill declaring war on June 17, 1812, was supported by only sixty-one percent of legislators, and Quebec's neighbouring New England states, including Vermont, were so indifferent as to be officially neutral. Lieutenant-General Sir George Prevost, who arrived in November 1811 as commander-in-chief of British forces in North America, made the defence of Lower Canada his priority, stationing most of his regulars there to further discourage an opening attack on the province. This, combined with a lack of military resources, forced the Americans into Upper Canada, where the British, with their Indian allies and local volunteer regiments, had a string of early successes. The American post at Mackinac Island (where Lake Michigan empties into Lake Huron) fell on July 17; Detroit made a surprise surrender to Major General Isaac Brock on August 16; and at Queenston Heights an invasion across the Niagara frontier was repelled by Brock on October 13. The action cost Brock his life, and Canada lost a popular officer who had been stationed in the country since 1802—he even appeared in Molson's customer accounts in 1808–9.

The offensive thrust towards Montreal did not come until the fall of 1813. Major General James Wilkinson advanced up the St. Lawrence in what was intended as a pincer movement with Major General Wade Hampton, whose army was based at Plattsburgh, New York, on the western shore of Lake Champlain. The rendezvous and joint assault on Montreal never happened, however. Hampton was repulsed on October 26 in a minor engagement on the banks of the Chateauguay River, some thirty miles southwest of Montreal. Refusing to have anything more to do with Canada, Hampton led his soldiers back across the border after suffering about fifty casualties. Wilkinson's advance was stopped in a more vigorous battle at Crysler's Farm, upriver from Cornwall, on November 11; this skirmish produced about 350 American casualties. The threat to Montreal was over.

The call to arms had sent three of the four Molson men into uniform. Only Thomas, twenty-one at the beginning of the war, was left behind to tend to the home front. As John Senior noted in his farm book, "I joined the 5th Battalion Incorporated Militia the 20th September 1812 went up to Coteau-du-Lac the 9th February 1813 and returned home the 2nd December 1814." Molson began his service as a lieutenant and was promoted to captain on March 25, 1813. William, the youngest, joined the 1st Battalion of Montreal Militia on October 15, 1812, while the oldest, John Junior, served as a cornet—a flag-bearing officer—in the Royal Montreal Cavalry under Captain (and erstwhile machinist) George Platt, and kept the rank until being promoted to lieutenant in the volunteer militia company in 1821.

None of the Molsons was ever called upon to spill American blood, though John Senior came the closest. Stationed at Coteau-du-Lac, forty miles upriver from Montreal, Molson's militia unit would have had to deal with Wilkinson's advancing army had it not been halted at Crysler's Farm. The skirmish at Chateauguay that turned back Hampton's army had occurred on the opposite side of the St. Lawrence, about fifteen miles from John Senior's position. With the invasion threat over, he resigned his commission on November 25 and returned to Montreal a week later. Like many of Montreal's leading anglophone citizens, the Molsons had dutifully turned out for the militia. But in the end, the glory of service belonged to the *habitants* serving with Lieutenant-Colonel Charles de Salaberry's Canadian Voltigeurs, who were largely responsible for halting Wilkinson's tepid advance at Chateauguay. The Molsons' main contribution to the war came from the *Swiftsure*, which was hired by the British Army to move men and supplies from Quebec City to Montreal. Receipts for two seasons of service during the war were almost £22,000, with revenues from troop transport exceeding £9,000.

When hostilities ended, all three Molson sons were in adulthood—William, the youngest, had turned twenty-one on November 5, 1814. In 1815 the family began divvying up its duties. William, who had served as the owner's representative aboard the *Swiftsure* during the war, tended to the brewery, while Thomas embarked on his grand tour, travelling first to New York in December 1815 and then to Britain to stock up on practical knowledge of brewing, steamboats, machinery and whatever else he judged pertinent. John Junior settled in Quebec City to oversee the family's interests there, mainly in the shipping line. A property was purchased from merchant Thomas White in July 1814 to serve as John Junior's home, and this appeared in John Senior's list of assets in December 1816 as "Garden & White's House" with a value of £2,000. John Junior was also operating the *Swiftsure* (in which his father gave him a half-interest), while John Senior oversaw the latest Molson steamboat, the *Malsham*. Her keel had been laid in September 1813, and she was launched the following autumn, entering service at the start of the 1815 season. At 145 feet on the keel and 160 feet overall, according to a report in the *Montreal Herald*, her passenger and freight capacity was one-third greater than that of the *Swiftsure*. The new ship was curiously named for the variant on "Molson" occasionally used by John Senior's great-grandfather, Thomas of Peakhill, in the early eighteenth century.

Through the 1815 and 1816 shipping seasons, John Senior and Junior ran their steamboats on the St. Lawrence. As soon as John Junior was operating in his own independent sphere, he became (or at least behaved like) his father's keeper and taskmaster, writing a stream of letters in which "I hope" was a constant refrain. He cajoled, reminded and outright ordered his father to respond promptly to obligations and opportunities. To cite just a few—on February 19, 1815: "You had better make enquiry into that lot next to Johnson's, and purchase it if you can get it reasonably cheap"; on September 20, 1815: "I hope you have got your money from Government [for the wartime steamboat services]. . . ."; on February 22, 1816: "I am informed that Mr. Pothier has purchased Mrs Campbell's house. I hope that you have seen him respecting it. . . ."; and on February 26, 1816: "I hope you have succeeded in doing something towards procuring a house for the Chief Justice."

One suspects that the ambitious John Junior thought of his father in the way his father had once thought of the attorney Philip Ashley: a good man who was a bit out of step with the times and needed constant prodding to get things done. The diarist and St. Mary's Current neighbour Jedidiah Hubbell Dorwin captured John Senior so memorably in one offhand observation in 1817: ". . . as the gate into the Brewery yard was directly opposite my store I had an opportunity to see him every day standing in the gate way with his wooden shoes or [sabots] on, with his blue cap and gray tunic [hailing] every habitant passing from the country into Town with

Grain for market. . . ." Gone was the sombre merchant dress of the 1810 portrait, and in its place was the unexpected garb of the farmers he greeted from the brewery gate as they headed down St. Mary Street. The eccentricity captured in the portrait helps illustrate the gap between the ambitious John Junior and the *faux-habitant* father who had long ago pronounced himself a "common brewer."

John Senior was approaching fifty-four when Dorwin captured him in full Canadien regalia. He had already outlived his own father by fourteen years. He could luxuriate in the novelty of being old enough to have capable adult children to whom he could begin handing over his many business interests. And the eldest, John Junior, approaching thirty years of age, displayed a complex approach to commerce that can only be described as wheeling and dealing.

The main purpose of the Molson steamboats was passenger service, which was becoming an increasingly important business as immigration to Canada grew substantially in the post-war years, although the amenities offered travellers on the *Malsham*—such as pears, plums and apricots, along with Molson beer—suggests an up-market focus. But John Junior took the smaller *Swiftsure* in entirely new directions. In addition to purchasing goods when it seemed advantageous, he was turning the *Swiftsure* into what amounted to a floating bank.

There were still no banks in the colony, chartered or not. Several attempts to create a proper bank in Montreal were stillborn. Three major North West Company trading firms—Phyn, Ellice & Inglis; Todd, McGill & Company; and Forsyth, Richardson & Company—had proposed creating a local bank, to be called the Canada Banking Company, in 1792. It apparently functioned briefly, as a private bank of deposit and issue in Montreal, with its paper notes authorized by the three firms. But for whatever reason, it died out quickly.[4] In 1808, John Richardson of Forsyth, Richardson & Company made an eloquent case in a petition to the provincial legislature to charter what was to be known as the Bank of Lower Canada, but it never materialized.

The British government had also suspended all shipments of specie to Canada in 1800 as a wartime measure, and the suspension would remain in effect through 1817. With the *Swiftsure* calling on the main settlements of Quebec—in addition to the principal ports of Montreal and Quebec City, the steamboats were stopping at Trois-Rivières and Sorel, among other places, to take on and discharge passengers and goods, refuel and even sell beer—John Junior discovered unprecedented opportunities to deal in bills of exchange at generous profit margins. It was a twist on an old fur trader's scheme, buying bills at great discount in distant outposts and remitting them for a profit once back in civilization. Rather than canoes, the Molsons were employing steamboats. By June 1815 John Junior, John Senior and William were buying and selling bills at considerable volume and value, with John Junior the main player. He was also instructing his father in the financial subtleties. As he wrote him on June 24:

> I have purchased the bills of Exchange and have taken them as Mr. Anderson said you mentioned, viz one of One Thousand, 4 of £300, 8 of 250 and the remainder in a bill of eight hundred and sixty pounds. I have also purchased a bill for William of 110 pounds. The interest of the bills I have not yet received amounting to £480.14.4 I have given Mr. Anderson an order to take it up and get a bill for it. . . . I was extremely happy to find that there was not a single forged bill amongst the whole of those I delivered & I wish yours may turn out the same. . . . The way to calculate the amount of your bills will be to ad 1/11 to the amount [of currency] and that will give you the amount Sterling at $17^1/_2$ per cent discount.

John Junior expanded on his bill dealings in a letter written aboard the *Swiftsure* to his father aboard the *Malsham* on September 20. He revealed that running the steamboats gave them privileged knowledge of supply and demand for funds in the province: "From what I can learn the public opinion is that there will be a premium [on the bills], but let that be as it may, my opinion is for us now to sell[. T]here are a great many who have bills to sell, who by the by have not so good an opportunity of selling as us, as we have a chance of knowing who sends down money to purchase."

These years were among the most exciting and turbulent in the history of the Molsons in Canada. The country's economy withered in the post-war years, just as the Molsons were expanding their enterprises and competition was rising all around them. By December 1816 there were at least three other brewers vying for the Montreal market: Miles Williams, Francis and John Chapman[5] and James Stevenson. The Molsons would confidently weather them all, but the appearance of a direct competitor in the St. Lawrence steamboat trade caused considerable concern.

The government's refusal to award a river monopoly to John Senior had encouraged a formidable competitor. News of the plan to build a steamboat with a fifty-horsepower engine was published in the *Quebec Gazette* on June 30, 1814. The *Car of Commerce* came together over the winter of 1814–15, rising from the ground in what must have been an ominous portent for the Molsons right next door to the brewery, at the shipyard of Hart Logan. A syndicate of thirty investors—most from Montreal, two from Quebec and a Yorkshire merchant[6]—spared little expense in building what was probably a knockoff of Robert Fulton's 175-foot *Car of Neptune*. The *Car of Commerce* ("car" then being synonymous with "chariot") was launched on October 7, 1815, and outclassed anything the Molsons had in size and performance, and probably in amenities as well. In her trials at Montreal that autumn, she must have demonstrated her daunting capabilities. With her fifty-horsepower Boulton & Watt engine, she became the first steam vessel on the river powerful enough to defeat the rapids at St. Mary's Current and call directly at the city of Montreal. Despite the major advances that the Molsons achieved with the *Swiftsure* and the *Malsham*, neither could surmount the rapids, and thus they could proceed no further upriver than the brewery. With the dismantling of the old defensive works completed in 1809, Montreal had turned outward to the river, with Commissioner's Wharf built to greet the traffic. The *Car of Commerce* partners had achieved a major coup in bringing their vessel right to Commissioner's Wharf.

John Senior responded almost immediately to the debut of the *Car of Commerce*. On October 25, 1815, he purchased a waterfront property in Quebec City's lower town, which gave him two wharves and warehouse facilities. He also began developing an ambitious new base of operations for his steamboat activities on the Montreal waterfront. He may have planned initially to lengthen a small wharf at the brewery property, as John Junior wrote him on September 20, "I wish you would inform me who it is that you have employed to get the grant to extend your wharf to [the] deep water mark. I should if possible wait up [on] his Excellency myself respecting it." But the arrival of the *Car of Commerce* demanded bolder plans. The ability of the *Car of Commerce* to steam right past the brewery and tie up on the city's new waterfront was a blow to the Molsons' pride and balance sheet. John Senior would need a substantial city property of his own to compete.

Among those suffering in the post-war economic downturn was Molson's St. Mary's Current neighbour Sir John Johnson, who owned a large waterfront property in the east end of the city, on rue St-Paul between St-Charles and Bonsecours. (Johnson had acquired it in 1796 from Colonel Fleury Deschambault, to whom Molson had sold a home and several lots on rue St-François-Xavier in 1807.) Its main building was a two-storey stone mansion measuring 5,439 "French" square feet, or about 6,350 English square feet. On December 16, 1815, Molson paid £3,500 for the Johnson property and began turning the main building into what he hoped would be the city's finest hotel, adding two wings and a stable, as well as a "canteen," which was probably meant to supply the steamboats.

Molson must have been one of the world's first integrated travel impresarios. To exploit his new hotel properly, he needed to build a wharf for the property that could accommodate a new generation of Molson steamboats powerful enough to overcome St. Mary's Current and deliver upbound passengers to the hotel's front door. But a wharf could not be built without accommodating the province's traditional public right of unencumbered transit along the shore. A vestige of the rapidly fading fur trade economy, the public right extended about 130 feet back from the high-water mark. And so another round of lobbying began in Quebec City, with John Junior monitoring its progress. Molson petitioned for the right to build a wharf 100 feet wide and extending far enough into the river to accommodate a vessel with twelve feet of draft. He promised that it would not interfere with the public shore right.

Fortunately, the petition did not have to come before a vote in the legislature, as the steamboat monopoly petitions had, and a fifty-year lease on the necessary water lot was drawn up on February 16, 1816. But it still required final approval of various committees and the legislative council. John Junior was tiring of keeping tabs on the government from his vantage point in the lower town and concluded they needed a man literally on the inside, within the citadel. The eighth session of the legislature ended on February 26, and the next day John Junior wrote his father, asking "if you see any prospect of getting elected as a member of parliament." In April, John Senior successfully stood for election in the riding of Montreal East (which included St. Mary's Current) for the ninth session, which would open on January 15, 1817. He replaced George Platt (who probably stepped down to make way for Molson), and it's believed Molson ran unopposed.

With the approach of the 1816 shipping season, which would throw the two Molson boats into full competition with the *Car of Commerce*, John Junior was filled with impatience and dread. "I hope you will try and commence on [paddle] boards [for] the Steam Boats, as I am very much afraid we will not have them ready in time," he wrote his father on February 26, referring to an attempt to improve the performance of their now outclassed vessels. "I feel anxious to leave this [monitoring approval of the water lot lease] for that purpose." Still waiting for news of the water lot lease, he confessed to his father on March 7, "I never was more uneasy in my life: doing literally nothing when there is so much work to do. I am like a person waiting for a fair wind to sail."

Meanwhile, Thomas had written his older brother from London, on February 6, as he prepared to travel to Birmingham to visit Boulton & Watt. He was enjoying himself thoroughly while John Junior fought persistent despair. "I am very much delighted with the Country and the women of this Country are very hospitable not like those of Canada," Thomas enthused. "And hope you are well and hearty give my kind love and affection to my Father, Mother and William and hope he has been attentive to business." But John Junior fretted that in Thomas's absence his youngest brother, William, was not up to the job of managing the brewery. "I am afraid William must be at a loss in the malt house, not being used to take charge there," he wrote his father on March 16.

Approval was finally received for the Montreal wharf on April 22. Molson's service to the province during the War of 1812 had stood him in good stead, for the legislative council was moved to grant the lease in part due to "the Zeal displayed by the Petitioner at the commencement of the late war with the United States of America and the benefit which the public service derived from the Introduction of the Steam Boat at that critical period at great Expense and Risk. . . ."

Two weeks later, the *Car of Commerce* made her first call at Quebec City. It quickly became clear that she was indeed a formidable adversary. In addition to her speed and ability to call directly at Montreal, she undercut the Molson ships on both freight and passenger rates. With the *Malsham* the newer and larger of the two Molson vessels, it fell to her—and John Senior—to meet the challenge directly. Cutthroat competition was new to the brewer, and John Junior pleaded with his father on May 16 not to be so obstinate about his pricing. "I hope that you have changed your prices for freight, as it will be giving them a decided advantage over us by not going at the same rate: your expenses are the same whether you go up and down loaded or empty, and your refusing the freight at their rate will make your friends send their goods by them, who never would have attempted it otherwise." John Junior then suggested that his father come to a collusive agreement with the *Car* syndicate on the rates charged for freight and passengers: "You may try and make an arrangement with the [*Car of Commerce*] and raise your passage money again which will make amend for the reduction of the freight. I saw clearly that every 6d you lost by refusing freight at their price was 6d clear profit to them—at their prices you can make more than by your passages. . . ."

Before the war with the *Car of Commerce* could proceed any further, however, John Junior was stunned by news from England: his brother Thomas had married their cousin Martha, youngest child of their late uncle Thomas. The upheaval the wedding brought to the Molsons' lives over the next twenty years would eclipse any terror the *Car of Commerce* summoned among them.

Chapter 19

Money, the cause of much mischief in the world, is the cause of most quarrels between fathers and sons; the former commonly thinking, that they cannot give too little, and the latter, that they cannot have enough; both equally in the wrong.
   —Lord Chesterfield, letter to his son, November 8, 1750

NEXT TO THE MYSTERIOUS ORIGINS of Sarah Vaughan, nothing in the early history of the Molsons in Canada has produced more confused speculation than the marriage of Thomas Molson to his cousin Martha at Gosberton on April 16, 1816. However loving the relationship or happy the occasion, there is no denying that the marriage was a root cause of the disruption and estrangement that plagued the second generation of Canadian Molsons in their relationships with each other and with their father. Little that transpired over the next few decades—even the decision of Thomas's son John Thomas to sail away from his opportunities and responsibilities in 1870—can be understood without being viewed through this lens.

Some of the confusion rests with the opinionated neighbour Jedidiah Hubbell Dorwin, whose observations on the marriages of the three Molson sons survived for posterity. As he recorded in his diary in 1817:

Mr Molson had three sons John[,] Thomas and William, William was the youngest and about my age during the summer. Thomas went to England to get a wife for himself and Brother

John. They were his cousins, as might be expected. Tommy had his choice and chose the best for it . . . from that the arrangement was all made by the father . . . before the young people became acquainted, so when Tommy arrived with his wife and her sister[,] John was dissatisfied, that is so the talk was. But he had no alternative and was married; Tommy's wife proved to be a splendid woman but Johns [not so much] . . . [however] she had children fast enough, to inherit the money, made by the Molsons. The Molson Family in England as well as here were [wealthy] and the intermarriage [was] to keep the money in the family. William married a Miss Badgley.

About the only things unequivocally true in this diary entry were who the Molson sons married: in 1816 Thomas wed Martha Molson and John Junior her older sister, Mary Ann Elizabeth; in 1819 William wed the daughter of Francis Badgley, Elizabeth. Beyond these obvious truths, the Dorwin diary is useful only as a record of the contemporary gossip: that John Senior had arranged the marriages of his two oldest sons to their first cousins "to keep the money in the family." Leaving aside the fact that the English Molsons were far from wealthy, this turned out not to be the case, for keeping the money in the family was the essence of the crisis that unfolded in poor Thomas's life.

While John Senior's neighbours may have imagined him capable of ordering his sons to marry the daughters of his late brother Thomas, his authority was anything but iron-fisted. The letters from John Junior to his father from 1814 to 1816, in which he blithely ordered John Senior around, show that the eldest son, at least, held no stock in any notion of unquestioned paternal authority. That John Senior could have commanded any of his children to marry against his will is inconceivable. John Senior's return to Lincolnshire in 1810 may have left him concerned about the future of his late brother's three children (although we have no evidence of this), but it is stretching credulity to think that he could have left England for Montreal in 1811 having assured his brother's widow that their children would one day wed.[1]

It is also evident from surviving letters that the brief romance between Thomas and Martha sparked a sudden marriage that caught the Molsons back in Quebec completely unawares. Thomas's opinion, given to his older brother on February 6, that "the women of this Country are very hospitable not like those of Canada," was a clue that his heart was destined to be won before the tour was over. He wrote to his brother again from London on February 21, informing him he expected to leave for Lincolnshire the next day "and only make a stay of about two weeks for the first time." It took precisely those two weeks for him to meet and decide to marry Martha. On March 6, Thomas wrote his father to announce the engagement to Martha and to ask for £2,000, "as I might have an insufficiency for all the things I may have to buy."

On May 26, John Junior, aboard the *Malsham,* wrote his father (who was aboard the *Swiftsure*), informing him that he had received a letter from Thomas that

> contains surprising news, viz of his being engaged to Miss Martha Molson, and that he had all matters arranged, that he had just come up to London with her sister Mary to buy furniture, and that he was to be married in about 3 weeks after the date of his letter, which was the 22nd March last: he mentions that he had wrote you a letter on the 6th inst. informing you of his intentions and requesting you would get him a house; that Mary was coming out with him and that he purposed leaving England soon after, via Quebec if there were any vessels to sail at that time. . . .

Thomas was inbound with his Martha's older sister, Mary. Martha was twenty-one in 1816 and Mary twenty-five, noticeably past the normal marrying age. Notwithstanding Dorwin's suggestion that John Junior was left with the lesser choice of spouse, something must have convinced him almost immediately that his cousin was worth marrying. In a letter to his father on July 20, John Junior noted: "While in Quebec [City] I assisted Martha & Mary in shopping to fit up the house" as Thomas and Martha prepared to move to Montreal, where Thomas could assume the primary responsibility for the brewery. John Junior gave no indication that any relationship yet existed between him and his cousin, but he was shortly fitting up his own house in Quebec City with Mary, as they were married on October 12.

The two eldest Molson sons had married just as John Senior prepared to enter into a formal partnership with his children. Perhaps John Junior and Thomas were chafing at their subservient status; now that they were married men and about to begin raising families, they would have demanded proper standing as partners in the multifaceted business that they had helped to flourish. In the agreement notarized on December 14, 1816, the father and his three offspring pledged to operate for seven years as John Molson & Sons. Ownership of properties brought into the operating sphere of the enterprise was retained, which meant that the vast majority of the underlying capital remained with John Senior. It was at this time that he drew up the list of assets which gave his net worth as £63,550—the equivalent of £3.4 million today. The only other partner to contribute any operating assets was John Junior, whose £6,000 represented his half-interest in the *Swiftsure*. John Senior's list of assets suggests that the numerous Upper Canadian and Quebec farm properties listed in the farm book in 1809 (as well as the mortgages and obligations he had held) were now gone, evidently liquidated to fund the steamboat service expansion.

Judging by the list of assets, the partnership's operations incorporated all of John Molson's activities. In addition to the brewery and the steamboats were the Montreal mansion-cum-hotel (which would open for business in January), the waterfront properties in Quebec City and the "Old Coffee House" on rue Capital, along with several miscellaneous properties.[2]

The partnership called for the four men to share equally in profits, and for those holding the fixed assets to be paid an additional return on equity of five percent per annum. For John Senior, this meant an annual bonus of £3,177 10s, a guaranteed income equivalent to about £170,000 today. John Junior would remain in Quebec City to oversee the shipping operations, while William tended to the brewery in Montreal under Thomas, with both of them coming under the ultimate direction of their father.

John Senior appeared to have laid the foundation for an orderly transformation of the family enterprise, but in fact Thomas's marriage to Martha the previous April lurked beneath it like an unexploded bomb. For Thomas, in his breakneck rush to marry his cousin without first consulting his father, had failed to sign a marriage contract.

Of the three Molson sons, Thomas is the most intriguing, and perhaps the most impressive. His art instruction by William Berczy made him a gifted draftsman, and he probably had as much right to be called an engineer as the portrait-miniaturist Robert Fulton ever had. With his facility for machinery and mechanical processes, the steamboats and brewing equipment of his youth would have been intellectually intoxicating. Thomas had a lifelong curiosity about technology—applying it, improving it, profiting from it. Distilling, the experimental pursuit shelved by his father, proved particularly alluring. No Molson son was better suited to the core business of brewing.

In 1841, Thomas Molson became famous for building his own Anglican church, conspicuously named St. Thomas's Church, near the brewery and stubbornly refusing to have it consecrated so that he could control the hiring of the priest.[3] Yet his independent streak had emerged much earlier. He already seemed set apart within the family when war broke out in 1812 as the Molson man not to take up arms (though perhaps it was simply his facility in the malthouse and brewhouse that nominated him as the one to carry on the business while everyone else prepared to oppose an American invasion). Largely isolated from his father and brothers at the brewery during the war years, the twenty-four-year-old seized on the trip overseas in 1815–16 to gain still greater freedom from the family. After the false start in New York, which drew his father's disapproval, once in Britain he was almost ravenous in his consumption of mechanical intelligence—and more eccentric knowledge, for as he wrote his brother John on February 6 from London,

"I saw Mr. Charles Loedel this evening and went to the dissecting room in Guys Hospital with him and saw the operations on the several dead bodies performed there and after that had the pleasure to take Tea with him. . . ."

Despite his second-class status in his father's will, Thomas had enjoyed special treatment from John Senior: first, he was granted what appears to have been the particular responsibility for the brewery during the war, and then he was allowed the unique opportunity to wander Britain in self-determined education—for neither John Junior nor William seem to have enjoyed this privilege. It's not certain, however, that Thomas was sent to England on merit alone. The war years could have frustrated similar plans for John Junior, and the pressing business of the steamboats would have discouraged him from making the journey in 1815–16, as he would not have been able to return in time for the opening of the 1816 shipping season in early May. And so the trip to England may have fallen to Thomas as much through expediency as through any favouritism by his father. Nonetheless, the privileges and responsibilities given to Thomas demonstrate that John Senior's estate is an imperfect device for divining the individual regard John Senior held for his sons. He plainly considered Thomas to be vital to the future prosperity of the family's collective enterprises, as his instructions on the knowledge to be gained on the trip covered every possible facet of their activities. Yet John Senior probably did not anticipate that the knowledge Thomas gained would extend far beyond steamships and brewing. Thomas quickly reasoned that in addition to producing commendable steam engines, England produced commendable wives.

Thomas's hurried decision to marry his cousin Martha suggests a determination not to return home as he had left: a second-born son whose future was fundamentally in the hands of his father and eventually his older brother. Marriage would not change the situation (at least for the better), but it made Thomas a first among siblings in finding a wife. It must have gnawed at Thomas's pride to know (as he surely must have known) that the brewery in which he toiled with such facility was destined to belong to John Junior, who was living 160 miles downriver, at Quebec City, and was busy with steamboats and speculating in bills of exchange. A resignation to the hard facts of his father's estate, as much as ignorance of the importance of what amounted to a prenuptial agreement, could have led Thomas to marry without a contract.

The marriage to his cousin Martha was a clarion call of his independence. And nothing better illustrates the fact that the marriage was not arranged by John Senior than the lack of a contract. But as a gesture of defiance, the wedding was a grave miscalculation by Thomas. John Senior had repeatedly revised his will since 1785, and there was no reason to suspect that he would not do so again once the responsibilities of his sons were fully determined. Thomas and William, after all, were still under age when the 1810 will was written; now, with the war behind them and the sons old enough to become business partners, John Senior could revisit the will with more detailed—and more equitable—terms. But Thomas's marriage paralyzed the estate. In the absence of a marriage contract, the civil code of the province dictated that half of any interest Thomas was given in the brewery was automatically the property of Martha; and in her own will, she could leave her share to whomever she pleased. This threatened John Senior's ambitions to keep the enterprise he had so painstakingly built within the control of his direct descendants. Thomas presented the worst possible scenario for his father. While being the son best suited to carry on the brewing business, he was also the son who could ultimately cause the family to lose outright control of it.

While Thomas's failure to secure a marriage contract must have caused his father concern, it did not interfere with the creation of the new family business partnership in December 1816. No family assets were at risk at this point, because all of the capital involved belonged to either John Senior or Junior and, under the 1810 will, everything was destined to belong to John Junior, who was careful enough to secure a marriage contract for his union with Mary. The father and three sons carried on with the duties of their partnership, but as time passed, the parallel partnership between Thomas and Martha threatened to undermine John Senior's aspirations for all involved.

After the partnership agreement was struck with his sons, John Senior dashed to England to visit family in Lincolnshire and call on Boulton & Watt in Birmingham—a trip that caused him to miss his first session of the legislature as an elected member for Montreal East. Molson was arranging to inspect and take delivery of a sixty-horsepower engine for their new steamboat, the *Lady Sherbrooke*. But after an initial visit to Boulton & Watt, he retreated to Lincolnshire, leaving the engine firm to await his return with increasing mystification.

"Mr. Molson is in Lincolnshire but [is] expected back daily," James Watt, Jr., informed William Creighton of the firm's drawing office, on April 1 from London. Watt was expecting to meet with Molson in London and travel to Birmingham with him, but on April 9, Watt informed Creighton, "I have seen nothing of Mr. Molson, who I believe is still in Lincolnshire." At last, on May 1, Watt informed Creighton: "Mr. Molson has at length made his appearance in town, and we shall come down together. . . . I hope his Engine will be completely ready for his inspection and for packing."

We do not know what delayed John Molson for a month in Lincolnshire. He left no clues of his own, but we can envision him making a persistent, ultimately fruitless, effort to somehow reverse Thomas's misstep in marrying Martha without a contract. He might have called on his late brother's widow, Ann Atkinson, hoping to broker a satisfactory ante-nuptial agreement. If he tried to do so, he returned home empty-handed. The damage Thomas had done to his own inheritance prospects could not be undone. The issue of bequest was like a great rock in the river on which Thomas's future had run hard aground.

After a season of head-to-head competition between the *Malsham* and the *Car of Commerce* in 1816, the respective owners acted on John Junior's suggestion, voiced to his father back in May 1816, that they come to an agreement on fares. In 1817, the two vessels began to appear in joint advertisements, but they did not create a monopoly. Another steamboat, the *Caledonia*, owned by a partnership led by the Montreal shipbuilder David Munn, was launched on August 26, 1817. The Molsons had already prepared to counter her with their most splendid vessel yet, the 170-foot *Lady Sherbrooke*, which was launched on July 30 and named for the wife of the governor general.

The *Lady Sherbrooke* had performed as hoped, both as a flagship of the Molson fleet and as a short-term stop-gap for the *Swiftsure*, which after only five seasons had deteriorated badly. Built with pine planks on oak frames, rot had set in. Her engine was salvaged for the replacement vessel, known as the *New Swiftsure*, which was built in the Logan shipyard over the winter of 1817–18.

The Molsons' St. Mary's neighbour, Jedidiah Dorwin, fondly described the *Lady Sherbrooke* in his diary, noting that she was the largest steamboat on the river. She was equipped with "one very large and tall mast which was used in a fair wind, and was a great help in [propelling] her[,] particular on leaving Quebec against an ebb tide." Dorwin wrote that the ship set a long-standing record for the fastest passage from Montreal to Quebec City, covering the 180 miles in only sixteen hours—an incredible improvement over the sixty-six hours required by the *Accommodation* on her maiden run. Her captain, a former Royal Navy officer, was famous for serving "John Bull"–style dinners on the passage—"Roast Beef and plumb pudding which make an English man [lick] his chops even [at] the sight of the dinner table. The *Lady Sherbrooke* was always a popular boat."

In the midst of heightened competition and the *Lady Sherbrooke*'s success came a traumatic incident off the water. The Molsons employed a clerk named John Bruce (not to be confused with the boatbuilder of the same name). According to Dorwin, the forty-year-old Bruce was "a very unassuming person, who used to come into my store of an evening after the days business was over and smoke his pipe, he appeared very happy and cheerful." On the morning of August 22, 1817, however, Dorwin was summoned by John Molson, who "wished me to go down to his office[. W]hen he took me into a small sideroom off the office . . . who did I see [but] Mr Bruce lying on the bed dead, with his throught [*sic*] cut from ear to ear and the rasor lying by his side[. A] coroner[']s inquest was held[,] JM Mondelet was the coroner[.] But [while] not anything was elicited to ascertain the cause of the rash act it was quite evident death was caused by his own hand. This was a sad affair. . . ."

Today, a man with his throat so brutally slit would immediately raise suspicions of homicide. Yet in Montreal in 1817, it was accepted that this was a suicide. John Bruce was buried the next day in Montreal; John Molson placed a notice in the *Montreal Herald* on September 27 in an effort to collect on and settle any debts Bruce might have had.

The 1818 season saw two more competitors appear, as a partnership comprising six Montreal and Quebec City investors launched the *Telegraph* and another syndicate launched the *Quebec*. With the *New Swiftsure* launched on July 11, the trade would have been even more overcrowded had not a surge in winter water levels forced the *Lady Sherbrooke* high onto land and removed her from service for the season.

Nevertheless, competition turned vicious. At the beginning of the season, according to a report in the *Quebec Mercury* of June 2, an unidentified saboteur of the *Quebec* "maliciously stuffed a piece of çanvas into one of the water pipes of the Engine, which caused the water to run in to the hold of the Boat, and damaged part of the cargo."[4] The *Car of Commerce* was accused later that season of deliberately ramming the *Quebec* in a serious collision.

At the same time, the Molsons' Mansion House Hotel had become the hub of the city's social scene, providing accommodations to all manner of dignitaries, including the governor general. It also hosted sumptuous dinners of the Beaver Club, the gathering of old fur traders (many of them now respectfully diversified merchants) whose membership depended on their having overwintered at least once at the North West Company's post at the head of Lake Superior.

The good cheer was sullied by the complicity of the North West Company in the massacre of twenty-two members of Lord Selkirk's Red River settlement (including Governor Robert Semple) at Seven Oaks in 1816. The repercussions of the atrocity led to the absorption of the North West partners by the Hudson's Bay Company in 1821. The Mansion House reigned unchallenged as Montreal's hotel of choice until a candle carried by a musician along a dark corridor accidentally started a fire that burned the building to the ground in March 1821, killing the headwaiter. Fifteen thousand pounds in insurance money helped abate the loss of the building, and another hotel, initially known as the New Mansion House, rose in its stead.

With the dawning of the 1820s, the seven-year term of the family partnership neared its conclusion. As the date approached, crucial changes in the business provoked corresponding changes in the activities of individual family members. The difficult competitive environment of the St. Lawrence steamboat trade set the realignments in motion. The Molsons' *Lady Sherbrooke* and the *Quebec* were engaged in a bitter public rivalry, and to make the *New Swiftsure* more competitive, her old engine was replaced by new twin engines from Boulton & Watt. The opening of the 1821 season saw all eight of the competitive steamboats race each other to Quebec City, producing debilitating collisions (including one between the *Malsham* and the *Lady Sherbrooke*) along the way. Passenger and freight rates were being pressed to unappetizing lows, and the taste for brawling competition rapidly faded.

In the spring of 1822, the St. Lawrence steamboat trade declared a collective truce. The initiator is not known, but the owners of the *Caledonia* were the first to blink. Already on February 28, 1821, her owners had advertised her sale at auction in the *Montreal Herald*, but without an acceptable bid they were forced to operate the vessel in the raucous 1821 season. On March 27, 1822, John Brown offered the *Caledonia* on behalf of his fellow owners to the Molsons on a three-year lease for £500 or in an outright sale for £3,500. The Molsons agreed to a one-year lease at £225, then on April 27 struck a merger agreement with the parties behind the *Quebec* and the *Car of Commerce*—John Caldwell (son of Henry Caldwell), John Davidson, Noah Freer, John Goudie and James McDouall, who were known as the Quebec Proprietors. Their new joint-stock company was called the St. Lawrence Steamboat Company, and two weeks after its formation, the *Caledonia* was purchased outright by Freer, Goudie and McDouall and brought into the venture as well. The final holdout, the *Telegraph*, was purchased by the company in June. Because the Molsons owned the majority of the assessed capital value of the company's ships, they held twenty-six of forty-four shares (after the *Telegraph* purchase), with each share valued at £1,000, and assumed responsibility for managing the steamboat line.

News spread quickly of the Molsons' successful acquisition of control of the steamboat service along the Montreal–Quebec City run. On July 22, John Molson & Sons was offered all fifty shares in the Lake Champlain Steamboat Company, which had exclusive rights to the lake until 1838. The sale offer noted that the company owned the steamboats *Phoenix* and *Congress*, seven good sloops, a large stone house and a wharf at Vergennes, as well as workshops and tools. John Senior held twenty shares in the Lake Champlain steamboat *Varennes* at his death, and it's possible he took a position in the Lake Champlain company.

By the summer of 1822, John Senior was in a position to retire gracefully from business life. The worst phase of the steamboat war on the St. Lawrence was over, and he appeared to have won. While a new rival stock venture, the Montreal Tow Boat Company, was formed at the end of the shipping season, the Molsons did not greet the news with outright alarm. The *Hercules*, equipped with a one-hundred-horsepower engine, was probably the most powerful vessel of its kind in North America when launched in 1823. While the St. Lawrence Steamboat Company would launch its own tow boats (among them the *John Molson*) to compete directly with the *Hercules*, the Molsons were gracious enough to offer their hotel for a celebratory feast (featuring a 125-pound turtle from British Guiana) in honour of the *Hercules*' launch.

The brewery meanwhile continued to dominate its market, and Thomas was exploring further opportunities in the distilling trade. John Molson was about to turn fifty-nine, and had purchased a farm on Île Ste-Marguerite in the Boucherville seigneury, just downstream from the brewery, where he could indulge himself as a gentleman farmer in agricultural experiments. He had withdrawn from political life. Despite missing the 1817 session of the legislature, he had become an active member, championing the construction of a public hospital in Montreal and advancing the cause of new canal construction at Lachine, among other initiatives. But he had decided not to stand for re-election in 1820.

The other family members had also been in motion over the past few years. On his marriage to Elizabeth Badgley in 1819, William had settled in Quebec City while John Junior returned to Montreal. But with the formation of the St. Lawrence Steamboat Company in 1822, John Junior had returned to Quebec City to work with William. This left Thomas alone in Montreal in charge of the brewery, where he had been acting as his own brewmaster since returning from his trip to England in 1816.

Thomas had long been the driving force at the brewery. According to Denison, he increased production to 100,000 gallons in his very first season, but at that point he had already begun gathering the knowledge to expand the brewery, once again, into distilled spirits. During his 1815–16 fact-finding mission to Britain, he had visited the distillery of George Hunter in Glasgow, taking notes and making drawings. A copper still that John Senior had purchased during his 1810–11 trip must have been the same one as the "still and worm" that appeared in the 1816 list of assets. John Senior had hired a Birmingham engineer named John Bennet to come to Montreal and install his first Boulton & Watt engines in the brewhouse and the *Swiftsure,* and the employment contract had also called upon him to operate the still if Molson so desired. But the still apparently sat unused. No later than October 1821, Thomas dusted off the still and began experimenting with the production of distilled spirits. In late November he sent "2 Puncheons [115 gallons each] of High Wines or Spirits of Whiskey" via the *Lady Sherbrooke* to his brother William at Quebec City, to forward to "Grayhurst & Hewatt" in London. Exports via William continued in 1822, and Thomas became so immersed in the new experimental art of whiskey production that in September 1822 an Upper Canadian brewmaster named Thomas Purcell had to be hired.

In 1823, the family partnership began to crumble as the expiry date approached, and Thomas was the one who brought it all down. His determination to diversify into distilling may have been a serious issue with his brothers, particularly John Junior. The returns had been disappointing, and Thomas's energies had been disconcertingly diverted from brewing. John Junior had an implicit veto as the partnership came up for renewal; everything was going to be left to him by their father, and he would not tolerate any divergence from the basic business plan that could deteriorate the value of the underlying assets. But having returned to Quebec City in 1822 to run the steamboat company with William, John Junior was completely removed from the day-to-day affairs of the brewery, which had fallen to Thomas. And by 1823, Thomas clearly was unhappy with his position, not only within the partnership but within his father's estate.

That spring, he and Martha and their son, Thomas, travelled to England. The family was back in Montreal on October 20, but in November, Thomas returned alone to England. The partnership was about to expire, and Thomas had not found a satisfactory role in the one that would succeed it.

During the summer visit, Thomas and Martha had decided to sell some copyhold land in Lincolnshire that she had inherited, but his return to England in November signalled a potential reversal: rather than cutting all ties with the mother country, Thomas was seriously considering relocating there with his young family.

Relations between Thomas and John Junior could not have been venal, as Thomas granted his older brother power of attorney on November 6, 1823, to tend to his affairs while he returned to England. The main source of friction was John Senior, who could not bring himself to promise Thomas any equity in the Molson brewery in the face of Martha's property rights.

On January 4, 1824, John Senior wrote his son in London a painful letter, which for three pages veered between mundane news from home—the amount of snow ("It keeps Snowing almost every day—have upwards of three feet in the Woods"), militia activities ("John's time is a great deal taken up in his drilling &

drilling his Troop") and the death of two horses at the farm on Île Boucherville—and the serious rift between them. The letter's circuitous contents indicate that Thomas had returned alone to England to consider establishing a business there. Thomas evidently was convinced that John Junior held an advantage over him in the family partnership that was based on outright preferential treatment by their father.

But Thomas's dilemma was not a matter of John Senior loving or respecting one son more than the other. It lay entirely in Thomas's failure, almost nine years earlier, to secure a marriage contract. In a family business, no one party could be indifferent to the issue of bequest: there was a collective responsibility to steer the underlying assets down the desired path of descent. With his impulsive marriage, Thomas had, if only unwittingly, endangered his father's plans. And Martha's first will, written in 1819, gave palpable dimension to John Senior's fears of losing the brewery to relations who were distant both geographically and in the family tree, and who had made no contribution to the prosperity they would enjoy.

Martha stated her understanding that provincial law gave her real and personal property, which "I may have a right to dispose by will." Martha then left the use and enjoyment of that property to her husband, Thomas, "for and during the term of his natural life," should he outlive her. If any of their children survived Thomas, all of her estate would then be shared equally among them. However, if no children survived Martha and Thomas, half of her estate would go to her sister, Mary, John Junior's wife, and her heirs forever, and the other half to the children, John and Mary Ann, of her brother, Thomas.

This created the scenario John Senior feared: that any portion of the brewery property left to Thomas would have to be shared with his spouse, and that through her own will a share of that property could pass out of the direct line of descent by going to her brother Thomas's two children.

On March 24, 1823, as she prepared for the trip to England with Thomas and their son, Martha drew up a more complex will whose provisions hinged on whether or not Thomas remarried if he outlived her. If he remained single, her share of the joint property (the "communauté") would be his to use and enjoy until his death, after which it was to be divided equally among any surviving children. But if Thomas remarried, her share of the communauté would be placed in trust to fund the "education and maintenance" of the children, who would then receive their equal shares when they turned twenty-one. If no children survived to adulthood, Martha's estate would be divided, as prescribed in the 1819 will, between the children of her sister and her brother.

The situation—in John Senior's eyes—was no better than in 1819. There was a chance that a substantial portion of the brewery could end up in the hands of Martha's English niece and nephew. And Thomas's 1823 will, drawn up jointly with Martha's, also agreed to divide his share of the communauté properties between the children of John Junior and those of his brother-in-law, Thomas, should none of his own children reach adulthood.

Martha was determined that her brother's children would benefit in some way from the Canadian Molson fortune if no children of her own survived—which was a real possibility. None of the first three children born to Martha and Thomas in Montreal, including the boy named Thomas, reached adulthood.

The only possible recourse for Thomas was to convince his wife to draw up a will that left everything to which she was entitled to his absolute ownership. John Senior had consulted with James Stuart, an eminent attorney, sometime politician and advocate of pro-mercantile political reforms. Stuart had travelled to England in 1822 as an agent of Montreal's merchant elite to advocate the union of the provinces. While there, he was named Lower Canada's new attorney-general. As John Senior advised Thomas in the January 4 letter, "James Stuart observed yesterday that by Martha's making her will in your favour would do away all the danger." But not only would Martha never agree to this, John Senior would not accept it as adequate protection. He reported to Thomas that he told Stuart: "I was fully aware of that but, [the fact is] that wills could be altered or destroyed every day—and that nothing human was perfectly certain—but of that judge for yourself."

John Senior was correct. Even if Martha had agreed to create such a will, there was nothing to prevent her from insisting on writing a new will with an entirely different set of provisions at some future date. And if she outlived Thomas, she could write another will then as well, leaving everything to her family back in England if she saw fit.

John Senior saw no way around the problem created by the lack of a marriage contract. He could not bring himself to leave his second-born son anything that represented capital in the family business. John Senior was reduced to arguing that his son should reconsider relocating to England, and he held out some hope that Thomas might agree to rejoin his father and brothers in a renewed partnership. He counselled, "If you have not made the intended purchase I should recommend you not to do it; I think there cannot be any danger of [John Junior] gaining any advantage of your residence in this country—Tom [Junior] being a fine Boy and Martha in the family way. . . ." He advised him that "Our Partnership is not not [sic] drawn out . . . it is not issued yet." In Thomas's absence, the brewmaster Purcell had been let go, and John Junior had "fancied he could manage the Brewhouse by himself. I told him not, have had William near a fortnight."

Even if Thomas did not agree to participate in the new partnership, his father dearly wished him back in Canada. "Our friends think it wrong that we should have separated," he volunteered, and he suspected that Martha was partly to blame for Thomas's plans to move to England.

> Now should you not purchase what you intended you have only consider whether you would reside at Quebec, Montreal, or Upper Canada & make your arrangements accordingly. Martha & Me have never spoke of your future Views, nor her wishes. A certain respect to her wishes may be proper—but I think there can not be the least doubt but that you will do better in Canada than in England—but that matter I leave to yourself. Your Mother finds it hard your separation from Her—but that is natural.

John Senior signed the letter as "your friend and father." It was a heroic and heartfelt effort, waged against his own intractability, to prevent what amounted to the loss of his second son. Had Thomas not chosen to return to Canada in 1824, John Senior might never have seen him again.

But he did return, either because his father's words had touched him or because he had concluded, as John Senior said, that England did not present nearly the opportunities Canada did. Still, Thomas refused to rejoin his father and brothers in the partnership, which was renewed and carried on as John Molson & Sons. All that remained was for him to decide where in Canada he would strike out on his own.

It has become a given that Thomas decided to leave Lower Canada specifically to escape the joint-property provisions of its civil code. But there's no evidence this motivated him in any way. Joint property was an issue only for John Senior. His refusal to alter his will to grant Thomas any business property drove his son out of the family partnership—but it did not necessarily drive him out of Lower Canada. Thomas had to find a place to establish his own business, and, as John Senior noted, that could be Montreal, Quebec City or somewhere in Upper Canada. John Senior did not imagine him having to leave Lower Canada.

The fact remained for Thomas that without a marriage contract, he could run, but not hide, from his obligations to Martha (if such evasion ever even occurred to him). Whether he relocated in England or Upper Canada, he would be subject to English common law. And under its terms, a wife, unless adequately provided for with a dower, was entitled to one-third of her husband's property upon his death—half if there were no children. While he might enjoy far more control over the distribution of his assets under English common law, he would still be required to leave a substantial portion of his property to his wife. A marriage contract could override this, but of course Thomas didn't have one. There was no safe haven for Thomas if he had some notion of directing his estate to his surviving children and leaving his wife with little or no real property if she outlived him—as his father had done in his marriage contract with Sarah Vaughan.

Thomas chose where to resettle on the basis of where the greatest opportunity lay. There was probably far too much brewing and distilling activity in Montreal and Quebec City for him to risk a venture of his own, and he would not have relished going into direct competition with his own family. And so he looked two hundred miles upriver, into Upper Canada, and chose Kingston.

The military and freight-forwarding outpost at the eastern end of Lake Ontario was a far cry from Montreal, which was aspiring to metropolitan status just as Thomas left it. In 1824, John Senior and Junior and other investors built the Theatre Royal opposite the Mansion House Hotel, to bring the performing arts to a city no longer defined by the fur trade. The merger between the North West and Hudson's Bay companies in 1821 had removed the trade entirely from the city, as only the northerly access route through Hudson Bay (of the latter company) was retained. Montreal was becoming increasingly industrialized; several foundries had been established since 1816, spurred by the construction of steamboats and engines not only for the lower St. Lawrence but for the Ottawa River and the upper St. Lawrence.

Kingston, meanwhile, had become the advance post of the commercial hum of Montreal, and the introduction of steamboat service had made the journey from Montreal, formerly left to stages negotiating bad bush roads, far less arduous. In 1822 the steamer *Dalhousie* began running twice-weekly between Kingston and Prescott, a distance of about sixty miles. In 1823 the *Cornwall* was introduced into service on Lake St. Francis, between Cornwall and Coteau Landing. This reduced overland travel to a rapids-riven gap of about thirty-five miles between the two steamer services.

The Kingston beer market was far from unserviced. The beverage had been produced in Kingston since the 1790s at a local brewery founded by the merchant and trader Joseph Forsyth. In 1826, the city's original brewery would be acquired by Philip Wenz and operated with his nephew Jacob Bajus. A man named James Bird was also advertising beer locally in 1824. And in 1819, Thomas Dalton had established both a brewery and a distillery in the town.[5]

Unperturbed by all this competition, Thomas Molson purchased a two-acre waterfront lot from Captain Henry Murney on July 5,

1824. An advertisement he placed in the *Upper Canada Chronicle* on November 12, 1824, notified farmers of his desire to purchase barley, charcoal, hops and a variety of building materials for "the Brewery lately occupied by Capt. Murney," which suggests that some sort of brewing operation already occupied the site. However, Thomas imported all the necessary brewing equipment from England, having purchased it on his last visit.

On April 14, 1787, Thomas's father had lectured Philip Ashley that "for a Father to wish a Son to keep anything of the kind contrary to his real interests is altogether repugnant to the duty of a Father to a Son—whatever I have said is barely to convince Mr. Ashley I have a will of *my own*." How much John Molson's circumstances had changed. As a young man new to Canada, he had fought the idea that he should be obliged to keep intact the generous estate his late father had left him. His own son Thomas, whose independent will was unquestionable, did not have to worry about making the same argument to anyone. John Senior had resolved not to leave him any of his own property, because he could never be certain from beyond the grave who ultimately owned it— whether it had been kept intact or divided among far-flung relatives and liquidated by them, as he had done with Snake Hall, in the name of some other pursuit. The duty of a father to a son had been obviated by the unfulfilled duty of a son to a father. The family's precious assets had not been protected by Thomas. John Molson was resigned to watch as the son born to brew, yet not to inherit, moved into the hinterlands that had intrigued Molson as a newcomer to the continent in 1782. So began the first great self-imposed exile among the Molsons of Canada.

Chapter 20

*In my mind it is only the strength of our passions, and the weakness
of our reason, that makes us so fond of life; but when the former
subside and give way to the latter, we grow weary of being and
willing to withdraw. . . . I may now walk off quietly, neither
missing nor being missed.*

 —Lord Chesterfield, letter to Solomon Dayrolles,
 February 28, 1757[1]

ON THE NIGHT OF January 10, 1836, John Molson lay alone in a
narrow bed in a small room at his farm on Île-Ste-Marguerite. The
full moon on January 4 would have set aglow the nightscape of
snow-smothered fields and river ice, which held captive the family's steamboats until spring breakup. For the past week the moon's
brilliance had been waning, each day giving way to a deeper night.
By the next evening, the moon would be in its final quarter. Molson
would not be alive to see it.

Back in Lincolnshire, the Soak rose and fell with the lunar tides,
the ocean pressing up through the soil in a persistent reminder of
the reclaimed Fen Lands' heritage as a saltwater marsh. Like the
Soak, the issues of heredity, kinship and bequest had proven to be
a persistent, repetitious upwelling in Molson's life. They were
inescapable, and in that lonely farmhouse bed Molson felt them
press up from beneath the frozen ground in the dead of night to cool
his veins and alarm his heart.

He was dying, and he knew it. He was seventy-two years old;
who knows what fatal condition or contagion had isolated him in

these cramped quarters. He had been sure he was about to die before, in 1795 and 1797, but this time his premonition was correct. Once again, the urge to set his estate to rights gripped him. After years of carefully managing his properties and interests, of resolving how best to provide for his descendants, he could not take leave of the world with a collected calm. On his last day on earth, his estate propelled him into action. Around midnight, as the calendar turned to January 11, he sent for the notary Henry Griffin.

His wife, Sarah Vaughan, had been dead for almost seven years; his sons were nowhere near him at this moment. Waiting for Griffin's arrival, Molson must have feared being unable to create a new will as much as he feared dying. For if he could not hold on long enough to dictate fresh terms of bequest, he would fail his son Thomas and leave the brewery's future in disarray. There was a promise he intended to keep, even if it was literally the last thing he would do.

For ten years following his departure from the family business in 1824, Thomas Molson had carried on in exile in Kingston, brewing and distilling. His first two children, John and Sarah Anne, had died in infancy in Montreal. Young Tom, whom John Molson so admired in the letter to his son Thomas in January 1824, would die at age twelve in 1833. As the letter noted, Martha was "in the family way" in 1824, and a daughter, christened Martha Ann, was born that year. She was the first of seven children to reach adulthood.

With steamboats having greatly improved travel along the upper St. Lawrence, the Thomas Molsons would not have been isolated from friends and family back in Montreal. The business ties with Thomas's father and brothers may have been severed, but presumably the social ones were not, and Martha would have welcomed visits with her sister, Mary, John Junior's wife.

It took only a few years for the solidarity of the family business to crumble further, more through distraction than any animosity. Its members' interests were diversifying beyond the brewery, and all of them became enchanted with banking, as legitimately chartered institutions made obsolete their speculating in bills of exchange from the decks of the steamboats.

After the War of 1812, pressure quickly mounted for Quebec to acquire the trappings of a modern commercial state, among which was a proper bank. John Richardson, who had unsuccessfully made the case for a bank charter in 1808, again was a prime mover, and this time the legislators listened. In 1818 a bill was passed granting a charter to the Bank of Montreal, for which stock had first been offered in 1817. None of the Molsons was involved at this stage, but as a member of the legislative assembly, John Senior had taken a positive interest in issuing its charter, and he also moved quickly to profit from the new venture. On October 10, 1817, he proposed to the founders that he build them their headquarters on a piece of land he owned in Montreal, leasing the property to them for twenty-one years, at a rate of eight percent of the capital value for the first year, six percent thereafter. Molson was unanimously rebuffed by the board of directors.[2]

A number of leading commercial figures known to the Molsons were involved in the bank. John Gray, through whom Molson had acquired land and financing opportunities in Upper Canada in the first decade of the century, served as the first president from 1817 to 1820, and the board of directors included George Platt, the machinist who produced the *Accommodation*'s engine. But the Molsons remained conspicuously aloof. Perhaps (as Denison suggested in *A History of the Bank of Montreal*) they initially remained steadfast to the idea of running their own pseudo-bank aboard the steamboats. By 1822 the Molsons had capitulated, taking a substantial equity position in the Bank of Montreal. A bank transfer register dated January 8, 1822, shows John Senior, John Junior and Thomas acquiring thirty shares each, with William taking another ten, giving the family more than twenty percent of the bank's stock. At £50 per share, the Molsons had collectively invested £5,000.

The family's position was much reduced by 1826, with Thomas having sold his shares, John Senior and Junior holding twenty each and William his original ten. But the Molsons acquired a leading role in boardroom politics. The merchant George Moffatt, a senior partner in Gillespie, Moffatt and Company, had been campaigning to install a new set of by-laws that would bring more fiduciary rigour to the bank's operations, and he was intent on gaining approval at the June 1826 general meeting. John Junior's election to the board in January 1826, which made him the youngest member (he was thirty-eight), may have been a preliminary move by Moffatt to secure a supportive majority, as at the general meeting Moffatt had John Junior firmly in his corner.

While Moffatt had the necessary votes on the board for the approval of the by-laws, he also needed a new president. For some reason, he didn't covet the position himself; he probably needed a neutral candidate to end the bickering with the dissenting board members. John Senior became his choice. The Swiss émigré Frederick William Ermatinger,[3] an original board member, resigned his position on June 9 to make room for Molson, and that day the freshly minted bank director was unanimously voted president. John Junior then sacrificed his board seat on June 20 to allow Ermatinger to return.

Denison suspected, with good cause, that Molson was selected for reasons of political expediency and not fiscal savvy. Molson was no fool, but he was in august company on this board of directors when it came to commercial acumen, and his own son, John Junior, would have made a far sharper chief banker. One only has to remember John Junior's instructions to his father on how to calculate interest on his bills of exchange, not to mention the extremely rudimentary bookkeeping of the brewery and its related ventures, to marvel that the brewery founder ended up at the helm of the province's leading financial institution. But in addition to his fundamentally diligent and incorruptible nature, John Senior was the right man for the times, which were troubled. Molson not only had to step into the breach of the squabble among the original directors, but also drew the unhappy assignment of presiding over the bank's business as the last vestiges of the city's fur-trading economy were dismantled.

For this he was also ideally suited, as unlike most of the board members he had no significant personal business history with the fur trade. As president until 1830, John Senior oversaw the liquidation of McGillvrays, Thain & Co., the last surviving partnership from the defeated North Westers, as new credit terms imposed by the Hudson's Bay Company in 1824 forced them into bankruptcy. (The end of the North West Company in 1821 may have been why Francis Badgley, William Molson's father-in-law, was hired as the Molson brewery's bookkeeper in 1822.)

The economy of the city had changed entirely during Molson's life. He had arrived in Montreal just before the nascent North West Company reconstituted itself in 1784; by 1825 all the celebrated principals who built the Montreal trade were either dead or (in the case of Thomas Thain) mad, and the enterprise that had linked Montreal to the seemingly limitless interior of the continent had been co-opted and crushed. The more clever merchants had shifted their focus with the times, and Molson joined their elite ranks just as the old order vanished.

The break had been made with the native networks that reached deep into the continent, but a new form of exploitable hinterland had risen in its place. The commercial focus of the city was now on the opportunities presented by the growing population of Upper Canada. There were goods to sell to the newcomers, and timber and wheat to sell overseas for them. Transportation cried out for development, and as canals and locks were completed, new opportunities for steamboat operators opened. But as the province's economy shifted, historic inequities remained, and Lower Canada's francophone majority began to raise its voice ever higher against the system of political and economic privilege from which it was largely excluded. At the same time, reformers in Upper Canada were pressing for greater accountability in government and its related institutions.

The bank presidency added further lustre to John Molson's expanding public stature. In March 1825, he established the Theatre Royal, which opened that December, complementing his rebuilt hotel. Having been named worshipful swordbearer for the Provincial Grand Lodge of Lower Canada, Molson was inspired to name the new building the Masonic Hall Hotel. With his hotel hosting the grand dinners of the last gasps of the Beaver Club, Molson was drawn closer to the affairs of fur trade merchants-cum-bankers like

John Richardson, John Forsyth and George Moffatt. He became vice-president of Montreal General Hospital, as well as a member of its committee of management and a life governor, and a director of the local agricultural society. A residence on the fringes of the city in the industrial suburb of St. Mary's was now beneath his station. In 1825 he assumed a conspicuous personal base of operations within Montreal by acquiring the ostentatious Belmont Hall, built by steamboat rival Thomas Torrance in 1818.

His only misstep came when he was lured back into politics by the 1827 election, which was forced by Governor General Lord Dalhousie in his ongoing struggle with the emerging *patriote* party, led by Louis-Joseph Papineau. Papineau had travelled to England in 1822 to argue against the Union Bill, which would have united the legislatures of Upper and Lower Canada, although the two provinces themselves would not have been merged into one. In addition to creating a single parliament, the bill provided a mechanism for determining Upper Canada's share of the customs duties collected in Lower Canada, and regulated trade with the United States. Montreal's leading merchants supported the bill, hoping the new political regime would improve the development and management of the locks and canals that were opening the interior. Papineau and his followers feared the submersion of francophone culture that a legislative union might cause, as well as its power to approve public expenditures on projects such as canals that they viewed as ultimately being of fundamental benefit to the anglophone merchant class.

The unobjectionable part of the bill, dealing with the division of customs revenues and trade with the United States, passed as the separate Canada Trade Act of 1822, while debate continued on the legislative merger. But thanks to the objections of Papineau and others, the provisions for a political union were defeated.

Despite the fondness Molson had shown for dressing in *faux-habitant* regalia while greeting farmers on the road at the brewhouse gate during his previous stint as an elected politician, his allegiances were with the Protestant mercantile elite and its Masonic brotherhood. He stood for election to one of the two seats in

Montreal East but withdrew his candidacy before polling was completed. The reformist candidate James Leslie was re-elected, along with the *patriote* Hugues Heney. Over in Montreal West, the bank director Peter McGill was in an ugly contest with Papineau; there was mob violence, a magistrate was beaten, and stones were tossed through McGill's windows. Papineau's *patriotes* triumphed, not only in Montreal West (where the reformist Robert Nelson was re-elected with Papineau) but throughout the province. When Lord Dalhousie refused to confirm Papineau as speaker of the elected assembly, the assembly resolutely continued to champion Papineau. Lord Dalhousie lost the standoff; he was recalled and reassigned as commander-in-chief of British forces in India in 1828, raising considerable hope among the *patriotes* that they would soon see reforms to reduce the power of the appointed legislative council.

Rebuffed by the electorate, John Molson nonetheless continued to move away from the day-to-day business of the brewery and the steamboats as he tended to bank affairs. The family forged ahead with thinning ranks. In 1828, a new partnership was formed between John Senior and his sons William and John Junior. We can only imagine what effect the death on March 18, 1829, of Sarah Vaughan had on the further fragmentation of the Molson family business.

Sarah's death preceded John Junior's withdrawal from the partnership by a matter of weeks; perhaps she had been the invisible glue binding a precarious alliance. Her influence no longer felt, John Junior departed before the existing partnership had reached its end of term, never to return. He established an import business with the brothers George and George Crew Davies, called Molson, Davies and Company. John Senior and William were left to form a new partnership, known as John and William Molson, that June, and it was essentially up to William to run the enterprise.

John Junior left just as the Molsons were confronting a challenge to their dominance of the steamboat trade, involving intriguing deceptions and collusion within the Bank of Montreal's board of directors. In 1826, the Montreal plumber James Greenfield had

entered into direct competition for passenger, freight and government contracts with the Molsons' St. Lawrence Steamboat
Company and the Montreal Steam Tow Boat Company. John
Torrance and his nephew David acquired control of the tow-boat
operation after the death of Thomas Torrance, and John assumed his
late brother Thomas's seat on the Bank of Montreal board. While
ostensibly competing with the Molson steamboat line, Torrance, the
bank board member, closed ranks with Molson, the bank president,
in an attempt to shut out Greenfield's *Lady of the Lake*.

In 1829 the Molsons dedicated one of their new boats, the
Waterloo, to compete head-to-head with Greenfield's *Lady of the
Lake* and force her from the trade. The standard steerage rate for
passengers from Montreal to Quebec City was driven down from
ten shillings to six pence that summer. Greenfield was also probably being squeezed by John Torrance, his partner in the transport of
military stores and men, and Greenfield accused him of diverting
business to the Molsons. That October, the river war ended when
Greenfield, the Molsons and the Torrances agreed to a cooperative
fare and freight schedule—an arrangement that continued through
the 1832 season, when Greenfield sold the Torrances and the
Molsons each a one-eighth share in his steamboat business for
£1,000 apiece.[4]

At the same time, the Molsons were expanding their steamboat
business above the Lachine Rapids, which had been defeated in
1825 by a new lock and canal in a public building program overseen by John Richardson. They prepared to enter the Ottawa
River trade[5]—the Rideau Canal, then under construction, would
create a "triangular" service between Montreal, Bytown (as Ottawa
was then known) and Kingston. It officially opened in May 1832,
and there was considerable manoeuvring to establish a dominant
position on the Ottawa. In 1828 John Molson & Sons formed a
joint-stock venture, the Ottawa Steamboat Company, in which
the family partnership was the leading shareholder. A minority
shareholder was the Bank of Montreal board member Horatio
Gates. The engines from the Molsons' old *Quebec* were installed
in a new vessel, the *Shannon*, being built at Hawkesbury, Ontario.

But a rival had silently arisen from within the ranks of the Bank of Montreal. Through a secret contractual agreement with Thomas Mears, bank vice-president Peter McGill had become the actual owner of the *William King* in August 1827, before she was moved to the Ottawa in 1828. To complicate matters, the same day that McGill signed the secret ownership agreement, he and Gates also signed a lumber contract with Mears. Why McGill wanted to conceal his involvement with the *William King* purchase is unknown, but he may have had intelligence of the Molsons' plans to expand to the Ottawa River and wished to hide his own ambitions for the service from the bank president, John Molson, Sr., and his fellow board member (and partner in the Mears lumber deal) Horatio Gates.

McGill and Mears were also partners with the Wright family of Hull in the badly ageing *Union* on the upper Ottawa. William Grant, a former co-investor and captain of the *Union,* broke with his partners in a dispute over the boat's accounts and signed on with the Molsons to operate the *Shannon.* As the *Shannon's* first season approached, Mears hoped to engineer a quick and profitable surrender of the *William King* and the *Union* to the well-financed Molson venture, but he was rebuffed. As he wrote to his partner Philomen Wright in February 1830, "I tried hard to sell out Both *Wm King* & *Union* to Molson But they would not Buy they Expect to drive us off of the River into Hudsons Bay."

The *Shannon* went into service in May 1830, and after only a month of direct competition, the Molsons' Ottawa Steamboat Company did buy out all its rivals in steam and stage service between Bytown and Montreal. Among them was McGill, who had made himself indispensable to the Molsons' monopolistic ambitions by purchasing the steamboat *St. Andrews* and her exclusive rights to the Vaudreuil lock. After the Rideau opened, the Ottawa Steamboat Company purchased three more boats in January 1835 and was reconstituted as a new stock company, the Ottawa and Rideau Forwarding Company, whose board of directors included Peter McGill and John Molson, Jr.[6]

With the death of Sarah Vaughan, the departure from the family partnership of John Junior, and the imminent end to his tenure as president of the Bank of Montreal, John Senior created his first new will in twenty years on January 30, 1830. It was also his first reasonably equitable distribution of assets since the 1795 and 1797 wills, as he strove once again to treat his sons impartially. The second-born William, however, was now selected to receive the brewery and its associated properties in St. Mary's suburb, as well as nearby lots Molson had purchased from Joseph Papineau and Thomas Barron. If William left no heirs, the brewery was to be shared by John Junior and Thomas and their respective heirs, and this provision indicated that John Senior was prepared to accept the possibility that Thomas's wife, Martha, could end up controlling the destiny of at least part of the brewery. John Junior was otherwise to receive the two large farm properties his father had acquired in the seigneury of Île Boucherville, which comprised the islands of St-Jean and Ste-Marguerite in the St. Lawrence, opposite the island of Montreal, as well as the Masonic Hotel (known later as the British-American Hotel) and his father's stake in the associated Theatre Royal (in which John Junior was already a shareholder). Thomas Molson would inherit three houses that stood on the rue Capital property in Montreal, as well as the various properties in the lower town of Quebec City, which were collectively referred to as Près-de-Ville. John Senior also left £100 to McGill College, the university chartered with funds from the estate of James McGill in 1821, and another £100 to be used specifically to expand the Montreal General Hospital. His nephew Samuel Rayment, son of his sister Martha, was to receive £100. Ten guineas were set aside for mourning rings for both his sister Martha and the widow Ann Elsdale. Everything else—his stock in the steamboat companies and the Bank of Montreal, as well as the remaining residue of the estate—was to be divided equally among his sons.

Conspicuously absent from the will was the palatial Belmont Hall. It's possible that Molson had already turned title of it over to John Junior, and had withdrawn from it following the death of Sarah Vaughan to alternate his residency with the changing seasons between the working farm at Île Boucherville and a house on the brewery property. (The will stated that he left to William "all that certain stone dwelling house, and wooden dwelling house, lot and premises lately occupied by me" in St. Mary's suburb.) Molson's 1836 will would indicate that there had been a property swap at some point, perhaps around 1829–30, between John Senior and Junior involving a farm that belonged to the son[7] and an unnamed property that belonged to the father, which may have been Belmont Hall.

Molson had displayed a commendable spirit of equanimity with the will, but this spirit had come to him too late to allow him to achieve in his own lifetime the cooperative family venture he had long envisioned. Thomas and John Junior were now gone, and even William was casting a wandering eye towards new horizons. Only four months after the will was written, William diversified by following his older brother into the import business. On May 30, 1830, while still retaining his duties at the brewery and steamboat business, William formed a partnership with his brother-in-law, John Thompson Badgley. John Senior put up funds to help with the venture's start-up, and because of loans he had already made to John Junior (and apparently to Thomas as well), he drew up a codicil to the will on June 25, which stated that any outstanding loans at the time of his death would have to be settled before the full bequests could be made.

The last gift John Molson had to make was his treasured portrait, painted in London in 1810–11. He wished it to be owned by whichever of his sons and heirs possessed the brewery after he died. But in the event that the brewery passed out of the family's hands, the portrait was to go to William and his heirs. John Senior could now imagine the brewery being abandoned by his sons as unceremoniously as he had sold off Snake Hall.

Sarah was gone and he was sixty-six years old; the boys, now men with families and ambitions of their own, were drifting away. The province was edging towards political and social conflagration. Nothing was certain any more, and he appears to have accepted the idea that he had lost the ability to determine anyone's destiny.

Molson was now shaping his estate to reflect the activities of his sons, not his ambitions for them. John Junior had no interest in brewing, and so it had become pointless to bequeath him the St. Mary's properties. With Thomas removed from the scene, William was the only one left to carry on the chosen trade of the patriarch.

In May 1832, in a by-election in Montreal West, British troops seeking to quell an agitated crowd fired into it, killing three fran-cophone Canadians. The first deaths had been recorded in what would build into an outright rebellion. It was a conspicuous time for John Molson to begin serving in the province's legislative council, to which he had been named that January. The appointment turned John Molson, common brewer, into the Honourable John Molson. Three years earlier, Louis-Joseph Papineau had called the appoint-ed upper houses of Upper and Lower Canada "the origin of all the abuses which impose strain on the provinces." Molson had risen to the inner circle of privilege just as the slide steepened towards insurrection.

On the far side of the Atlantic, Britain made a belated step towards a more egalitarian society with the Reform Bill of 1832. Meanwhile, Upper Canada's leading radical, the politician and publisher William Lyon Mackenzie, was railing against the insular power of the Family Compact (known as the chateau clique in Lower Canada), an interrelated and intertwined elite of legislative appointees who were unaccountable to the electorate. It was a peculiar coincidence that the small Lincolnshire town of Moulton produced both John Molson and D'Arcy Boulton, two of the most prominent members of the privileged ranks in the two provinces. In fact, the extended Boulton family had become one of the most notorious examples of nepotism, and Mackenzie singled them out for particular vilification in *Sketches of Canada and the United States*, published in Britain in 1833.[8]

In depicting for right-thinking Englishmen the flagrant self-dealing within his province, Mackenzie made D'Arcy Boulton the first name on his list of power-hoarding cronies. After being freed in 1813 from a French prison at Verdun, where he had languished for three years after his capture by privateers, Boulton was admitted to the English bar, making it possible for him to lobby for the attorney-generalship of Upper Canada, which he secured at the end of the year. He had retired in 1827, and Mackenzie noted how he had been pensioned off at £500 per annum; of his sons, Mackenzie revealed that D'Arcy Junior was auditor-general, Henry was attorney-general,[9] William was a church missionary and King's College professor, and George was the registrar at Northumberland and assembly member for Durham. Furthermore, the brother-in-law of D'Arcy Junior was John Beverley Robinson, chief justice of Upper Canada and member for life and speaker of the legislative council—and a long list of influential positions cascaded through the Robinson family tree.

In Lower Canada, Molson joined the appointed council at the same time as his fellow failed candidate for the legislative assembly of 1827, Peter McGill. In 1831, George Moffatt had been added to the council upon the death of John Richardson. As Creighton has noted, though Mackenzie denounced the concentration of power in Upper Canada as nepotism, the so-called Family Compact in both provinces "was less a company of blood-relations than it was a fraternal union of merchants, professional men and bureaucrats. The group was relatively small, and the names of a few dozen persons turned up again and again, with almost equal regularity in the affairs of business and of government, until the extent of their monopoly control suggests the practical identification of the political and commercial state."[10]

Molson, McGill and Moffatt were a perfect example of this collegiality in commerce and politics. They formed a united front on the council in pressing the causes of the merchant elite, a group that had been all but shut out of the elected assembly by the increasing successes of the *patriotes* at the polls. It fell to this trio, along with Matthew Bell and John Forsyth, to further the cause of the merchants, bankers and transportation interests (often the same people) from their positions of appointed privilege.[11] Whatever ill feelings McGill might have risked by secretly going up against Molson on the Ottawa in 1828 were gone. He became president of the Bank of Montreal in 1834 (after the death of Molson's successor, Horatio Gates), and he remained linked to the Molsons not only by their stock holdings in the bank and the Ottawa River steamboat trade but by a new transportation venture in 1831, the Champlain and St. Lawrence Railroad. The company set out to build the country's first rail line, a run of about fifteen miles from La Prairie to St. Johns. McGill served with William Molson as a director, while John Molson, Jr., was president and John Senior participated as a shareholder.

The struggle for power and reform in Lower Canada was not neatly divided along language lines. There were moderates among the francophones and radicals among the anglophones. Papineau's *patriotes* were an unusual blend of political revolutionaries and social paternalists. They not only championed elemental rights for the francophone majority but resisted any changes thought likely to endanger the survival of the culture. Lower Canada was to remain distinct from Upper Canada, and the seigneurial system was to continue. Papineau's *patriotes* consistently frustrated any legislative attempts to improve the transportation system linking the two provinces, improvements that merchants like Molson and his allies desperately wanted, to avoid having vital trade siphoned away by the Erie Canal in New York. (Mackenzie was happy to see Upper Canadian goods go to market through the United States if it meant denying profits to members of the merchant elite who were developing and profiting from the St. Lawrence system.)

At the same time, Upper and Lower Canada were locked in a bitter dispute about the divvying of import duties collected by Lower Canada on behalf of both provinces, a dispute the Canada Trade Act of 1822 failed to resolve. The economic momentum of Canada lay in the upper province, but without a seaport of its own, it could not gain a satisfactory share of the tithes. Soon, Upper Canadians increased their demands from simply receiving a more generous share of the duties to securing a seaport—by annexing Montreal, which in addition to having access to the Atlantic had become the commercial centre of the provinces. The legislative council had already passed an 1826 resolution calling for the annexation of Montreal. D'Arcy Boulton's son Henry, the province's attorney-general, played a leading role in efforts to pry Montreal loose from Lower Canada. Boulton was a key speaker in the initiative's favour in the assembly of Upper Canada in February 1833. Naturally the annexation plan also came before the legislature in Lower Canada, with debate divided along predictable lines. The *patriotes* vociferously opposed it, while in the legislative council the Molson-McGill-Moffatt bloc sided with its mercantile elite brethren in Upper Canada by proposing that the counties of Montreal and Vaudreuil be annexed by the neighbouring province.

The stances of the *patriotes* were often reactionary and economically stunting. They were blind to the benefits of improving the transportation corridors, for example. Having to spend public funds to complete the Lachine Canal offended them, as they opposed any government expenditure that they viewed to be principally of benefit to the merchants who dominated the unelected legislative council, and to influential British trading houses that drew their profits from Canada and spent them in the mother country. But their politics arose from an undeniable truth about the marginalized role of francophones in the businesses that men like John Molson, Sr., were often so eager to support with public spending. In banking and transportation, two sectors in which the Molsons were especially prominent, francophones were woefully underrepresented. In 1831, only 2.9 percent of Bank of Montreal stock was held by francophones, and in the nine leading transportation ventures, just 2 percent of stock was in francophone hands.[12] Critics of the tightly held reins of political, economic and legal power in both provinces found hopeless conflicts of interest.[13]

Into this dismal landscape of rival factions and ambitions sailed a true calamity: the cholera epidemic of 1832, carried into Upper and Lower Canada by waves of British immigrants, sped along by the efficient new locks and canals. An estimated 66,000 immigrants reached the Canadian provinces in 1832 alone, with the majority bound for Upper Canada. The disease swept up the St. Lawrence with them, claiming thousands of lives, and reappeared in 1834. On August 11, 1834, John Senior wrote a letter from his farm on

Île-Ste-Marguerite to account for his absence from a recent meeting of St. Paul's Masonic Lodge. He complained of "the situation of the health of the people at Boucherville—making us short of labourers (tho not a single instance of Cholera at this place to this period)."

A few weeks after John Senior wrote his letter, Thomas reappeared in Montreal, ending his ten-year self-imposed exile.

The return of the prodigal son invites no simple explanation. The calamities facing Upper and Lower Canada at the time were almost biblical in scope. Atop the political strife and the deadly presence of cholera came a serious economic reversal caused largely by American president Andrew Jackson's war with the Federal Bank of the United States. Jackson hated the institution and was determined to kill it off. He used his veto to revoke a renewal of its charter in 1832, and in the late summer of 1833 all federal deposits were withdrawn from it. The resulting financial panic spread to Canada, and business failures were recorded in Montreal and Quebec City—and Kingston, where Thomas Molson had been quietly building his own modest empire.

Because Thomas left behind no financial records from his brewing and distilling business in Kingston, it cannot be said for certain that the economic downturn of 1833–34 sent him, at age forty-three, scrambling back to Montreal with his wife and children. He had expanded his operation, buying out the rival Dalton brewery and distillery in 1831, in addition to acquiring several hundred acres of land in Upper Canada. Kingston was thriving famously at the time, its economy boosted by the construction of the Rideau Canal. Although he paid only about £250 for the Dalton brewery, it's possible Thomas overextended himself in an effort to keep up with his former apprentice, James Morton, who in 1831 established the Kingston Brewery and Distillery with partner John Drummond. Thomas may also have been hobbled by his participation in a banking crisis whose repercussions surpassed those of Andrew Jackson's war on the Federal Bank of the United States.

Kingston had a rocky history in early provincial banking. A close friend of Thomas in the town was Thomas Markland, who inspired the name of Thomas's son William Markland, born in 1833, just before Thomas returned to Montreal.[14] As early as 1813, Markland was issuing his own paper currency at Kingston to smooth dealings in his forwarding business. In 1817, he and a group of fellow Kingston businessmen petitioned the government of Upper Canada for the first bank charter in the country. The bill incorporating the Bank of Upper Canada was passed on March 27, months before the Bank of Montreal received its own charter from Lower Canada. The charter for the Kingston bank was granted, however, on the condition that it receive royal assent by January 1, 1819—which it did not.

As time passed without the royal assent, the Bank of Montreal's founders moved quickly to establish a foothold in Upper Canada. In 1818, Markland in Kingston and William Allan in York were secured as agents for the bank—and Markland was supplied with $10,000 in bank notes to put into circulation.[15] The Bank of Upper Canada was then strangely revived with the arrival in July 1819 of the new lieutenant-governor, Sir Peregrine Maitland, who announced that he had the royal assent for the bank charter, even though the deadline in the original bill had passed. The bill went back to the legislative council and emerged unrecognizable. The Family Compact had connived to rewrite the Kingston bank bill so that the principals were now Compact members and the location was changed to the "seat of government"—namely, York. The bank now also benefitted from a twenty-percent equity stake held by the government. Most of the board positions were filled by government members, who also had their own private holdings of shares.

The Kingston group, which had been robbed blind, was granted a bank of its own, called the Bank of Kingston. But the shareholders refused to give up the original Bank of Upper Canada name. Thus there were two Banks of Upper Canada in the province—the one controlled by the Family Compact and the "pretended" bank in Kingston.

Mismanagement drove the Kingston bank under in 1822, just before Thomas Molson relocated there. The Family Compact then put an end to Thomas Markland's business as an agent for the Bank of Montreal by forbidding any bank chartered by a government outside the province to operate in Upper Canada—in the process creating a convenient monopoly for their own bank.

The blatant conflicts of interest in the management and ownership of the Bank of Upper Canada, as well as the potential weaknesses in its financial structure, drew the ire of William Lyon Mackenzie. Having been trained in a Scottish counting house, he had a highly informed sense of outrage which was not unlike that of William Rayment, who had enjoyed a similar counting-house apprenticeship. And like Rayment, he wrote persuasively, with his attacks turning the political into the personal.

Mackenzie soon had two potentially malignant banks in the province to criticize. A group of Kingston merchants, Thomas Molson included, petitioned the legislature in 1830 for permission to establish a new bank there, with branches in outlying towns. Mackenzie initially approved of the initiative as a monopoly-breaker, but he became disenchanted with the bank's financial structure and feared a failure in the making. In 1832, the legislative council of the province approved the charter for the new Kingston bank, to be called the Commercial Bank of Midland District, and permitted a capitalization increase for the Bank of Upper Canada.[16]

Mackenzie took his objections to Upper Canada's latest banking legislation to the British government, and found willing listeners. In early 1833, Upper Canada was awash with rumours—stirred up by Mackenzie himself—that Westminster was about to revoke the capitalization increase for the Bank of Upper Canada and terminate the charter of the Commercial Bank of Midland District. Both banks reined in their activities as a result and probably contributed to the economic slump. Although the home government sent out a new eight-point set of conditions for new charters to meet, it did not actually put an end to the Commercial Bank. But anticipation of a serious reversal for the bank, in addition to the other poor economic signposts, may have helped Thomas decide to return to Montreal in the fall of 1834.

Whatever the economic underpinnings of Thomas's return, it may have come at the invitation of his brother William, who had suddenly decided to take the Molson brewery once more into the distilling business in 1833. William had probably recognized that the Molsons were missing out on overseas trade with a brewery business focused entirely on the domestic market. The mercantile economy was founded on goods moving back and forth across the Atlantic.[17] Turning Canadian grain into whiskey for sale in Britain was a natural opportunity—albeit one that Thomas had unsuccessfully attempted to exploit while running the Molson brewery in the early 1820s. William, who had arranged the exports of Thomas's spirits in those years, had come around to Thomas's point of view. Thomas now had considerable experience with distilling in Kingston—and perhaps had been exporting his product—and William must have welcomed his expertise.

Thomas returned for a fresh round of electoral violence. Already that year the Tories had been routed in Upper Canada, and Papineau's *patriotes* were poised to make a virtual sweep of Lower Canada's legislative assembly. Papineau had tabled his famous "92 Resolutions" during the 1834 session, which enraged the Protestant elite with its republican and anti-merchant sentiments and took specific aim at the legislative council on which John Senior sat. Both Mackenzie and Papineau despised the banks in their respective provinces, and encouraged voters to cause their ruin by making a "run" on them, demanding specie for their notes. In his Montreal West campaign, Papineau argued, "The most efficacious and most immediate means which the Canadians have to protect themselves against the fury of their enemies, is to attack them in their dearest parts—their pockets—in their strongest entrenchments, the Banks." Papineau and his Montreal West running mate, the reformer Robert Nelson, captured the riding as mob violence plagued the polling. On November 16, the second-last day of polling, William Molson wrote his father at his Boucherville farm: "The election for the West Ward still remains unsettled, but am sorry to say every night there are disturbances in the streets, people beaten, and Glass or windows of Houses broken, Mr. English's House was almost made a write off on Friday night and . . . a party were on their way to Papineau's House for retaliation."

As soon as the election was over, concerned Tories in Montreal West formed the Constitutional Association to oppose the *patriote* policies that were enjoying free rein in the legislative assembly. Both John Junior and Senior participated in this new organization, along with Peter McGill and George Moffatt. The province was proving ungovernable, with the elected legislative assembly and appointed legislative council deadlocked in the 1835 session. That spring, delegates from the Constitutional Association were dispatched to London to argue against the reforms demanded by Papineau—in particular the one that would make the upper house an elected body.

In the midst of this political turmoil, the Molsons drew up their new partnership. Written against the backdrop of dangerous unrest, as Upper and Lower Canada staggered towards genuine revolution, the agreement felt like a defensive retrenchment. Returning to Montreal, Thomas abandoned the outright proprietorship and independence he had enjoyed at Kingston (which would not have been a concern if his own ventures were in fact failing). He advertised the sale of his brewery and distillery property, complete with a stone house on Church Street ("commanding a most extensive and delightful view of Lake Ontario") and wharf and stores, in the *Montreal Gazette* on February 14, 1835. Thomas pitched the property as being "well adapted to the Forwarding Business, whether by the St. Lawrence or the Rideau Canal. . . ." It appears to have been at least initially leased or purchased by James Morton.[18]

On February 21—one week after Thomas Molson advertised his Kingston properties—the new Molson family partnership was struck, backdated to June 1834. John Junior remained apart, concerned with his banks, his railway and the Constitutional Association. But John Senior, William and Thomas came together in a partnership devoted to brewing and distilling known as John Molson & Sons. The sons each received three of eight shares, with the remaining two going to John Senior, who would enjoy an annual rent of £1,100 from the St. Mary's suburb property, based on a six percent return on capital value. The profits (or losses) would be divided in proportion to the shares.

Thomas could not have returned to Montreal and assumed a place in a family partnership without his father addressing the old thorn of Martha's rights to joint property in Lower Canada. Perhaps it was thought the problem would go away with the proposed annexation of Montreal and Vaudreuil by Upper Canada, which would have eliminated the old French civil code and the property rights Martha enjoyed under it. The Constitutional Association delegates who travelled to London that spring included the annexation on their list of proposed solutions to the political crisis, although for some reason they did not present it to the home government. Certainly, having Montreal deposited in Upper Canada would solve a major inheritance problem for John Senior, allowing him to reunite his family without complications of bequest. His desire to have Thomas back in Montreal could well have been a factor in his advocacy of the annexation proposal in the legislative council.

But no annexation came to pass, and a more practical solution to the bequest problem was required. Where it came from—or when it was decided on—isn't known, but the issue must have been settled before the new partnership came about. Thomas's branch of the family would now receive the brewery property upon John Senior's death. For whatever reason, William would not retain any of the brewery bequest he had just been granted in 1830, even though he had dissolved his import partnership with John Thompson Badgley in February 1834. He remained involved with John Junior in the Champlain and St. Lawrence Railroad. William, like John Junior, apparently saw his future and that of his heirs lying beyond the brewery. Or he may not have had a choice. Thomas could have returned from Kingston because William was the one who was struggling and John Senior was desperate to have Thomas back to save the operation.

But there was still that matter of Martha's property rights. John Senior's main concern was that the brewery remain in the possession of his direct descendants. If leaving the brewery to Thomas was not an option, then why not have the bequest leap-frog the second generation and proceed directly to the third? Instead of leaving the brewery directly to Thomas—which would have meant giving half of it to Martha—John Senior would bequeath it to Thomas's eldest son, John Henry Robinson. And because the bequest involved only the property and not the actual business, any associated operations (such as a new distillery on separate land) started by Thomas would belong to him (and Martha) and be distinct from the bequest to John Henry Robinson, even though they might be included in an operating partnership. Thomas would also enjoy the profits from whatever partnership he maintained with his brother William (and eventually with his son, when he came of age).

It was a simple, ingenious solution. But when John Molson awoke at midnight on January 11, 1836, ten months had passed without his having revised his will so that the bequest could flow as planned. With death only hours away, Molson devoted his last breaths to satisfying his pledge to Thomas.

Chapter 21

All I desire, for my own burial, is not to be buried alive.
    —Lord Chesterfield, to Mrs. Eugenia Stanhope,
        March 16, 1769

SOMETIME IN THE EARLY hours of January 11, 1836, the notary Henry Griffin arrived at John Molson's home on Île-Ste-Marguerite to begin hurriedly drafting a new will for the dying patriarch. Griffin started working with the 1830 will, pencilling in Molson's desired changes. After he went off with the revisions, he was sent for again by Molson around nine in the morning to receive further directions. Griffin then drew up a fresh will, and returned to Molson's room at ten to read it to him in the presence of two witnesses. One was Dr. Robert Nelson, whose care actually may have been killing Molson, as Thomas Molson would later complain of the "quack pills" that claimed his father. The other was a gentleman of Montreal named Frederick Gundlack.

This deathbed reworking of the 1830 will essentially swapped two property packages between William and Thomas Molson. William would now receive the holdings at Quebec City known as Près-de-Ville, while Thomas (or at least his son) would get the brewery property at St. Mary's Current. John Senior directed that the brewery was to descend to "my grandson John Molson, son of my son Thomas Molson." If John did not live to twenty-one, or chose not to enter the brewing business, then the brewery would pass instead to "my next grandson named John Molson." At the time, the only alternative candidate was John Junior's eldest son,

John, born in 1820—William had named his only son, born in 1822, after himself.

John Junior would still receive the hotel and associated theatre property in Montreal, as well as his father's farm holdings in the Boucherville seigneury and another farm at Côte-de-la-Visitation. Finally, John Junior was left the St. Mary Foundry, located next door to the brewery, which had been acquired in 1835 and was already being run by him.[1]

The residue of Molson's estate was to be divided equally among his three sons. This included several additional properties around St. Mary's Current, as well as Molson's shares in the Bank of Montreal, the Champlain and St. Lawrence Railroad, and the various steamboat companies. And in the event that no grandson named John proved eligible to inherit the brewery, it was to be considered part of the residue and so divided equally among the sons. Unlike the 1830 will, no mention was made of Samuel Rayment or mourning rings for Martha Molson and Ann Elsdale. (We know that the widow Elsdale, at least, was still alive.) And Molson's directions about who should receive his oil portrait were gone.

The will was read to Molson by Griffin, who stooped by him at the head of the bed while Nelson and Gundlack watched and listened. There were several interruptions as John Molson made comments that required initialled margin notes. The three men present then all signed the will as witnesses. Yet, having stood at close quarters around the dying Molson, with his words clearly stated for all of them to hear, they could not subsequently agree on what he had wished to become of the brewery.

With Molson dying, there had been no time to make a clean copy of the final will. Instead, the document, as drafted by Griffin and amended with margin notes, had to serve as his last will and testament. At some unknown hour after the will was drafted, John Molson died. Molson's three sons—who in addition to being the principal legatees were also named as executors, along with Peter McGill and George Moffatt—were confronted by a document that was a morass of ambiguity, both in its phrasing and in the condition of the margin notes. It demanded an unusual amount of interpretation, which only meant that there would be much for the brothers to fight about.

They fought for seven years.

John Molson's funeral at Christ Church on January 14 was a major occasion for his fellow members of the Protestant mercantile elite and the public at large. While his politics had been solidly on the side of appointed privilege, his contributions to the general quality of life in the province were too great for even his opponents to ignore. The newspaper *Le Canadien* of Quebec City set aside its *patriote* sentiments long enough to salute him:

> We hasten to associate ourselves with the regrets which have been expressed by our Montreal contemporaries, on the loss experienced by Canadian industry through the death of the Hon. John Molson, to whom Lower Canada owes the introduction of steam in inland navigation, and who at all times was a zealous supporter of every important commercial and industrial enterprise. Few men have rendered better service to their country in connection with its material development.[2]

At the same time, the reform-minded Montreal publication *La Minerve* (named for the Roman goddess of wisdom) grasped the obituary as an opportunity to argue subtly that Molson's wealth was accumulated through the labour of the francophone underclass: "Mr. Molson belonged to that small number of Europeans who, coming to settle in Canada, reject all national distinctions; just as he had started his fortune with those born in this land, so he always had a large number of Canadians in his employ, whose loyalty must have helped to ensure his considerable profit."[3]

He was buried in the cemetery of the St-Laurent suburb; when a family mausoleum was established in Mount Royal Cemetery in 1860, his remains, along with those of Sarah Vaughan, were reinterred there. The Bank of Montreal followed its own tradition by announcing a thirty-day period of mourning for the former president—in 1834 the bank had announced a similar period for the (early) death of Horatio Gates.

The funeral provided but a momentary pause in the escalating controversy over the terms of the deathbed will. After the probate was petitioned by John Junior on January 16, the three men present at the will's creation were called upon to testify to its meaning and authenticity.

No one disputed the fact that Molson wished the brewery to descend to a grandson named John, beginning with Thomas Molson's son of that name. What should become of the brewery in the years before the legatee came of age was another matter. It was clear from the will and the witnesses' testimony that Molson did not wish his death to terminate the 1835 partnership, which had brought Thomas back into business with his father and brother William. But beyond his desire for continuity, virtually everything was in dispute.

As the will stated, the brewery was "to be enjoyed by my two sons Thomas and William in co-partnership which shall be conducted under the terms of the memorandum of partnership" set down by Griffin in 1835. But this provision left an empty chair between Thomas and William. The brothers held six of eight shares. The other two—one-quarter of the partnership—had belonged to their father, who also drew an annual rent from the property.

What was to become of their late father's shares in the partnership until a grandson inherited the property? Were they still supposed to pay out the one-fourth share of the profits, and to whom? And what of the rent payments on the property to which John Senior had been entitled?" Did they continue, and to whose benefit? And how long was the co-partnership mentioned in the will even supposed to last? If it was to adhere to the 1835 memorandum, then it would have to expire in June 1837. But the will seemed to entertain, instead, the idea that Thomas and William should continue to operate the brewery until its heir came of age, which in John Henry Robinson's case would not be until 1847. In that case, another decade of operations had to be negotiated after the present partnership lapsed. Would rent still have to be paid by the succeeding partnership—and again, to whom?

The will provided only the most curt direction, stating that the partnership "shall be continued for the benefit of my three sons in the proportions therein set forth." But all three sons were not party to the 1835 agreement—John Junior had not been involved at all. Had a fundamental error been made in hurriedly drafting the will?

While the will was spectacularly inadequate in its directions, it made sense when "John Molson" was thought of as an entity to be possessed by successive generations of men of the same name. The dying Molson was the first one, and he intended that eventually the "John Molson" role would be fulfilled by a grandson named John. No other grandson, no matter how interested in or capable of assuming the brewery's stewardship, was eligible. John Senior was not simply plotting the future of Molson's brewery; it was *John* Molson's brewery. Ironically, it seemed that Molson had not learned the lesson embodied in his son Thomas—that neither the eldest offspring nor a descendant with the proper echo of his own name was necessarily the right person to take over the business.

A phantom John Molson evidently occupied the empty chair between Thomas and William in the brewery partnership. With the patriarch dead, someone else would have to sit there. That person appeared to be John Junior. He would in essence become "John Molson" for the duration of the partnership when it came to sharing in the profits, while the actual living members of the 1835 partnership would continue to run the business. But what about the rent? If the terms of the memorandum were to be followed, then the £1,100 rent still had to be paid—but to whom? A considerable sum was at stake. When the partnership was struck in 1835, the annual rent was the equivalent of £75,000 today.

A major problem with the will was that it simply gave the brewery property to the first eligible grandson named John. It did not say that ownership would only be vested when the legatee turned twenty-one. There was no trust mechanism—nothing about the brewery property being operated by Thomas and William for the eventual benefit of the first eligible grandson named John, the way Snake Hall and its associated lands were overseen by Samuel Elsdale on behalf of the young John Molson. Thus there was no suggestion that the grandson was entitled to any proceeds of the brewery operation from the years leading up to his twenty-first birthday. The brewery was to be "enjoyed" by the sons in the intervening years.

Thomas and William evidently were expected to maintain and manage the brewery property in the interest of its owner, the grandson legatee, until he came of age, while enjoying any profits it generated. This raised the issue of brewery profits from the first year of the existing partnership. John Senior had died before the first year was completed, on February 21, and so no profits had been divided according to the partnership shares. Was the "John Molson" share to go to John Junior?

A serious dispute gathered around the presence of three loaded words written into the margin of the will by Henry Griffin: "free from rent." They were meant to indicate that the partners were to continue operating the brewery after Molson's death without having to pay the annual £1,100 rent, but there was some question as to whether the provision began with Molson's death or would have to wait until the 1835 partnership expired. More important, it wasn't even certain that they belonged in the will. They had been initialled by Molson and partly obliterated. Were the words struck out before or after Molson signed his assent?

As Griffin testified, the very use of the words had been his idea. "In drawing the will I myself inserted the words. . . ." He had taken the initiative to "obviate a difficulty which might arise under the new copartnership. . . . I conceived at first that the testator did not intend to charge his sons after his death with rent."

The three witnesses could not agree on what the words meant, and whether John Molson had even agreed to them. Having put them in the draft will himself, Griffin said Molson wanted them taken out. When he read the will aloud to Molson and reached the words "free from rent," Molson said, "No, no," and so the margin note was struck—or at least seemed to have been, for the deletion was ambiguous.

But neither Gundlack nor Nelson heard Molson say, "No, no." To the contrary, Gundlack testified that Molson said, "Yes, free from rent," and noted that "I cannot say whether the three words 'free from rent' were struck out when the testator put his initials to the said marginal note. . . ." Dr. Nelson was equally opposed to Griffin's version. He said the words "free from rent" must have been obliterated "through error and mistake," as "several interruptions to the reading of the clause of which these words form a part took place on part of the Testator." In Dr. Nelson's opinion, Molson was anxious to be explicit on the brewery's ownership and its steward-ship in the years before an heir came of age. Molson wished the partnership of William and Thomas to continue until that time, but he also wanted the existing partnership to have a specific term, after which a new partnership would be formed, which could then begin operating the brewery free from rent. In that case, rents still had to be collected—and paid to somebody—until June 1837.

John Junior submitted the will to the local court on January 29, to be filed in the register of wills and testaments of the district of Montreal, and noted that copies were to be available to all parties, with the words "free from rent" to be included, as two of three wit-nesses to the will had testified. But the arguing had only begun. John Junior launched legal action against his two brothers to settle his father's intentions.

In addition to his determination to collect all profits from the brewery to which he was conceivably entitled, John Junior dis-agreed with William about the Près-de-Ville inheritance. Some of the properties identified as Près-de-Ville in the 1830 will had been sold by their father before drafting the new will. There were rents and invested income from the properties that had been sold which John Junior felt belonged in the estate's residue and should not be considered part of the bequest to William.

John Junior also believed that the words "free from rent" should be struck from the will, although his own lawyer, Alexander Buchanan, could not fathom his objection. In an opinion written for John Junior on March 14, 1836, Buchanan observed that the words actually "seem to operate to the benefit of Mr. John Molson." Striking them out would mean Molson, as one of the co-partners, would be responsible for paying a share of that rent from the profits he would otherwise enjoy. But John Junior may have been thinking that, if rent had to be paid, then surely it should be placed in trust to the benefit of the property's owner when he came of age. And with the sickly J.H.R.'s survival in doubt, John Junior's son, John III, stood to inherit the brewery and would collect those rents.

The brothers' feuding over their father's will quickly drove off the two other executors, Peter McGill and George Moffatt, who wanted nothing to do with the internecine battle.[4] In February 1837, more than a year after the patriarch's death, the brothers were at least able to gather and divide the essential components of the estate's residue.[5]

Included in the residue were ten shares in the British American Land Company, which had been formed in London in 1832, ostensibly as a public-spirited effort to encourage immigration to Canada. Predictably for a venture in which Molson was involved, Peter McGill and George Moffatt were named its resident commissioners. More than one million acres were acquired in the Eastern Townships, and its activities enraged Papineau's *patriotes,* who saw the company's activities as a plot to crowd out the province's francophone majority.[6] The land company became a flashpoint for antagonism between the *patriotes* and the anglophone commercial oligarchy. John Molson's sons were still squabbling over his legacy when these tensions erupted into lawlessness and bloodshed.

When the Molsons' steamboat *Varennes* burned at St-Ours on the Richelieu in June 1837, *patriote* sabotage was immediately suspected. Although the loss proved to be an accident, it heightened hysterical fears in the Canadian commercial community that strategic assets were under siege by rebels. The Molsons were particularly vulnerable: in addition to the burned *Varennes,* the Champlain and St. Lawrence Railroad had begun operating on July 21, 1836, its imported British locomotive (christened the *Dorchester* in honour of the governor and the railway terminus at the renamed St. Johns) riding its steel rails into the heart of *patriote* resistance along the Richelieu valley. Attacks by revolutionaries were also feared on the Rideau system, where the Molsons held shares in the Ottawa and Rideau Forwarding Company.

Both William and John Junior were active members of the Constitutional Association of Montreal, which was pressing for a union of the Canadian provinces in order to rid the elected assembly of francophone control. The association openly celebrated the domination of Lower Canada's economy by the anglophone minority, which in their opinion was more a case of leadership than evidence of a commercial oligarchy. "It must also be observed that the general trade of the Province is carried on almost exclusively by the Colonists of British origin," the association stated in a representation made on a union of the provinces in 1837. "The French-Canadian inhabitants have never had much share in it, and the general indisposition evinced by them to commercial pursuits, has almost become an anti-commercial spirit." By way of proof of the importance of the anglophone minority in commerce, the representation included a list of prominent stock ventures in which francophones held only two percent of the capital value. Most of the companies were involved in transportation and banking, and were practically a blueprint of the Molsons' investment activities.[7]

The fuse to the powder keg of *patriote* anger was lit by the British government's rejection on March 1, 1837, of Papineau's demands for political and economic reforms, as expressed in the 92 Resolutions passed by the legislative assembly in 1834. The colonial secretary, Lord John Russell, then introduced to the House of Commons on March 2 new resolutions for the administration of Lower Canada that reversed a previously conciliatory approach to *patriote* demands. In 1831, the British government had transferred control of most revenues to the legislative assembly, but in 1833 and 1834 the assembly used its power to refuse to pass bills to pay for government supplies. Lord Russell's resolutions granted the governor the right to ignore the legislative assembly and use funds from the treasury as he saw fit.

The actual detonation of *patriote* anger came in November, after clashes in Montreal with Tories on October 31 sent Papineau and other reform leaders to the Richelieu valley, where rebel forces were encamped at St. Johns. Warrants were issued for the arrests of the rebel leaders. The railway president, John Junior, marched into combat with other volunteer militia, and he is thought to have been wounded in an engagement on the Chambly–Longueuil Road. While British regulars suffered a stunning defeat at St-Denis on November 23, a loyalist force at St-Charles two days later inflicted a demoralizing loss on the rebels, killing twenty-eight of them. Papineau, a reluctant figurehead in the violent rebellion, fled the country.

The rebellion would not bypass Caldwell's Manor. John Molson's old haunt, now unequivocally known as Alburgh, Vermont, was the scene of torchings and cross-border raids as republican-minded *patriotes* found sympathizers among Americans whose enthusiasm for invading Canada stretched back to the American Revolution. A *patriote* party launched one such raid from Alburgh into Quebec "and plundered the first house across the line, belonging to a family named Vosburgh," according to the local historian Allen Stratton. "They were robbed of everything, the father was struck with a sabre, laying his face open from ear to ear, the son was bayoneted in six or seven places. They stole a team and fired the barn[,] letting the rest of the stock to be roasted alive. The son managed to escape out the rear door."[8]

One of the local *patriote* sympathizers was Benjamin Mott, a son of Joseph Mott, the man who had purchased John Molson's lands on the Missisquoi Tongue. Mott was arrested by the British Army and taken to Montreal, where he was tried and condemned to death. Lobbying by friends had his sentence commuted to exile to Australia, and he arrived in Sydney in March 1840. He was eventually allowed to return home, and he reached Alburgh in 1845— only to find, as tradition has it, that his wife, thinking him dead, had remarried.

In Upper Canada, William Lyon Mackenzie's armed uprising was quickly subdued by local militia and he fled to the United States. On December 13, an army of 1,300 under Governor Sir John Colborne set out in deep snow from Montreal to confront a rebel force in nearby St-Eustache. Attached to the governor was Frederick Marryat, the sea captain turned novelist who was in the midst of a publicity tour of North America. The tour was an unrelenting disaster. Despite his celebrity, which foreshadowed that of Dickens in the new world, Marryat managed to offend an impressive number of people who were otherwise disposed to admire him. His arch-Tory politics and habit of making inflammatory public pronouncements on sensitive issues caused him to be pursued by a lynch mob, have his books burned in public bonfires and twice witness his own effigy set alight.

The tour began Marryat's professional decline, which ended nine years later with his juvenile novel *The Privateersman*, lifted from the journal of Robinson Elsdale.[9] By strange coincidence, the commander of British forces at Montreal, Sir George Augustus Wetherall, shared his last name with Elsdale's privateer captain. Marryat's fame and his experience as a naval officer allowed him to join Wetherall and Colborne in the march on St-Eustache.

The British Army had a mean streak when it came to armed uprisings and was inclined to view opponents as traitors rather than as proper military rivals. At the Battle of Long Island in August 1776, British soldiers bayonetted rebels who had surrendered, under the approving gaze of their officers. "You know all stratagems are lawful in a war, especially against such vile enemies of the King and country," one British officer said in dismissing the atrocities. In Lower Canada in 1837, the British regulars were in an especially vicious mood owing to the brutal murder of one of their own, Lieutenant Jack Weir. He had been carrying dispatches in the conflict along the Richelieu valley when captured by *patriotes* on November 23. His bound body, weighted with stones, was discovered in the Richelieu a week later. The troops who filed into St-Eustache with Marryat would give no quarter.

The rebels had holed up in the local church. They set fire to a nearby house, hoping the smoke would camouflage their escape, but the British troops had the church surrounded. Marryat described the scene:

> The poor wretches attempted to get away, either singly or by twos and threes, but the moment they appeared a volley was discharged, and they fell. Every attempt was made by the officers to make prisoners, but with indifferent success; indeed,

such was the exasperation of the troops at the murder of Lieut. Weir, that it was a service of danger to attempt to save the life of one of these poor deluded creatures. The fire from the house soon communicated to the church. Chenier, the leader, with ten others, the remnant of the insurgents who were in the church, rushed out; there was one tremendous volley, and it was all over.[10]

When the fire was extinguished, Marryat entered the smouldering church.

The floor had been burnt to cinders, and upon and between the sleepers on which the floor had been laid, were scattered the remains of human creatures, injured in various degrees, or destroyed by the fire; some with merely the clothes burnt off, leaving the naked body; some burnt to a deep brown tinge; others so far consumed that the viscera were exposed; while here and there the blackened ribs and vertebra were all that the fierce flames had spared.[11]

The *patriote* army made one of its last stands on the Missisquoi Tongue. A force of about six hundred rebels first raided Potton in the Eastern Townships and then Plattsburgh, New York, before crossing Lake Champlain to take refuge in Alburgh in late February 1838. That spring, the rebel force was trapped between British troops on the forty-fifth parallel and the U.S. Army and Vermont militia arrayed at its back, and chose to surrender to the Americans.

The definitive end to the armed rebellion in Lower Canada did not come until November 1838, when a *patriote* force gathered at Boucherville dispersed without a fight. Not counting the rebels cut down at St-Eustache, more than a dozen ultimately were executed; fifty-eight were sent to join Benjamin Mott in Australia. Upper and Lower Canada were united, as the Tory merchants had hoped, in 1841. But while the rebellions were over and the Canadas were united, the Molsons were still very much apart.

Epilogue

As fathers commonly go, it is seldom a misfortune to be fatherless; and considering the general run of sons, [it is] as seldom a misfortune to be childless.

　　　　　—Lord Chesterfield, letter to his son, July 15, 1751

THE WILL DRAFTED BY John Henry Robinson Molson in 1866 was a model of brevity and clarity. Where the notarial copy of his grandfather John's hurried and much-disputed 1836 will was five pages long, J.H.R.'s will contained only five paragraphs, even though it was equally concerned with making sure the brewery landed in the proper hands. And only one paragraph was necessary reading:

> I give and bequeath to my brother John Thomas Molson, the whole of my estate and effects, real and personal, moveable and immoveable, of every nature and kind whatsoever belonging, due, or accruing to, me at the time of my decease. The same to be, and remain his property absolutely and unconditionally.

Thirty years after the death of the patriarch, J.H.R. Molson, having no children of his own and embittered by the behaviour of every one of his siblings but John Thomas, was determined that the brewery should pass on to the only person he thought deserved it. His choice of an heir had nothing to do with who might be the most fit actually to operate the brewery, for John Thomas had none of his father's or his grandfather's enthusiasm for the trade, much less for what might be called an honest day's work.

John Thomas had grown up knowing that he was the spare heir created by his father, Thomas, one year after the patriarch's death. J.H.R.'s health was considered so frail that Thomas had seized upon the birth of another boy in 1837 to doubly ensure that a son of his—and not of his brother John, with whom he was locked in litigation over their father's estate—would qualify to inherit the brewery. He did so simply by naming this boy John as well, thereby creating two offspring who met the 1836 will's primary direction that the brewery pass to "John Molson, son of my son Thomas Molson."[1] In the endgame played by the brothers Thomas, John Junior and William over the patriarch's estate, each contestant had his own definition of victory; for Thomas, the birth of John Thomas was checkmate. There were still five more years of antagonism over the terms of the will, but in the larger context of the family's destiny as brewers, the path along the middle branch of Thomas Molson had been all but fixed with John Thomas's birth.

The birth of John Thomas did not deter John Junior from pressing forward with a lawsuit over the terms of his father's will, in which his brothers were named as defendants. After the interruptions of the rebellion, John Junior received a favourable judgment in February 1838 on one of his claims. He was entitled to his father's one-quarter share of the 1835 partnership, and hence of any profits for the year between his father's death and the striking of a new partnership between Thomas and William in 1837. The court ordered Thomas and William to turn over to John Junior by April 1 all necessary records to determine the monies owed to him. When Thomas and William failed to comply, John Junior had them found in contempt of court on April 20.

No satisfactory settlement arose from the legal actions that embroiled the brothers. According to Denison, the only significant resolution had come in 1837, when the issue of John Junior's entitlement to shared profits was addressed, at least for the future, as Thomas and William bought out John Junior's one-quarter interest in the brewery partnership. To settle the outstanding disputes in 1842, the brothers were able to enlist Peter McGill and George Moffatt, who had earlier withdrawn as executors of John Molson's estate, to serve as arbitrators.

The two esteemed old friends of their father, who were also business partners of the sons in a number of ventures, brought a Solomonic wisdom to their duties. They agreed with John Junior's claim, backed by the 1838 court decision, to profits from the brewery partnership that existed at the time of his father's death. But they sided with William in ruling that the credits generated by properties sold at Quebec City before their father's death belonged to William, and not to the residue of the estate.[2] The issue of rental payments on the brewery had also been settled: the provision "free from rent" was considered to have been struck from the will, and the partnership using the St. Mary's Current brewery property was obliged to pay rent to its owner, J.H.R. Molson, which was held in a trust account for him until he came of age.[3]

By then, the brewery partnership of 1835 had been succeeded by two different agreements. One, created in 1837 and called Thomas and William Molson, carried on operating the brewery establishment that was to be inherited by J.H.R. Molson, but the following April 25, five days after Thomas and William suffered the contempt-of-court ruling, they created another partnership, Thomas and William Molson and Company, which was to last ten years.[4] The copartnership was backdated to January 15; the distillery and other parts of the St. Mary's operation had been gutted by a fire on January 5, and as restorations proceeded, the brothers apparently decided to create an accounting firewall between the old operations and the new. "It is clear, from the various account books, that the sole object of the partnership of 1837 was to administer the brewery on behalf of young John Henry Robinson, whereas that of 1838 managed the distillery and brewery establishments, built after the fire, for the exclusive advantage of William and Thomas," the historian Alfred Dubuc has written.[5]

About the only aspect of the late patriarch's life that did not provoke an estate battle was the steamboat trade, for the family's direct involvement in it was all but over. In 1836, the Ottawa and Rideau Forwarding Company came under attack from Bytown-area merchants for poor service and high rates, and lost more than £7,000 that season. The company responded in the spring of 1837 by entering into a common schedule of freight rates with several other forwarding companies and turning management of the entire operation over to the forwarders Macpherson, Crane & Co. of Montreal. After two disastrous seasons, the company failed in 1842.[6] On the St. Lawrence too, the Molsons' involvement in the steam trade had faded after the merger of the Torrance and Molson lines in 1833.

Whatever estrangement existed between John and William as a result of the long-standing feud over their father's will must have been assuaged by the marriage between John's son John III and William's daughter Ann in 1845. It was the third first-cousin marriage in the family in two generations. With the bloodlines of John and William fused through their children, the brothers went on to create the Molsons Bank in 1853. (William and Thomas's efforts to create a bank in the late 1830s had failed to secure regulatory approval.) Molsons Bank was a highly successful venture that prospered right up to its absorption by the Bank of Montreal in 1925.

William also maintained a lengthy partnership with Thomas in the brewing and distilling business, and only left it in 1853 as he prepared to create the bank with John. By then, J.H.R. was involved in the brewery partnership. After coming of age in June 1847, J.H.R. had assumed ownership of the brewery property, and was taken on as a minority (one-quarter) partner on June 30, 1848, when the existing partnership between Thomas and William expired. But the young man may have been badly treated in the process, cheated by his own father and uncle. Dubuc has argued that Thomas and William improperly accounted for the insurance monies collected on the 1838 fire, paying J.H.R. only the principal and not the interest that had accumulated over the past ten years. Dubuc also states that J.H.R. was shortchanged in the handling of his apprenticeship contract. J.H.R. had signed the contract on November 15, 1844, retroactive to November 1, 1843, and according to Dubuc, J.H.R. should have received his indentures and been, at the least, taken on as a salaried employee after turning twenty-one. Instead, J.H.R. collected no pay for the period from his birthday on June 5, 1847, until the new partnership was drawn up one year later. "These actions would influence John Henry

Robinson's behaviour towards his father and his uncle William," states Dubuc.[7]

Despite another bout of animosity, the family continued to work together in its various ventures. When William withdrew from the brewing and distilling partnership in 1853 (as the ten-year 1848 partnership agreement allowed him to do within five years), Thomas and J.H.R. continued in a new partnership together. And when the Molsons Bank became a chartered (joint-stock) operation in 1855, the brothers John, Thomas and William, as well as J.H.R., were among the shareholders, with William serving as president and John as vice-president.

In 1859, Thomas surprised his family by remarrying—Martha had died in 1848. With his new wife, Sophia Stephenson, Thomas withdrew from day-to-day business, and in 1861 a new partnership was formed, called John H.R. Molson and Brothers, involving J.H.R., William Markland and John Thomas. At some point, certainly no later than the death of Thomas Molson in 1863, when the expanse of his estate was laid bare—Dubuc has estimated its worth at a minimum of $1 million[8]—John Thomas may have grasped the fact that he was so wealthy that work was not only unnecessary, but almost unseemly if the only purpose of the exertion was to make himself wealthier still. Thomas was as much self-made as his father had been. He and William had built an impressive distillery operation in addition to the brewery, and Thomas had diversified into real estate around Montreal and expanded his presence in Upper Canada. He owned three distilleries there, two of which he leased out, and also operated a sawmill and flourmill. Back in Montreal, he served as president of the New City Gas Light Company, in addition to sitting on the board of the Molsons Bank, and was also a shareholder in the Grand Trunk Railway.

Through his inheritance and an apprenticeship with a New York State distiller, John Thomas had been set up to continue the family business in spirits while J.H.R. turned out beer. Denison has suggested that corruption in the distilling industry soured John Thomas's enthusiasm for his appointed profession, but Denison was also obliged to note that attached to the surviving

apprenticeship contract is the transcription of a temperance lecture made in 1860:

> Woe, woe to the drunkard—to the rum seller and distiller—
> on the last day. When Thomas Molson shall be chairman
> and William Dow secretary. Sorry I am to say that Thomas
> Molson, a classical man, a man of education, has a college
> for education!—a church for salvation!—and a distillery for
> damnation![9]

"Whether John Thomas Molson took these preposterous sentiments seriously has not been established," Denison commented,
although he allowed that he was evidently "never altogether happy
in his inheritance." The temperance movement had a powerful following in the Montreal Protestant community—a majority
favoured a complete ban on distilled spirits—and John Thomas may
have blanched at the thought of presiding over the late nineteenth-
century equivalent of today's cigarette business. As soon as he was
able, he sold the Longue Pointe distillery to J.H.R., who persisted
with it until 1866. The following year, the partners began refining
sugar on the premises, but the venture was doomed. It would be
shut down in 1871, its machinery sold off to its principal rival,
Redpath and Son.

The sugar refinery was a considerable source of friction between
J.H.R. and William Markland, but the animosity was already well
developed by the time J.H.R. decided to leave the entirety of his
estate to John Thomas in September 1866— for as he explained to
John Thomas then, their brother's "untruthfulness & dishonesty
[made] any bequest to him not to be thought of."

Refining had scarcely begun before William Markland Molson
was pressing in April 1867 for them to stop any further investments
in the operation. J.H.R. defended the venture, but John Thomas
was soon fearing a continuing erosion of his assets as the refinery
stumbled badly. At the same time, William had liquidated the mill
property he had inherited from his father at Port Hope, Ontario, to
invest in a mining venture on the north shore of the Gulf of St.

Lawrence at the Moisie River. The Moisie Iron Company, which attempted to turn a profit from the iron-rich sands—an indication of the massive yet unexploited deposits at the Moisie's headwaters in Labrador and northern Quebec—was run by his uncle William. But like the sugar refinery, the mining venture eventually failed, its closure around 1875 being attributed by Denison to U.S. duties that made its export business untenable.

With the brewery partnership scheduled for renewal in 1869, John Thomas decided to withdraw from the family business altogether. He had intended, as he explained in an 1868 letter to J.H.R., to get on with arranging his "retirement" in 1864, although he was then only twenty-seven. The death of his bride, Lillias Savage, in childbirth in 1866 must have steeled his resolve to withdraw completely. The *Nooya* commission followed in 1870, and he sailed away in her, his brother J.H.R.'s promised bequest of the brewery tucked away for whatever rainy day awaited him.

However unlikely it seemed that John Thomas would ever actually run the brewery, J.H.R. cared only that someone he judged deserving of its fruits should come to possess it. It was as if J.H.R. had decided that, after personally suffering so many years of rancour, he was determined something good should come of the place. If it purchased John Thomas's freedom from the miseries the enterprise had visited on him, then he could die satisfied.

John Thomas spent the better part of the 1870s disengaged from the workaday world, sufficiently confident in the ability of his investments to generate income to ignore the onset of a worldwide recession. From 1871 to 1878, when he was not in England or making appearances in Montreal or hunting in the Canadian hinterlands, he cruised the Gulf of St. Lawrence aboard the *Nooya*, sometimes venturing as far as Labrador. He maintained a summer cottage at Cacouna on the Gaspé Peninsula, and the *Nooya* would ride at anchor in the shelter of Percé Rock while John Thomas entertained guests, among them the governor general.

He made his globe-girdling vacation through the superlatives of civilizations past and present in the winter of 1871–72, and in early

1874 he remarried, taking as his bride the twenty-four-year-old Jane (Jennie) Baker Butler of Waterloo, Quebec. That prompted a sumptuous European honeymoon in which the new John Thomas Molsons travelled from July until January, 194 days in all. John Thomas's expenditures included £50 for rhodonite in St. Petersburg, £240 for paintings in Munich, £100 for a coral mosaic and other unspecified extravagances, and £350 for "dresses etc." These honeymoon expenditures, which totalled £1,500, would cost £88,500 today.

John Thomas and Jane Butler raised seven children, and their christenings could not have made a more emphatic break with the family's history. The Molsons had been naming their sons John, Thomas and William since at least the sixteenth century, and among the daughters, the names Mary and Martha were routinely found. John Thomas pointedly ignored all precedents. His sons were named Herbert, Kenneth, Percival and Walter, his daughters Naomi, Mabel and Evelyn. The chain of John Molsons that the patriarch had envisioned owning the brewery would stop with John Thomas.

Aboard the *Nooya*, circa 1870. (The Molson Archives Collection/National Archives of Canada/PA-127502)

In the fall of 1878, the *Nooya* recorded a passage all the way to Halifax and back. It was the last significant cruise in almost a decade of John Thomas's wandering around the Gulf. Despite his determination to lead a gentleman's life of leisure, John Thomas was being forced back into the workaday world. He realized his lifetime vacation was over.

The ongoing global recession may have made it impossible for John Thomas to continue living off his investments, and the brewery was struggling, too, plagued by spoilage, which Denison has noted created a rate of returns of up to four percent of sales. The problem was solved in 1880 when the brewery began producing its own yeast under a new brewmaster, John Hyde, but J.H.R. still needed relief from his extensive duties. He was overextended, having taken on the vice-presidency of the family bank in 1879. The burden of overseeing the brewery had already been relieved by Adam Skaife, who had come to work for the Molsons in 1852 and had risen to chief clerk. He had proved so fundamental to the business that in 1872 he was taken on by J.H.R. as a minority partner, becoming the first non-Molson to share in the management and profits of the enterprise.

William Markland was by then well removed from the personal and professional lives of J.H.R. and John Thomas. Having withdrawn from the brewery partnership, he then withdrew from Canada altogether, relocating to Portland, Oregon, in 1877 with his wife and children to pursue mining opportunities. He would not return to Montreal for more than twenty years. Yet another self-imposed exile had struck the Molsons.

The second generation of Canadian Molsons were also by then gone, John Junior having died in 1860, Thomas in 1863, William in 1875. J.H.R. had at last got married, to Louisa Godard Frothingham in 1873, but there were no children. John Thomas, a sailor reluctantly home from the sea, remained the only apparent hope for a continuation of the Molson brewing dynasty.

As for the brewery's future, much of the credit for its recovery from the spoilage crisis and its continued good health likely belonged to the dutiful Adam Skaife, who had been with the

Molsons twenty-eight years in 1880, when his share of the operating partnership was increased from one-sixth to one-quarter (a share equal to that of the new partner, John Thomas, while J.H.R. retained half). John Thomas dutifully put in his office time as J.H.R.'s attentions were torn between the brewery, the family bank and other investments. In 1889, J.H.R. became the bank's president. In 1897, he became another Molson gripped by a deathbed urgency.

The Molson fondness for aphorism was doubtless cultivated by the patriarch John's careful reading of Lord Chesterfield. Even in 1824, when his son Thomas teetered on the brink of relocating to England, John Molson could not help but lecture his thirty-two-year-old offspring on some elemental truth: "Knowledge is Strength, Knowledge is every thing when properly applied."

At some unknown date, Thomas took the time to write down what he called "Jefferson's Rules of Life"—an imprecise rendition of Thomas Jefferson's oft-quoted "Ten Rules for the Good Life,"[10] which owed some philosophical debt to Chesterfield:

> Never put off till tomorrow what can be done today.
> Never trouble others to do what you can do yourself.
> Never spend your money before you have it.
> Never buy what you do not want because it is cheap.
> Pride costs as much as hunger, *thirst* and cold.
> We never repent of eating too little.
> Nothing is troublesome that we do willingly.
> How much pain those evils cost us that never happens.
> Take things by their smooth handle.
> When angry count ten before you speak.

As death approached, it was J.H.R.'s turn to dictate a philosophy of life to guide the future generations of Molsons. His words were recorded in the family bible:

> The Molson Family has maintained and preserved its position and influence by steady, patient industry, and every member

should be a real worker and not rely upon what it has been. All that is good and great of the family should not be underground.

Your private life should be pure, make no compromise with vice, be able to say "No" in a firm manly manner.

Character [is] the real test of manhood, live within your income no matter how small it may be. Permanent wealth is maintained by vigilance, prudence and not by speculation. Be just and generous when you have the means, wealth will not take care of itself if not vigilantly cared for.

There was to have been more, but time ran out for J.H.R. He died on May 28, 1897, at the age of seventy. Whatever else he felt was crucial for future Molsons to understand and obey, they would have to figure out on their own.

Since promising his brother John Thomas the entirety of his estate more than thirty years earlier, much had changed in J.H.R.'s life, including a rapprochement with his once-loathed brother William Markland. J.H.R. left separate life annuities to William Markland and his wife, as well as cash, bank stock and properties to their children, Harry Markland and Frederick William. Harry Markland had never gone west, choosing instead a career with Molsons Bank, and William Markland returned to Montreal with the rest of the family the year after J.H.R.'s death. But J.H.R. remained true to the core of his 1866 promise to John Thomas in leaving him the brewery.

According to Denison, an illness had left John Thomas infirm and incapable of actually running the brewery. But the brewery's future had already been imagined. J.H.R. looked to the fourth generation of Molsons in Canada in specifying that upon John Thomas's death, the brewery was to pass to his son, Herbert.

In 1894, Herbert Molson received a Bachelor of Applied Science degree from McGill, then graduated from the United States Brewers' Academy in New York City the following year. He also took over the management of the brewery in 1895. When a new partnership was created after J.H.R.'s death, as the brewery property's new owner the invalid John Thomas was granted half the shares, and Adam Skaife continued with a one-quarter interest. Herbert now took a one-eighth share, equal to that of his cousin Frederick William, son of William Markland. An efficiency expert, Frederick William combined with Herbert, the chemist and brewmaster, to guide the brewery into the new century and out of the rancorous uncertainties that had plagued the enterprise through the family's second and third generations.

The plant was modernized and the product line was overhauled. The first modern Molson brand, Export Ale, appeared in 1903. Between 1898 and 1909, total production increased from 14,625 to 81,334 barrels. In 1909, Herbert and Frederick resisted joining a consolidation of fourteen Quebec brewers into National Breweries, which rendered the Molsons a minority regional player in Quebec, holding perhaps twenty percent of the provincial market.

When John Thomas died in 1910, the opportunity arose to reorganize the family business, to abandon the vexatious tradition of separate property ownership and operating partnerships that dated back to John Molson and Thomas Loid in 1783. A new venture, Molson's Brewery Limited, was formed as a private joint-stock company in 1911. Herbert and Frederick converted their properties to stock, and Adam Skaife, who joined them as a director, was compensated for his long-standing interest in the partnership with a bond issue.

Molson's Brewery had acquired a nominally modern shape, although the company would not be transformed into a leading national brewer for more than forty years. The impetus came not from the Molsons themselves, but from E.P. Taylor's often ruthless acquisition and consolidation of regional breweries.

E.P. Taylor, a principal in Brading's Brewery of Ottawa, began the reinvention of the Canadian brewing industry by swallowing twenty-three Ontario operations between 1930 and 1953. By 1949, his Canadian Breweries Ltd. dominated the Ontario market, its best-known components being Carling and O'Keefe's. Taylor had also created a formidable affiliate in the prairie provinces, Western

Canada Breweries Ltd. For better or worse, Taylor was driving the modernization of the beer industry, eliminating small local breweries in favour of large-capacity plants that turned out a select number of national brands. Marketing of these streamlined brands capitalized on new opportunities in mass-market advertising created by television, radio and publishing. The post-war beer market was also being transformed by the rise in household consumption, as suburban barbecues began to eclipse taverns as the breweries' most important revenue source.

Provincial laws permitted beer to be sold only in the province in which it was produced. In the new age of mass marketing, which de facto required the development of national brands, brewers needed to have separate production facilities in each provincial market to satisfy the demand that advertising was creating. Taylor next turned his attention to Quebec, where the Molsons had been enjoying recent successes against that province's National, whose individual breweries included Dow, Frontenac and Dawes. In 1949, National Breweries and its flagship brand, the Dawes brewery's Black Horse ale, held 45.9 percent of the provincial market, while Molson's was second with 40 percent.[11] In only two years, Molson's overtook National with a lighter ale recipe; in 1951, Molson's held 50.5 percent of the Quebec market, while National dropped to 34.3. Canadian Breweries had an also-ran presence in Quebec through the Carling bottling plant in Montreal. With only about 12 percent of the Quebec market, Taylor was dissatisfied.

In 1951, both Taylor and Labatt's Brewery, which had been established in London, Ontario, in 1849, made plays for a larger share of the Quebec market, just as National Breweries was moving to shed excess capacity. National wanted to sell its Frontenac Breweries operation in Montreal, and Taylor's Canadian Breweries outbid Labatt's to acquire it that October. At the same time, Canadian Breweries was negotiating a share exchange with National's shareholders. In March 1952, Taylor was able to wrest control of National, and made its Dow Brewery the focal point of his Quebec operations. The number of brands was slashed from nine to four, and through a complex series of closures, expansions and plant exchanges, National-Dow was left operating four plants in the province. Their total capacity in 1952 of 35.5 million gallons, however, was dwarfed by the 43.7 million gallons of the single Molson plant, which stood on the historic St. Mary's Current property.

The Canadian Breweries' National-Dow was operating at only 64.9 percent of capacity, while the Molson plant was running at 93.8 percent. National-Dow had room to grow, and Taylor was willing to spend on an unprecedented scale to market his Quebec brands. Dow became the first Canadian brewery to advertise on television ("Wouldn't a Dow go good now?") and also increased radio and newspaper advertising. By the year-end of October 31, 1954, Dow had spent an incredible $3.2 million on advertising and sales promotion. The National-Dow operations of Canadian Breweries delivered a textbook lesson on how promotion translated into sales in the new era of streamlined brands and mass-market advertising. From January 1952 to August 1954, National-Dow's share of the Quebec market increased from 28.2 to 35 percent, while Molson's dipped from 53.4 to 48.5 percent.

Molson's was under siege and had no choice but to counter-attack. It could not survive as a single, mammoth brewery in Montreal. A new plant was established in Toronto in 1955, just as Labatt's was preparing to open a plant of its own in Montreal in 1956. The national brand war began, and with the new Toronto plant, Molson's rolled out a new lager called Canadian.

At the same time, Molson's established a presence in the national psyche through the family's ownership of the Montreal Canadiens of the National Hockey League and the brewery's sponsorship of the national television broadcast property Hockey Night in Canada. Senator Hartland Molson, grandson of Herbert, and his brother, Thomas Henry Pentland, purchased the Canadian Arena Company (owner of the Canadiens and the Montreal Forum) in 1957, and the franchise and arena remained in family hands until 1971, when they were sold to the Bronfman family of Montreal. In 1978, the treasured sports property was reacquired, this time by the company Molson's Brewery.

In January 2001, Molson Inc. sold 80.9 percent of the Canadiens and all of the new Molson Centre to the Colorado businessman George N. Gillett, Jr. Losses on the team and on the arena had become intolerable for a company in the midst of an about-face in its business plan. Molson had suffered a diversification misadventure in the 1990s, transforming itself into a holding company with such interests as "big box" retailing (Home Depot) and industrial cleaning. In 1998, the company began refocusing on its brewery operations.

Molson's Brewery became a public company in February 1945, when it began trading on the Montreal Stock Exchange, but the business has remained under the family's control. Three direct descendants of the brewery's founder are on the Molson Inc. board of directors: Eric Herbert (chairman of the board since 1988), Stephen Thomas (secretary of the board, as well as a member of the board of the charitable Molson Foundation) and Robert Ian. Eric and Stephen are sons of Thomas Henry Pentland, and so are descended from Herbert; Robert Ian is a descendant of Frederick William. Eric Molson remains the single largest shareholder in Molson Inc., with about one-third of the common Class B shares; no one else holds more than ten percent of the voting shares. In all, more than half the common shares are controlled, directly or indirectly, by Molson family members through estates or trusts.

It has long been a matter of pride within the organization that the heritage of the company is a living one, not just a marketing device. Molson Inc. dates the brewery's beginning to 1786, when John Molson returned from settling his inheritance in Lincolnshire and brewed his first batch of ale. For 215 years, John Molson's direct descendants have been prominently involved. (Inside Molson Inc., employees are wont to dismiss the Canadian arch-rival Labatt's as "the Belgians"—the brewery having been purchased by the Belgian giant Interbrew.) The majority of Molson voting stock remains within the family, and the brewery's headquarters continues to occupy the plot of land at St. Mary's Current first purchased by Thomas Loid in 1782 and acquired by John Molson in a sheriff's auction in 1785. The company and the family have no real rivals in the nation's commercial heritage. And to their credit, the Molsons have continued the charitable support of community institutions begun by John Molson, his sons and grandsons in their contributions to McGill University, Montreal General Hospital and other worthy causes.

"My expectations grow every day more sanguine on this Speculation & I presume it will in short time prove very lucrative & not without sufficient reason," John Molson assured Philip Ashley on October 22, 1786, as he completed his first malting in the log malthouse at St. Mary's Current. On March 31, 2001, Molson Inc. reported from the same plot of ground that gross revenues for the past year were $2.5 billion, with a net profit of $134 million.

$\mathscr{N}otes$

CHAPTER 1

1. It has been argued that John Thomas Molson made the first transatlantic crossing in a steam-powered private yacht, but he did nothing to publicize it, and when Lord Brassey made the crossing two years later in a steam yacht twice the size of *Nooya* in eighteen days, the honour would be claimed for him. In hindsight, John Thomas was right not to assert a historic first, as *Nooya* was an auxiliary-powered schooner, and relied mainly on her sails for that passage.

CHAPTER 2

1. *The Interesting Narrative of the Life of Olaudah Equiano, or Gustavus Vassa the African* (1789).

2. The problem with tracing Molsons (and all their variants) is the fact that the name means "son of Moll," a diminutive of Mary, and England had an ample supply of Marys producing male offspring. The name is a matronym—a surname based on the mother rather than the father. (Peterson, in contrast, is a patronym.) By the seventeenth century, England was broadly adopting the fifteenth-century French custom of a woman taking her husband's surname, and so whoever was born a Molson by then owed his or her name to some distant male whose father's surname was unavailable. The most obvious reason for this unavailability would be illegitimacy, but a matronym (as B.K. Sandwell explained in his Molson monograph) could also be used in cases of adoption, or where the father's identity was so disagreeable that the mother's given name was thought preferable. Molsons (and their spelling variants) can be found in christening records not only in Yorkshire and Lincolnshire, but in London and Liverpool and in Sterling, Scotland, in the early eighteenth century.

3. The renowned parliamentary commander Sir Thomas Fairfax wrote to the speaker of the House of Commons on May 23, 1643, informing him that royalist forces under the Earl of Newcastle had taken Rotherham and Sheffield, towns about twelve and eighteen miles, respectively, to the west of Cantley. The letter noted how the earl's forces "do now range over all the south-west part of this country, pillaging and cruelly using the well-affected party. . . ."

4. It suggests there was a first-born Thomas who died, and that the name was then given to this youngest of five children, who was nineteen years junior to the eldest surviving male, Richard, born in 1599.

5. We might even know their principal contact: a family named Sansom. On December 5, 1664, a letter (a 1720 transcript of which survives in very poor condition) was written by a Yorkshire Molson to a man named Sansom in the south Lincolnshire village of Cowbit. Both Cowbit and the Sansom family would figure prominently in the Molson family's future. Thomas of Peakhill's daughter Elizabeth, born in 1697, married Richard Sansom in 1720. Sansom's signature then appears on a bond of obligation signed by Thomas Molson in 1733, and as a co-leasee of some Peakhill property in 1731. He was also chosen as a guardian for the children of the lone male heir of Thomas of Peakhill and Mary—John, born in 1700. The 1664 letter was written the same day that the will of Thomas Mouldson of Brampton (county York)—a distant cousin of the Thomas Moulson who came to Crowland—was executed. Fragmentary surviving phrases (such as ". . . the will of Thomas Andrew was well proved. . . ." and "By the decree you find you have got more than was expect viz that the lands . . .") suggest that there was a relationship between the Molsons and Sansoms based at least in part on land ownership that could have been at the heart of Thomas Moulson's relocation to south Lincolnshire.

6. Samuel Lewis, *A Topographical Dictionary of England,* 1831.

7. The Molson family papers preserve a 1737 document that provided for the continuation of payments for flood controls in the Moulton Common Marsh, and another in 1741 concerns improvements to the same marsh.

8. Grammar schools were a popular form of what Canadians would know as a public, or free, school. These sprang up in communities around England in the mid-sixteenth century. The Moulton school was founded in 1561.

9. Edward Coke, a parliamentarian and jurist who became Lord Chief Justice of England in 1613 and is remembered as the "father" of English common law through his contributions to the Petition of Right of 1628, nonetheless in his *Institutes* defined a husband and wife as one person—the male person. *The Law's Resolutions of Women's Rights,* which was written in 1642, "made explicit that women existed as married or to be married and were subject to their husbands," according to Anderson and Zinnser (*A History of Their Own: Women in Europe from Prehistory to the Present,* Volume 1). *The Law's Resolutions* stated that women "have no rights in Parliament, they make no laws, they consent to none, they abrogate none."

10. It may not be the home in which our John Molson lived—we know, for example, from a repair bill in 1788 that the house at the time, while built using brick and lime mortar, had a thatched roof. A Canadian descendant, Hugh Molson, visited south Lincolnshire on a genealogical fact-finding mission in 1930, and wrote a memorandum in which he expressed his scepticism

of the age of the surviving home. "In my opinion the present house dates entirely from after John Molson emigrated. It is not unlikely that an earlier house stood on the site which in much earlier times was occupied by a considerable house belonging, I believe, to a monastic house, perhaps Crowland Abbey, and it was surrounded by a moat which is now in the process of being filled up." His "moat" was probably part of the drainage and irrigation system of the reclaimed Fen Lands.

11. In North America the conflict, which had begun in 1754, was known as the French and Indian War.

CHAPTER 3

1. I have calculated modern equivalencies for this book using the British House of Commons research paper "Inflation: The Value of the Pound 1750–1998" (issued February 23, 1999). Conversions are calculated using the price index (PI) for the historical year and the "modern" PI (1998). The modern equivalencies should be taken as a general guide. Absolute values are difficult to determine when many monetary units that appear in this book represent not only British pounds but the Halifax exchange rate used in Quebec, and the funds often are being applied in Quebec, whose price index would not necessarily have been the same as in England. It should also be noted that the swiftest decline in purchasing power of the pound occurred between 1970 and 1998. While one needed almost £14 in 1970 to purchase the goods £1 could secure 220 years earlier, in 1750, nearly £9 were required in 1998 to buy the same goods that £1 could purchase just 28 years earlier, in 1970. Thus, the £64,600 value in "today's" money (1998) that I have given for the £600 dowry of 1760 would have been only £7,440 in 1970.

2. For a full discussion of the naval officer's training and career, see N.A.M. Rodger's *The Wooden World: An Anatomy of the Georgian Navy*.

3. Britain might not have lost the Thirteen Colonies had not the prime minister, Lord North, seen to it that his brother-in-law, Rear Admiral Thomas Graves, secured command of the British fleet based at New York in 1781. That autumn, Graves bungled the Battle of the Chesapeake Capes and allowed a French blockade to maroon Cornwallis's seven-thousand-man army at Yorktown. Cornwallis's surrender effectively ended the rebellion in the Continental Army's favour and brought down North's government.

4. The Reform Bill of 1832 and the associated Boundary Bill resulted in Holland gaining its own Member of Parliament.

5. No genealogical records confirm the dates of birth or parentage of John or Samuel Elsdale, but other records indicate that on September 15, 1741, a child named Edward Elsdale, son of Samuel and Mary Elsdale, was christened at Surfleet. Another Edward Elsdale is recorded as having been christened at Surfleet on September 17, 1747, again a child of Samuel and Mary. Evidently,

the first Edward died, and his name was used again for Mary's last known child. Presumably this Edward did not survive either.

6. Elsdale had entered naval service just as the British Navy was introducing an important new method of training and managing its onboard manpower. Called the divisional system, it was introduced around 1755, and was intended to improve the efficiency of a ship's company and the welfare of its sailors. At the time, the navy was so flooded with wartime recruits like Elsdale that the men were scarcely known to their officers. Under the new manpower system, a ship's company was given divisions of command and responsibility: a midshipman like Elsdale was expected to train men in his subdivision in the use of cannons and small arms, while he in turn was overseen by a lieutenant.

7. Privateering was so enticing to American sailors during the Revolutionary War that the rebel union could scarcely man a proper navy. Most of the effective American naval action against the British was achieved by marauding privateers, the most famous of which was John Paul Jones.

8. A photocopy of the original manuscript was graciously made for the author by Robinson Elsdale's descendants in England. The manuscript, bound in leather by Elsdale's wife, remains in the family's private possession.

9. How Marryat got hold of the material is revealed in a letter written by W. Harrison Ainsworth (who apparently had taught at Manchester Grammar School) to one of Robinson Elsdale's grandchildren in 1872: "Mr. Robinson Elsdale, your Grandfather, appears to have been a very remarkable man. The volume (in MS.) containing his early adventures, was sent to me for publication by Dr. [Robinson] Elsdale [grandson of the privateer]. I lent it to Capt. Marryat, who based upon it his story, entitled 'The Privateer's-Man.' The early chapters of that Tale, are actually a transcript from your Grandfather's most curious narrative."

10. Elsdale's liberties with truth in his manuscript raise flags of concern for the work as a whole, even for the authenticity of his career. But a 1769 letter of congratulations preserved in the Molson Archives supports his privateering experience—the only document beyond Robinson's collection of anecdotes thus far unearthed to do so. His manuscript does provide clues to the veracity of his career. His captain's name was Wetherall. No one named Wetherall (or its many spelling variants) survives in British Admiralty record indices, but Treasury records contain a certificate dated October 29, 1757, signed by Thomas Wetherell affirming "that he has received on board his ship the *Enterprize* beef, tobacco, rice and brandy to be delivered to Stade," a North Sea port on the Elbe downstream from Hamburg. Other Treasury records indicate the *Enterprize* was one of four ships specified in a contract issued by the Commissioners of Victualling to merchant John Biggin to carry provisions to Stade between October and December 1757, presumably in support of the army of Britain's subsidized ally in the Seven Years War, Frederick II of Prussia.

(Biggin was also required to sign an affidavit on November 4, 1757, swearing that he would not bribe the inspectors appointed to examine the beef he supplied.)

Biggin (or his heirs) appears to have been in the provisioning business for the British military for a number of years. Wherever Britain's forces established a base, private contractors necessarily followed, and the foundation of the British merchant class in post-conquest Quebec was laid largely by such contractors. It was a trade John Molson was destined to enter, as he provided beer to the British troops in and around Montreal.

Another Treasury document notes the expiration of a victualling contract for Senegal and Senegambia in April 1768 that had been held by "Biggin and Bacon." The slaving forts of the Senegal coast had been captured from the French in 1758 and were held until their return in the Treaty of Paris of 1783. The forts opened more of west Africa to the wretched business of slavery for British merchants, and Liverpudlians in particular seized the opportunity. Robinson Elsdale suggested a possible connection to Liverpool in his manuscript by asserting he participated as a crew-member on at least one slave expedition to Senegal.

While the name of Elsdale's privateering ship, the *Revenge*, was almost a boilerplate name for privateers—Edward Teach, alias Blackbeard, wreaked havoc as a buccaneer aboard *Queen Anne's Revenge*—it is worth noting that on November 15, 1756, the owners of the privateer *Revenge* of Liverpool petitioned the Treasury Department for permission to release the flour contained in a captured French ship to relieve the shortage in the city. Thus it is possible that much of the activity Elsdale recounted in his anecdotes took place under the auspices of a Liverpool shipowner. And Marryat, in fact, was specific in placing the fictional Elsdale's employer in Liverpool.

11. Reverend Robinson Elsdale spent thirty-two years at Manchester Grammar School, the last three as master; his youngest son, Daniel, became a dockside priest in London. Samuel Elsdale served as master of Moulton Grammar School and warranted special mention in his father's DNB listing as "a frequent contributor to magazines, and the author of a volume of sacred poetry entitled *Death, Judgment, Heaven, and Hell; a Poem, with Hymns and other Poems.*" Samuel's son Robinson served as a surgeon at Moulton for thirty years.

12. Marryat presented the same passage thus: "Retreat being cut off, the French struggled with all the animosity and rage of mingled hate and despair; while we, infuriated at the obstinate resistance, were filled with vengeance and a thirst for blood. Wedged into one mass, we grappled together,—for there was no room for fair fighting,—seeking each other's hearts with shortened weapons, struggling and falling together on the deck, rolling among the dead and the dying, or trodden underfoot by the others, who still maintained the combat with unabated fury."

13. There was a grim epitaph to the action. After the *Revenge* was recaptured from French and Spanish privateers, the injured Elsdale was consigned to hospital in Port Royal. There he encountered the widowed Frenchwoman, who was watching over her wounded son in the same hospital. She recognized Elsdale and lambasted him for killing her husband. One of Elsdale's fellow crewmen silenced her by punching her son in the head, killing him.

14. While a proper census of Britain would not be conducted until 1801, its leaders had begun to fear—wrongly—that the kingdom was running a deficit in subjects, as the new world offered fresh opportunities, particularly once a hostile French presence had been eradicated. The government estimated that between 1700 and 1750, Lincolnshire had lost 19,800 of its estimated 180,000 residents, and that was before the Seven Years War wrested Quebec from the French. The 1801 census would actually indicate a Lincolnshire population on the increase, to 215,500.

15. Only Father John's youngest sister, Martha, born in 1740 and married at nineteen in 1759, yet survived, and appeared to be thriving famously, or at least producing heirs at a furious rate. She and her husband, Matthew Clarke (or Clark), had fourteen children between 1760 and 1780.

16. A connection between a Pell family and the Elsdales is suggested by the third (and final) marriage of John Molson's grandfather Samuel Elsdale. Elsdale's first known wife, Mary Robinson, had died in 1757. His second wife, Eleanor Stanroyd, whom he had married in 1772 when he was sixty-seven, died in 1783. In 1784, at seventy-nine, the widower Elsdale married a milliner named Mary Albin (or Albon). In Boston, Lincolnshire, in 1753, a woman named Mary Albin had wed a man named Isaac Pell. Thus, Samuel Elsdale and Mary Albin could have been widower and widow, with Mary's late husband, a Pell, having provided a long-standing social bridge.

17. A James Pell was born at Bicker in 1757 to a father named James, which would have made this James Jr. two years older than James Gibbins's offspring of the same name.

18. Their welcome in Montreal presumably was warmer than the one extended to some of the Loyalists claiming to be refugees from rebel mobs. Allan McLean, the British Army's commanding officer in Montreal, wrote to headquarters in Quebec in the fall of 1779 to complain that he was plagued by "royalists real and pretended." During the winter of 1779–80 he ordered about three dozen able-bodied refugees who had turned up at Varennes in what is now northern Vermont to join a militia unit at St. Ours. He then went so far as to try to imprison forty other recent arrivals who resisted his attempts to recruit them for military duty. General Frederick Haldimand, Quebec's lieutenant-governor, refused to let him lock them up. But Haldimand did feel that such arrivals should be made to resettle around the upper military posts, especially Detroit, and he did relocate some Loyalist families in 1780.

CHAPTER 4

1. Miller, *Broadsides*, p. 90.

2. Denison erroneously stated that the *Preston* escorted Molson's convoy to Quebec.

3. Peter Livius was dismissed as chief justice after his ruling in a dispute involving two Montreal merchants who had offended Governor Guy Carleton. Livius had returned to England to seek and receive vindication through an order-in-council in March 1779, but he had never been able to make it back to Quebec. A storm off Newfoundland in the autumn of 1780 dismasted his ship and forced him back to England. He was supposed to return to the colony in the spring of 1782—he could have become a member of John Molson's convoy—but ended up remaining on the wrong side of the Atlantic, serving in absentia until 1786.

4. Creighton, *The Empire of the St. Lawrence*, p. 39.

5. Burt, *The Old Province of Quebec*, Vol. II, p. 27.

6. Molson also never identified the convoy's warships in his correspondence, and mistakenly referred to James Worth as "Wake."

7. Molson's description of his voyage, set down in letters to his uncle Robinson and his grandfather Samuel several months later, are confused in timing. When correlated with observations in Captain Worth's log, many critical events appear to have been dated a full week after the fact in his letters.

8. The engagement endures for the innovative tactics employed by Rodney. Rather than being satisfied with the traditional parade of lines of battle firing at each other, Rodney took advantage of a ragged French line to split it and attack it mercilessly from both sides, thereby anticipating Nelson's successful strategy at Trafalgar by more than two decades.

9. The Articles of War ran to thirty-six separate disciplinary transgressions, and more than half specified death as the punishment, which included the shipboard crimes of theft, spying, murder and sodomy. It seems today a harsh code, but the brutality of naval discipline must be set in the context of justice on land, where flogging was also a popular punishment, and death was still the penalty specified for 160 types of felonies at the beginning of the nineteenth century. On land, judges showed no hesitation in applying the law to its fullest—public hangings were common and popular forms of entertainment. Most appalling was the practice of hanging children for simple thefts. There is a case of a child of six being sent to the gallows in England, and in February 1814, five children (one of them eight years old) were condemned to death at London's Old Bailey.

10. John Paul Jones's *Bonhomme Richard* had achieved a sensational victory against the forty-four-gun British warship *Serapis* off the east coast of Britain as she was escorting a convoy to the Baltic in 1779. But Jones was no longer active in privateering when Molson's convoy sailed.

CHAPTER 5

1. The island is traditionally discussed in terms of east and west, although its layout is more north-south.

2. The present Nôtre-Dame Basilica was consecrated in 1829.

3. The seigneurial system that gave the Sulpicians control of the island of Montreal has long since been abandoned, but the order still administers Nôtre-Dame Basilica, erected in the early nineteenth century on the site of the original seventeenth-century church.

4. Data compiled by the Montreal Research Group of the Canadian Centre for Architecture indicates there were 406 residences within the walled town in 1805. Using a multiple of 7.5 residents per household, the MRG estimates a population of 3,045.

5. Creighton, *The Empire of the St. Lawrence*, p. 24. More recent analysis by the Montreal Research Group into the professions of 402 property owners in 1765 was forced to qualify 144 of them as "unknown."

6. Under the Quebec Revenue Act of April 1775, the British Parliament introduced a new duty system aimed solely at rum, spirits and molasses, in an effort to strengthen the North American colonies' trade with Britain. Quebec was being drained of specie by trade with New Englanders, who swapped fish for rum and molasses in smuggling operations to the French and Dutch Caribbean sugar colonies. Under the new act, rum shipped from the British West Indies to Britain could be imported by Quebec duty-free. If the rum came to Quebec directly from a British West Indies possession, the duty was six pence per gallon; nine pence if it came via one of the American colonies; and a full shilling—then worth twelve pence—if it came from a non-British domain such as the French or Dutch Caribbean possessions. Molasses was dutiable at three pence per gallon if transported on British or Canadian ships, six pence otherwise. Importing duty-free rum from Britain was cheaper than bringing it in from the West Indies under the duty. But initially at least, cheaper still was importing molasses from a French or Dutch Caribbean possession at three pence per gallon (plus a one-pence imperial customs charge) and distilling it in Quebec. By 1787, there were four distilleries in the colony, one of them in Montreal, with a total capacity of 420,000 gallons. See A.L. Burt, *The Old Province of Quebec*, Vol. II, pp. 167–69, for details of the rum trade, Quebec Revenue Act and domestic distilling business.

7. The arrival of Loyalists introduced, to a limited degree around Montreal, the inflated "York rate" (eight shillings to the Spanish dollar, devised in New York), but Molson appears never to have used it. And his occasional reference to dollars in his first years in Quebec would have meant Spanish dollars, not the hugely deflated American paper dollars printed to fund the revolution. An American dollar coin did not appear until 1792.

8. The Cochrane debacle is discussed in *The Old Province of Quebec*, Vol. II, pp. 33–36, and in *The Empire of the St. Lawrence*, pp. 95–96.

9. This money would actually have been worth about £7,200, based on the 1782 British price index, but I have used a multiple of eighty for the entirety of the 1780s. There was an immediate drop in the value of the pound in 1783 of twelve percent as the American Revolution ended, and the price index remained relatively stable for the rest of the decade.

CHAPTER 6

1. John Waite's son George testified to the family's ouster from Tryon County. His name appears on a petition (as Wait) signed by members of the King's Royal Regiment of New York on June 13, 1778. The soldiers complained to the British commander in Quebec, Guy Carleton, that they were being treated as regular enlistments rather than as volunteers, and "having left there Families behind them In the province of New York, Suffering through poverty and Nakedness being Script and plundered of all they had by the Rebels," they asked to be deployed in New York rather than continue to serve garrison duty in Quebec. A man named Thomas Wait appeared in the muster roll of Captain Allan Cameron's Company of New York Volunteers at Savannah on November 29, 1779.

2. An alternative to this John Waite as Thomas Loid's brewery labourer is a member of the Wait family who settled at the north end of Isle La Motte in northern Lake Champlain, close by the four hundred acres Molson acquired at Caldwell's Manor. However, the Wait clan did not settle at Isle La Motte until 1788, although they could have been in the area before then.

3. Denison asserted, without citation, that a brewhouse twelve feet square could be found at Snake Hall.

4. This charge was moved to May 28, 1784, in the final accounting (Molson Archives, Vol. 35, Accounts 1783–85). Thus it applied to visits to Caldwell's Manor in either the fall of 1783 or the spring of 1784.

5. Another Ostrander, named John, was born at Albany and served in the revolution on the opposing side with the First Canadian Regiment, which the American forces raised during the 1775–76 invasion of Quebec. Men like John Ostrander augmented the true Canadians in the ranks, and he returned to Albany after the war.

6. It's also possible Loid and Molson were put in touch with McGlemoyl (or Loyalists who knew him) through John Johnson, the superintendent of Loyalist refugees and Indian affairs, who was a brewery neighbour.

7. A privately compiled genealogy submitted to the Mormon church dates Caldwell's birth to 1737 in Ross Bey, Ireland.

8. The biographical details for Caldwell are drawn substantially from the *Dictionary of Canadian Biography*.

9. Foucault made some attempts at settling the land, but King George's War of 1744–48 put an end to his efforts. After visiting the area in July 1749, Pehr Kalm observed that "a Wind Mill built of stone, stands on the east side of the Lake on a projecting piece of ground. Some Frenchmen have lived near it; they left when the War broke out, and are not yet come back to it. The English, with their Indians, have burned the houses here several times, but the Mill remained unhurt." The windmill, which was in ruins when Loyalist settlers arrived, gave the name to present-day Windmill Point.

10. A ninety-nine-year lease for all the properties was granted to Caldwell at an annual rent of £520 for the first twenty years, £640 thereafter, with the option to buy the properties outright within the first twenty years for £16,000—which Caldwell did not do, although, as Allen Stratton noted, financially it made the most sense, as the first twenty years of lease payments alone amounted to more than £10,000. The details of Caldwell's land deals with Murray are presented in Stratton's *History of Alburgh, Vermont*.

11. The properties belonging to the religious order, which had been seized by the Crown after the conquest, included ten seigneuries that generated income of about £1,000 to £1,200 per year, according to A.L. Burt. Caldwell thus robbed the Crown of about eight years of the Estates' revenues. Based on the British price index of 1810, Caldwell's thefts amounted to the modern equivalent of £1.6 million from the Crown and £320,000 from the Jesuit Estates.

12. According to Stratton's published translation of the *Registre d'Intendance* (Fief No. 9, Folio 30) in the Archives nationales du Québec.

13. Molson's will of 1785 referred to "my Interest & Improvements made on [a] Certain Tract of Land known by the name of the Tongue or Caldwells Manor Situate in Vermont State." While no survey survives from Caldwell's activities, the lot numbers 27 and 28 cited by Molson in his settling of accounts with Loid can be found on an undated survey produced by the Vermont Forest and Parks Department labelled "1781 Town Lotting Plan of Alburgh, Vt." The lots are located precisely where the subsequent purchaser of Molson's land, Joseph Mott, accumulated 1,000 acres. Their position on the lotting plan also agrees with a reference Molson made in a 1786 notebook to "my lands opposite Point au Fair."

14. In 1774, Ethan Allen had hatched a scheme with Philip Skene, owner of a vast tract of upstate New York, to create a new British colony, of which Skene would be governor, by combining New York territory above the Mohawk River with the New Hampshire Grants. It would have been a speculator's bonanza, but the revolution left the proposal stillborn.

15. Ethan Allen's performance was decried by rebel commanders, who realized it probably hardened Canadian resolve against the revolution and made firm allies of the British and the native tribes. General Montgomery, who succeeded in taking Montreal on November 12 from a depleted garrison

of about 150 men without firing a shot, cursed Allen's "imprudence and ambition." General Washington ventured the opinion that Allen's "misfortune will, I hope, teach a lesson of prudence and subordination to others who may be too ambitious to outshine their general officers and regardless of order and duty rush into enterprises which have unfavorable effects to the public and are destructive to themselves."

16. George Washington eyed the Vermont lobbyists warily. On February 6, 1782, General Washington, while in Philadelphia, wrote General Philip J. Schulyer, who had been in charge of the ill-fated Canadian invasion of 1775. "[I] am informed Mr Ira Allen and Mr [Jonas] Fay have arrived in this Town from Vermont on some public business to Congress, what the object of their Mission is I know not, should any thing interesting transpire I shall communicate it to you."

17. Burt, *The Old Province of Quebec*, Vol. II, pp. 9–10.

18. The firm was actually Phyn & Ellice, one of the great trading houses, and a partner in the North West Company. The associated firm George Ellice & Co. had an office in Montreal.

CHAPTER 7

1. No tavern licence records survive for Montreal from this period.

2. Smith, *Legend of the Lake*, p. 103.

3. Ibid, p. 109.

4. No payroll for the crew of the *Ontario* survives. Jim Brainsby (or Brainby) was probably related to the boatswain Robert Brainby, who appears on the Naval Department payroll at Carleton Island on December 31, 1779. The loss of the *Ontario* coincides with Molson's observation that Brainsby had drowned three years earlier. And the fact that a neighbour of Molson's, John Johnson, had been closely associated with the *Ontario* and the Carleton Island base suggests that Molson learned of Brainsby's loss from Johnson.

5. In their final accounting, in March 1785, for expenses incurred since the interim accounting around June 1784, £13 was added to Molson's credit, "To Sundries Journeys from Montreal to Manor Articles bought etc," and dated January 30, 1784. In the summary of all credits dating back to September 1783, this credit was moved to May 28, 1784. The final accounting also noted an expense for Molson of £66 4s 8d on May 17, 1784, "To Sundries as per Bills & provision etc for the use of Mr. Loid," which had not appeared in the interim accounting.

6. Later, the bill would be entered as a credit to Molson of £88 18s, reflecting the actual draw of £80 on the Gosling account and his discount loss of £8 18s.

7. The production figures are a very rough estimate, made with input from brewery historian Ian Bowering. An Upper Canadian brewer reported in 1832

and 1833 being able to produce 9.6 to 11 Imperial gallons of ale for each bushel of malted barley, which would represent a six to ten percent reduction in weight of the barley purchased from the farmer. Because Molson and Loid were brewing wheat using an unknown process, it's difficult to draw a firm conclusion about the brewery's output based on Molson's grain purchases. But if he bought eighty-six bushels of wheat and barley, we could expect the partners to produce around 900 to 1,000 gallons of beer, or eighteen hogsheads.

8. The volume of wheat was entered as "soixant minots" in the movables inventory. A minot was a measure used in Quebec until at least the 1830s that was equal to 1.07 Imperial bushels.

9. Donald Fyson, *Criminal Justice, Civil Society and the Local State: The Justices of the Peace in Quebec and Lower Canada*, Ph.D. thesis, Université de Montréal, 1995.

10. Ibid.

11. Ibid.

12. The fact that Waite claimed wages dating back to January 1783 has led some writers to believe that Molson must have been in business with Loid at this early date. But there's no evidence that Molson began formally working with Loid any earlier than September 1783, when they began maintaining the joint account of their expenditures. An error in the joint-account ledgers may also encourage this misinterpretation. An entry of expenses for Loid that appears to be for February 2, 1783, was corrected to February 2, 1784, in the revised summary. It's likely that Waite's claim for outstanding wages simply extended back to when Loid first hired him, and that to get satisfaction in the courts he had to sue both Loid and Molson. The fact that expenses borne exclusively by Loid were deducted from Waite's settlement indicates that the responsibility for Waite's hiring lay with Loid alone. Items on Waite's 1784 account paid for by Loid included veal, venison, beef, currants, ale, beer, tobacco, cash, and shoe repairs.

13. Denison wrote (incorrectly) in *The Barley and the Stream* (p. 30) that the first attempt to auction the brewery property took place October 22. But the notice in the *Quebec Gazette* of August 26, 1784, and the indenture of sale of January 31, 1785, specify the December 31 date as the first attempt to hold an auction.

14. In one of his more imaginative pronouncements, Chesterfield wrote his son on January 8, 1750: "It is most certain, that the reputation of chastity is not so necessary for a woman, as that of veracity is for a man; and with reason; for it is possible for a woman to be virtuous, though not strictly chaste, but it is not possible for a man to be virtuous without strict veracity. . . . For God's sake be scrupulously jealous of the purity of your moral character; keep it immaculate, unblemished, unsullied; and it will be unsuspected."

15. Loid's credits for expenditures logged after the interim settlement came to £189 11s 10d, but they were all incongruously attributed to one day—

February 2, 1784 (initially mislabelled as 1783), which was well before the interim settlement. As noted, several credits logged for Molson after the interim settlement were also given dates that preceded that settlement. Loid, in fact, had no actual credits after February 7, 1784 (the expenditures for which date were all then transferred to February 2 in the summary of total historic credits), while Molson recorded incidental credits of about £12 after the interim settlement. This, as noted, suggests that after the suit, Molson was no longer living with Loid; otherwise he still would have been paying Loid room and board.

16. What is striking about this amount is that it far exceeds the funds we know Molson received from home during his first two years in Quebec. He sold a £60 bill of exchange in 1782 and an £80 bill in 1783, which, with discounts, might have netted him around £125 in cash. Presumably he brought some money with him from England, but it could not have been much if he had been compelled to sell the £60 bill soon after he arrived. How, then, was he able to spend £234, according to the joint account, between September 1783 and December 1, 1784—all but £12 5s 8d of which was spent by May 28, 1784? Possibly he had funds available to him from working with the Gibbins men in butchering and with Loid in brewing, but we have already seen that the brewery had a disastrous 1783–84 season and could not have produced the sort of revenues that would give Molson such spending power. Optimistically, shared revenues could have accounted for one large Molson credit of £66 4s 8d. It was entered in the ledgers after the interim settlement, even though it was attributed to May 17, 1784. The credit was "To Sundries as per Bills & Provision etc. for the use of Mr. Loid." Shared brewery revenues may also have covered another backdated credit of £13 "To Sundries Journies from Montreal to Manor, Articles Bot etc.," which was logged initially for January 30, 1784, and then moved to May 28 in the summary of all credits since September 1783. But that would still seem to leave Molson short of the revenues to take his spending to £234.

The answer may lie in bad bookkeeping. Molson may have "double dipped" on the £80 bill of exchange he sold to Loid in September 1783. It's significant that the bill was not entered as a credit to Molson before the interim settlement of June 1784, but rather was logged on a subsequent ledger page, backdated to its date of sale, and included in the final settlement tally of March 2, 1785. Molson claimed £88 18s, which combined the face value of the bill with the discount loss on the sale to Loid. But Molson should only have been credited against Loid for the £8 18s discount on the bill, if the cash he received was then used for expenditures credited to him. Otherwise he was claiming the bill's value twice. This may have been what happened. Molson and Loid's accounting was so simplistic and confused that it's possible Molson asserted that the money his grandfather had to provide Ashley to satisfy the bill represented a debt against his estate, for which he deserved a credit. Both men were too fiscally naive to realize that Molson was claiming the expense a second time by doing so. Ironically, a double claim on the bill of exchange would mean that Molson was the one seriously indebted to Loid, and that Loid surrendered both the brewery and the land at Caldwell's Manor on the worst possible terms.

CHAPTER 8

1. Beyond what may have been disappointing personal news, the Wilsons could have caught wind of the coming radical revisions to the British Acts of Navigation, which would bar virtually all American-made ships—and ships having an American among their owners—from being registered in Britain. (American ships taken as prizes were exempt.) The new regulations were enacted in 1786.

2. The identity of "Mrs. Jacobs" is not certain, but the Jacobs name appears in a number of marriages around Caldwell's Manor.

3. He may have been referring to Robert Hunter, Jr., who left the province about this time and wrote an account of his travels, *Quebec to Carolina, 1785–86.*

4. During the American Revolution, James Phyn acquired the first of a series of ships named the *Everetta,* which were also referred to in various records as the *Ewretta* and (in one Molson letter) the *Eweretta.* Eweretta was a woman's given name found in the Phyn family. The second one, purchased in 1781, was the former *Latium,* a 350-ton vessel. In 1792, a third *Everetta,* of 342 tons, was built for Phyn on the Thames. See Denison, *A History of the Bank of Montreal,* Vol. 1, Appendix D, p. 437.

5. John Molson's entry in the *Dictionary of Canadian Biography* states that he made trips to England in 1795 and 1797, but this is highly unlikely. No documents survive that support the visits, and a number of documents rule them out. The authors may have been led to conclude that he made the trips because he produced wills in those years, and in 1785 and 1810 Molson wrote wills before making the Atlantic crossing. But his 1795 and 1797 wills were more in character with his 1836 will—he thought he was about to die and had to put his affairs in order. He could not have visited England in 1795 because he provided his friend George Stansfeld, who took his own trip that year, with power of attorney to collect all his (Molson's) personal papers. And Molson's correspondence gives no hint of a trip in 1797. In fact, he was entering the lumber business in the summer of 1797—and writing a deathbed will that June—and so could not have been overseas.

CHAPTER 9

1. The more complete title was *Theoretic Hints on an Improved Practice of Brewing Malt-Liquors; Including Some Strictures on the Nature and Properties of*

Water, Malt, and Hops; the Doctrine of Fermentation; the Agency of Air; the Effects of Heat and Cold. . . .

2. "A List of the Principal Civil Officers of Vermont from 1777 to 1918," published under the direction of the Secretary of State in 1918.

3. While Molson made no mention of it, James Gibbins, Jr., was also set-tled at Missisquoi Bay, raising a family. A genealogy compiled by the Sinclair family of Canada cites as one of its distant ancestors a man named James Gibbons Pell, thought to have been born in Lincolnshire around 1760. James Gibbins, Jr., alias Pell, was christened at Spalding on October 12, 1759. This Sinclair ancestor married, at an unknown date, a woman named Margaret Brisbin Mills, at Caldwell's Manor. The Sinclair genealogy indicates they raised two sons, William and George—the fact that these were also the names of James Junior's brothers further supports the likelihood that James Gibbins, Jr., alias Pell, and James Gibbons Pell were one and the same person.

4. John Molson entry, *Dictionary of Canadian Biography*.

5. The Reverend John Bethune's third son, also named John, born in 1791, was ordained as an Anglican priest, and in 1818 became minister of the new Christ Church and first rector of the Anglican parish of Montreal. In 1835, he was appointed principal, pro tem, of McGill University—the educational institution founded by the estate of James McGill. In 1850, Bethune became rector of Christ Church Cathedral, then its Dean, the first Anglican in Canada to receive that dignity. Bethune's ministry in Montreal lasted more than fifty-four years, until his death in 1872.

6. A cousin, Guy Johnson, held the post between father and son. All three were eventually knighted.

7. *Joseph Brant 1743–1807: Man of Two Worlds*, p. 68.

8. John Molson entry, *Dictionary of Canadian Biography*.

9. This reply was included in the published collections of Chesterfield's letters.

10. As the editor of the Oxford University Press edition of Lord Chesterfield's letters notes, Chesterfield was apparently unconcerned that the speaker of this line (from *Othello*) is Iago, who is responding to Desdemona's query of what a woman "ever fair and never proud" was good for.

CHAPTER 10

1. "Spinster" did not carry the "old maid" connotation it has today. An agreement of June 14, 1759, signed by John Molson's grandfather John, to pro-vide a £600 dowry for his daughter Martha in her marriage to Mathew Clarke, identified the bride as "Martha Molson Spinster," even though she was only nineteen. "Spinster" was also a job description, for a woman who spun wool as a cottage trade or was apprenticed to become one. Any young unmarried woman by default was a labourer in training, and so could earn the "spinster"

label. Cottage trades were so few for women that "spinster" was employed as a generic description for unmarried women of any age.

2. The Vaughans in the British Naval and Military Records, Series C, were enlistees with the Prince of Wales American Regiment, Loyal New Englanders, Volunteers of Ireland, Guide and Pioneers, King's Orange Rangers, Maryland Loyalists, Pennsylvania Loyalists, New Jersey Volunteers and King's American Regiment.

3. The genealogy presented here on the Vaughans of Caldwell's Manor is based on research by David Bell, a published family history by Vaughan descendant Herbert Derick, information in the Vaughan fond at the National Archives of Canada (MG25 G 129) and privately compiled family trees submitted to the International Genealogy Index.

4. Amos Hawley Vaughan was a surveyor whose work, according to documents in the Archives nationales du Québec, included a survey of the former Foucault seigneury, then known as Allard's Manor, in 1847–48, and the path across Ash Island of the Champlain–St. Lawrence Rail Road, in which the Molsons invested.

5. While there is no specific Sarah Vaughan in this family tree who would match John Molson's spouse, there are possible connections to someone named Insley. There are a few signs of Inslee marriages into the greater Vaughan family circle, through the Ward and Crosby families. Rebecca Towner's mother was Amy Ward of New Haven. On January 4, 1775, a Samuel Ward Burnham married an Elizabeth Inslee in Hartford—a slim connection, but possibly a relevant one. The possible link to the Vaughans via Crosby comes from Rebecca's brother Ithiel, who married a Sara Crosby around 1764 in Putnam, N.Y. A Samuel Inslee married an Ann Crosby in Boston on December 20, 1768. But beyond similarities of names, none of these family connections can be proved, and they still don't offer up a Sarah Vaughan who could have married John Molson.

6. There is some confusion about the identity of various men named John Vaughan in the early history of the Massachusetts Bay Colony. Johan Vahan may have been the man known as John of Waterton, and family researchers are still trying to decide if these Vaughan men are the same person.

7. One family pedigree filed with the Church of Jesus Christ of Latter-day Saints asserts that she died on May 13, 1843, but it does not give a place of death or any supportive documentation, and this has not been confirmed by other Vaughan family researchers. These pedigrees can be rife with errors, and the pedigrees for the Sweets and the Vaughans are full of contradictions, inconsistencies and impossibilities. In some cases, family members are asserted to have been born in Rhode Island more than a decade before the colony was settled.

8. I am indebted to David M. Bell for his genealogy of the Kinsley/Kingsley family of Vermont, produced in July 2000.

CHAPTER 11

1. Denison stated that there was a combined malthouse and brewhouse, 36 by 60 feet (p. 27), when Molson joined forces with Loid, but there is no apparent evidence for this. Denison's preliminary notes in fact stated, "The assumption has always been that the first buildings were made of logs, possibly white cedar from the famous stands on the south shore of Lake St. Louis above the Lachine rapids since Montreal Island itself provided mainly hardwoods. The assumption seems reasonable." Denison modified this in the book to a combined brewhouse-malthouse of a specific dimension, built with squared cedar logs, without providing any evidence. As noted, more than one building stood on the property in the fall of 1783, and comments by Molson in letters written in 1787 make it clear the brewhouse and malthouse had been separate.

2. The Cooks may have come from Caldwell's Manor, as a man named Jacob Cook appears on the 1786 list of applicants for Loyalist land grants in Sutton and Potton townships. Jacob Cook had lived "south of ye line" in Caldwell's Upper Manor since 1777, according to the application. The name Cook had appeared in the joint account between Molson and Loid as part of Loid's expenses—a 14s 6d payment on November 15, 1783, and a £1 3s 4d outlay logged, among many expenses, on February 2, 1784.

3. This chapter's discussion of historic brewing practices is drawn from consultation with the brewery historian Ian Bowering.

4. Alexander Morrice, *A Practical Treatise on Brewing the various sorts of Malt Liquor; With Examples of each Species, and the mode of using the Thermometer and Saccharometer; the whole forming A Complete Guide to Brewing London Porter, Brown Stout, Reading Beer, Amber, Hock, London Ale, Windsor Ale, Welch Ale, Wirtemberg Ale, Scurvy-Grass Ale, and Table and Shipping Beer to which are included, General Instructions for Making Malt; and Tables of the net duties of excise on Strong and Table Beer Payable by Common Brewers, in Town and Country*, 7th edition (London: Sherwood, Gilbert and Piper, 1827).

CHAPTER 12

1. The first detailed listing of Molson's brewery clients in his "waste book" does not begin until 1788, and so a proper portrait of his market in 1787 cannot be drawn.

2. Allen Stratton identified the men in a 1794 petition to the Land Committee of Governor Dorchester, calling for grants in the Quebec townships of Sutton and Potton. The Land Committee pronounced the chief petitioner, Alexander Taylor a "disturber of the peace and a seditious person," and the petition failed. In any event, the townships had already been granted. Evidence within the list points to a date of 1786 for the residencies. Stratton's list indicates the vast majority (fifty-eight) were from Caldwell's Upper Manor ("South of ye line"), with four from St. Johns, three from "North of ye line," one from

"Missiquoi Bay," four from "Mississquoi River" and one simply from "Missisquoi." Six had served in "Jessup's Corps" (the King's Loyal Americans regiment, led by Lieutenant-Colonel Ebenezer Jessup and Major Edward Jessup), one in the Royal Navy, one in "Major Roger's [sic] Corps" (the King's American Rangers, led by Major James Rogers), and one in an unidentified militia. As well, Captain John Savage had been a British Army regular. The total garnered from Loyalist land-grant applications did not include men like Thomas Loid and James Gibbins, Sr., who were also living in and around the Upper Manor at the time. While settlers who received their lands from Ira Allen were also present, it's impossible to know how many, as the first state census wasn't conducted for Alburgh until 1790. That census identified ninety heads of families, fifteen of whom had been on the circa-1786 Loyalist land-grant application rolls. Clearly, as freehold lands became available to Loyalists, they moved out of the Upper Manor.

3. Burt, *The Old Province of Quebec*, Vol. II, p. 166.

4. Ibid., p. 163.

5. The petition, signed and dated at Bennington, called for "an Act for extending the circuit of the post rider from Bennington to Rutland, in the County of Rutland, thro' such towns in the County of Addison as may best serve the interest of said county. . . ." The postal service the petition called for had nothing to do with Alburgh—the northernmost point in the proposed route, Addison County on the east shore of Lake Champlain, was some fifty miles south of Alburgh.

CHAPTER 13

1. A Loyalist named David Logan was settled at Caldwell's Upper Manor about 1786 and appeared in the 1790 Alburgh census. This reference could also be to John Logan, who inherited his family's Montreal property in 1784. The name "Logan" also appears in the brewery account book in 1788.

2. Other men named Mott—Richard and Jacob—appear in the muster rolls of the New York Volunteers in Savannah in November 1779.

3. Kelsey, *Joseph Brant 1743–1807: Man of Two Worlds*, p. 301.

4. Several men named Joseph Mott appear in the New York census for Dutchess County in 1800.

5. The exhaustive and often contradictory testimony from all parties was preserved by Allen Stratton in his *History of Alburgh, Vermont*.

6. William may have remained and gone by the name Gibbins Pell as well, as a man by that name was a subscriber to the War Fund in Montreal, according to an item in the *Quebec Gazette* of June 20, 1799. He also signed (along with John Molson) a public tribute in Montreal to the departing Lord Robert Prescott, published by the *Gazette* on July 25, 1799. James Gibbins Pell became active in the militia, and in 1823 was appointed major, battalion of

troops. What became of George Gibbins is unknown.

Denison asserted that two Pell sons, James and William, relocated to the United States. He wrote that "there is some reason to believe that one of them, William, later became the owner of Fort Ticonderoga, now the most impressive monument to the French regime in America and still owned by members of the Pell family." But genealogical records and historic documents suggest that these Pells were not descended from the Pells known to Molson. The ruins of the fort were purchased in 1820 by William Ferris Pell, whose ancestors in America can readily be traced back into the 1740s. The Pell genealogy is confused by the presence of the Ferris Pells in land deals in Quebec's Eastern Townships. Documents in the papers of the Ruiter family (who settled initially at Caldwell's Manor) at the National Archives of Canada (MG 23 G III Vol 2) detail the brothers Benjamin and William F. Pell purchasing land in Bolton Township and the seigneury of St. Armand on January 23, 1806. The Ruiter papers also include a pledge of security dated February 23, 1806, by three men for about £100 in which they acknowledge they are indebted "unto Benjamin Pell of the Citty [*sic*] of New York and William Ferris Pell of Burlington in the State of Vermont Merchants and partners."

7. While Molson made no mention of Sarah Vaughan or their children in letters home, one might argue that he mentioned them in letters since lost. But there is little doubt he said nothing about them. If he ever conveyed these facts, one would expect an "echo" of them in letters Molson received. It's impossible to imagine his sister Martha ever writing to him without including the basic salutation "Give my love to the children" if she knew they existed. This did not happen, in fact, until 1811.

CHAPTER 14

1. In an alternative draft of the letter, Molson allowed himself more description: "The climate in itself is agreeable (tho' the Winters are Severe & Summers hot) in the summer they have what are called Calashes which is a kind of an one horse chair with this alteration that there is a seat in the front for the driver & in the Winter the Carioles which are calculated to travel on the snow have no Wheels the form of them is nearly the same as the body of a Calash."

2. *The Gentleman's Magazine*, March 1788, "Being the third number of Vol LVIII, Part I., (Sylvanus Urban, gent., London, Printed by John Nichols, for D. Henry, late of Saint John's Gate.)"

3. The dispute over an estate was all too familiar in the life of the late Samuel Elsdale. In 1737, Samuel and his new bride, Mary Robinson, sued a number of members of Mary's family over the will of her father, John Robinson. According to a surviving statement by one of the defendants,

Mary's sister Ann, which has been preserved in the Public Record Office, Samuel and Mary had sought a share of a £500 bequest based on the role Mary had played as estate administrator after the death of her sister Prudence at age eight.

4. In responding, Molson also noted that a letter written by Rayment on March 5, since lost, had arrived in September. It was probably the duplicate of the March 2 letter Rayment said he was sending in case the first went astray.

CHAPTER 15

1. John Molson entry in the *Dictionary of Canadian Biography*.

2. Production figures from Denison, *The Barley and the Stream*, p. 47.

3. Francis Badgley's surveying work earned him immortality through Badgeley [*sic*] Island, Badgeley Point and Badgeley Rocks at the eastern approach to Georgian Bay's North Channel.

4. Although there were a number of hospitals called Bethlem, this was likely Bethlem Royal Hospital, an asylum south of London, in Surrey.

5. The only other strategy available—suggested, it appears, by Stansfeld—was an action of ejectment, a legal ruse to establish title that had become popular in the seventeenth century. That Molson even considered such a move has been misinterpreted as an attempt to have Ann Elsdale and the children forcibly removed from the estate, which it wasn't—and in any case they weren't even living on the property. To pull this off, a person would take the role of the intended plaintiff (someone acting with Molson's power of attorney) and walk onto the property just long enough to present a lease to another person, who would become the nominal plaintiff. This nominal plaintiff would then have to actually move to occupy the land under the terms of his lease, inviting an ejectment from the purported owner, in this case Ann Elsdale. For the nominal plaintiff to prove the validity of the lease in a subsequent action against the defendant (Ann Elsdale), all relevant documents would have to be brought before the court. In the process, the true ownership could be determined. While it probably represented Molson's best bet for settling the matter, he does not appear to have gone ahead with it.

CHAPTER 16

1. Almost nothing is known of what became of them. In 1823, Rayment advised Molson that the two children were still unmarried.

2. In addition to the $400, Sheppard was also entitled annually to six hogsheads of "table" beer, one hogshead of "strong" beer, one hogshead of "mild ale" and "as many Grains as may be necessary for one cow, also the use of the House and Stable belonging to the said John Molson and now in the occupation of him the said William Sheppard, and likewise the use of that

quarter of the Garden which is contiguous thereto, with all which the said William Sheppard did and does hereby declare himself to be content and satisfied." Sheppard pledged that he "shall not nor will himself do, nor suffer knowingly others to do any damage or injury to any of the property of the said John Molson, nor to waster, embezzle or purloin the same." That the payment was in dollars indicates the important role of American trade in the Canadian colonial economy. The Americans had issued a silver dollar coin in 1792. Spanish-milled dollars also continued to be popular, and when Sir Isaac Brock issued army bills in Lower Canada to help finance the War of 1812, they were given a denomination of Spanish dollars.

3. In the Molson Archives, there is a gap in brewery accounts from 1791 to 1797. Volume 38 is a "waste book"—a small hand-stitched notebook listing sales to individual customers from 1786 to 1790, although the orders substantially begin in 1788. Volume 39, a full brewery account book, covers 1798–99.

4. Denison, p. 52.

5. The farm book contains entries for a Longue Pointe farm "between Peter Robertson & self" beginning October 1, 1802; in 1803, expenses appear for a farm at St. Catharines and for "Ranjards Orchard & Farm" in an unknown location. The final farm surfaces in a note made June 26, 1807, in which Molson wrote: "Sold the farm at La Chine to Francois Martineau and his wife L100 currency payable in nine years."

6. The acquisition date must have been after 1805 because the ADHÉMAR Research Project does not list Molson as a property owner on the street for that data year.

7. One of the successful grant applicants was Captain John Savage of Caldwell's Manor, who received the entirety of Shefford County and settled it in 1792.

8. Biographical information has been drawn from the *Dictionary of Canadian Biography*, as well as Andre's *William Berczy* and Tovell's *Berczy*.

9. The descriptions of John Small, Samuel Heron, William Willcocks, and D'Arcy Boulton in this chapter are drawn substantially from the *Dictionary of Canadian Biography*.

10. Firth, *The Town of York, 1793–1815: a collection of documents of early Toronto*.

CHAPTER 17

1. Molson had become involved as an executor and trustee for the estate of a Montreal merchant named William Horner, who had died on March 4, 1808, and among the papers of Horner that Molson acquired was a letter written to Horner in 1801 by a man named John Jackson in Marham, England. The letter had nothing to say about steamboats, but it may be more than coincidence that a mechanic named John Jackson was a principal figure in the

steamboat effort. As well, among the papers Molson had collected from the Horner estate was an "act of promise and donation" by Horner to a woman named Janet Kay dated March 31, 1806, thereby adding the name Kay to that of Jackson in Horner's affairs. (William and John Kay also appeared as customers in Molson's 1808 accounts.) And so it is possible that Horner, and not Molson, was involved initially in the steamboat venture.

2. Two curious components of his assets are £1,230 marked "Geo. Davison legacy" and £583 6s 8p marked "Alex. Davison." The brothers George and Alexander Davison had been prominent Quebec merchants. In the early 1780s George Davison, who served under Haldimand on the executive council, acquired a large tract in the seigneury of Rivière-du-Loup at Trois-Rivières, site of the St. Maurice Forges, and Davison secured the lease for the Forges with Bell and Munro in 1793. The presence of a "legacy" from George Davison—he died in 1799—in Molson's asset list begs the question of what this substantial sum represented. Perhaps it was an interest in the Forges, or some of Davison's lands. On August 21, 1800, an advertisement in the *Quebec Gazette* had announced the private sale of Davison's properties at Rivière-du-Loup, Machiche and Maskinonge.

Alexander Davison was best known for securing the lucrative contract as the supply agent for all British forces in North America—irregularities in the execution of which earned him a twenty-seven-month prison sentence. His brother George assisted him in this enterprise, and Alexander also used as his local agents Bell and Munro, lessees of the St. Maurice Forges, as well as John Gray, financier to William Willcocks and Samuel Heron. (William Berczy visited with Davison in London in 1799 and gained the merchant's sympathy for his land-grant struggle.) As noted, Gray's presence is suspected in many of Molson's real estate and financing deals in Upper Canada. Like other Montreal merchants, Molson may have worked with Gray, when he was acting as Davison's agent, to sell his product to British troops. How Alexander Davison came to be obliged to Molson for almost £600 isn't clear, but Gray may have been a conduit.

3. Sir John Ross, *A Treaty on Navigation By Steam* (1837), cited by George H. Wilson in "The Application of Steam to St. Lawrence Valley Navigation, 1809–1840."

4. Wilson, "The Application of Steam."

5. Quoted by Wilson in "The Application of Steam."

6. W.R. Riddell, "Transportation from Schenectady to Quebec in 1810." Quoted in Mackay, *Steamboat Connections*, p 11.

7. Quoted by Wilson in "The Application of Steam."

8. *The Life of John Fitch, the Inventor of the Steamboat.*

9. Fitch had left technical drawings in France after his failed efforts there, and these came into the possession of Fulton. Fulton had also been living in Philadelphia when Fitch was experimenting with his designs in the 1780s. In

1801 Fulton travelled to Scotland's Forth and Clyde canal to see the pioneering work of William Symington and Patrick Miller, and he was given a ride on their vessel in addition to being allowed to make drawings of its engine and machinery.

10. According to Westcott, one critic, Bennett Wooderoft, charged that Fulton's so-called invention as patented in the United States was a pastiche of British innovations: "He had a cylinder, with steam acting on each side of the piston, the air pump, and detached condenser ([James] Watt's invention), connecting rods, and cranks, to obtain a rotary motion, and a fly wheel, to get over the dead point ([James] Pickard's invention), improved paddle wheels ([Patrick] Miller's invention), and the combination of these instruments together for the first time ([William] Symington's invention). In fact, if these inventions, separate or as a combination, were removed out of Fulton's Boat, nothing would be left but the hull."

11. *Robert Fulton: Engineer and Artist.*

12. Quoted by Wilson in "The Application of Steam."

CHAPTER 18

1. Molson travelled in style, for this latest *Everetta* was an admired vessel. Thomas Ridout praised her in a letter home to York, Upper Canada, after making the Atlantic crossing in 1809. "We have not experienced the least misfortune or accident. The *Everetta* is the best vessel I have seen. . . . Yesterday we dined on board on a dish of beef steaks, 'Quebec beef.' We have crossed the ocean *alone,* without a *company.*" On July 5, 1811, Ridout remarked on seeing her in Quebec City: "In coming to anchor, we passed close under the stern of the *Everetta.* She is the prettiest vessel here." See Thomas Ridout, *Ten Years of Peace and War in Upper Canada.*

2. The original portrait still hangs in the boardroom of Molson Inc. in Montreal. The copy is in the collection of the McCord Museum of Montreal, bequeathed as part of Thomas Molson's papers and effects.

3. The *Swiftsure* was built by John Bruce at Hart Logan's shipyard in St. Mary's Current, where Bruce had found employment after the *Accommodation* was laid up and John Molson had gone to England in 1810–11. According to Mackey (*Steamboat Connections*), Bruce was the inspector for the timber on the *Frontenac,* which entered service on Lake Ontario in 1817, and built the *Ottawa* in 1819 for the river trade above the Lachine Rapids. He died "all but forgotten" in the Montreal General Hospital on December 26, 1825.

4. Denison, *A History of the Bank of Montreal,* Vol. I, p. 31.

5. Their relation to the Chapman fired by Molson in 1789 is unknown.

6. There is some confusion over the ownership of the *Car of Commerce.* Denison states that Montreal merchant Thomas Torrance was the principal investor, and this has been repeated by other authors. But the *Register of*

Shipping indicates that the owners as of her registry at Quebec on May 6, 1816, did not include Torrance. Instead, Torrance appears as one of the owners of the *Caledonia* in November 1817. (See Wilson, "The Application of Steam.")

CHAPTER 19

1. The mechanics of the introduction of Mary and Martha to John and Thomas have also been confused. The *Dictionary of Canadian Biography*'s entry on John Junior states: "At the end of 1815 he moved to Quebec [City]... That year he went to England, apparently to settle a matter related to the building of the *Lady Sherbrooke* and the *New Swiftsure*, ships that would be launched in 1816 and 1817 respectively. It is thought that he met Mary Ann Elizabeth Molson, his first cousin, on this trip; her sister, Martha, married Thomas, John's brother, in England in April 1816. The following month, Mary Ann Elizabeth arrived at Quebec, and on 12 October she and John were married."

This timeline is impossible. John Junior could not have visited England on business of any kind in these years (and the *Lady Sherbrooke* would not be launched until 1817, the *New Swiftsure* until 1818). His regular letters to his father make it clear that John Junior was in Quebec in the years following his military service in the War of 1812. It was Thomas who was travelling in England in 1815–16. And as the family's letters indicate, Mary came to Quebec with her sister and Thomas.

2. The additional properties consisted of the home and land at St. Mary's Current purchased from François Desautels, the White property in Quebec City, "Barons Lot or Barn Lot," possibly acquired from notary Thomas Barron (who had witnessed Molson's marriage contract), and "Upper lot from Papineau (No. 31)."

3. The construction of the church, in which William participated, ushered in years of dispute with two successive bishops of Montreal, George Jehosaphat Mountain and Francis Fulford. Thomas wanted to name his own priest and the bishops wouldn't let him. In retaliation, he refused to have the church consecrated so he could retain control, even though it meant paying property taxes. After the church burned down in the catastrophic Montreal fire of 1852, he held off replacing it, but after a visit to England in 1857 he decided to build a new St. Thomas's on the site of the old, dedicated to a new Protestant faith he imported from the old country: the Countess of Huntingdon's Connexion, a Methodist-Anglican hybrid founded in 1748 and legally established in 1783. The Connexion granted individual churches autonomy, and autonomy was Thomas Molson's signature enthusiasm. He brought back from England 750 copies of the Connexion hymnal as well as a set of chimes for the new church that were identical to those in London's Royal Exchange and cost as much as the entire original church. He also built

an adjoining seminary, Molson's College, to train ministers, but the initiative was a failure. In 1860, when the church's minister, Alfred Stone, resigned and the Civil War erupted south of the border, Thomas rented the college and several houses as billets for the British Army. His grand exercise in obstinacy ended with his bequest of the church and eleven houses to the Church of England, which by then had come around to acknowledging the objections of faithful like Thomas and allowed parishioners to own churches and appoint priests. (Information on St. Thomas's Church is drawn from Thomas Molson's entry in the *Dictionary of Canadian Biography* and "Thomas Molson Built and Owned a Church," a column in the *Montreal Gazette* by Edgar Andrew Collard.)

4. Quoted by Wilson. Mr. Wilson's unpublished master's thesis, "The Application of Steam . . . ," was an invaluable source of information about the St. Lawrence steamboat trade in the years discussed in these pages.

5. See Bowering, *The Art and Mystery of Brewing in Ontario*.

CHAPTER 20

1. Despite Chesterfield's certainty that he was dying, he lived another sixteen years.

2. Details of the early history of the bank are drawn from Merrill Denison's *A History of the Bank of Montreal*.

3. A sheriff of Montreal, Ermatinger oversaw property sales to John Molson, Sr., on June 14, 1825, and April 4, 1826.

4. The St. Lawrence steamboat rivalry is described by Mackey in *Steamboat Connections*, pp. 36–37. I have added the significance of the Bank of Montreal directorships.

5. The manoeuvring to dominate the Ottawa steamboat trade is ably detailed by Mackey in *Steamboat Connections*, pp. 92–93.

6. Ibid., pp. 136–37.

7. In an 1824 letter to Thomas, John Senior noted that he had purchased a farm from a man named Clarke for £1,300 and had given it to John Junior: "He has let it for £80 per annum for Seven Years; & Reserved a Large house to himself with a right of Stone and Lime."

8. One of the anecdotes Mackenzie included in *Sketches* was his firsthand experience of being aboard the Molsons' *Waterloo* when she sank after being caught in pack ice on the St. Lawrence in 1832. No lives were lost.

9. Mackenzie's protestations doubtless were a factor in the summary removal of Henry Boulton, Jr., as attorney-general in 1833.

10. Creighton, *The Empire of the St. Lawrence*, p. 265.

11. Ibid., pp. 265–66.

12. J.L. Finlay, *Pre-Confederation Canada: The Structure of Canadian History to 1867*, p. 239.

13. In Upper Canada, Henry Boulton was not only the attorney-general, but the solicitor both for the Welland Canal Company, which was in the process of linking Lake Ontario and Lake Erie, and for the Bank of Upper Canada, the majority of whose board of directors came from government ranks. In addition to the government-supported bank holding a twenty-five-percent interest in the canal company, the bank's directors, appointed as government overseers, were also private shareholders in the canal. (See Creighton, pp. 266–67.)

14. For an excellent overview of Thomas Markland's activities, and of the events surrounding the Bank of Upper Canada and the Commercial Bank of Midland District, see Denison, *A History of the Bank of Montreal*, Vol. I.

15. The dollar bank notes, which could be redeemed on demand for coin, were indicative of the prevalence of Spanish and American dollars in the Canadian provinces in the early 1800s, despite the official monetary units of pounds, shillings and pence. American bank notes in dollar denominations were in wide circulation in Upper Canada at this time.

16. In 1830, the government in Lower Canada had refused to permit such an increase for the Bank of Montreal as its charter was renewed and extended to 1837. The demand for funds at a time of prosperity led to the petition in February 1831 for a new bank, the City Bank of Montreal, which received royal assent in 1833. Among the investors were a number of Bank of Montreal shareholders, including John Molson, Jr., who were seeking a fresh opportunity for their money in response to the freeze on the capitalization of their existing bank investment.

17. In his entry for William Molson in the *Dictionary of Canadian Biography*, Alfred Dubuc argued, "In a mercantile economy, the whole structure is centred on export and import trade. The principal source of public revenue is customs, customs duties on exports and on imports. A tacit agreement is established between the state and the large merchants, encouraging foreign trade and discouraging national production." Thus the Molson distilling business was counter to what was considered to be the best economic interests of the province. While there was nothing wrong with exporting whiskey, producing it for domestic consumption denied the state duties on imports.

18. Morton is thought to have been the sole owner of the 4.75-acre lakefront site incorporating the old Dalton facility by 1840. In addition to brewing and distilling, Morton was operating a sawmill, a foundry, locomotive works and a shipping facility. He was bankrupted in the 1859 recession but ran successfully for the Canadian legislature in 1861. When he died in 1864, his debts exceeded $250,000. Details on Morton, Molson and the history of brewing in Kingston can be found in Ian Bowering, *The Art and Mystery of Brewing in Ontario*, pp. 58–61.

CHAPTER 21

1. The foundry had been established in 1816, in an old horse mill, as the Montreal Air Furnace by Joseph Lough, one of the partners in the steamboat *Vermont* in 1807. He had come north to Montreal with a number of other Americans to expand the steamboat trade on the St. Lawrence above Montreal. When Lough's initial foundry venture failed, it was taken over in 1819–20 by the Scottish merchant Thomas Andrew Turner, a founding vice-president of the Bank of Montreal who became the publisher and owner of the *Montreal Gazette* in 1822. Under the guidance of Lough, the business, renamed St. Mary Foundry, produced its first steam engine in 1820.

In 1822, after Turner shifted his attention to the *Gazette* and his business partner Alexander Allison died, the foundry came under the control of a familiar name in Molson affairs, the Montreal merchant John Gray. The path is unclear for the foundry in the 1820s; Gray apparently leased it for three years from Allison's estate, and in 1829 it was purchased from Turner by John Bennet (who had come to Montreal from England to oversee the installation of Molson's first steam engines, in the *Swiftsure* and the brewery) and his partner, John Henderson. Bennet & Henderson gained distinction in 1831 by producing the engines for the *Royal William*, the first Canadian steamship to make the Atlantic crossing. But the partnership failed in 1835, at which point the foundry came into the hands of the Molsons. See Mackey, *Steamboat Connections*, for the full details of the foundry's history.

2. Translation from Denison, *The Barley and the Stream*, p. 164.

3. Translation from Alfred Dubuc's entry for John Molson in the *Dictionary of Canadian Biography*.

4. *Dictionary of Canadian Biography*.

5. The residue of the estate consisted of the lands in St. Mary's suburb that were not included in the brewery property or attached to the foundry, and the shares in the Ottawa and Rideau Forwarding Company (as the expanded Ottawa Steamboat Company had become known in 1835), the St. Lawrence Steamboat Company, the Quebec Fire Insurance Company, the Montreal Library, the Bank of Montreal, the steamboat *Varennes* (which operated on the Richelieu and Lake Champlain) and the British American Land Company.

6. Creighton, *The Empire of the St. Lawrence*, pp. 276–78.

7. The companies listed were the Bank of Montreal, the City Bank, the Champlain and St. Lawrence Railroad Company, the Montreal Water Works, the St. Lawrence Steamboat Company, the Montreal Steam Tow Boat Company, the Ottawa and Rideau Forwarding Company, the St. Lawrence Steamboat and Mail Coach Company, the Montreal Gas Works (probably the Montreal Gas Light Company, of which John Junior was president) and St. Ann Market. The list also noted £50,000 worth of capitalization, all held by investors of British origin, in "other Steam Boats and capital invested in the

forwarding establishments on the Saint Lawrence, above & below Montreal." The only significant francophone institutions cited, the Mutual Insurance Company and the Banque du Peuple, were presented as having almost forty percent of their total capitalization in the hands of anglophone investors.

8. Stratton, *History of the Town of Alburgh, Vermont*, Vol. I, p. 125.

9. It's difficult to say for certain whether or not Marryat had read Robinson Elsdale's journal at this point. The original manuscript in the possession of the Elsdale family is inscribed with the note that his widow, Ann Elsdale, made a gift of it to her fifteen-year-old grandson, Robinson, in 1827, on the death of the grandson's father, the Reverend Samuel Elsdale. (Ann Elsdale died in 1837.) We know that the manuscript was shown to Marryat on an unknown date by W. Harrison Ainsworth, who is believed to have taught at Manchester Grammar School, where the grandson Robinson's uncle, the Reverend Robinson, served as headmaster. (See also Note 9, Chapter 3.) By the time Ainsworth acquired temporary custody of the manuscript and loaned it to Marryat, the grandson Robinson appears to have been established as Dr. Robinson Elsdale, surgeon in Moulton. Dr. Robinson practised in Moulton for thirty years, and having died in 1867, he may not have been established in Moulton until 1837. Circumstances suggest that Marryat did not read the manuscript until the 1840s, shortly before using it as the basis for his *Privateersman* novel of 1846. Thus, when Marryat came to Montreal during the rebellion, the fact that the Molsons, descendants of Robinson Elsdale's sister, were living there would have meant nothing to them.

10. Marryat, *Diary in America*, p. 163.

11. Ibid., p. 164.

EPILOGUE

1. As eccentric as the strategy might now seem, it was not unheard of at the time for parents to give their children identical first names in order to satisfy the terms of a bequest. This was probably why the Davies brothers, the business partners of John Junior, were named George and George Crew.

2. The arbitration process is described by Dubuc in his William Molson entry in the *Dictionary of Canadian Biography*. No arbitration records survive in the Molson Archives.

3. Denison mentions (p. 222) the trust account and payments over a period of about twelve years—which would backdate them to 1836. No trust account record appears to be preserved in the Molson Archives.

4. The existence of two different partnerships, created in 1837 and 1838, is cited by Dubuc in his William Molson entry in the *Dictionary of Canadian Biography*. Only the 1838 partnership is preserved in the Molson Archives.

5. William Molson entry, *Dictionary of Canadian Biography*.

6. See Mackey, *Steamboat Connections*.

7. William Molson entry, *Dictionary of Canadian Biography*.

8. Thomas Molson entry, *Dictionary of Canadian Biography*.

9. William Dow was a prominent Montreal brewer and distiller. The "college" referred to was the seminary attached to St. Thomas's church.

10. Jefferson's actual "Ten Rules for the Good Life" are: 1. Never put off till tomorrow what you can do today; 2. Never trouble another for what you can do yourself; 3. Never spend your money before you have it; 4. Never buy what you do not want because it is cheap; it will never be dear to you; 5. Pride costs us more than hunger, thirst, and cold; 6. Never repent of having eaten too little; 7. Nothing is troublesome that we do willingly; 8. Don't let the evils which have never happened cost you pain; 9. Always take things by their smooth handle; and 10. When angry, count to ten before you speak; if very angry, count to one hundred.

11. Production and market-share figures come from the *Restrictive Trade Practices Commission Report Concerning an Alleged Combine in the Manufacture, Distribution and Sale of Beer in Canada* (Department of Justice, Ottawa, 1955).

$\mathcal{Bibliography}$

PRIMARY SOURCES

Canada

ARCHIVES NATIONALES DU QUÉBEC

Birth, marriage, death records, Christ Church (Anglican), Montreal district, 1766–1899.

Loyd vs. Bolton, 1783, Court of Common Pleas, July 1780–February 1784, TL16, S4.

John Molson marriage contract, Jonathan A. Gray Papers 1796–1812, Reel 8779.

MCCORD MUSEUM, MONTREAL

Molson family fonds.

NATIONAL ARCHIVES OF CANADA

British Military and Naval Records. Series C, 1759–1906 (RG 8).

Haldimand Papers (MG 21).

Jedidiah Hubbell Dorwin Diaries (R 4080 0 6 E).

John Molson vs. Thos. P. Loyd (RG 4 B17. Vol. 7, File 5).

Molson Archives, incorporating microfilm of Molson family papers of McCord Museum (MG 28 III 57).

Quebec and Lower Canada land petitions, 1764–1841 (RG 1 L 3L).

Royal Navy and Provincial Marine 1779–1849 (C 3242).

Ruiter Papers (MG 23 G III. Vol. 2).

Vaughan family fond (MG 25 G 129).

Waite, John. Loyalist compensation claims, Audit Office (AO 13 16 22, AO 12 109 316).

NATIONAL LIBRARY OF CANADA
Quebec Gazette.

ENGLAND

ARCHIVES OF SOHO, BIRMINGHAM CITY ARCHIVES
Letters of James Watt, Jr.

PUBLIC RECORD OFFICE, KEW, RICHMOND, SURREY
Banaster vs. Richard (William) and John Molson (C 1/604/31).

Biggin documents (T 1/463/220, T 1/375/38, T 1/375/58, T 1/384).

Biggin and Wetherell (T 1/319-388, 429-436).

Boulton estate papers (J 90/1236).

Captain's log, HMS *Assistance* (ADM 51/72).

Captain's log, HMS *Preston* (ADM 51/721).

Captain's log, HMS *Surprize* (ADM 51/950).

Elsdale vs. Robinson (C 11/1828/15).

Privateer Revenge of Liverpool (T 1/365/89).

WIRRAL ARCHIVES, BIRKENHEAD
Laird Bros. papers.

UNITED STATES

VERMONT STATE ARCHIVES
Alburgh inhabitants' petition for new trial, October 13, 1794. Vol. 19, p. 153.

Letter, Henry Caldwell to Governor Chittenden, March 29, 1785. Vol. 24, p. 13.

Petition of Alburgh settlers for title to land, October 26, 1796. Vol. 22, p. 218.

Petition signed by Thomas P. Loid. Vol. 17, p. 308.

SECONDARY SOURCES

Anderson, Bonnie S., and Zinsser, Judith P. *A History of Their Own: Women in Europe from Prehistory to the Present*. Vol. I. Harper & Row (Perennial Library), 1989.

Andre, John. *William Berczy: Co-founder of Toronto*. Borough of York, 1967.

Armstrong, James. *A treatise on the law relating to marriages in Lower Canada* [pamphlet]. 1857.

Blakeley, Phyllis R., and Grant, John N., eds. *Eleven Exiles: Accounts of Loyalists of the American Revolution*. Dundurn Press, 1982.

Bowering, Ian. *The Art and Mystery of Brewing in Ontario*. General Store Publishing House, 1988.

British Atlas: Counties of England, 1840. Pigot & Co. Reprinted by Salamander Books, 2000.

Brock, Leslie V. "The Colonial Currency, Prices, and Exchange Rates," *Essays in History*. Vol. 34. Corcoran Department of History, University of Virginia, 1992.

Brooke, Frances. *The History of Emily Montague*. J. Dodsley, 1769.

Burt, A.L. *The Old Province of Quebec*. Vols. I & II. McClelland and Stewart (Carleton Library), 1968.

The Canadian biographical dictionary and portrait gallery of eminent and self-made men: Quebec and the Maritime provinces. H.C. Cooper, Jr., 1881.

Carruthers, Richard. *Molson Family* (geneology). Privately published, 1995.

Cary, George Thomas. *The Lower St. Lawrence, or Quebec to Halifax via Gaspé and Pictou: to which is appended Mr. Wood's description of the River Saguenay. . . .* 1862.

Caya, Marcel. Henry Caldwell (c. 1735–1810) entry, *Dictionary of Canadian Biography*.

Colledge, J.J. *Ships of the Royal Navy: An Historical Index.* Vol. I. Newton Abbot, 1969.

Creighton, Donald. *The Empire of the St. Lawrence: A Study in Commerce and Politics.* Macmillan of Canada, 1970.

Denison, Merrill. *The Barley and the Stream: The Molson Story.* McClelland and Stewart, 1955.

———. *A History of the Bank of Montreal.* Vol. I. McClelland and Stewart, 1966.

Dickinson, H.W. *Robert Fulton: Engineer and Artist.* London, 1913. Text published online by the University of Rochester Steam Engine Library.

Dubuc, Alfred. John Molson (1763–1836) entry, *Dictionary of Canadian Biography*.

———. Thomas Molson (1791–1863) entry, *Dictionary of Canadian Biography*.

———. William Molson (1793–1875) entry, *Dictionary of Canadian Biography*.

Dubuc, Alfred, and Robert Tremblay. John Molson (1787–1860) entry, *Dictionary of Canadian Biography*.

Elsdale, Robinson. Unpublished memoirs. Elsdale family collection.

Equiano, Olaudah. *The Interesting Narrative of the Life of Olaudah Equiano, or Gustavus Vassa the African.* 1789.

Finlay, J.L. *Pre-Confederation Canada: The Structure of Canadian History to 1867.* Prentice-Hall Canada, 1990.

Firth, Edith G. *The Town of York, 1793–1815: A Collection of Documents of Early Toronto.* Champlain Society, 1962.

Fyson, Donald. *Criminal Justice, Civil Society and the Local State: The Justices of the Peace in the District of Montreal, 1764–1830.* Ph.D. thesis, Université de Montréal, 1995. Published online by Donald Fyson at www.hst.ulaval.ca/profs/dfyson/crimjust/.

Grant, George Munro. *French Canadian Life and Character: With Historical and Descriptive Sketches of the Scenery and Life in Quebec, Montreal.* A. Belford, 1899.

Henry, Alexander. *The Journal of Alexander Henry the Younger, 1799–1814.* Vol. I. Barry M. Gough, ed. Champlain Society, 1988.

James, Lawrence. *The Rise and Fall of the British Empire.* Abacus, 1995.

Jenks, Edward. *A Short History of English Law.* 2nd ed. Methuen, 1920.

Kalm, Pehr [Peter]. *Travels into North America, containing its natural history . . . with the civil ecclesiastical and commercial state of the country. . . .* 2nd ed. Translated by John Reinhold Forster. Lowndes, 1772.

Kelsay, Isabel Thompson. *Joseph Brant 1743–1807: Man of Two Worlds.* Syracuse University Press, 1984.

Keegan, John. *Battle at Sea: From Man-of-War to Submarine.* Pimlico, 1993.

Kyte, Eleanor. Francis Badgley (1767–1841) entry, *Dictionary of Canadian Biography.*

Lewis, Samuel. *A Topographical Dictionary of England.* S. Lewis, 1831.

Lownsbrough, John. D'Arcy Boulton (1759–1834) entry, *Dictionary of Canadian Biography.*

Mackenzie, William Lyon. *Sketches of Canada and the United States.* E. Wilson, 1833.

Mackey, Frank. *Steamboat Connections: Montreal to Upper Canada, 1816–1843.* McGill–Queen's University Press, 2000.

Mackintosh, Charles Herbert. *The Canadian parliamentary companion and annual register, 1877.* Citizen Printing and Publishing Co., 1877.

Mackintosh, W.A. "Canada and Vermont: A study in historical geography." *Canadian Historical Review,* 1927.

Malcomson, Robert. *Lords of the Lake: The Naval War on Lake Ontario, 1812–1814.* Robin Brass Studio, 1998.

Marryat, Frederick. *The Privateersman: Adventures by Sea and Land, in Civil and Savage Life, One Hundred Years Ago.* Syndicate Trading Co., n.d. Originally published in 1846.

———. *Diary in America: The Complete Account of His Trials, Wrangles, and Tribulations in the United States and Canada, 1837–1838.* Nicholas Vane, 1960.

Mercer, Graeme. *Prominent men of Canada: a collection of persons distinguished in professional and political life, and in the commerce and industry of Canada.* Canadian Biographical Publishing Co., 1892.

Miller, Nathan. *Broadsides: The Age of Fighting Sail, 1775–1815.* John Wiley & Sons, 2000.

Morgan, Henry James. *Sketches of celebrated Canadian Persons connected with Canada: from the earliest period in the history of the province down to the present time.* R. Worthington, 1865.

Morrice, Alexander. *A Practical Treatise on Brewing the various sorts of Malt Liquor....* 7th ed. Sherwood, Gilbert and Piper, 1827.

Murray, Venetia. *High Society in the Regency Period, 1788–1830.* Penguin Books, 1999.

Phillips, Kevin. *The Cousins' Wars: Religion, Politics, & the Triumph of Anglo-America.* Basic Books, 1999.

Phillips, Michael. *Ships of the Old Navy: A History of the Sailing Ships of the Royal Navy.* Published online at www.cronab.demon.co.uk.

Powell, James. *A History of the Canadian Dollar.* Published online by the Bank of Canada.

Restrictive Trade Practices Commission Report Concerning an Alleged Combine in the Manufacture, Distribution and Sale of Beer in Canada. Department of Justice, Ottawa, 1955.

Ridout, Thomas. *Ten Years of Upper Canada in Peace and War, 1805–1815: Being the Ridout Letters.* W. Briggs, 1890.

Roberts, David, ed. *Lord Chesterfield's Letters.* Oxford University Press, 1992.

Robeson, Virginia R., gen. ed. *Documents in Canadian History: Lower Canada in the 1830s.* The Ontario Institute for Studies in Education, 1977.

Rodger, N.A.M. *The Wooden World: An Anatomy of the Georgian Navy.* W.W. Norton, 1996.

Rose, George Maclean. *A Cyclopaedia of Canadian biography: being chiefly men of the time....* Rose Publishing, 1886.

Sandwell, Bernard K. *The Molson Family.* Private monograph. Montreal, 1933.

Scheer, George F., and Rankin, Hugh F., eds. *Rebels & Redcoats: The American Revolution Through the Eyes of Those Who Fought and Lived It.* Da Capo Press, 1957.

Smith, Arthur Britton. *Legend of the Lake: The 22-Gun Brig-Sloop* Ontario, *1780.* Quarry Press, 1997.

Snider, C.H.J. *Annals of The Royal Canadian Yacht Club, 1852–1937.* Ross & Mann, 1937.

Stratton, Allen L. *History of the Town of Alburgh, Vermont.* Vol. I. Northlight Studio Press, 1986.

———. *Unfinished Typescript for History of the Town of Alburgh, Vermont.* Vol. II. Vermont Historical Society, 2000.

Tovell, Rosemarie L., gen. ed. *Berczy.* National Gallery of Canada, 1991.

Twigger, Robert. *Inflation: The Value of the Pound 1750–1998.* Research paper 99/20, House of Commons Library. Issued February 23, 1999.

Westcott, Thompson. *The Life of John Fitch, the Inventor of the Steamboat.* Philadelphia, 1857.

Wilson, George H. *The Application of Steam to St. Lawrence Valley Navigation 1809–1840.* Unpublished M.A. thesis, McGill University, 1961.

Winton, John, ed. *An Illustrated History of the Royal Navy.* Salamander Books, 2000.

ONLINE RESOURCES

(All sites verified July 2001)

ADHÉMAR—Groupe de recherche sur Montréal
cca.qc.ca/adhemar

American Historical Association
www.theaha.org

American Memory, Library of Congress
memory.loc.gov/ammem/amhome.html

Ancestry.com
www.ancestry.com

Archives de Montréal
www.ville.montreal.qc.ca/archives

Archives nationales du Québec
www.anq.gouv.qc.ca/ANQ-K.html

ARCHON—Archival Resources Online
www.hmc.gov.uk/archon/archon.htm

Bank of Canada
www.bankofcanada.ca

British Library
www.bl.uk

A Century of Lawmaking for a New Nation: U.S. Congressional Documents
    and Debates, 1774–1873, Library of Congress
lcweb2.loc.gov/ammem/amlaw/lawhome.html

Concordances of Great Books
www.concordance.com

Early Canadiana Online
www.canadiana.org

FamilySearch Internet Genealogy Service
www.familysearch.org

Heritage Lincolnshire
www.lincsheritage.org

Institute of Historical Research
ihr.sas.ac.uk

Lake Champlain Maritime Museum
www.lcmm.org

Lincolnshire Look-up Exchange
www.excel.net/~nclark/lincs.html

Loyalist Institute Home Page
www.royalprovincial.com

Marine Museum of the Great Lakes at Kingston
www.MarMus.ca

MilitaryHeritage.com
www.militaryheritage.com

Montreal Research Group—see ADHÉMAR

National Archives of Canada
www.archives.ca

National Library of Canada
www.nlc-bnc.ca

Public Record Office (UK)
www.pro.gov.uk

Royal Naval Museum
www.royalnavalmuseum.org

University of Rochester Steam Engine Library
www.history.rochester.edu/steam/

Vermont Historical Society
www.state.vt.us/vhs

Vermont State Archives
vermont-archives.org

Index

Accommodation (steamboat), 1, 14–15, 324, 324–43, 355, 373, 387, 457(n3)
Albemarle, HMS, 16–18
Albin (Albon), Mary, 136, 160, 167, 263, 289–90, 440(n16)
Allan, Bryce, 9–10, 11
Allan, Sir Hugh, 9, 13
Allan, William, 401
Allcock, Judge Henry, 314
Allen, Ethan, 126–27, 444(n14,15)
Allen, Ira, 119, 125–29, 129, 155, 156, 164–65, 178–80, 211, 241, 242, 249, 250, 256, 258–59, 262, 445(n16), 451(n2)
Allen, John, 258
Allison, Alexander, 461(n1)
Amherst, General Jeffrey, 96
Arnold, Benedict, 80, 122, 251
Articles of War, 75–76, 79–81, 441(n9)
Ashbridge, Sarah, 315
Ashley, Reverend James, 171, 266–67, 272–91, 298–300
Ashley, Philip, 102–7, 112, 115, 118–19, 131, 137, 139, 141, 146–47, 156, 159–60, 167–83, 214–16, 221, 223–24, 228–38, 243–49, 259–60, 266–67, 271, 278–80, 284, 286–88, 298–99, 358–59, 384, 434, 447(n16)
Assistance, HMS, 55–82, 56, 70, 164
Atkinson, Ann, 286, 349, 372

Badgley, Elizabeth, *xxv*, 366, 377
Badgley, Francis, *xxv*, 283, 293, 366, 389, 454(n3)
Badgley, James, 293
Badgley, John Thompson, 395, 405
Bajus, Jacob, 383
Baker, Martha, *xxi*, *xxii*, 26, 28

Bank of Lower Canada, 359
Bank of Montreal, 387, 391–93, 394, 398–99, 401–2, 408–10, 422, 460(n16), 461(n1,5,7)
Bank of Upper Canada 401, 402, 460(n13)
Banking. *See* Bank of Lower Canada; Bank of Upper Canada; Banque du Peuple; Canada Banking Company; City Bank of Montreal; Commercial Bank of Midland District; Federal Bank of the United States; Gosling & Son; Molson "banking" (steamboats); Molsons Bank
Banque du Peuple, 461(n7)
Barfleur, HMS, 74
Barron, Thomas, 394, 458(n2)
Baxter, Boaz, 45, 167, 254
Baxter, Jack, 48–49, 167–69, 177, 183–87, 197, 200, 232, 274, 291
Beaubien, Benjamin, 325, 341
Beaver Club, 374, 389–90
Beek, Gerbrand, 300–1, 344
Beer: ale (traditional), 222; as domestic drink, 114; India Pale Ale, 217; Molson Canadian lager, 114, 432; Molson Export Ale, 430; as naval ration, 114; porter, 216–17, 222, 226; "small," 225, 282; spruce, 96–97, 282; "two-penny" (amber), 222, 226; wheat, 134, 137, 141, 143
Bell, David M., 204
Bell, Matthew, 325, 397–98
Bennet, John, 377, 461(n1)
Bennett, William, 216, 236
Bennet & Henderson, 461(n1)
Bennington, Battle of (1777), 210–12
Berczy, Charles Albert, 312

Berczy, Charlotte, 312
Berczy, William, 310–16, 313, 352, 369, 456(n2)
Berczy, William Bent, 312, 352
Bethune, Reverend John, 190, 203, 449(n5)
Biggin, John, 438(n10)
Bird, James, 383
Bolton, Henry, 145
Bolton, William, 297–98
Boswell, Arthur Radcliffe, 7–8
Boulton, Alice, 103, 105, 136–37, 159–60, 316
Boulton, D'Arcy, Jr., 397
Boulton, D'Arcy, Sr., 316–19, 342, 396–99
Boulton, Henry, Jr. (of Moulton), 159–60, 316–17
Boulton, Henry, Jr. (of Upper Canada), 397, 459(ch20/n5), 460(n13)
Boulton, Matthew, 54
Boulton & Watt, 54, 320–21, 328–29, 334, 340–41, 351–52, 361, 363–64, 372, 375, 377
Brading's Brewery, 430–31
Brainsby, Jim, 134, 135, 189, 202, 282, 445(n4)
Brant, Joseph, 91–92, 191, 251
Brant, Molly, 191
Brewing, Loid and Molson production in 1784, 143–44; Molson production in 1786, 223–24; in 1791, 282; in 1816, 377; from 1898 to 1909, 430; in 1952, 432; Molson process c. 1786, 216–28, 220, 227; in Quebec during French regime, 96–97; at Snake Hall, 113–14; transformation of Canadian industry in 20th century, 430–34
Bridge, Samuel, 333, 334, 340–41
British American Land Company, 414, 461(n5)
British-American Hotel, 394. See also: Mansion House Hotel, Masonic Hall Hotel
Brock, Major General Sir Isaac, 356, 454(ch16/n2)
Bronfman family, 432
Brooke, Frances, 119–20
Bruce, John (clerk), 373–74

Bruce, John (shipbuilder), 323–33, 341, 343, 457(n3)
Buchanan, Alexander, 413–14
Burgoyne, General John, 127, 293
Burt, A.L., 101, 127, 444(n11)
Butler, Benjamin, 257
Butler, Jane Baker, xxv, 426
Byrne, St. Clare, 6, 10–15

Caldwell, Henry, 115–29, 155–56, 164–65, 178, 179, 203, 211–12, 240, 242, 249–59, 262, 443, 444(n10), 444(n11)
Caldwell, John, 259, 375–76
Caldwell's Manor, 111, 115–41, 153–56, 154, 162–65, 178–80, 186, 195–98, 203–5, 211–13, 231, 238–42, 249, 252, 255–56, 259, 262, 272, 416, 443(n2), 444(n13), 445(n5), 447(n16), 449(n3), 450(n3), 451(ch11/n2,ch12/n2), 452(n1,6), 455(n7)
Caledonia (steamboat), 372–73, 376, 457(n6)
Cambridge, HMS, 297–98
Canada Banking Company, 359
Canadian Arena Company, 432
Canadian Breweries Ltd., 430–32
Cannington, William, 215–16
Car of Commerce (steamboat), 361–64, 372–76, 457(n6)
Car of Neptune (steamboat), 336, 361
Carleton, Guy, 120, 127, 241, 441(n3), 443(n1). See also Dorchester, Lord
Carruthers, Richard, 199–200
Cartier, Jacques, 87, 96
Catholic rights, 60, 61, 90
Champlain, Samuel de, 23–24, 123
Champlain and St. Lawrence Railroad, 398, 405, 408, 414, 461(n7)
Chapman(brewery employee), 254, 282, 457(n5)
Chapman, Francis and John, 361
Chapman, George, 41–43, 282
Chateauguay, Battle of (1813), 356–57
Chesapeake Capes, Battle of, (1781) 57–58, 437(n3)
Chesterfield, Lord, 29, 152, 175, 177–86, 192–94, 215, 228, 262, 428, 446(n14), 449(n10), 459(n1)

Chittenden, John, 127, 129, 155–56, 164–65, 258

Cholera epidemic (1832–34), 399–400

Christ Church (Montreal), 149, 187–91, 195, 199, 312, 409, 449(n5)

Christall, William, 7

City Bank of Montreal, 460(n16)

Civil War (England), 22–24, 207

Clark, James, 332–33

Clark(e), Matthew, 136, 440(n15), 449(n1)

Clark, General Rogers, 59

Clay, Henry, 355

Clermont (steamboat), 320–22, 327–29, 336

Clinton, Colonel James, 251

Cochrane, John, 101, 163, 443(ch5/n8)

Coddington, William, 207

Coit, William, 254

Coke, Edward, 436(n9)

Colborne, Governor Sir John, 416–17

Commercial Bank of Midland District, 402, 460(n14)

Congress (steamboat), 376

Conroy, Patrick, 255–58

Constitutional Association, 404, 405, 415

Cook, Christopher, 197, 219, 226, 228

Cook, Captain James, 90

Cook, John, 197, 219–26

Cornwall (steamboat), 383

Cornwallis, Charles, Earl (General), 48, 57, 437(n3)

Creighton, Donald, 61, 310, 397

Creighton, William, 372

Cromwell, Oliver, 22

Cruisers and Convoys Act (1708), 64

Crysler's Farm, Battle of (1813), 356–57

Currency, in colonial North America, 97–98

Cutter, Ezekial, 324, 329, 33

Dalhousie, Governor General Lord, 383, 390, 391

Dalton brewery and distillery, 383, 400, 460(n18)

Davidson, John, 375–76

Davies, George and George Crew, 391, 462(n1)

Davison, Alexander and George, 456(n2)

Dawes brewery, 431

De Bonne, Pierre Amable, 312

de Grasse, Comte, 58, 73, 74

de Salaberry, Lieutenant-Colonel Charles, 357

Dearborn, Major General Henry, 355

Dechambault, Captain Francis, 240, 257–58

Defoe, Daniel, 23

Delisle, Reverend David Chabrand, 189

Denison, Merrill, 52, 94, 97, 195–99, 203, 308, 377, 387, 388, 420, 423–25, 427, 429, 441(n2), 443(n3), 446(n13), 451(ch11/n1), 452(n6), 457(n6), 462(n3)

Desautels, Francois, 281, 308, 347, 458(n2)

Desautels, Pierre, 281, 308, 355

Deschambault, Colonel Fleury, 309, 362

Dickinson, H.W., 336

Dispatch (merchant ship), 56, 62–71, 81

Distilling. *See* Molson distilling activities; Rum trade; Whiskey trade

Dobie, Richard, 293

Dorchester, Lord, 239, 241–42, 248, 261

Dorwin, Jedidiah Hubbell, 130, 358–59, 365–68, 373–74

Dow brewery (National-Dow), 431–32

Dow, William, 424, 463(n9)

Dubuc, Alfred, 181, 421, 422–23, 460(n17)

Duke of Ancaster (privateer), 41, 42, 323

Dunmore, Lord, 126

Ejectment, action of, 256, 454(n5)

Electoral reform (Great Britain), 33, 396–97, 437(n4)

Elsdale, Ann (1743–65), *xxiv*, 35, 275, 284, 299, 300

Elsdale, Ann (Gibbins) (1757–1837), *xxiv*, 43, 47, 159, 163, 166, 170–73, 178, 183–87, 196, 266–69, 272–79, 282, 286–87, 291–94, 299–303,

349, 350, 394, 408, 454(n5), 462(n9)
Elsdale, Edward, 437(n5)
Elsdale, John (of Ipswich) (1724–88), xxiv, 34, 268–69, 272–73, 283, 285, 437(n5)
Elsdale, Mary (Robinson) (1711–57), xxiv, 28, 34, 299, 440(n16), 453(n3)
Elsdale, Mary (1739–72). See Molson, Mary (Elsdale)
Elsdale, Robinson (1744–83), xxiv, 13, 28–54, 37, 64, 68, 71–72, 81, 93, 102, 106–9, 115–19, 132–38, 143, 146–47, 165, 172, 177, 266, 270, 275, 277–78, 282–84, 299–301, 322, 323, 417, 438(n9,10), 441(n7), 462(n9)
Elsdale, Dr. Robinson (1812–67), 439(n11), 462(n9)
Elsdale, Reverend Robinson (1783–1850), xxiv, 39, 272, 349, 439(n11)
Elsdale, Samuel (c.1705–88), xxiv, 28, 32, 34–35, 44–46, 51–52, 99, 102–3, 104–7, 114–15, 130, 131, 136–40, 147, 161, 167–69, 215–16, 230, 260, 263, 267–72, 275, 279, 283, 284, 287–91, 294, 299, 323, 411–12, 437(n5), 440(n16), 441(n7), 453(n3)
Elsdale, Samuel (of Pimlico), xxiv, 34, 269, 283–91, 437(n5)
Elsdale, Reverend Samuel (1780–1827), xxiv, 39, 272, 349, 351, 439(n11), 462(n9)
Equiano, Olaudah, 19
Erie Canal, 398
Ermatinger, Frederick William, 388, 459(n3)
Everetta (merchant ship), 163, 170, 176, 177, 183, 214–15, 233, 236–37, 340–41, 342, 448(n4), 457(n1)

Fame (merchant ship), 174–76
Featonby, Captain George, 163, 183, 233, 237, 261
Federal Bank of the United States, 400
Fields, Susannah, xxiv, 43, 51
Finlay, Hugh, 59

Finlay, James, 145
Fitch, John, 335, 456(n9)
Flamand, Jean Baptiste, 148–49
Forster, Elizabeth, 316
Forsyth, John, 390, 397–98
Forsyth, Joseph, 383
Forsyth, Richardson & Co., 359
Foster, Thomas, 298–99, 300
Foucault seigneury, 119–24, 128, 450(n4). See also Caldwell's Manor
Franklin, Benjamin, 57, 137
Freemasonry, 184, 192, 305, 389–91, 400. See also St. Paul's Masonic Lodge (Montreal)
Freer, Noah, 375–76
Frobisher, Benjamin, 145
Frobisher, Joseph, 145, 189, 261
Frontenac Breweries, 431
Frothingham, Louisa Godard, 427
Fulton, Robert, 320–29, 334–43, 351, 361, 369, 456(n9), 457(n10)
Fur trade. See Beaver Club; Forsyth, Richardson & Co.; Frobisher, Benjamin and Joseph; Henry, Alexander; Hudson's Bay Co.; McGill, John and James; McGillvrays, Thain & Co.; McTavish, Frobisher & Co.; Merchant class of Quebec (protestant); North West Company; Phyn &Ellice; Todd, McGill & Company; XY Company

Gates, Horatio, 392, 393, 398, 410
Genesee tract, 311
Genevay, Louis, 312
George Ellice & Co., 445(n18)
Germain, Lord, 62, 127
Gibbins (Pell), George (1761–?), xxiv, 49–51, 93, 162–63, 185, 452(n6)
Gibbins (Pell), James, Jr. (1759–?), xxiv, 49–54, 56, 59, 62, 67, 70–72, 78, 80, 84–86, 92–94, 118–19, 160–63, 185, 249, 260, 440(n17), 449(n3), 452(n6)
Gibbins (Pell), James, Sr. (1731–?), xxiv, 42, 43, 48–54, 56, 59, 62, 65, 67, 70–72, 78, 80, 84–86, 92–95, 118–19, 134, 154, 161–65, 170, 174–80, 185, 205, 212–17, 221,

234, 240, 245, 249–74, 279, 286, 344, 447(n16), 451(n2)

Gibbins, Luke, *xxiv*, 161, 270

Gibbins (Pell), William (1762–?), *xxiv*, 49–51, 92–94, 118–19, 185, 260, 452(n6)

Gibbon, Edward, 178

Gideon, Sir Sampson, 122

Gillespie, Moffatt and Co., 387–88

Gillett, George N., Jr., 433

Good, George Thomas, 12

Gosling & Son (Robert and Francis Gosling), 102–3, 112, 156, 168, 177, 216, 230, 231, 237, 244, 278, 280, 445(n6)

Goudie, John, 375–76

Grand Trunk Railway, 423

Grant, Captain David Alexander, 238–47, 259–60

Grant, Captain John, 239–47, 259–60

Grant, Major John, 256–57

Grant, William (merchant), 238

Grant, William (steamboat captain), 393

Graves, Admiral Thomas, 437(n3)

Gray, Edward William, 144–53, 310

Gray, John, 310, 314–16, 387, 456(n2), 461(n1)

Gray, Jonathan, 310

Gray, Robert Isaac Dey, 314, 318

Green Mountain Boys, 126–27, 239

Greenfield, James, 391–92

Griffin, Henry, 386, 407–13

Gundlack, Frederick, 407–13

Gzowksi, Sir Casimir, 8

Habeas Corpus Act, 60, 62

Haldimand, General (Governor) Frederick, 59–62, 77–78, 80, 101, 122–23, 127, 129, 163, 440(n18), 456(n2)

Hall, Will Tudor, 331

Hamilton, Lieutenant-Governor Henry, 59, 156, 163

Hampton, Major General Wade, 356–57

Harley & Drummond, 101

Haw, William, 48, 134

Hawke, Admiral Edward, 18, 73

Henderson, John, 461(n1)

Heney, Hugues, 391

Henry, Alexander, 307

Hercules (steam towboat), 376

Heron, Samuel, 310, 315–16, 456(n2)

Holm(es), Ann, 197

Home Depot, 433

Hood, Admiral Samuel, 58, 74

Hope, Lieutenant-Colonel Henry, 59

Horner, William, 333, 455(n1)

Howe, Lord Richard, 16–18

Hoyle, Rosseter, 309

Hudson's Bay Co., 89, 90, 375, 383, 389

Huffman, Peter, 197, 228

Hunter, Robert, Jr., 163, 448

Hutchinson, Anne, 207

Hyde, John, 427

Inglis, Ellice & Co., 351

Inglis, Captain John, 77–78, 81

Inheritance: primogeniture vs. gavelkind, 26–27. *See also* Spousal rights

Jackson, President Andrew, 400

Jackson, John, 323–33, 341, 343, 455(n1)

Jackson, Paul, 41, 323

Jamestown settlement, 23–24

Jarvis, William, 314–15

Jay's Treaty (1794), 242, 258

Jefferies, Thomas, 197

Jefferson, Thomas, 59, 258, 428, 463(n10)

Jesuit Estates, 123, 444(n11)

John Molson (steam towboat), 376

Johnson, (Sir) John, 113, 135, 191, 202–3, 238, 251, 362, 443(n6), 445(n4)

Johnson, Samuel, 178

Johnson, (Sir) William, 191

Jones, John Paul, 78, 438, 441(n10)

Kalm, Pehr, 83–84, 444(n9)

Kay, John, 323, 325, 333, 456(n1)

Kelly, Isabel Thompson, 191

Kingsley (Kinsley) family (Connecticut and Vermont), 209–12, 249, 347

Kingston Brewery and Distillery, 400

Knickerbacco, John, 256

Knightley family (Northamptonshire), 201–2, 316–17

Labatt's Brewery, 431–34
Lachine Canal, 377, 392, 399
Lady Maria, HMS, 242, 258
Lady of the Lake (steamboat), 392
Lady Sherbrooke (steamboat), 372–77, 458(n1)
Laird Bros., 6–7, 10–14
Lake Champlain Steamboat Company, 376
Lauson seigneury, 123
LeMoyne, Marie-Charles, 238–39
Lenox, Lord George, 297
Leslie, James, 391
Lilly, Charles, Elizabeth and John, *xxv*, 283
Livingston, Robert, 334–38, 343, 351
Livingstone, David, 10
Livius, Chief Justice Peter, 441(n3)
Loedel, Charles, 370
Logan, David, 249, 452(n1)
Logan, Hart, 361, 373
Logan, John, 452(n1)
Loid, Thomas Pelgrave, 48–51, 59, 67, 71, 80–81, 86, 92–96, 104, 106, 110–19, 124, 130, 133–35, 140–55, 154, 159, 164, 165, 169, 179–80, 216–18, 223–24, 229, 231, 240–43, 249–54, 259–62, 272, 281, 322, 333, 338, 344, 430, 433–34, 443(n6), 444(n13), 445(n5), 446(n12,15), 447(n16), 451(ch11/n1,ch12/n2)
London (merchant ship), 77–78, 174–78
Long Island, Battle of (1776), 417
Longue Pointe distillery, 4–5, 424
Longueuil seigneury, 239
Lough, Joseph, 321–22, 461(n1)
Loyalists: American strongholds, 48, 50, 198, 203; as brewery customers, 95, 97, 103, 116, 240; compensation for wartime losses, 242; and crop failures of 1786–87, 276–77; demands for freehold land, 92, 121, 122; migration to and settlement in Quebec, 50–51, 92, 115–16, 118, 121, 123, 124, 127, 128, 203, 239,

250, 309–10, 440(n18), 442(n7), 444(n9), 451(n2), 452(n1); military activity, 135, 190, 202, 209, 240, 250–51, 256, 293, 440(n18), 450(n2), 451(n2); settling of Royal Townships and Upper Canada, 91–92, 121, 202–3, 240

Macdonald, Sir John A., 8
MacDonnell, Angus, 314–15
Mackenzie, Alexander, 90, 100
Mackenzie, William Lyon, 396–98, 402–3, 416–17, 459(n9)
Macpherson, Crane & Co., 422
Madison, President James, 355
Maitland, Lieutenant-Governor Sir Peregrine, 401
Malsham (steamboat), 324, 358–61, 364, 367, 372–75
Malting, 220. *See:* Brewing: Molson process c. 1786
Mansion House Hotel, 374, 375, 383, 394. *See also* British American Hotel, Masonic Hall Hotel
Markland, Thomas, 400–2, 460
Marriage contract, John Molson and Sarah Vaughan, 195, 310, 344–47
Marryat, Captain Frederick, 38–42, 119, 416–18, 438(n9,10), 439(n12), 462(n9)
Marvin, Benjamin, 255–58
Masonic Hall Hotel, 389–90. *See also* Mansion House Hotel, British American Hotel
Massachusetts Bay Colony, 22–24, 205–7, 450(n6)
May, Captain William, 47–50, 89–90, 134, 136
McBeath & Sheppard, 306
McCarthy, Jeremiah, 117, 154
McDouall, James, 375–76
McGill College (University), 394, 429–30, 434, 449(n5)
McGill, James, 145, 189, 312, 394, 449(n5)
McGill, John, 145, 261
McGill, Peter, 391, 393, 397–99, 404, 408–9, 414, 420
McGillivray, William, 312
McGillvrays, Thain & Co., 388–89

McGlemoyl, James, 117–21, 124–25, 128, 211–12, 252, 443(n6)

McLean, Brigadier-General Allan, 59, 440(n18)

McLintock, Francis, 10

McPherson, Sir David Lewis, 8

McTavish, Frobisher & Co., 306–7

McTavish, Simon, 189

Mears, Thomas, 393

Mercantile system, 97–98

Merchant class of Quebec (protestant), 89–91, 100–3, 163, 185, 233–34, 256, 276–77, 312; demands for political, legal and economic reform, 60–62, 216, 241, 248, 380, 390–91; diversification away from furs, 364, 367, 374, 385; domination of provincial economy, 399; and fur trade, 89, 91, 100, 103, 185, 293, 366–67, 374, 385, 388; and judicial appointments, 144–45, 148; new opportuntities in Upper Canada, 364, 369–70; political privilege, 396–99, 403

Mitchell, Peter, 8–9

Moffatt, George, 387–88, 390, 397–99, 404, 408–9, 414, 420

Moisie Iron Company, 425

Molson brewery partnerships:
John Molson and Thomas Loid (1783), 112–18, 130–34, 137–55

John Molson & Sons (1816), 368–82

John Molson & Sons (1824), 382–91, 392

John and William Molson (1829), 391–404

John Molson & Sons (1834), 404–21

Thomas and William Molson (1837), 421

Thomas and William Molson & Company (1838), 421–22

Thomas and William Molson & Company (1848), 422–23

Thomas and William Molson & Company (1853), 423

John H.R. Molson and Brothers (1861), 423–24

John H.R. Molson and Brothers (1872), 427

John H.R. Molson and Brothers (1880), 428

John H.R. Molson and Brothers (1897), 429–30

Molson enterprises:
"Banking" (steamboats), 359–60, 386–87

Distilling, 306–7, 312, 369, 376–78, 383, 386, 400, 403, 404, 422–24, 460(n17).

Lumber, 307–8

Molson Inc., 433–34

Molson's Brewery Ltd. (1911), 430

Molson's Brewery Ltd. (1945), 433

Molson, Davies and Company, 391

Molsons Bank, 422, 423, 429

St. Mary Foundry, 408, 461(n1)

Steamboats. *See Accommodation, John Molson, Lady Sherbrooke, Malsham, New Swiftsure, Quebec, Swiftsure, Varennes, Waterloo. See also* Ottawa and Rideau Forwarding Company, Ottawa Steamboat Company, St. Lawrence Steamboat Company

Sugar refining, 424

William Molson and John Thompson Badgley, 395, 405

See also Champlain and St. Lawrence Railroad

Molson properties in Canada: Belmont Hall, 390, 394–95; rue Capital (Montreal), 309, 325, 368, 394; farm properties (miscellaneous, Lower Canada), 309, 408, 455(n5); Montreal properties (miscellaneous), 309; Quebec City, 357–58, 394, 407–8, 413, 458(n2); St. Mary's Current (including brewery), 3–5, 94, 144–53, 158, 161, 163, 181, 214–15, 218–19, 240, 261, 281, 282, 300, 306, 308, 330, 344, 347, 348, 355, 362, 379, 394, 395, 405, 407, 411–12, 421, 422, 429, 446(n13), 458(n2), 461(n5); Ste-Maguerite (Île Boucherville) farms, 376, 379, 385, 394–95, 400, 403, 407, 408; Upper Canada, 310, 310–19. *See also* Caldwell's Manor; Mansion House Hotel

Molson, Elizabeth (1820–94), *xxv*, 8

Molson, Frederick William (1860–1929), *xxv*, 429–33

Molson, Harriet (1830–1913), *xxv*, 5

Molson, Harry Markland (1856–1912), *xxv*, 429

Molson, Herbert (1875–1928), *xxv*, 429–33

Molson, John (1699–1767), *xxi, xxii*, 26, 28, 30, 44–45, 53, 92–93, 449(n1)

Molson, John (1730–70), *xxii, xxiii*, 28–30, 43–45, 52–53, 104, 139

Molson, John (1760–90), *xxii*, 53, 131, 139–40, 161, 167

Molson, John, (1763–1836), *xxiii, xxv, passim*. *See also* Marriage contract; Wills

Molson, John (1787–1860), *xxv*, 2, 4, 13, 286, 294, 312, 319, 342–49, 354–73, 377–81, 386–88, 391–96, 404–16, 420–23, 427, 458(n1), 459(n7), 460(n16), 461(n7), 462(n1)

Molson, John (1820–1907), *xxv*, 4, 408

Molson, John Henry Robinson (1826–97), *xxv*, 1–6, 406–8, 419–29

Molson, John Thomas (1837–1910), *xxv*, 2–15, 365, 419–30, 435(ch1/n1)

Molson, Martha, (1740–?), *xxii*, 136, 440, 449(n1)

Molson, Martha (1767–?), *xxiii*, 44, 47, 49, 52–53, 130, 135–40, 160, 167, 168, 171, 182, 262–79, 283–86, 292–96, 302–3, 349–51, 394, 408, 453(n7)

Molson, Martha (1795–1848), *xxiii*, *xxv*, 3, 364–72, 378–82, 386, 394, 405–6, 423, 458(n1)

Molson, Martha Ann, (1824–1900), *xxv*, 5, 386

Molson, Mary, (1766–96), *xxiii*, 44, 52–53, 136, 140, 160, 167, 171, 182, 263–64, 267–74, 288, 292, 302–6

Molson, Mary (Elsdale) (1739–72), *xxii, xxiii, xxiv*, 28–30, 35, 43–45, 53, 113, 131, 139, 275, 284, 299

Molson, Mary Anne Elizabeth (1791–1862), *xxiii, xxv*, 366–68, 371, 379, 386, 458(n1)

Molson, Mary Anne Elizabeth (1828–1922), *xxv*, 5

Molson, Samuel Elsdale (1764–92), *xxiii*, 44, 53, 160, 267–86, 290–94, 299, 300

Molson, Thomas (1732–72), *xxii*, 45, 53, 104–7, 131, 139–140, 288

Molson, Thomas (1768–1803), 44, 52–53, 160, 167, 170, 215–16, 233–36, 246, 266–67, 271–74, 286, 288, 294, 302, 305, 349, 364

Molson, Thomas (1791–1863), *xxv*, 2–4, 5, 292–94, 312, 336, 342–44, 348–49, 352–58, 363–72, 376–88, 394–96, 400–13, 420–24, 427–28, 457(n2), 458(n3), 459(n7)

Molson, Thomas (1793–1854), *xxiii*, 379–80

Molson, Thomas (1821–33), 3, 378, 381, 386

Molson (Mouldson), Thomas, of Crowland (1618–82), *xxi*, 22–27, 201, 436(n5)

Molson (Moldson), Thomas, of Kylhome (C14), 20–21

Molson (Moulson/Malsham), Thomas, of Peakhill (1652–1740), *xxi*, 22–28, 49, 201–2, 358, 436(n5)

Molson, William (1741–72), *xxii*, 44–45, 92–93

Molson, William (1793–1875), *xxv*, 5, 294, 312, 342–44, 348–49, 354, 357–71, 377–78, 387–91, 394–415, 420–27, 458(n3), 460(n17)

Molson, William Markland (1833–1913), *xxv*, 2–5, 401, 423–30

Monarque, Pierre, 94, 146–47, 151–52, 161, 163, 181, 214, 240, 261, 281, 282

Mondelet, Jean-Marie, 312, 374

Monetary system in Quebec, 97–103, 359–60. *See also* Currency; Banking

Montgomery, Brigadier General Richard, 122–23, 4449(n15)

Montreal: diminishing importance of fur trade, 304; election of 1816, 363; of 1820, 377; of 1827, 390; of 1832, 396; of 1834, 403; post-Conquest character, 83–93; proposed annexation by Upper Canada, 398–99, 405; removal of defensive works, 304, 361; in Revolution of 1837–38, 415, 416; surrender to British in 1760, 18, 88, 96; to Americans in 1775, 88, 127; waterfront development, 361; in War of 1812, 355–57

Montreal Gas Light Company, 461(n7)

Montreal General Hospital 390, 394, 434, 457(n3)

Montreal Library, 461(n7)

Montreal Tow Boat Company, 376

Montreal Water Works, 309, 461(n7)

Morgan, John, 183–86, 232, 274

Morrice, Alexander, 219–23

Mott, Benjamin, 416, 418

Mott, Joseph, Sr., 250–57, 416, 444(n13)

Mott, Joseph, Jr., 257–58

Mott, Samuel, 255–58

Munn, David, 308, 332, 373

Munro, David, 325, 456(n2)

Murney, Captain Henry, 383–84

Murray, Brigadier General (Governor) James, 61, 98–99, 120–24, 128–29, 259, 444(n10)

Mutual Insurance Company, 461(n7)

National Breweries, 430–32

Naval Department (Lake Ontario and Lake Champlain), 135, 190, 202, 445(n4)

Nelson, Horatio, 16–20, 36, 65, 355, 441(n8)

Nelson, Robert, 391, 403

Nelson, Dr. Robert, 407–8, 412–13

Nelson, William, 354

New City Gas Light Company, 423

New Swiftsure (steamboat), 373–75, 458(n1)

New York state: dispute over Vermont land grants, 125–28

92 Resolutions (1834), 403, 415

Nooya, SV, 6–15, 7, 425–27, 426, 435(n1)

North River Steam Boat Company, 320–21

North West Company, 89–92, 100, 145, 163, 236–37, 293, 306–7, 359, 374–75, 389, 445(n18)

North, Lord, 57, 437(n3)

Nôtre-Dame de Montréal, Société de, 87

Ontario, HMS, 135, 445

Ostrander, Everard, 116

Oswald, Robert, 57, 73

Ottawa and Rideau Forwarding Company, 393, 414, 421–22, 461(n5,7)

Ottawa Steamboat Company, 392, 393, 461(n5)

Pandora, HMS, 77–82

Papineau, Joseph, 332, 394, 458(n2)

Papineau, Louis-Joseph, 332, 343, 390–91, 396, 398, 403, 404, 414, 415–16

Parker, Gerrard, Ogilvy & Co., 309, 326

Pavey, Edward, 215–16, 275

Perreault, Joseph, 282

Phoenix (steamboat), 376

Phyn & Ellice, 131, 163, 236–37, 445(n18)

Phyn, Ellice & Inglis, 351, 359

Phyn, James 163, 236–37, 448(n4)

Pilgrim, Alphonso, 331

Platt, George, 293, 324–25, 329, 334, 357, 363, 387

Platt, John, Jr., 293

Platt, John, Sr., 223–24, 293, 324

Plymouth colony, 205–7

Porter, James, 309

Prescott, Governor General Robert, 312, 452(n6)

Preston, HMS, 58–59, 441(n2)

Preston, Mary, 316–17

Prevost, Lieutenant-General Sir George, 356

Privateering, 15, 36–41, 51–52, 57–59, 63–68, 77–81, 314, 342, 397, 438(n7,10), 440(n13), 441(n10)

Purcell, Thomas, 377, 381

Puritans, 22, 205–6

Quebec: character, c. 1782, 83–84, 93–94; governance issues, legal and judicial system (post-conquest), 59–62, 144–48; Quebec Act (1774) 60, 90; Quebec Revenue Act (1775), 442(n6); invasion by Americans in 1775–76, 88, 122, 251; political unrest and election violence, 390–91, 396–99, 403–4, 414–18; territory in 1763 and 1774, 90–92; trade with Vermont 155, 241–42, 248; in War of 1812, 355–57. See also Rebellion of 1837–38; Seigneurial system
Quebec (steamboat), 374, 375–76, 392
Quebec Fire Insurance Company, 461(n5)
Queenston Heights, Battle of (1812), 356
Quiberon Bay, Battle of (1759), 18, 73

Randall, James, 197, 219
Rayment, Samuel, 394, 408
Rayment, William, xxiii, 254, 266–305, 311–12, 349, 350, 402, 454(ch14/n4)
Rebellion of 1837–38: in Lower Canada, 414–18; in Upper Canada, 416
Récollet order, 88–89
Reform Bill (1832), 396, 437(n4)
Regulations and Instructions relating to His Majesty's Service at Sea, 76
Richards, John, 45
Richardson, John (brewer), 177–78, 218, 225
Richardson, John (merchant), 359, 387, 390, 392, 397
Rideau Canal, 392–93, 400, 404, 414
Roanoke settlement, 23–24
Robinson, John Beverley, 397
Robinson, William, 46
Rockingham, Marquis of, 57, 73
Rodger, N.A.M., 34, 76, 114
Rodney, Admiral George, 58, 72–74, 87, 441(n8)
Rogers, Major James, 293, 451(ch12/n2)
Rooseveldt, Nicholas, 335
Royal Canadian Yacht Club, 7–9

Royal George, HMS, 18–19, 57
Royal Navy: discipline, 32, 75–76, 79–82; disrepair c. 1782, 57; escort duties, 64; signalling, 65; training and advancement, 32–37, 438(n6). See also various ships (HMS); Naval department
Royal Sovereign, HMS, 18, 57
Rum trade, 97, 101, 276, 307, 424, 442(n6)
Russell, Elizabeth, 315
Russell, Lord John, 415

St. Andrews (steamboat), 393
St. Ann Market, 461(n7)
St-Charles, Battle of (1837), 416
St-Denis, Battle of (1837), 416
St-Eustache, Battle of (1837), 416–18
St. Lawrence Steamboat Company, 375–77, 392, 461(n5,7)
St. Lawrence Steamboat and Mail Coach Company, 461(n7)
St. Mary Foundry. See: Molson enterprises
St. Maurice Forges, 324, 325, 329–34, 456(n2)
St. Paul's Masonic Lodge (Montreal), 192, 400
St. Thomas's Church (Montreal), 369–70, 424, 458(n3), 463(n9)
Saintes, Battle of the (1782), 56, 73–75, 79
Saisie, writ of, 146, 216, 241
Sanderson, Roxby & Co., 305
Sansom, Richard, xxi, 436(n5)
Savage, Captain John, 240, 250–58, 451(ch12/n2), 455(n7)
Savage, Lillias, xxv, 2, 425
Schulyer, General Philip J., 445(n16)
Scots Presbyterian Church (Montreal), 190, 192, 203, 305
Scott, Sir Walter, 20–21
Seigneurial system, 59, 60, 92, 117–18, 121–22, 309–10, 398
Selkirk (Red River) settlement, 374–75
Seven Oaks massacre (1816), 374–75
Sewell, Stephen, 343
Shannon (steamboat), 392, 393

Shay, Isaac, 309, 325–26
Sheppard, William, 306–8, 454–55
Simcoe, John Graves: Colonel, 242; Lieutenant-Governor, 311–14
Skaife, Adam, 427–28, 430
Skene, Philip, 444(n14)
Small, John, 312–15, 318
Smith, Captain John, 62–68
Smith, Chief Justice William, 248
Snake Hall, 26–30, 27, 38, 43–46, 52–53, 106, 113–14, 118–19, 158–60, 166, 201–2, 213–14, 216, 230, 231, 234, 236, 246, 264, 271, 274, 275, 280, 282, 302, 317, 322, 346, 384, 395, 411–12, 436(n10), 443(n3)
Solomon (Solomans), Lucius Levy, 110, 112
Southern, John, 351–52
Speedy (merchant ship), 318
Spousal rights: English common law vs. Lower Canada, 189–90, 345–46
Stansfeld, George, 228, 249, 280, 282, 295–301, 309, 448(n5), 454(n5)
Stark family (Vermont), 239
Steam engine, development, 53–54, 322, 328–29, 333–34
Steamboats, development, 320–21, 334–36, 456(n9,10)
Steamboats, service: on Hudson River, 320–23, 329, 335, 361; on Lake Champlain and Richelieu River, 321–23, 326, 329, 332, 336, 340, 343, 376, 414; on lower St. Lawrence River, 322–41, 354–55, 357–64, 368, 372–76, 391–92, 422; on upper St. Lawrence River, 383; on Ottawa River and Rideau Canal, 383, 392–93, 414, 421–22; on Mississippi River, 337, 340
Stevens, John Cox, 335
Stickney Estate, 275–79, 284–94, 298–301, 350
Stratton, Allen L., 179, 254, 259, 416, 451(ch12/n2)
Stribling, Colonel Thomas, 297
Stuart, Attorney-General James, 380
Sulpicians (Order of Saint-Sulpice), 84–85, 87–89, 151, 442(n3)

Surprize, HMS, 55, 56, 64, 66, 70–82
Sweet family (Massachusetts, Rhode Island and Vermont), 204–13
Swiftsure (steamboat) 324, 355–61, 367–68, 373, 377, 457(n3), 461(n1)

Talon, Jean, 96–97, 103
Taylor, E.P., 430–32
Teasdall, John, 309
Telegraph (steamboat), 374, 376
Temperance movement, 424
Thain, Thomas, 389
Theatre Royal, 389–90, 394
Theed, Reverend John, 292, 299
Thompson, P.L., 230
Tichenor, Governor Isaac, 258
Todd, McGill & Company, 359
Torrance, David, 392, 422
Torrance, John, 392, 422
Torrance, Thomas 390, 392, 457(n6)
Totchley (Tetchley), David, 199–202, 212
Townley, Samuel (H. Townley & Son), 233, 236–38, 245–46, 261, 278
Trafalgar, Battle of (1805), 16–20, 65, 441(n8)
Triumph (merchant ship), 156–57, 216
Turner, Thomas Andrew, 461(n1)
Tuzo, Thomas, 331

Union (steamboat), 393
Union Bill (1822), 390
Upper Canada: and activities of Montreal merchant elite, 364, 369–70; Family Compact, 319, 396, 397, 401–2; settlement, 91–92, 121, 202–3, 240, 310–16. *See also* Loyalists; Molson properties (Upper Canada); Rebellion of 1837–38; Steamboat service

Varennes (steamboat), 414, 461(n5)
Vaughan family: Connecticut and Vermont, 203–4, 450(n4,5); Massachusetts and Rhode Island, 204–13, 450(n6)
Vaughan, Sarah (1761?–1829), *xxiv*, *xxv*, 187–94, 195–213, 215, 228, 232, 240, 246–49, 260, 264–66,

270, 274, 283, 286, 292–93, 301–2, 312, 342, 344–47, 352, 354, 363–65, 381–82, 386, 391, 394–95, 409–10, 453(n7)

Vaughan, Reverend Thomas, 199–200

Vermont: border with Quebec, 111, 125, 128; declaration of independence, 127; incursions by British military in 1788, 255-5;, in 1792, 256-58; in 1793, 258; negotiations for recognition as American state, 126–28, 242, 445(n16); negotiations for status as British province, 127, 242; political origins, 125–28; in Rebellion of 1837–38, 416, 418; strategic role in American Revolution, 126; trade with Quebec, 112, 155, 242, 248; in War of 1812, 356

Vermont (steamboat), 321–28, 332, 336, 343, 461(n1)

Victory, HMS, 18, 19, 57

Ville de Paris (French warship), 58, 73, 74

Waddington, Thomas, 215–16, 234

Waite (Wait), John, 113, 133–34, 141–51, 216, 218, 251, 443(n1,2), 446(n12)

Walker, James, 145–52

War of 1812, 343, 355–57

Washington, George, 50–51, 110, 258, 445(n16)

Waterloo (steamboat), 392, 459(n8)

Watt, James, Jr., 351, 352, 372

Watt, James, Sr., 53–54, 351, 457(n10)

Weir, Lieutenant Jack, 417–18

Wentworth, Benning, 125–26

Wenz, Philip, 383

Westcott, Thompson, 335, 457(n10)

Western Canada Breweries Ltd., 430–31

Wetherall, Captain *(Revenge)*, 39–40, 438(n10)

Wetherall, Sir George Augustus, 417

Wetherell, Captain Thomas, 438(n10)

Whiskey trade, 306–7, 338, 377, 403, 460(n17)

White, John, 312–14

White, Thomas, 357–58

Whitsed, Abraham, *xxiii*, 274, 288, 291, 303, 305–6

Wilkinson, James (engineer), 334

Wilkinson, Major General James, 356–57

Willcocks, William, 314–16, 456(n2)

William King (steamboat), 393

Williams family (Vermont), 239–40

Williams, Miles, 361

Williams, Roger, 206–7

Wills:
  Elsdale, Samuel, 268–79, 283–92, 298–300
  Molson, John (1699–1737), 44
  Molson, John (1730–70), 44–45, 53
  Molson, John (1760–90), 105, 114
  Molson, John (1763–1836): of 1785, 130, 154, 161, 166, 444(n13); of 1795 and 1797, 188, 191, 200, 202, 209, 301–3, 344, 347, 348, 386; of 1810, 46, 344–49, 370–71, 382; of 1830, 394–95, 407–8 ; of 1836, 3–4, 386, 405–6, 407–14, 420–21
  Molson, John Henry Robinson: of 1866, 5, 419; of 1897, 429
  Molson, Martha (1795–1848), 379–81
  Molson, Thomas (1791–1863), 5, 380, 423

Wilson, George H., 332

Wilson, John, 158–59

Winans, John and James, 321–23, 327, 329, 332, 340, 343

Wincely, Mary, *xxi*, 26, 201–2

Wood, Enos, 256–57

Wood, Samuel, 280, 317

Worth, Captain James, 55–82, 70, 441(n6)

Wright, Philemon 307–8, 393

XY Company, 307

Young, John, 306